THE LOGIC
OF WILLIAM OF OCKHAM

by

ERNEST A. MOODY

New York

RUSSELL & RUSSELL

1965

67 - A 0425

FIRST PUBLISHED IN 1935
REISSUED, 1965, BY RUSSELL & RUSSELL, INC.
BY ARRANGEMENT WITH ERNEST A. MOODY
L.C. CATALOG CARD NO: 65—17914
PRINTED IN THE UNITED STATES OF AMERICA

PREFACE

At a time when mediæval philosophy is receiving more serious attention than for some hundreds of years, no apologies need be offered for undertaking a detailed first hand study of Ockham's logic. His reputation, as the foremost of the nominalists and as the mediæval philosopher whose thought was in many respects responsible for fundamental and characteristic attitudes and methods in modern science, exhibits him as the most significant philosopher of the later Middle Ages.

Despite Ockham's fame, and the admitted importance of his nominalistic restatement of the *Organon*, no modern exposition of his logic, with any pretence at thoroughness or close analysis, exists. Furthermore, texts of Ockham's philosophical writings are extremely scarce, so that it is not easy for those who wish to acquire a clear and adequate understanding of Ockham's thought, to do so. The present study is designed to reveal, through a careful analysis carried out with adequate source material, the philosophical content, and the essentially aristotelian inspiration, of Ockham's theory of science.

In addition to this purely historical interest, a twentieth century re-reading of Ockham's logical discussions has direct interest from the philosophical point of view. One cannot for long study his discussions of quantity, quality, time, place,

and relation, without being struck by the relevance of his
analyses of logical and physical problems to the speculative
interests of contemporary science. Though Ockham's language,
and the aristotelian background of his thought, are largely
absent from current statements of scientific problems, his
interests are surprisingly "modern," and remarkably free
from the theological preoccupations which, in the case of
most mediæval philosophical writings, obscure their scientific
content to modern secular readers. The direct philosophical
interest, for our own times, of Ockham's discussions, is
heightened by the fact that he not only deals with problems
that seem pertinent to us, but offers analyses of these problems,
and modes of solution, which possess great philosophic power
—though they are for the most part unfamiliar to contemporary
philosophers of science.

The reader's indulgence is asked for the unavoidable
difficulties attendant on the attempt to render Ockham's
thought accurately, in a language which to him would have
seemed almost hopelessly diffuse and equivocal. The
niceties of rhetoric have been sacrificed to what seemed
a more important end—namely, to get to the bottom of
Ockham's discussions, as far as possible, and to reveal,
even at the cost of unusual terminology and seemingly
needless restatement, *what* Ockham's much heralded
"nominalism" *is*.

My indebtedness to Dr. Richard McKeon, for his aid in
the task of elucidating Ockham's thought within the context
of Greek and mediæval tradition, and for his kindness in
lending me his much prized photostatic copies of Ockham's
writings, is hereby acknowledged with the utmost gratitude.
I am also much indebted to Professor F. J. E. Wood-
bridge, of Columbia University, for many illuminating ideas

communicated with rare felicity in the course of his discussions of philosophical empiricism. And for her immense patience, sympathy, and encouragement, without which this book could not have been finished, I thank my wife.

E. A. M.

Greenwich, Conn.
  Sept., 1935.

TABLE OF CONTENTS

CHAPTER ONE

I. The "place" assigned to Ockham in historical studies of mediæval philosophy—as innovator, sceptic, "subjectivist," and destructive critic of scholastic aristotelianism. Doubts concerning this estimate —Ockham's opposition to the *moderni*, his constant appeal to Aristotle against them. An alternative hypothesis of historical orientation—Ockham as critic of neo-platonist, arab, and augustinian corruptions of Aristotle.

II. Mediæval interest in logic not merely pedagogic, but philosophical. Scholasticism as a single organic philosophy *vs.* scholasticism as a conflict of philosophies. St. Thomas' critique of averroism and augustinism; Duns Scotus' critique of Aquinas. Ockham's "nominalism" originates in his statement of logic, and in his analysis of the term "universal." Porphyry's questions and his fifth predicable— the "problem of individuation" and the "sixth predicable." Ockham, like Aquinas, a critic of the logical realism of the augustinian and arab traditions, revived after Aquinas by the scotists.

III. Ockham's life and writings. Authors cited and positions criticized by him. The terminist logic—Petrus Hispanus *vs.* Michael Psellos as author of the *Summulae logicales*.

IV. Problems of aim and method involved in the study of Ockham's logic and of his "nominalism." Historical *vs.* philosophical approach; synthetic *vs.* analytic methods of study. Judgments of comparison, and historical estimates, of little value unless preceded by detailed analysis from the philosophical point of view. Aim of present study: to make clear, in Ockham's own terms and in contrast to alternative "aristotelianisms" which he opposed and criticized, what Ockham's interpretation of aristotelian logic was. We cannot *judge* Ockham's aristotelianism by the "real Aristotle," but only by our own, or by some other, interpretation of Aristotle.

CONTENTS

CHAPTER FOUR

CHAPTER SEVEN

CONTENTS

NOTE ON ABBREVIATIONS

S. tot. log. refers to Ockham's *Summa totius logicae*, 1508 edition.

Exp. aur. refers to Ockham's *Expositio aurea super artem veterem.* The Roman numerals, I, II, and III, indicate respectively those portions of the "Golden Exposition" concerned with Porphyry's *Isagoge*, Aristotle's *Categoriae*, and Aristotle's *De interpretatione.* The page references are to the 1496 edition.

WILLIAM OF OCKHAM

CHAPTER ONE

OCKHAM AND THE SCHOLASTIC TRADITION

I

HISTORIANS of philosophy tend, as a rule, to look for con-
tinuities in the chronicle of human speculation, in order that
abrupt transitions, or gaps in what might otherwise be a
progressive unfolding of a major point of view, may be avoided.
Like "nature," they abhor a vacuum and discontinuity.
Historical research is often a search for missing links, and for
"fore-runners" of certain events or attitudes which, according
to the philosophy of the historian, represent the peaks of
significant social, intellectual, or religious development, in
terms of which the intervening events and attitudes are to be
interpreted and represented as periods of transition.

William of Ockham, who flourished during the first half of
the fourteenth century, has been fated to play the rôle of a
transition figure and missing link, in historical studies of late
scholastic and early modern philosophy. Had he lived in the
middle of the thirteenth century, judgments concerning the
import and value of his philosophical writings would undoubtedly be radically and surprisingly different from what
they have been. But because the fourteenth century witnessed
the beginnings of modern experimental science and of its
mathematical method, and because it was also characterized
by the growth of scepticism and by the tendency to make a
radical separation between natural knowledge and religious

faith, a serious breach of historical continuity would be involved in any interpretation of Ockham's philosophy that failed to disclose in his thought the seeds of scepticism, of empiricism, and of the revolt against scholastic intellectualism which was the glory of the renaissance.

If we turn to the histories of philosophy, and to the studies which have been made of Ockham's philosophy during the past century, we find an almost unanimous agreement concerning the general tendencies of his thought, which, if not dictated by the desire for historical continuity, at least yields an interpretation that nicely satisfies the requirements of the historian.[1] Practically all agree that Ockham was of a sceptical turn of mind; that he was filled with a thirst for novelty; that he departed from the metaphysical foundations of the aristotelian theory of science through his criticism of various scholastic theories of the universal and the "intelligible species"; and that he was, whether he knew it or not, the father of the modern empirical and experimental point of view, sowing the seeds that came to flower in Francis Bacon, Locke, and Hume.

Ockham's sceptical tendencies are associated, in these accounts, with a sophistic spirit that delighted in logical subtleties and "vain disputations," and with a dialectical manner of questioning all first principles which recalls the "academic doubt" and which anticipates the Cartesian *method* of doubt. To him, throughout, is attributed a rebellious spirit that took pleasure in questioning all authority, and in every opportunity for novelty and dialectical display.[2]

[1] Michalski, in a series of monographs concerned with the critical and sceptical tendencies of the fourteenth century (see Bibliography for titles), is an excellent example of the historical method of interpreting fourteenth century philosophy. He concerns himself only with those elements in Ockham's writings which can be exhibited as anticipatory of later developments, and which give to fourteenth century thought the appearance of a continuous and progressive development— progressive from the standpoint of experimental science, retrogressive from the viewpoint of scholastic metaphysics.

[2] Characterizations of Ockham as one who thirsted for novelty are to be found in most of the general histories of philosophy. Cf. Ueberweg-Geyer, *Grundriss der Geschichte der Philosophie*, II (Berlin, 1928), p. 571: "Die Richtung der ockhamischen Philosophie ist kritisch und skeptisch." Cf. also Ehrle, *Peter von*

That Ockham's criticism of the various scholastic doctrines of *universalia in re*, or *ante rem*, as objects of knowledge, is equivalent to a rejection of the foundations of science as it was conceived by Aristotle, seems to be doubted by few modern interpreters of Ockham. In spite of the fact that it is hard to find, among the theories explicitly attacked by Ockham, many that are, *in the sense in which they were attacked*, authentically attributable to St. Thomas Aquinas, it is usually taken for granted that Ockham's criticisms applied with almost equal force to thomism, scotism, and to the entire tradition of scholastic aristotelianism. It is further concluded that his criticisms were, consciously or unconsciously, aimed at Aristotle himself, and at the very heart of aristotelian metaphysics and theory of science.[1]

Candia, p. 110: "Wollen wir das innerste und allgemeinste Prinzip der nominal-istischen Eigenart aufweisen, so können wir wohl einen ungesunden, übertriebenen Drang nach Neuern und Eigenen als solches bezeichnen." He adds that the stages of this tendency are (1) Duns Scotus, (2) Durandus and Aureoli, (3) Ockham, and (4) Nicolas of Autrecourt and John of Mirecourt. Cf. also De Wulf, *Hist. of Med. Phil.*, II, pp. 186–7: "The philosophy of William of Ockham had the success of a novelty and a reaction. . . . It represented a new method, that of subtleties and dialectical *finesse*."

[1] Ritter, Stöckl, and Gilson all state that for Ockham science is no longer of the universal and necessary, but of the particular—a position which, if actually characteristic of Ockham, would thoroughly justify the statement that he was essentially anti-aristotelian in his theory of science. Cf. Ritter, *Gesch. d. christl. Phil.*, VIII. Teil, (Hamburg, 1845), p. 582: "Dieser Richtung schliesst Occam sich an, indem er erklärt, dass die reale Wissenschaft nicht vom Allgemeinen sei, sondern nur vom Besondern." Stöckl, *Gesch. d. Phil. des Mittelalters*, 2, p. 1004: "Ebenso ist es klar, dass nach Ockhams Theorie die reale Wissenschaft sich in keiner Weise auf das Allgemeine, sondern nur auf das Besondere bezieht." Gilson, *La philosophie au moyen âge*, p. 253: "Mais du point de vue auquel Occam s'est placé, c'est le particulier qui est l'objet de la science."
    The only support given for these statements from Ockham's writings (by Ritter and Stöckl; Gilson gives none) is the following sentence from Ockham's *Comm. in IV Sent.*, I, Dist. II, Qu. 4: "Scientia realis est de rebus, sed non de rebus universalibus. . . . Sed scientia isto modo est de rebus singularibus." In its context this sentence means merely that *scientia realis* is distinguished from *scientia rationalis* by the difference that in propositions of the real sciences, the terms denote things that are not terms or concepts, while in propositions of logic or *scientia rationalis*, the terms stand for terms or concepts or other parts of human discourse. Since for Ockham the word "universal" is properly applicable only to terms or concepts, since only terms or concepts can be said to be "predicable of many," it follows that no real science can be about universals, since a real science is not, like logic, about terms or other parts of discourse.
    That this is the proper interpretation of the passage cited by Ritter and Stöckl is evident from other statements made in the very same paragraph of Ockham's

WILLIAM OF OCKHAM

It was not new, in the history of scholasticism, for aristotelian
principles to be attacked, but almost invariably the attack had
been founded on a positive predilection for the augustinian
point of view.[1] Ockham, however, is said to have had no
more use for the augustinian theory of knowledge, with its
multiple variations of the illumination theory, than for the
more aristotelian doctrine of the abstraction of the universal
by the active intellect. He would seem, to judge from the
usual accounts given, to have been purely a negative critic of
both the augustinian and aristotelian elements of the scholastic
tradition, with nothing constructive to offer beyond an
empiricism of thoroughly atomic and agnostic character.[2]

Such an empiricism, like that of Hume, would be practically
the only remaining alternative after a rejection of both the

---

discussion. E.g., "Scientiam esse de rebus potest intelligi . . . quod res sint
illa, pro quibus partes sciti supponunt, et sic scientia realis est de rebus." Again:
"Scientia quaelibet, sive sit realis sive rationalis, est tantum de propositionibus."
As will be seen later, in Ockham's analysis of the term or concept, the extension
of the terms of a scientific proposition is determined by the meaning of the terms,
and hence, since scientific propositions are always of universal character and never
particular, the supposition of the terms of propositions in the real sciences is
determined by the intentional character of the universal term or concept which
is a univocal sign of many individuals.

Against the view of Ritter, Stöckl, and Gilson, that for Ockham science is of
the particular and not of the universal, we may cite Ockham as follows: Exp.
aur., I, 16v: "nulla scientia proprie dicta est de individuis sed de universalibus
pro individuis." Also S. tot. log., I, 31, 12r: "Tertio modo dicitur predicatum
illud quod predicatur de aliquo subiecto predicatione directa, de quo subiecto
potest esse scientia proprie dicta, et sic Philosophus accipit predicatum primo
Topicorum, ubi distinguit quattuor predicata, scil. genus, diffinitionem, et accidens. Et sub genus comprehendit differentiam, ubi non enumerat speciem,
quia quamvis species predicatur de individuo, quia tamen individua non possunt
esse subiecta in propositionibus scitis scientia proprie dicta, ideo inter illa pred-
dicata non enumeratur species."

[1] This is well illustrated in St. Bonaventura. Cf. Gilson, *La philosophie de S.
Bonaventure* (Vrin, Paris, 1929), ch. ii ("La critique de la philosophie naturelle")
and ch. vii ("L'analogie universelle").

[2] Cf. Federhofer, "Ein Beitrag zur Bibliographie u. Biographie des W. von
Ockham," in *Philosophisches Jahrbuch*, XXXVIII (1925), p. 28: "In der Auf-
fassung des Erkenntnisursprunges liegt ja der Schlüssel seines Weltanschauung.
Als ausgesprochener Gegner der platonisch-augustinischen Illuminationstheorie,
ebenfalls eines intellectus separatus und der aristotelischen Abstraktion durch
Intuszeption der Formen, beginnt Ockham jene Richtung in der Erkenntnislehre
einzuleiten, die für den mathematisierenden Subjektivsmus eines Hobbes, den
erkenntnistheoretischen Rationalismus Descartes, und den Empirismus von
Locke und Hume charakteristisch ist."

augustinian and aristotelian metaphysics and theories of knowledge. There is empiricism in Aristotle, and a doctrine of intuition; but it is held that Ockham's empiricism, and his doctrine of the intuitive cognition of individuals, lacks the metaphysical foundation present in Aristotle, this foundation having been destroyed by his criticism of *universalia in re*. For Aristotle, intuition (νοῦς) is the apprehension of the essential nature of a thing in abstraction from its accidental and sensible determinations.[1] It is held that Ockham, in denying the existence of universal natures *in* things distinct from the principle by which they are individuals, inevitably denied that we can have intellectual apprehension of essential nature through universal concepts univocally applicable to many individuals.

On these general points, then, we find an almost unanimous agreement among modern authorities: that Ockham was a sceptic, that his convictions with respect to universals were equivalent to an attack on aristotelian metaphysics and on realism in science, and that the only positive aspect of his thought that is of interest is to be found in an empiricist and subjectivist orientation akin to that of Francis Bacon, Locke, Hume, and to the philosophical background of modern experimental science.[2] While there are some rather startling differences in the way in which modern scholars support

[1] Arist., An. Post. II, 100a 3–100b 17. Cf. Ockham, Exp. aur., I, 16v, whose account of the process of coming to grasp the universal is almost a literal paraphrase of Aristotle's account.

[2] For an interpretation of Ockham's philosophical writings as a whole, based on the conviction that the key to his thought is an empiricist point of view anticipatory of Locke, Hume, and of Francis Bacon, see N. Abbagnano, *Guglielmo di Ockham*, p. 53: "Il tratto essenziale e caratteristico del metodo e della dottrina di Ockham è il ricorso continuo ai dati immediati dell' experienza. . ." p. 56: "egli stabilisce la teoria della conoscenza intuitiva, nella quale il dualismo di realtà e spirito è superato con un netto ricorso all' experienza, cioè all' intuizione immediata dell' attuale e individuale realtà delle cose," pp. 104–5: "L'induzione di Ockham si scosta quindi dal concetto aristotelico, di quanto si avvicina a quello baconiano."

Federhofer, Siebeck, and Hauréau also find in Ockham's "empiricism" the chief significance of his work. Cf. Siebeck, *Occams Erkenntnislehre in ihrer historischen Stellung*, p. 330: "Nach allem bisherigen könnte Occam in seiner Beziehung zur Entwickelung der neueren Philosophie unter den mittelalterlichen Denkern als derjenige erscheinen, der noch innerhalb der Scholastik selbst die Grundlagen des nachmaligen Empirismus geschaffen hat." Hauréau, *Hist. de la phil. scolastique,*

6 WILLIAM OF OCKHAM

these more general conclusions, when they take up specific points of interpretation,[1] the final characterization of Ockham as sceptical, "modern," anti-aristotelian, and empirically or positivistically minded, is the accepted characterization, comfortably established on the shelves of our libraries. It is, incidentally, thc characterization that is most helpful in exhibiting the transition from thirteenth century scholasticism to modern empiricism as a continuous development, without serious gaps or reverse motions such as might be displeasing to the historically minded.

The hypothesis that Ockham was the missing link between thirteenth century scholasticism and the experimental and mathematical view of science that characterized the nominalists and that became dominant in the modern era, seems *prima facie* a reasonable assumption, for the reason that the school known as nominalists in the fifteenth century, looked upon William of Ockham as its founder.[2] Furthermore, Nicolas of Orêsme and Albert of Saxony, who applied the experimental and mathematical methods to physical investigations with results that anticipated the work of Galileo, Copernicus, and Descartes, were followers of Ockham whose period of education fell within his own lifetime.[3] On the other hand, many a philosopher has had followers and interpreters, and possibly more than one class-room student, that he himself

---

II, 2, p. 430, says enthusiastically: "C'est donc, en realité, sur le sol si bien preparé par le prince des nominalistes que François Bacon a fondé son éternel monument."

E. Hochstetter, *Studien zur Metaphysik u. Erkenntnislehre Wilhelms von Ockham* (Diss., Berlin, 1927) is one of the few who question the usual view of Ockham as a non-aristotelian empiricist. Prantl, *Gesch. d. Logik im Abendlande*, III, p. 332, also thinks Ockham's theory of science is basically aristotelian, though he (Prantl) tends to express this "aristotelische Empirismus" in rather Kantian language.

[1] E.g., Federhofer (*Phil. Jahrbuch* XXXIX, p. 277): "Dieses Bestreben, Denken und Sinnlichkeit in unmittelbare Nähe zu bringen, hat Ockham von Scotus übernommen." De Wulf, op. cit., II, p. 182: "In Ockham's ideology, the collaboration between sensation and thought which is so close in the systems of the other scholastics becomes purely external. . . ."

[2] Cf. Ehrle, *Peter von Candia*, p. 107, for an account of the origins of the names "terministae," "conceptistae," and "nominales" as applied to a school. The earliest use of the name "nominales" appears to have been at Cologne, around 1425.

[3] Cf. Pierre Duhem, *Etudes sur Leonard de Vinci*, III, pp. 346-405; 481-92.

would have repudiated. The fact that the nominalist school regarded Ockham as its founder, does not necessarily imply that his philosophy was adequately interpreted by the nominalist school. Nor is it sufficient, in any case, to call him a nominalist, until we have obtained an adequate grasp of what the word "nominalist," as applied to Ockham's philosophy, means.

In spite of the *prima facie* plausibility of the characterization of Ockham as a promoter of the experimental and mathematical methods of science, and hence (by a generous inference) as an advance guard of the baconian and cartesian philosophies of science, nevertheless the application of this hypothesis to the detailed interpretation of Ockham's writings runs up against many difficulties. Even a superficial reading of Ockham's works, let alone a systematic study, gives reason for doubt concerning the accuracy of the usual characterization of him. For instance, if Ockham had actually been inspired by a desire for novelty and by a spirit of rebellion against tradition, it is strange that he did not keep up with the progressive movements of his own times, and number himself among the *moderni*. It is strange that he constantly criticized them and stated his own preference for the opinions of the *antiqui*, on the ground that they (the *antiqui*) stayed closer to the authentic thought of Aristotle.[1]

Again, if Ockham were actually an empiricist of the "atomic proposition" variety, interpreting the universal propositions of the sciences as mere generalizations of singular contingent propositions known by experience, how is it that he considered

---

[1] S. tot. log., I, 41, 14v: "Ponuntur ab omnibus auctoribus decem predicamenta; sed in modo ponendi, ut mihi videtur, multi moderni discordant ab antiquis . . . unde . . . fingunt nomina abstracta, sicut de 'quando,' quod est adverbium, fingunt tale abstractum 'quandeitas,' etc. . . . Et quia intentio antiquorum mihi videtur rationabilior, ideo ipsam persequendo primo ostendam quod haec fuit eorum intentio," etc. I have found fifteen or more references to the *moderni* in Ockham's logical writings, and all of them are criticisms of the *moderni* for ignorance or misinterpretation of Aristotle, most of the theories criticized being characteristic of 14th century scotists, like Francescus Mayronis, or of impure thomists like Walter Burleigh or Aegidius Romanus. Aquinas' own positions are scarcely mentioned, and he would seem to have been one of the *antiqui* whom Ockham preferred.

the principal utility of logic to be in enabling us to distinguish necessary propositions—in the real sciences—from those which are contingent or merely probable?[1] And if his empiricism undermined the aristotelian conception of science as of the universal, how are we to account for his explicit denial that science is of the particular? Finally, if Ockham were really in revolt against the aristotelian metaphysics and theory of science, it is strange that his criticisms of scholastic doctrines are in practically every instance supported by direct appeals to the arguments and authority of Aristotle.[2]

Ockham's constant appeal to Aristotle, in his criticism of doctrines held by his contemporaries—doctrines which were themselves upheld in the name of Aristotle—suggests an alternative hypothesis concerning his philosophical orientation and his place in the history of mediæval aristotelianism. We might, for example, take him at his word and assume that he was seeking to effect a return to a pure aristotelianism—the scholastic interpretations of the peripatetic philosophy being, in Ockham's eyes and in his time, encrusted with alien elements derived from the augustinian tradition and from the arab commentators. If this were really Ockham's attitude and aim, it would be quite natural to find him ranged against the *moderni*, as represented by the scotists and by many of the thomists of his own day. We might also, on this supposition, expect to find that his criticisms bore more directly on the doctrines of Duns Scotus, whose peripateticism was more deeply tinged with augustinian elements, than on the authentic doctrines of St. Thomas, who, in philosophy, was less affected by augustinism.

---

[1] Exp. aur., I, Proem., 1r: "ista scientia perfecte habita faciliter iudicatur quid verum quid falsum, et hoc quantum ad illa quae per propositiones per se notas possunt sciri, cum in talibus non oporteat nisi ordinate procedere a propositionibus per se notis ad alia quae consequuntur ex eis, et tale processum seu discursum docet logica. . . . Alia utilitas est pro modis arguendi et respondendi," etc.

[2] Cf. *ante*, p. 3, Note 1. S. tot. log., I, 44, 17r: "Et quia ponuntur communiter a modernis quod quaelibet quantitas est quaedam res distincta realiter et totaliter a substantia et a qualitate. . . . Volo igitur primo ostendere quod illa opinio est contra mentem Aristotelis. Secundo ponam aliquas rationes contra eam. Tertio recitabo opinionem contrariam quae mihi videtur esse de mente Aristotelis. . . ."

This, as a matter of fact, is precisely what we find. Among the theories criticized by Ockham it is hard to discover any that were, in the sense in which he attacked them, essential to the philosophy of St. Thomas. On the other hand, many of his criticisms, though not as a rule directed at the teachings of Duns Scotus himself, attack principles which are essentially involved in the scotist position. If Ockham had been interested, as many of the modern interpreters of his thought would have us believe, in undermining the aristotelian theory of science, and the aristotelian metaphysics, would he not have chosen as his principal opponent the scholastic doctor, Thomas Aquinas, who stayed closest to Aristotle? If he had been interested in exhibiting natural knowledge, and human intelligence, as insufficient for the attainment of truth and certainty, would he not have supported this position by appeals to St. Augustine, as many a member of his own *Order of Friars Minor* had done before him? But in point of fact, he rarely cites St. Augustine in matters of epistemology, but on nearly every point goes back to the text of Aristotle.

Professor Gilson, in an extremely interesting and scholarly article that appeared in 1926, discussed a problem of historical interpretation that is in some respects analogous to that which presents itself when we consider Ockham's attitude toward Aristotle.[1] According to Professor Gilson, St. Thomas was driven to what seemed like a criticism of St. Augustine, by the fact that augustinism had become associated, in an almost inextricable manner, with the epistemological theory of Avicenna. In a subsequent study Professor Gilson indicated the important influence which Avicenna exerted on Duns Scotus, in the interpretation of Aristotle—an influence which had for some time been quite natural to those scholastics whose taste or tradition was largely augustinian.[2]

With William of Ockham we have what appears to be a criticism of very fundamental aristotelian doctrines, or let

[1] Gilson, "Pourquoi St. Thomas a critiqué St. Augustin," in *Archives d'histoire*, etc., 1926, pp. 5–128.
[2] Gilson, "Avicenne et le point de départ de Duns Scot," in *Archives d'histoire*, etc., 1927, pp. 89–150.

us say of doctrines that had been developed and stated by scholastic philosophers who professed to follow Aristotle in matters of natural knowledge. On the other hand, we find that Ockham not only refrains from criticizing Aristotle himself, as St. Thomas had refrained from direct criticism of St. Augustine, but we find him constantly defending his criticism of scholastic aristotelianism by the text and principles of Aristotle.

From a superficial standpoint, at least, a situation of this kind suggests that Ockham had no intention of undermining the authentic doctrines of the Stagyrite; and the keenness and admitted ability of the Venerable Inceptor (as Ockham was called) makes it improbable that he did not know what he was doing, or that he attacked aristotelianism without knowing it. A more likely solution might be one similar to that suggested by Professor Gilson in the case of St. Thomas' criticism of augustinism—that is, that Ockham found scholastic peripateticism so subtly and inextricably coloured by augustinian or arab meanings and interpretations, that he found it necessary to attack these scholastic statements as generally presented and understood, being unable to use the traditional terminology and modes of expression, aristotelian though they had been in their origin, without incurring the danger of their being given a non-aristotelian turn. [1]

In support of this hypothesis we may mention most of the features of Ockham's writings that have been used to support the contrary contention. His use of a novel terminology developed from the terminist logicians, as well as his emphasis on terms and concepts and on their definition, have been taken as indications of his "thirst for novelty" and for "dialectical subtleties," and of a spirit of revolt against the traditions of

[1] Perhaps the term "augustinism" is too narrow as a characterization of the immense variety of doctrines that sprang, in mediæval discussions, from the writings of St. Augustine himself, from the application of christian theological doctrines and viewpoints to natural philosophy, and from the mixture of neo-platonism and aristotelianism that characterized mediæval arab and jewish philosophical literature and which became so influential in the latin West during the thirteenth century. Prof. Gilson has coined the term "augustinisme avicennisant" to signify what we might call augustinism and neo-platonism in aristotelian dress.

scholastic aristotelianism. But if his revolt were against an interpretation of Aristotle that was adulterated with augustinian and arab elements of a neo-platonist tendency, so that the very terminology of scholastic discussion had become infected with mixed significance and equivocation derived from attempts to synthesize aristotelianism and augustinism, his use of new modes of expression, and his meticulous care in the unequivocal definition of terms, would be equally well explained. In the same way, his attacks on various realist theories of *universalia in re*—which in so many cases resulted in an identification of the objects of human knowledge with *universalia ante rem*, or with eternal ideas or exemplars in the divine intellect, or which involved such intricate and non-aristotelian theories as the scotist formal distinction within the thing—can be explained as an attack on an un-aristotelian aristotelianism, just as well as they can be explained from the contrary standpoint.

In short, there is sufficient superficial evidence for both characterizations of Ockham, to invite a more adequate examination of his discussions concerning logic and science, for the purpose of determining, on evidence less superficial, which of these two interpretations, if either, is the more tenable. Only by an analysis of Ockham's theory of science motivated by philosophical, rather than historical, interests, aiming to reveal the principles underlying his exposition of logic and his criticisms of his contemporaries, can the problem receive a determinate answer.

II

The extensive preoccupation of mediæval philosophical literature with logic, and the mediæval habit of discussing philosophical problems in the terminology of Aristotle, have long been noted by historians. Until recently it was assumed, indeed, that scholasticism, insofar as it was concerned with philosophical as distinguished from theological interest, was little more than an academic restatement of aristotelian "dogmas," carefully petrified into syllogisms, overlaid with hair-splitting verbal disputes and "logic-chopping," and utterly devoid of any critical examination of basic principles or premises.[1]

First-hand investigation of mediæval philosophical literature has, in recent years, brought about a considerable change in the attitude of competent scholars and historians of philosophy with respect to the character of the mediæval period. The mediæval interest in logic is now seen to have been not so much an interest in argument for argument's sake, as a preoccupation with the nature and grounds of scientific certainty, and an attempt to discover and to formulate the criteria by which science might be distinguished from opinion.[2]

The study of primary sources has also revealed in mediæval discussions a variety of philosophical points of view, stemming from diverse traditions—a variety that can scarcely be reconciled with the older notion that mediæval philosophy was an uncritical restatement of aristotelian formulas within limitations allowed by christian theology and by the authority of St.

[1] Cf. A. Weber, *Hist. of Phil.* (transl. by Thilly, Scribners, N.Y., 1925, revised ed.), p. 187: "As soon as Aristotle's system received recognition as the only authentic expression of human reason, its authority naturally transcended that of free thought," p. 188: "Henceforth the question no longer is to prove the agreement between the dogma and natural reason, but its agreement with the letter of Aristotle's writings." The tradition of scholastic "barrenness" goes back to Francis Bacon, and indeed to his 13th century name-sake Roger Bacon; cf. Francis Bacon, *Advancement of Learning* (Everyman ed., N.Y., 1915, p. 26): "This kind of degenerate learning did chiefly reign amongst the schoolmen; who having sharp and strong wits, and abundance of leisure, and small variety of reading, but their wits being shut up in the cells of a few authors (chiefly Aristotle their dictator) as their persons were shut up in the cells of monasteries and colleges, and knowing little history, either of nature or time, did out of no great quantity of matter and infinite agitation of wit spin out unto those laborious webs of learning which are extant in their books." Cf. also John Locke, *Essay* (Fraser's ed., Oxford, 1894), vol. II, p. 127: "This, though a very useless skill, and that which I think the direct opposite to the ways of knowledge, hath yet passed hitherto under the laudable and esteemed names of *subtlety* and *acuteness*, and has had the applause of the schools," etc.

[2] The work of Ritter, Stöckl, Hauréau, Prantl, Ueberweg-Heinze, and other pioneers in the first-hand study of mediæval philosophy, laid the ground for more detailed and accurate understanding of the period, found now in the work of scholars like Gilson, Duhem, Grabmann, Mandonnet, etc. The publication of mediæval philosophical treatises and *Quaestiones* has done much to show that the charges of hair-splitting verbalism and of slavery to Aristotle, do not apply to 13th century and only in part to 14th century scholasticism.

Augustine. The mediæval discussions of logic, physics, psychology, ethics, and metaphysics, though formulated in language that was largely aristotelian, disclose points of view and principles of analysis and criticism characteristic of diverse traditions. In a single and adequate philosophical language, and within a comparatively short period of time, augustinism, neo-platonism, and aristotelianism, in an immense variety of forms found in greek, latin, arabic, and jewish philosophical literature, faced each other and were subjected to profound and acute criticism. Though the language and background of these discussions are not ours—so that we may often fail to recognize the philosophical problems with which we are familiar in our modern discussions—once the barrier of language and terminology is crossed, and the translation of problems from one set of terms to the other accomplished, it is hard to find any important philosophical question that was not raised, and subjected to thorough-going analysis, in the literature of scholasticism.

While there are still some scholars who seek to portray scholasticism as a more or less homogeneous development with an intrinsic and organic doctrinal unity, the philosophical discussions of the thirteenth century are being more and more recognized as expressions of a fundamental conflict of principles and methods.[1] As the enormous influence of the arab and jewish syntheses of neo-platonic principles and aristotelian terminology, on the scholastics of the thirteenth century, is more clearly recognized, the criticisms levelled by St. Thomas Aquinas against the doctrines of Averroes and Avicenna are seen to apply to a very large part of the scholastic tradition itself.

The aristotelian principles espoused in philosophy by St. Thomas, were then subjected to a penetrating and subtle criticism by Duns Scotus. Did Duns re-introduce, in a refined

---

[1] For the view of mediæval philosophy as a homogeneous synthesis with an organic doctrinal unity, cf. De Wulf, *Hist. of Med. Phil.*, Introduction. For the view of it as the expression of conflicting traditions, issuing in several distinct, opposed, and coherent systems of thought, cf. Gilson, "Pourquoi St. Thomas a critiqué St. Augustin," in *Archives d'histoire, etc.*, 1926, p. 5, Note 1, and pp. 125-7.

and perhaps attenuated form, the neo-platonist influence present in the arab restatements of aristotelianism, which St. Thomas had attacked and largely eliminated from his own aristotelian philosophy? This is a problem that requires the most careful analysis, and thorough study, on the part of the historian. Professor Gilson, in a recent study, has pointed out some significant features of Duns' thought that have close affinity with the thought of Avicenna, and which indicate as probable the conclusion that the scotist synthesis marks a return, in an original and subtle form, to the un-aristotelian aristotelianism inspired by the arab tradition, that had been rejected by Aquinas.[1]

The critical character of thirteenth century philosophy, and the diversity of principles and traditions involved in it, make necessary a rather careful analysis of the arguments and criticisms of such a writer as William of Ockham, in any attempt to determine his philosophical orientation. It is not enough to enumerate the authorities which he quotes, or to look for epigrammatic statements of principle here and there in his writings. Such a method can lead, as indeed it has done, to a variety of opposed estimates, each one plausible and supported by textual citations, but unable to explain the citations on which the other opposed estimates are based. Ockham's works are of a critical and analytical character; our task, in seeking to determine his position in the history of mediæval thought, involves the procedure of discovering what theories and positions he criticizes, by what principles his criticisms are regulated, and of tracing, to the extent required, these opposed points of view to their sources in the diverse philosophical traditions which entered into mediæval thought.

To pursue this analysis in terms of Ockham's exposition of logic has certain advantages. For one thing, Ockham's extant works include a relatively complete treatment of logic. He wrote no treatises on metaphysics, and his works on physics,

[1] Gilson, "Avicenne et le point de départ de Duns Scot," in *Archives d'histoire, etc.*, 1927, pp. 89–150.

though extensive, are not so immediately connected with the epistemological aspect of mediæval discussion in which we are here interested. In the second place, logic was prominent in mediæval philosophy throughout the whole period of scholastic writing, so that the principles and methods of mediæval writers from Boethius up to the beginning of the modern era can be brought to a focus, as it were, on certain recurrent problems of logic which were dealt with in the earlier as well as the later centuries.

The most famous, if not notorious, of these recurrent problems, was the so-called "problem of universals," discussed by practically every commentator on Porphyry as a metaphysical question relevant to the understanding of Aristotle's treatise on the categories. Are genera and species substances? Are they corporeal or incorporeal? If the latter, are they in sensible things or separated from them? These three questions raised by Porphyry, at the beginning of a treatise designed as an introduction to Aristotle's analysis of terms, had a double effect, whose importance can scarcely be over-estimated, on the aristotelianism of the Middle Ages. Its effect on mediæval logic was to give to scholastic interpretations of Aristotle's *Organon* a metaphysical orientation, and emphasis which, in Aristotle's own logical treatises, is carefully avoided. Its effect on mediæval metaphysics was also important, since it tended, by reading problems of logic as problems of metaphysics, to cause metaphysical questions to be discussed in forms borrowed from logic.

These effects are illustrated in innumerable forms distinctive of the chief syntheses of augustinism, aristotelianism, and the arab interpretations of Aristotle, that appeared in thirteenth century literature. The discussions concerning a principle of individuation, a problem that seemed of great importance to the thirteenth century, turn on a problem resulting largely from the porphyrian interpretation of Aristotle.

Porphyry regarded the *species* as a fifth predicable, of the same logical status as *definition*, *property*, and *accident*. The primary subject of predication, which is the individual "first substance," thus became distinguished from the *infima species*. The effect of this distinction was to make necessary some principle of individuation, whereby the primary subject of predication could be distinguished formally, and essentially, from the species, just as the species is distinguished from its proximate genus by the essential differentia. In other words, a sixth predicable became necessary. It is not found in Porphyry, but appeared later in two apparently independent sources— in Abelard and in Avicenna.[1] This sixth predicable was the "individual," and the primary subject of predication thus became indeterminate with respect to universality and individuality, as was the case in the scotist tradition.[2]

When, against this background, the aristotelian thesis that nothing exists apart from individuals is adopted, it becomes impossible to maintain the aristotelian theory that knowledge, which is of the universal, is of the sensible and changeable things which exist by nature. For the primary subject is no longer the individual nature apprehended through sense experience, but a form indeterminate with respect to individuality, and prior to it, like an exemplar according to which God creates existent individuals, and by which the soul is illumined in its act of understanding.

The affinity of this point of view, developed from Porphyry's interpretation of Aristotle's *Categories*, with the theological and metaphysical tendencies of augustinism, is obvious. The philosophy of Avicenna, in which the same problems were faced in the attempt to understand Aristotle in terms of a neo-platonist metaphysical background, provided the thirteenth century scholastics with concepts and arguments admirably adapted to the elaboration of the porphyrian point of view.

---

[1] This interesting and significant addition to the predicables is discussed by R. P. McKeon, in his *Philosophy in the Middle Ages* (soon to be published). It seems to have escaped other scholars and historians of mediæval philosophy, since in no other secondary source have I found mention of it.

[2] Cf. Duns Scotus, Qu. in Met., Qu. 18, n. 8: "Est ergo natura in potentia remota ad determinationem singularitatis, et ad indeterminationem universalis; et sicut a producente coniungitur singularitati, ita a re agente, et simul ab intellectu agente, coniungitur universalitati. Et isto modo bene intelligitur illud dictum Avicennae, V. Met., ch. 1, quod natura de se non est universalis, nec particularis, sed tantum natura."

This neo-platonist manner of interpreting Aristotle, which was inherited from Porphyry and reinforced by augustinism and by the arab commentators, received at the hands of St. Thomas Aquinas a thorough-going critique, bearing chiefly on the metaphysical issues, and on the illumination theories of knowledge developed from augustinian and arab sources. The platonist doctrine of separated forms, the arab theory of a separated active intellect, and the augustinian theory of knowledge by illumination or by exemplars, were linked together by St. Thomas, and attacked on the general ground that they entailed or presupposed the denial of the reality of the created world and the efficacy of finite causes, and consequently the denial of the "firstness" of the first principles of natural knowledge.[1]

The opponents criticized by St. Thomas were the averroists and those augustinians who had been influenced by arab doctrines of platonic or neo-platonic character. Aquinas' battle could be fought with weapons forged in a generous fashion from the principles of aristotelian metaphysics. Duns Scotus, who came later, conceded these principles of aristotelianism, and then proceded to qualify them, and to reintroduce, in his analysis of each philosophical or scientific problem, distinctions and qualifications which were inspired by the older augustinism and by Avicenna, and which permitted a return, in a refined and subtle form, to the essentials of the augustinian point of view.

William of Ockham professed to be a pure aristotelian, and through a painstaking analysis of logical questions he sought to uncover, and to dislodge, the non-aristotelian elements which in his eyes corrupted mediæval interpretations of Aristotle—elements which gave rise to problems and difficulties that have no place in the works of the Stagyrite, but arise only as a result of the attempt to make a philosophical synthesis of aristotelianism and augustinism. Ockham could not, like Aquinas, carry out his critique along broad metaphysical lines, because the scholastics whose doctrines he was criticizing were

[1] Cf. Gilson, "Pourquoi St. Thomas a critiqué St. Augustin."

perfectly willing to concede most of the theses upheld by St.
Thomas, even while they qualified them and re-interpreted
them, in application to questions of logic and of natural
science, in an augustinian and avicennist manner.

Ockham found it necessary to track down the point of view
which he was criticizing, and which St. Thomas before him
had also attacked, to its roots in the porphyrian and boethian
interpretations of Aristotle's logic. A neo-platonist theory
of knowledge had been insinuated into the interpretation of
Aristotle by almost every teacher of aristotelianism that the
Middle Ages had—by Porphyry, by Boethius (who thought
to make a synthesis of platonism and aristotelianism), by
Avicenna, Averroes, Avencebrol, Maimonides, and even by
Proclus, whose "Book of Causes" was for a long time attributed
to Aristotle and used as a guide to understanding aristotelian
metaphysics. Aquinas attacked this neo-platonist attitude in
the doctrines of the arab and jewish writers, and in the
augustinism that had assimilated important elements from
these sources. Ockham tracked it down to Porphyry's introduction of a metaphysical status to the purely logical
distinctions and orderings of terms with which Aristotle had been
concerned in the *Categories*; and in each logical question that
he treats, the interpretations criticized by him reveal their
roots in the porphyrian confusion between τὰ ὄντα and τὰ
λεγόμενα. His criticisms themselves are, by the same token,
grounded in the constant effort to maintain the distinction
between logic, natural science, and metaphysics, and between
modes of signification and the things signified.

III

William of Ockham, like so many mediæval writers, has
very little biography beyond the record of his ideas, as contained
in his works. He was born probably between 1290 and 1300,
and his home appears to have been the village of Ockham,
in the county of Surrey. He entered the Order of Friars
Minor, and received his education at Oxford, obtaining his

baccalaureate around the year 1318. During the following two years he read the *Sentences* of Peter Lombard, as part of the customary requirements for the Master's degree. Theological students who had completed these requirements, but who had not yet received their license to teach theology, were said to be *inceptores*, their academic grade being that of *baccalaureus formatus*—whence the title by which Ockham was known by later generations, as the *inceptor venerabilis*, a name that originally had no connection with the idea of Ockham as the founder, or *inceptor*, of nominalism.

In 1324, probably before receiving his licentiate as a Master, Ockham's academic career was interrupted by a summons to the papal court at Avignon. Certain statements, in his philosophical and theological writings, had been challenged as heretical, and he was called to the papal *curia* to defend himself against these charges. The wheels of ecclesiastical condemnation sometimes move very slowly, and the investigation of Ockham's alleged heretical views ran on for three years from the time of his arrival in Avignon, without resulting in a condemnation. During this period, from 1325 to 1328, Ockham made the acquaintance of two prominent Franciscans who were attending on the papal court in order to defend their views concerning the vow of poverty, and the manner in which it was to be applied in practice. One of these men, Michael Cesena, was General of the Franciscan Order at that time; the other was Bonagratia, from Bergamo. Ockham's sympathies were won for their cause, so that soon after Pope John XXII decided the question unfavourably to their views, Ockham was excommunicated (June 6, 1328) along with Cesena and Bonagratia, all three of them having registered their protest, in writing, against the papal decision. Thus, although Ockham's summons to Avignon rested on accusations against his theological orthodoxy, his excommunication was not a consequence of these accusations. It resulted from his association, on the question of the Franciscan vow of poverty, with the views upheld by the General of his Order, and by Bonagratia. As far as is known, Ockham's theological orthodoxy, apart from the question of obedience to the Avignon papal authority, was never officially denied: and the charges which had occasioned his visit to Avignon were dropped.

Ockham, Cesena, and Bonagratia did not wait for the sentence of excommunication, but escaped from Avignon toward the end of May, 1328, seeking the protection of the Emperor Louis of Bavaria, who at that time had broken with the Avignon papal authority. Already the Emperor had given shelter to two other prominent teachers, Marsilius of Padua and John of Janun. Ockham and his companions settled down at the Franciscan headquarters in Munich, in 1330, and it was here, during the following eight years, that Ockham wrote his great mass of political treatises against the subordination of the civil authority to the papacy.

The course of Ockham's life and activities, after the Emperor's death in 1338, is a matter of mystery as far as our present knowledge is concerned. There is some evidence to indicate that he took up teaching activities, and possibly wrote his *Quodlibetal Questions*, at Strasbourg; it has even been argued that he returned to the University of Paris during the last decade of his life, on the ground that Paris became such a centre of Ockhamism at that time.

It is fairly certain that a few years before his death Ockham sought to be reconciled with his brother Franciscans who had remained loyal to the Avignon *curia* rather than to their General, Michael Cesena. After Cesena's death, in 1342, Ockham had taken over the seal of the Order and had acted as "Vicar of the Order" (i.e., of that part which did not recognize the Avignon authority); but in 1348 he sent the seal to William Farnier, who was General of the other faction. The tradition that at this time Ockham also sought to be restored to communion with the Holy See, has no documentary support, though it seems probable that he should have done so, since he was willing to surrender the seal of his Order to those who were in communion with the Avignon line of Popes. Whether or not he died excommunicate, is

not known—his death occurred on April 10th, 1349 (or 1350—
here again we are in ignorance), presumably because of the
plague which was decimating Europe at that time.[1]

Ockham's longest single work, and probably one of his
earliest, is his commentary on the *Sentences* of Peter Lombard.
This, likewise, is his principal theological work; his politico-
theological writings, written after his flight from Avignon,
form a considerable part of his total literary production, but
have little direct bearing on his nominalism and philosophical
views. Those of his writings that can be called strictly
philosophical in character, are concerned with logic and natural
philosophy. They include a *Summulae in libros physicorum*,
Quaestiones in octo libros physicorum, and two works on logic—in
addition, several shorter treatises on questions of natural
philosophy and logic are attributed to Ockham. His *Quodlibeta
septem* are also of direct philosophical, as well as theological,
interest. The same may be said of his commentary on the
Sentences, and to a lesser degree of the treatise *De sacramento
altaris* and of his *Centiloquium theologicum*.

The two works on logic, which are of most immediate
interest in the study of Ockham's theory of science and of
what is called his "nominalism," are the following: (1) *Summa
totius logicae*, written, according to its dedication, at the request
of a certain Brother Adam, who had expressed the desire to
see Ockham's logical theories presented in a single systematic
work; (2) *Expositio aurea super artem veterem*, which consists
of textual commentaries on Porphyry's *Isagoge*, and on
Aristotle's *Categoriae* and *De interpretatione*.[2] In these works

---

[1] For biographical data on Ockham, cf. Federhofer (*Phil. Jahrbuch* XXXVIII,
1925, pp. 39–48); also Abbagnano, ch. i, and Ueberweg-Geyer, pp. 572–4, containing references to all the principal sources of our scanty knowledge of Ockham's
life.

[2] The editions used for the present study are the following: "Summa totius
logicae Magistri Guielmi Occham Anglici logicorum argutissimi nuper cor-
recta. Venetiis 1508." This edition was edited by Marcus de Benevento, a
prominent nominalist of the time, and, according to Prantl (p. 329, Anm. 740) it
was worked over, if not rewritten, by this editor. Ehrle, *Peter von Candia*, p. 99,
also remarks: "Der Text ist im Druck von dem bekannten Nominalistenhaupt
Markus von Benevent humanistisch etwas überarbeitet." The "Golden Exposition" is here used in the 1496 edition: "Expositio aurea et admodum utilis super

is found Ockham's *ex professo* treatment of logic and of the nature of discursive science, though parts of his quodlibetal questions and of his commentary on the *Sentences*, also discuss logical and epistemological questions, and can be used as relevant sources. To take these latter works as the sole or principal source for Ockham's theory of science, neglecting the logical works and particularly that part of the *Summa totius logicae* which deals with demonstration, is likely to give a rather distorted view of Ockham's position. His constructive statement is in the logical works, whereas the *Quodlibeta*, and the commentary on the *Sentences*, touch on the nature of science either incidentally in the discussion of theological or other questions, or else by way of arguing detached problems removed from the context of the systematic exposition of logic.[1]

The order of composition of Ockham's works is a matter of considerable interest, but until further research is made into the manuscript tradition, the question can scarcely be settled with any degree of accuracy. It is generally conceded that the commentary on the *Sentences* is an early work, written at Oxford prior to Ockham's summons to Avignon in 1324; but the order and dates of composition of the other works are matters of extremely divergent opinions. From the time

---

artem veterem edita per venerabilem inceptorem fratrem Guilielmum de Occham cum quaestionibus Alberti parvi de Saxonia. Bononiae 1496." Prantl (ibid.) also questions the complete authenticity of this text, but Abbagnano, pp. 28–9, questions the evidence on which Prantl's opinion is based, and points out that the editor (Marcus de Benevento) is careful to indicate his own interpolations, keeping them distinct from the text of Ockham.

The "Brother Adam" in the dedication of the S. tot. log., is Adam Wodeham, according to Pelzer ("Les 51 articles de G. Occam censurés, en Avignon, en 1326," in *Revue d'histoire ecclésiastique*, 1922, pp. 240–70), and Michalski ("Les sources, etc . . .", Cracovie 1927) who had previously questioned it.

[1] Those parts of the *Quodlibeta* dealing with epistemology have been translated into English by Prof. Richard McKeon, in *Selections from Mediæval Philosophers*, vol. II, pp. 351–421 (Scribners, 1930), with an introductory sketch of Ockham's philosophical orientation which is worth more than one careful reading.

Ritter, Stöckl, Siebeck, Federhofer, and indeed practically all modern writers on Ockham, including even Prantl, appear to have given very little attention to the part of Ockham's *Summa totius logicae* dealing with demonstration. Yet it is here, if anywhere, that a direct statement of Ockham's theory of science ought to be sought.

when Ockham left Avignon (1328) until the end of the following decade (around 1340), he produced so many political writings that he would scarcely have had much time for philosophical composition. He did not die, however, until 1349 (or possibly 1350), and little is known of his activities during this last period of his life. Whether his *Quodlibeta*, his logical treatises, and his writings on physics, were written before he left Oxford in 1324, or during the last decade of his life, is a disputed and open question. That some of these works were written later seems likely, since otherwise his literary activity at Oxford would have been immense.[1]

The nature and extent of Ockham's own library is another question that must remain largely a matter of conjecture. In his logical works he refers constantly, of course, to Aristotle, and, in his commentary on Porphyry, to the author of the *Isagoge*. A fairly frequent use is made of Boethius, whose logical works were standard elements of a mediæval education, and of Avicenna and Averroes, of whom the same may perhaps be said. On logical questions Ockham makes more use of the authority of Averroes than of Avicenna, but on the whole he draws far less on the arab commentators than was usually the case among scholastic writers, and where he does draw on them it is only to add their support to a position already established by reason and by aristotelian principles. St. John Damascene is quoted occasionally, as is St. Anselm. In the part of the *Summa totius logicae* dealing with demonstration, Ockham makes rather frequent reference to Robert Grosseteste's commentary on the *Posterior Analytics*. St. Augustine, whose name appears so frequently in most mediæval treatises even when they are on logic or on natural philosophy, is

---

[1] On the manuscript tradition, and a list (not completely accurate) of Ockham's extant writings, cf. A. G. Little, *The Grey Friars at Oxford*, pp. 225–34. On the order and dates of composition, Federhofer (*Phil. Jahrbuch* XXXVIII, 1925, pp. 29–39) and Abbagnano (ch. i) have much to say, but rather insecure evidence for their conclusions. Cf. also Hochstetter, *Studien zur Metaph. u. Erkenntnislehre W. v. Ockham* (Diss. Berlin 1927), pp. 1–11; and Pelzer, *Les 51 articles, etc.*, pp. 245–6. Ockham's treatises are full of references to his own works, but since the manuscripts and editions are all of relatively late origin, and contain interpolations by copyists and editors, it is unsafe to base conclusions concerning the order of composition on such evidence, though this is the method employed by Federhofer.

mentioned only a few times in Ockham's logical works. Indeed, one looks in vain in Ockham's writings for the interest in the historical origins of philosophical theories, which is found, for example, in St. Thomas. Ockham, more than most of the great mediæval writers, seems content to deal directly and analytically with the philosophical problems and arguments which his age inherited from the past, without bothering to attach labels, or to indulge in historical inquiries, with respect to their authors or their origin.

The opinions and arguments introduced by Ockham for purposes of analysis and criticism, without mention of their authors, are many, but seem where they are identifiable at all to be derived chiefly from the works of his own contemporaries. Prantl and Abbagnano have attempted to identify some of these protagonists, among whom may be mentioned Duns Scotus, Franciscus de Mayronis, Durandus de St. Porcianus, Aegidius Romanus, Walter Burleigh, and Henry of Harclay.[1] Until further research, and the publication of critical editions of the works of the numerous Masters of the early fourteenth century, has taken place, positive identification of the arguments and opinions criticized by Ockham is scarcely possible. A rich and varied field of investigation awaits future historians and scholars, in this period, with many an unpublished and perhaps unknown manuscript waiting to see the light. Meanwhile we have to be content with the arguments themselves, anonymous though they be.

A further question of historical interest is that of the origin of the terminist logic which Ockham used and developed in his own restatement of the *Organon*. It has for a long time been a matter of debate whether the *Summulae logicales* written by Peter of Spain was a latin version of the *Synopsis of Aristotle's Logic* of Michael Psellos of Byzantium, or whether the latter was a greek version of the treatise of Peter of Spain. Prantl, who held with great tenacity to the former opinion, considered

---

[1] Prantl, *Gesch. d. Logik*, vol. III, pp. 330–61; Abbagnano, *Guglielmo di Ockham*, ch. ii, and especially pp. 75–85. Cf. also L. Baudry, "Les rapports de G. d'Occam et de Walter Burleigh," in *Archives d'histoire doctrinale et litteraire du moyen âge*, t. IX, 1934.

that the entire development of late thirteenth and early fourteenth century logic, in the latin West, was inspired by what he called the "Byzantine logic." In recent years, however, the balance of scholarly authority seems to favour the second hypothesis, so that the *Synopsis* of Psellos is regarded as a free translation of the *Summulae* of Petrus Hispanus.[1]

In any event, Prantl discovered fairly substantial traces of the terminist logic in Lambert of Auxerre (fl. ca. 1250) and in William Shyreswood (died 1249), both of whom included in their expositions of logic treatises on the *proprietates terminorum*.[2] If we assume that these writers were not borrowing or translating from Byzantine sources, the most probable hypothesis is that the terminist logic developed from the activities of the grammarians, who, during the thirteenth century, began to break away from unquestioning subservience to Priscian and Donatus, and to construct a philosophy of grammar. Grammar, in ancient times, had been the handmaiden of rhetoric; now it became the handmaiden of logic.[3]

Most of the terms and distinctions used by Ockham in his logical works are found also in the works of other scholastic writers of his time, and in the logical treatises attributed to Duns Scotus.[4] Ockham's originality is not to be sought

---

[1] The principal arguments against Prantl's position are given by Thurot, in *Rev. Archéol.*, N. S. X, pp. 267–81; and in *Rev. Critique*, XIII, pp. 194–203; by Valentin Rose, in *Hermes* II (1867), pp. 146–7 and pp. 465–7; and by R. Stapper, *Papst Johannes XXI* (Munster, 1898), pp. 16 ff. That the author of the *Summulae logicales* was not Pope John XXI, but another Petrus Hispanus who wrote the work around 1311, has been argued very convincingly by H. D. Simonin, O.P., in *Archives d'histoire doctrinale et litteraire du moyen âge*, 1930, pp. 267–78.

[2] Prantl, *Gesch. d. Logik*, vol. III, pp. 10–32.

[3] Cf. Paetow, *The Arts Course at Mediæval Universities with Special Reference to Grammar and Rhetoric* (Illinois Univ. Press); also ch. v of "Les Œuvres de Siger de Courtrai" by G. Wallerand (*Les Philosophes Belges*, t. VIII, Louvain, 1913).

[4] The characteristic innovations of the terminist logic, such as *suppositio, copulatio, restrictio, ampliatio, appellatio, distributio*, and *relatio*, which were the distinctions dealt with in treatises "de proprietatibus terminorum," are used to a considerably greater extent by Duns Scotus in the *Qu. sup. Perih.*, and the other logical works attributed to him and included in vol. I of Wadding's edition, than by Ockham. Indeed, Ockham makes practically no use of these terminist distinctions, beyond the distinction between *significatio* and *suppositio*, which goes back to Aquinas and even earlier; there is in Ockham's works no treatise on the "proprietates terminorum," beyond an analysis of modes of supposition. For the meanings of these terminist distinctions, cf. Prantl, vol. III, pp. 17–9, 31–2, and 51–68.

in the invention of terms or distinctions, but rather in the use he made of them in giving a new statement of the aristotelian logic. Whether this statement is to be regarded as a mediæval corruption of the authentic thought of Aristotle, or as a mediæval discovery of an aristotelianism freed from the corruption of an augustinian and neo-platonist interpretation, is a question of considerable interest and significance for the history of philosophy. The present study of Ockham's· exposition of logic aims to contribute, through a philosophical analysis of the content of his logical works, to the solution of this question.

IV

It is well, at the outset, to consider the alternative methods of pursuing the study of Ockham's logic, and to indicate the method chosen and the reasons favouring it. Ockham, in his logical works, is primarily concerned to give a clear and accurate statement of the characteristics of discursive thinking as such —and insofar as we make this interest predominant in our study of Ockham, the subject of inquiry is logic or the nature of discursive signification. But Ockham, in presenting his statement of logic and his philosophy of science, was not only a logician and philosopher, but also a critic of his contemporaries, and a professed interpreter of Aristotle. Insofar as we are interested in these aspects of Ockham's discussions, the subject of our inquiry is no longer logic itself, or discursive signification as such, but it is *Ockham's logic* as an interpretation of the *Organon*, and as a criticism of alternative interpretations of the *Organon* such as were prevalent in Ockham's time. In the same way, our material suggests two different sorts of question: first, what are the primary concepts and principles presupposed by Ockham's analysis of the character of discursive science, and how adequate or how intelligible is his

---

When Ockham's logical works are compared with the treatises on logic produced by his contemporaries and by many who were his predecessors, he is seen to have been less of an innovator and fabricator of verbal distinctions, than a critic of the innovations and verbalism of his times.

analysis when grasped in function of its own intrinsic principles and aim? Secondly, stressing the historical interest, we may ask how accurate an interpreter of Aristotle Ockham was, and whether his interpretation of the *Organon* is more faithful, or less, than the alternative interpretations which he criticized and rejected.

To attempt to give an answer to the second question, without previously answering the first question, is equivalent to an attempt to build a house without knowing whether the materials put together are stone or wood or metal. To judge concerning Ockham's accuracy as an interpreter of Aristotle, one must first possess an accurate and adequate understanding of the aristotelian philosophy that Ockham was interpreting, *and* of the philosophical principles regulating Ockham's interpretation. To possess such understanding, to a degree sufficient to give any great measure of objective validity to one's judgments and estimates, is surely no easy matter. Aristotle himself was *the* authentic aristotelian, and all other aristotelians are *interpreters* of the Stagyrite. Such was Ockham, and such were the scotists, thomists, and other mediæval writers whose interpretations of Aristotle were rejected or modified by Ockham. To compare these alternative interpretations to the "real Aristotle," is only to measure them by still another interpretation set up, implicitly or explicitly, by the historian who makes the comparisons, and who offers, as the fruit of his inquiries, his "conclusions."

The disadvantages of this method of direct comparison and synthetic judgment, both from the viewpoint of historical accuracy and from that of philosophic value, are fairly obvious. But if we decline to use the method of comparison and judgment by reference to our own version of the "true Aristotle," what method remains? How investigate Ockham's aristotelianism? There remains the method of analysis and exposition—the detailed study of Aristotle's *Organon* through *the eyes of Ockham*, in his own terms and by the light of his own principles. Here our task is not that of judging the work of one man by the standards of another, or by what we judge to be the standards of the other—rather it is to seek to understand the content of a philosophical work by following its author in his own analysis of philosophical problems, and by seeking to grasp his analysis in terms of the subject matter itself and of its own principles.

In the case of Ockham, this alternative method—that of exposition and analysis—has much to recommend it. For one thing, despite the fact that Ockham's "nominalism" has played an extremely prominent part in historical judgments concerning late mediæval and early modern philosophies, a survey of the secondary literature on Ockham shows a surprising absence of detailed or analytic studies of what Ockham's nominalism was. Though many mediæval scholars appear to concur in the judgment that Ockham's nominalism had a corrosive effect on scholastic philosophy, and that it was responsible for many of the characteristic attitudes and problems of seventeenth century thought, few of these scholars seem to agree on a definite *philosophical* basis, in Ockham's writings, for the conclusions which they share. It is easy to learn, from secondary sources, that Ockham's nominalism was responsible for countless scientific and philosophical tendencies of early modern times—but it is not easy to learn, from these sources, what Ockham's nominalism was.

Furthermore, the scarcity of texts of Ockham's philosophical works, by which historical estimates of his influence and of the directions of his thought might be checked, makes an expository and analytic treatment of his logic particularly desirable. Aristotle's writings are everywhere available, and hence, if the reader wishes to reach a considered opinion of his own, as to whether Ockham was a good interpreter of Aristotle or not, he is not forced to depend on any secondary source for his understanding of the Stagyrite. He is, however, forced in most instances to depend on secondary sources for his understanding of Ockham. Consequently, next to bringing out a critical edition of Ockham's works, the publication of a detailed analytic exposition of Ockham's theory of science, in his own terms and in function of the discussions in which he was himself engaged, can provide part of the foundation required for sound judgments concerning Ockham's aristotelianism.

In the present work, consequently, we propose to use historical comparison and contrast only to the extent justified by Ockham's text. Insofar as he presents his theory of science by way of criticizing alternative views upheld by his predecessors and contemporaries, the discussion of the problems dealt with by Ockham, in terms of the concepts and convictions of other thinkers, is justified—indeed, it is to some degree required for the clear grasp of Ockham's own position. Thus we will have occasion to consider, along with Ockham's analysis of discursive signification, the alternative statements offered by Porphyry, Averroes, Avicenna, Duns Scotus, and others. We will not, however, find it necessary, for the purpose of understanding Ockham's exposition of logic or the metaphysics involved in it, to translate his discussions into the language and context of seventeenth century philosophy— for while it is possible that some of the seventeenth century thinkers were concerned to defend, or to criticize, Ockham's logic, it is not possible that Ockham was trying to defend, criticize, or *anticipate*, Locke, Berkeley, or Descartes.

Ockham also presented his exposition of logic as an interpretation of Aristotle's *Organon*, and consequently constant reference to the aristotelian text is justified, and indeed required, for the understanding of his exposition. Much of this exposition consists of explicit discussions of Aristotle's text, in which Ockham seeks to justify his own mode of interpretation and to invalidate conflicting interpretations. Ockham's arguments, in such cases, rest not on a merely philological basis, but rather on an appeal to what he considered to be the *principles* of Aristotle's philosophical analyses. Hence our use of the aristotelian texts, in expounding Ockham, will be guided by the aim of *clarification* of Ockham's interpretation, rather than by the aim of judging his interpretation through a grammatical analysis of particular sentences or paragraphs in Aristotle.

In general, the method which has been adopted for our present study of Ockham's logic, is determined not by the aim of passing judgment on Ockham's principles or conclusions, but by the aim of understanding what they are. In the same way, where material from Aristotle's writings is brought in, or where references to Aristotle are given in the notes, the purpose is not to *judge* Ockham's aristotelianism by our own choice of citations from Aristotle, but to make "Ockham's Aristotle" more evident to the reader.

The above method of studying Ockham leaves to the reader, for the most part, the task of deciding whether or not Ockham's conception of science was aristotelian, or whether it was more so, or less so, than the scotist and other mediæval interpretations that Ockham rejected. If the exposition and analysis of Ockham's work in logic, undertaken in the pages which follow, provide a more accurate foundation than has hitherto been available, for the reader's judgment on this question, our efforts will have been sufficiently justified. And if, by chance, some should feel the philosophical power of Ockham's analysis of discourse, as a thing of value and significance even in the twentieth century and in the age of relativity physics, the ends of philosophy, as well as of the history of philosophy, will have been served.

CHAPTER TWO

THE LOGIC OF TERMS

THE fundamental preoccupation of William of Ockham, in his exposition of aristotelian logic, is in maintaining the distinction between those forms or characters of discourse attributable to the voluntary operations of the human mind, and those elements which cannot be exhibited as products of synthetic rational operations, but which are apprehended by the mind as indivisible principles of its knowledge of nature. This preoccupation is indicated, at the start of Ockham's treatment of logic, (I) in his discussion of the status of logic among the sciences; (II) in his discussion of the nature of the term or concept; and (III) in his discussion of the distinctions between absolute and connotative terms, and between concrete and abstract terms.

I

In the *Proemium* to his commentary on Porphyry, Ockham states what logic is, its causes, its utility, its distinction from other sciences, and its status as an art rather than as a speculative discipline. Like any science whatever, logic is something present in the intellective soul, and hence is not a substance but rather an accidental determination or qualification of a substance. More precisely, it is a collection of habits of knowledge (*collectio habituum*) in the mind of anyone who can be said to possess the science.

Like any science, logic has only two essential causes— efficient and final. Its efficient cause, insofar as it is a discipline acquired by instruction, is the teacher; its immediate final

cause is the actual understanding of the propositions of which
logic is composed, and by which the habitual understanding
of the science is in the first instance acquired. Its mediate
end, or ulterior purpose, is that for the sake of which logic
exists—namely, the science of nature. It is worth noting that
Ockham here speaks as if logic were the instrument only of
the philosophy of nature, and not of *philosophia prima* or
metaphysics, a view which receives considerable confirmation
from his later discussions.[1]

The utility of logic is two-fold. As instrument of demonstrative science, it enables us to distinguish principles from
conclusions, necessary propositions from contingent and
impossible ones, and truths which are known from truths
which are merely believed. Its other utility is in enabling us
to recognize the implicative connections between propositions
hypothetically assumed in dialectical argument or inquiry.
The truth attributed to probable or hypothetical premises,
being neither self-evident nor demonstrable, is attributed
to them by analogy, the evident principles of demonstrative
science being the standard or exemplar, so to speak, by
analogy with which the meaning of "hypothesis" or of
"probable truth" is understood.[2]

The differentia between logic and the other sciences, whereby

---

[1] Exp. aur., I, Proem., 1r: "Logica . . . est una collectio multorum habituum."
"Sciendum est quod istius scientiae, sicut cuiuslibet alterius scientiae, sunt tantum
duae causae essentiales, proprie loquendo de causis, cuius ratio est quia nulla res
simplex non composita ex partibus alterius et alterius rationis potest habere nisi
duas causas, scilicet efficientem et finalem." The final cause "est actus cognoscendi
ex quo talis habitus generatur, finis autem illorum actuum, qui est finis mediatus
habitus vel habituum, est ille propter quem ellitiuntur; de hoc tamen pertinet
tractare ad scientiam naturalem." For a discussion of the question of the non-
discursive character of metaphysics, and of logic as an instrument only of discursive
science, see ch. iv, section I.

[2] Exp. aur., I, Proem., 1r: "videndum est de istius scientiae utilitate, circa
quod est sciendum quod istius scientiae multae sunt utilitates, inter quas una est
facilitas discernendi verum a falso, unde ista scientia perfecte habita faciliter
iudicatur quid verum quid falsum, et hoc quantum ad illa quae per propositiones
per se notas possunt sciri, cum in talibus non oporteat nisi ordinate procedere a
propositionibus per se notis ad alia quae consequuntur ex eis, et tale processum seu
discursum docet logica. . . . Alia utilitas est pro modo arguendi et respondendi,
nam per istam artem docetur quae est propositio repugnans, quid consequens et
quid antecedens, quibus faciliter notis repugnans negatur, consequens conceditur,
et ad antecedens secundum sui qualitatem sicut ad impertinens respondetur."

logic is called "rational science" and the other sciences are called "real sciences," is the following: Whereas the propositions of logic state truths about the terms, propositions, and arguments used in the real sciences, the real sciences *use* such forms of discourse to state truths about things that are not concepts or parts of discourse, but which exist by nature, and are principles of natural knowledge. Logic, in other words, is the analysis of discursive science *qua* discursive, while the real sciences, which *are* discursive, are *about* things that exist by nature and not by the operations of reason. The things that exist by nature are individual things, but they are signified *per se* (in abstraction from this or that time, place, or other accidental determination or circumstance) by concepts which are called universal, because they are univocal signs of many. Hence, since only terms or concepts are properly called "universals," it follows that only logic treats of things which can be called universals, while the real sciences state propositions which are universally true of the individuals signified by their terms.[1]

It is to be noted that the terms which logic *uses* (called terms of second intention, because they signify terms and not things), do not signify concepts *qua* "psychic states," but only as modes of signification. If logic were concerned with psychic states as such, it would be a part of psychology, and its terms would stand not for terms *qua* signs of things, but *qua* "real things." On the other hand, though the logician must distinguish terms or concepts by their characteristics as signs of things, he does not found his distinctions between terms on the distinctions between different kinds of individuals signified by such terms or concepts, but confines his attention to the differences in *modes* of signification. If this were not the case, the logician, to know his own science, would have to know

[1] Exp. aur., I, Proem., lv: "de aliis est ista scientia et de aliis aliae scientiae, nam ista scientia saltem principaliter tradit notitia conceptuum et intentionum per animam fabricatarum, non extra se quomodo fabricantur res artificiales, sed intra se . . . cuiusmodi sunt sillogismi, propositiones, termini . . ." Logic is called *scientia rationalis* "quia determinat de hiis quae sine ratione esse non possunt, aliae autem scientiae de rebus extra animam existentibus determinant." Cf. also Sent. I, Dist. II, Qu. 4 M (cited by Prantl, p. 352, Anm. 797) on this distinction.

the natures of all the "real things" of which the natural sciences treat.[1]

Since logic, according to Ockham, is concerned neither with the things signified by concepts, nor with concepts as "things" (in the sense of "psychic states"), it is not a speculative science. Rather it is a set of rules concerning the ways in which the human reason, through voluntary operations of synthesis or analysis, can construct sciences *about* things, and exhibit its constructions (i.e., the demonstrations of the science) as determinate kinds of syntheses of determinate elements which are the principles of the science. Logic, in other words, is an art, concerned with the ways in which the human mind can construct forms of significant expression from pre-existent elements, just as a plastic art is concerned with the ways in which the artist can construct statues and portraits, etc., out of pre-existent elements. In the words of Ockham, logic deals principally with those concepts and intentions "fabricated by the mind, not outside of itself as artificial things are fabricated, but within itself"; and it is called *scientia rationalis* because it treats of "those things which cannot exist without the reason."[2]

The use of the word "fabrication," in describing the aspect of discursive thought with which logic deals, is most significant. Fabrication is not creation; it requires and presupposes elements or principles which are the starting points of the fabrication of different products. If logic deals with human discourse insofar as it is a procedure of fabrication, it deals with it insofar as it can be exhibited as a set of voluntary synthetic operations dependent on pre-existent elements or principles which control these operations and which are not produced by them. In other words, the existence of logic, as Ockham understands it, presupposes the existence of real

---

[1] S. tot. log., III, ii, 22, fol. 68v. Speaking of such propositions as "animal est genus," "homo est species," etc., Ockham says: "si tales propositiones per se ad logicam pertinerent, . . . logicus non posset perfecte scire logicam nisi cognosceret naturam omnium rerum, imo etiam nisi cognosceret omnes conclusiones et omnia principia omnium scientiarum." A proposition of logic would be such as "genus predicatur de specie universaliter et non e converso."

[2] Exp. aur., I, Proem., lv; cited *ante*, p. 33, Note 1.

science, and real science, in turn, presupposes the existence of determinate natures the grasp of which yields the principles of the science.

Each real science, insofar as it is demonstrative, is concerned with making its conclusions and demonstrations (which are the "fabrications" proper to that science) known by its principles (which are not "fabrications" but are the pre-existent elements or starting points of the discursive structure). Logic is concerned with the ways in which *conclusions as such* can be exhibited as formally dependent on *principles as such*; it does not make known either conclusions or principles, but teaches the ways in which any discursive science may be analysed in terms of its own principles and of the forms of synthesis characteristic of discursive signification as such. It is therefore a universal discipline, to precisely the extent that discursive science as a whole is universal. And to the extent that it is concerned with discourse *qua* rational construction from principles known but not constructed by reason, it is an art, and an instrument of real science.

While it is stated by Ockham that logic deals *principally* with those concepts and intentions of the mind which are fabrications, or products of voluntary rational operations, he does not state that logic deals exclusively with them. For just as the fabrication of a product by an artist presupposes the existence of the elements out of which his product is made, so the art which gives the rules of such fabrication presupposes the recognition of the elements insofar as their character determines or limits the *kinds of operations* taught by the art. Hence logic deals partially, and as if by way of introduction, with the elements or *principia* of discursive science insofar as these elements determine the character of discursive knowledge as such. It need not differentiate between the principles of this or that science, but only between ultimate kinds of principles or elements that are distinguishable in *any* discursive science.

Thus, since every discursive science requires not only its subject genus, but also attributes which it demonstrates of

its subject, logic requires, for the formulation and understanding of its rules, the recognition of the distinction *in
nature* of substance and accident—i.e., of principles by which
the existence of things is apprehended by man through sense
preception or intuition, and of principles by which the things
so apprehended can be understood to be what they are
independently of our ways of coming to apprehend their
existence.

Whether this distinction is properly included within logic,
or belongs only to natural science as a "real distinction,"
so that logic to this extent presupposes a distinction that belongs
to physics, is not explicitly stated by Ockham, and is perhaps
not of great importance. What is significant, however, is
Ockham's statement that the book of *Categories*, in which this
distinction is made to the extent required for the analysis of
forms of incomplex signification, is "partly speculative."[1]
An art which presupposed no speculative knowledge, and which
could teach how to produce things without requiring recognition of pre-existent elements out of which to produce them,
would be no longer a human art, but a divine one—for it
would be the art of creation *ex nihilo*. Ockham's characterization of the things of which logic principally treats, as
"fabrications" of the human mind, and as products of pre-
existent elements recognized by the mind but not produced
by it, indicates his basic realism, and his full acceptance of
the aristotelian view of scientific knowledge as dependent on
indemonstrable and immediate understanding of essential
nature—an understanding that is "neither innate in a determinate form, nor developed from other higher states of
knowledge, but from sense-perception."[2]

Ockham quotes Avicenna to the effect that logic is a
"practical" rather than a speculative science, because it
deals with things done by us (*de operibus nostris*), whereas

---

[1] Exp. aur., II, Proem., 37r: "dicendum est quod iste liber (*scil.* Categoriae)
pro aliqua sui parte est speculativus et pro alia sui parte est practicus . . . nam
aliqua pars est de operibus nostris sicut illa quae est de sermonibus. . . . Alia
pars non est de operibus nostris, et illa est speculativa. . . ."
[2] Arist., An. Post., II, 19, 100a, 9-11.

speculative sciences are concerned with things that are not products of human operations. The term "practical science," as here used, has the generalized meaning of any discipline that is not speculative. Among practical sciences there is a distinction between "dictative" and "ostensive" sciences: the former, which are the moral disciplines, state what things *ought* to be sought or avoided, while the latter, which are the arts, state how things *can* be done. Logic is chiefly concerned with stating how terms can be combined significantly, and with the analysis of conclusions as such into principles as such, and of kinds of terms into kinds of elements or *principia* of definition. All forms of discourse, however, which can be exhibited by logic as products of the synthetic and voluntary operations of reason, or as equivalent to such syntheses, are "things done by us." Hence, though logic presupposes the speculative recognition of the distinction between substantial and accidental being, as the starting point for its analysis of the forms of discursive knowledge, it is properly characterized as an "ostensive practical science," which is to say, as an art.[1]

These remarks of Ockham concerning the nature of logic, and its distinction from the "real sciences," are worth weighing against the statement made by some modern historians of philosophy that Ockham's point of view tended to be anti-metaphysical. To give a metaphysical status to the forms of discourse, by erasing the distinction between forms of statement

---

[1] Exp. aur., I, Proem., lv: "dicendum est sicut Avicenna dicit in principio suae Metaphysicae quod distinctio inter scientias practicas et speculativas est, quia scientiae practicae sunt de operibus nostris, scientiae autem speculativae non sunt de operibus nostris. Ex quo patet quod logica est dicendum practica, quia cum scientia logicae tractet de sillogismis, propositionibus, et huiusmodi, quae non nisi a nobis fieri possunt, sequitur quod est de operibus nostris. . . ." Cf. Sent., Prolog., Qu. 4, 11 N (Prantl, p. 331, Anm. 741): "Logica, rhetorica, et grammatica sunt vere notitiae practicae et non speculativae, quia vere dirigunt intellectum in operationibus suis, quae sunt mediate voluntate in sua potestate, sicut logica dirigit intellectum in sillogizando, discurrendo, et sic de aliis. Potest tamen distingui de practica, quia quaedam est dictativa et quaedam tantum ostensiva; prima est illa, quae determinate dictat, aliquid esse faciendum vel non faciendum . . . et isto modo nec logica nec rhetorica est practica nec etiam ars quaecunque mechanica. . . . Ostensiva non dictat aliquid fugiendum aut persequendum, sed tantum ostendit quomodo opus fieri potest. . . ."

and the things of which statements are true or false, has much the same effect as the tendency, usually attributed to nominalism, to characterize *all* concepts as mental constructs and to deny to science any principles other than the rules of logical construction. Both tendencies are, in the aristotelian sense, anti-metaphysical, and both were criticized and combated by Ockham. What was important to him was the maintenance of the distinction between concepts whose determinate character is a function of the essential or individual ("undivided") natures of the things they signify, and concepts whose character is in part determined by human ways of apprehending things or by synthetic operations of the mind. On this distinction, in Ockham's view, depends the distinction within the natural sciences between first principles and the truths known by them, a distinction that is all important to Aristotle, and to the maintenance of which the principal arguments of the *Posterior Analytics* are devoted.[1]

II

Logic, according to Ockham, treats of terms, propositions, and arguments insofar as they can be exhibited as "fabrications" of reason—as products of the voluntary operations of synthesis and analysis that characterize discursive thought *qua* discursive. This is much the same as saying that logic is concerned with the propositions of the sciences not from the standpoint of their accordance with fact or existence, but from the standpoint of their formal character as kinds of

---

[1] The characterization of Ockham as anti-metaphysical in tendency is found in De Wulf, *Hist. of Med. Phil.*, vol. II, p. 185: "The conceptualist terminism, and the impoverishment of metaphysics, are the most significant elements in Ockham." Whether this "impoverishment" is or is not a purification, effected by Ockham's desire to maintain, without qualification, and in accordance with Aristotle's principles as expressed in the Posterior Analytics, the "firstness" of the first principles of the sciences, is a question worth keeping in mind in our analysis of his logical works. M. De Wulf, who likes to speak of scotism as "metaphysically rich," would perhaps, from Ockham's point of view, be open to the accusation of wanting to enrich metaphysics by clothing it with things not rightfully or essentially its own. The danger of course is that of the rich man in general—to take care of his possessions he is all too likely to become the servant of them.

synthesis of terms. Similarly, logic is concerned with terms
not from the standpoint of the things which they signify,
but from the standpoint of exhibiting them as different forms
of signification determined by principles of signification such
as are primary and unanalysable. In both respects logic
differs from the natural sciences, which, though they *use*
terms to signify things and *use* propositions to state facts, are
concerned with things and with facts, and not, like logic,
with modes of signifying things and of stating facts.

Since logic is the analysis of modes of signification into
such elements as cannot be exhibited as products of the
synthetic operations of the mind, and since all arguments are
reducible, by analysis, to propositions, and all propositions
to terms, it follows that the starting point of logic, in its
statement of the principles of discursive signification, is the
term. What the term is, what forms it may have and the
relation between these forms, as well as the properties of
the term as an element of discursive signification or statement,
are questions to which Ockham gives a precise answer, and
which reveal fundamental and characteristic features of his
interpretation of Aristotle.[1]

In the *Prior Analytics* Aristotle defines the term as that into
which the proposition is resolved, as into subject and predicate.
Taking this definition as a starting point, Ockham refers to
Boethius' distinction between the three forms that a given
term may have, and discusses the relation between them. A
term may be written, spoken, or simply understood in the
mind. Now it is said that the written and spoken forms are
subordinate, in some sense, to the concepts corresponding to
them. In what sense, precisely, is this subordination to be
understood? Boethius states that the spoken word signifies the
concept, and that the written word signifies the spoken word;
and most mediæval logicians followed him in giving this
interpretation to Aristotle's statement in the *De Interpretatione*,

---

[1] S. tot. log., I, 1, 1r: "Omnes logicae tractatores intendunt astruere quod
argumenta et sillogismi ex propositionibus, et propositiones ex terminis componuntur. Unde terminus aliud non est quam pars propinqua propositionis."

that "Spoken words are the symbols of mental experience
and written words are the symbols of spoken words."[1]

Ockham concedes that in the broadest sense of the word
"sign," the spoken word is a sign of the concept. In this broad
sense anything is a sign of its cause, or of whatever comes
into the mind when it is itself apprehended; and since the
spoken word is an indication of the presence, in the mind of
of the speaker, of the concept corresponding to it, we may in
this sense say that it "signifies" the concept. But we cannot
say that the spoken word signifies the concept in the sense
that it *means* the concept, or in the sense that it denotes it—
in this sense of the word "signify," the spoken word signifies not
the concept, but rather the thing or things signified by the
concept. The spoken or written word, in this sense, is a sign
of the thing or things which it can denote, just as much as the
concept is. It is subordinate to the concept only·because the
signification of the written or spoken word is established by
convention, whereas the signification of the concept is
established by the act of understanding which brings it into
existence. The concept, in other words, is a *natural sign* of
what it means or of the things it can denote, whereas the
written or spoken word is instituted by convention to be a
sign of what the concept corresponding to it signifies by
nature.[2]

Since a sign, whether a natural or conventional sign, is
something in itself, besides being a sign of something other

---

[1] Arist., De int., 1, 16a 4–5. Ockham, S. tot. log., I, 1, 1r: "Diffiniens enim
terminum Aristoteles primo Priorum dicit: 'Terminum voco in quem resolvitur
propositio, ut in predicatum vel de quo predicatur. . . .'" Cf. Arist., An. Priora I,
1, 24b 16–18. Ockham, ibid.: "Est itaque sciendum quod sicut secundum
Boetium primo Perihermenias triplex est oratio, *scil.* scripta, prolata, et concepta
tantum habens esse in intellecta; sic triplex est terminus: scriptus, prolatus,
conceptus. . . . Unde isti termini concepti . . . sunt illa verba mentalia quae
beatus Augustinus dicit quinto De Trinitate nullius esse linguae, quae tantum in
mente manent et exterius proferri non possunt, quamvis voces tanquam signa
eis subordinata pronuntientur exterius." Cf. Boethius, *In libr. de int. ed. prima*
(Migne PL 64, cl. 297 B–C): "rem concipit intellectus, intellectum vero voces
designant, ipsa vero voces litterae significant."

[2] S. tot. log., I, 1, lv: "Dicimus autem voces esse signa subordinata conceptibus
vel intentionibus, non quia proprie accipiendo hoc vocabulum 'signum' ipsae
voces significant ipsos conceptus primo et proprie, sed quia voces imponuntur ad

than itself, a sharp distinction is drawn between two ways in which it can enter into discourse. The word "man," for example, or the concept corresponding to it, is used quite differently in the proposition "Man is an animal" from the way it is used in the statement "Man is a noun." In the first case it is taken as standing for the individual real things of which it is a sign; in the second case it is taken as standing for itself as a determinate kind of sign, and it does not stand for the individual things (*scil*. Socrates, Plato, etc.) which it means. Where a term is used to stand for the things which it means, it is said to be used significatively, or to have "personal supposition" in the proposition of which it is subject or predicate. If, however, it does not stand for what it *means*, but for the kind of sign (whether conceived, spoken, or written) that it *is*, then it is said to be used non-significatively, or to have "simple or material supposition"—"simple" if it is taken as an instance of the kind of *concept* that it is, and "material" if it be taken as an instance of the kind of *spoken or written sign* that it is.[1]

significandum illa eadem, quae per conceptus mentis significantur, ita quod conceptus primo naturaliter aliquod significat, et secundario vox illud idem significat, in tantum quod voce instituta ad significandum aliquod signatum per conceptum mentis, si conceptus ille mutaret significatum suum, eo ipso vox sine nova institutione suum significatum mutaret; et pro tanto dicit Aristoteles quod voces sunt earum quae sunt in anima passionum notae, sic etiam intelligit Boetius quando dicit voces significare conceptus." " . . . conceptus sive passio animae naturaliter significat quicquid significat. Terminus autem prolatus vel scriptus nihil significat nisi secundum voluntariam institutionem. . . . Propter tamen protervos est sciendum quod signum dupliciter accipitur. Uno modo pro omni illo quod apprehensum, aliquid aliud in cognitionem facit venire, quamvis non faciat mentem venire in primum cognitionem eius . . . et sic vox naturaliter significat aliquid sicut quaelibet effectus significat saltem suam causam . . . sed tam generaliter non loquor hic de signo. Aliter accipitur signum pro illo quod aliquid facit in cognitionem venire et natum est pro illo supponere vel addi in propositione, . . . vel quod natum est componi ex talibus, cuiusmodi est oratio vel propositio, et sic accipiendo hoc vocabulum 'signum,' vox nullius est signum naturale."

[1] S. tot. log., I, 63, 24v: "restat dicere de suppositione quae est proprietas conveniens termino sed nunquam nisi propositione. . . . Dicitur autem suppositio, id est *pro aliis positio*, ita quod quando terminus in propositione stat pro aliquo, utimur illo termino pro illo, *scil*. de quo sive pronomine demonstrante ipsum, ille terminus . . . verificetur." "Suppositio personalis universaliter est illa quando terminus supponit pro suo significato. . . . Suppositio simplex est quando terminus supponit pro intentione animae, sed non tenetur significative. . . . Suppositio

Having established the distinction between the significative and non-significative use of words, Ockham makes Aristotle's definition of the term more precise, through stating that a term is that which, taken significatively (or having personal supposition), can be subject or predicate of a proposition. In this way syncategorematic words, which cannot if taken significatively be complete subjects or predicates of a proposition, are excluded. For though we might form the proposition "Every is an adjective," in such a statement the word "every" is not taken significatively, but has material supposition, being used not for what it means, but rather as an instance of the kind of word it is.[1]

---

materialis est quando terminus non supponit significative, et supponit vel pro voce vel pro scripto, sicut patet hic 'homo est nomen,' ubi 'homo' supponit pro se ipso, et tamen non significat seipsum."

The distinction between different kinds of supposition of terms is an old distinction in mediæval logic, but the earlier writers merely distinguished "material" from "formal" supposition. In William Shyreswood (see Prantl, p. 18, Anm. 61) *suppositio materialis* is distinguished from *suppositio formalis* in the customary manner, but the latter is subdivided into *suppositio simplex* and *suppositio personalis*. This is perhaps the earliest use of this distinction within "formal supposition." Michalski, (*Le criticisme et le scepticisme, etc.* . . . Cracovie, 1926, pp. 118–21) mentions that these distinctions are found in Petrus Hispanus, who defines *suppositio simplex* as "acceptio termini communis pro re universali significata per ipsum terminum." Michalski considers that the difference between Peter of Spain's definition, and that of Ockham, marks the point of transition from aristotelianism to nominalism. But to Ockham the notion of a *res universalis*, distinct alike from a thought in the mind and from individuals outside the mind, is utterly un-aristotelian, and suggestive of the separated forms criticized by Aristotle, or of the eternal exemplars of the augustinian and arab illumination theories of knowledge. If Ockham's position is justified, the transition here noted is not from aristotelianism to nominalism, as Michalski holds, but from platonism to aristotelianism.

[1] S. tot. log., I, 2, iv: "Tertio modo accipitur (*scil.* terminus) praecise et magis stricte pro illo quod significative sumptum potest esse subiectum vel predicatum alicuius propositionis. . . . Multa etiam nomina non sunt termini, ut nomina syncategorematica, quia talia quamvis possint esse extrema propositionis si sumantur materialiter vel simpliciter, tamen quando sumuntur significative non possunt esse extrema propositionum. . . . Et illo modo accipit Philosophus terminum primo Priorum."

The distinction between categorematic and syncategorematic terms, which is found in modern "traditional logic" as well as in mediæval logic, is expressed by Ockham as follows, S. tot. log. I, 4, 3r: "Termini cathegoreumatici sunt qui finitam et certam habent significationem, sicut hoc nomen *homo* significat omnes homines, et hoc nomen *animal* significat ómnia animalia, et hoc nomen *albedo* omnes albedines. Termini autem syncathegoreumatici sunt tales: *omnis, nullus, aliquis, totus, praeter, tantum, inquantum*, et huiusmodi, qui non habent finitam significationem et certam, nec significant aliquas res distinctas a rebus significatis per cathegoreumata; imo sicut in algorismo cifra per se posita nihil significat,

The distinction between the significative and non-significative supposition of terms is required for the avoidance of equivocation and of sophistical refutations such as rest on the fact that we not only use words or concepts to signify things, but can, by the reflective power of the mind, also consider the same words or concepts *as* acts of signification or of understanding. What we cannot do is to use a word or concept significatively and non-significatively at the same time, as would be the case if this argument were valid: "Man is a species, Socrates is a man, therefore Socrates is a species." Similarly, the "vicious circle fallacy," for whose avoidance the "theory of types" was developed in recent times, is easily obviated by the distinction between the significative and non-significative supposition of terms. Thus in the statement "What I am saying is false," the subject term stands either for itself as a term (in which case the statement is false because the predicate "false" cannot signify anything that is not a proposition), or else it stands for something other than itself (e.g., for "what I have just said,") in which case there is no vicious circle.

In the propositions of the real sciences, and in the propositions which belong properly to logic, the terms are always used significatively. For though the terms in the propositions of a real science stand for things which are not terms, while those of logic stand for terms or other forms of discourse, in both cases the terms stand for what they mean, and hence have personal supposition. Thus "a genus is predicable of the species ordered under it" is a pure proposition of logic, in which both subject and predicate are used significatively. But "animal is predicable of the species ordered under it," or "animal is predicable *per se* of man," are not properly propositions of logic nor of real science, but appear when

---

sed addita alteri figurae facit eam significare, ita syncathegoreumata proprie loquendo nihil significant sed magis addita alteri termino faciunt aliud significare; sive faciunt ipsum pro aliquo vel aliquibus determinato modo supponere, seu aliud officium circa cathegoreuma exercent." E.g., "every", taken alone, has no definite reference to anything, but "every man" has; "every" is syncategorematic, and "man" is categorematic.

logical rules are applied, as to their instances, to the propositions of real science.[1]

Science, whether it is of things that exist by nature, or of
concepts or parts of discourse that exist only by human operations of signification, is of the universal, and not of particular
instances. Hence the logician, stating rules about predication
and about genera and species, does not need to know all
the particular terms that can be predicated as genus of their
species, any more than the physicist, who states truths about
changeable bodies, has to know each moveable body that
exists or that may exist. Where particular instances are
mentioned, either by the physicist or by the logician, it is for
the sake of illustration. Such illustrations, though useful in
teaching a science, are not what the scientist is trying to
teach.

Ockham, as we have already seen, distinguishes logic from
the real sciences by the fact that logic states truths about forms
of discourse, while the real sciences use such forms of discourse
for the statement of truths about things which are not signs.
This distinction can be stated in another way, by saying that
the propositions that strictly belong to the real sciences are
composed of *terms of first intention*, taken significatively, while
the propositions that strictly belong to logic are composed of
terms of second intention, also used significatively.

A term is used significatively, as we have seen, when it is
used to denote, or to "stand for," the things of which the concept, by which its meaning has been established, is a *natural
sign*. A concept is a natural sign of what it can denote, and
not a conventional sign, because its meaning is not imposed
on it by convention, but it is itself the act or habit of meaning
the things which it can denote, or of identifying the things that
can be identified by it. Thus we might, by agreement, decide
to use the *words* "whiteness" and "blackness" as synonyms,
but we could not by voluntary agreement make the ideas or
concepts, which correspond to these words according to their
present usage, cease to be distinct and contrary.

[1] Cf. *Ante*, p. 34. Note 1.

All terms therefore, whose denotation is determined by some determinate concept or intention of the mind, are terms either of *first* or of *second intention*.[1]

Terms of second intention are significant categorematic words, or the concepts corresponding to them, such as can stand only for things that are terms or forms of discourse. For example, the words "proposition," "term," "subject," "predicate," etc., are words which can, when taken significatively, stand only for parts of discourse—written, spoken, or thought. All significant categorematic words, or the concepts corresponding to them, such as are not terms of second intention, are *terms of first intention;* that is to say, all terms which signify things that exist by nature, apart from human acts of signifying them, are terms of first intention. These are the terms used in the propositions of the real sciences, which can stand only for things that can exist by nature, and not for things that exist only through the operations of human discursive thought.

In addition to the terms used in the pure propositions of natural science (terms of first intention), and to the terms that belong properly in the propositions of logic (terms of second intention), there is a group of metaphysical terms convertible with "being," that signify not only the things signified by terms of first intention, but also the things signified by terms of second intention. These metaphysical terms, called by

[1] In addition to these, there are a few terms used as symbols for conventional groupings of words, such as the grammatical terms "declension" or "third conjugation," whose denotation is not determined by any single concept or act of understanding, but purely by convention and by enumerating the particular things they can be used to denote. These terms whose denotation is purely conventional, and to which no concept corresponds, are called *words of second imposition:* they are few, and of interest chiefly to grammarians. All other terms, whose denotation is determined by concepts which are natural signs of the things denoted by them, are called *words of first imposition*, and are sub-divided, according to whether they naturally signify terms or things that are not terms, into terms of second intention, and terms of first intention.
S. tot. log., I, 11, 5v: "Stricte . . . dicitur nomen secundae impositionis illud quod non significat nisi signa ad placitum instituta, ita quod non potest competere intentionibus animae quae sunt naturalia signa; cuiusmodi sunt talia, 'figura,' 'coniugatio,' et huiusmodi . . . sola nomina cathegoreumatica quae non sunt nomina secundae impositionis vocantur nomina primae impositionis. Nomina autem primae impositionis stricte accipiendo, sunt in duplici divisa, quia quaedam sunt nomina primae intentionis, et quaedam sunt nomina secundae intentionis."

mediæval writers the "transcendentals," are six in number: namely, *ens* (that which is), *res* (thing), *aliquid* (something), *unum* (that which is one or "individual"), *verum* (that which is, *qua* intelligible), and *bonum* (that which is, *qua* desirable). These are predicates of absolute universality, predicable convertibly of each other, and predicable significatively and *per se* of every significant term.[1]

Ockham's basis of distinction between metaphysics, the discursive real sciences, and logic, and his concern to maintain the distinction between these sciences without compromise or equivocation, is nicely indicated by this division of significant terms or concepts, into (1) terms of second intention (which alone can enter into the propositions of logic), (2) terms of first intention (which alone belong in the propositions of the real sciences), and (3) the six transcendental terms of absolute universality (which alone belong in the propositions of metaphysics).

From Ockham's point of view, and by his understanding of Aristotle, the possibility of science and of demonstration rests on the possibility of an analytic reduction of the synthetic constructions of discursive thought to principles grasped through experience, and understood in abstraction from the contingent circumstances in which they came to be apprehended. Such principles are concepts of *indivisible* or *individual*

---

[1] S. tot. log., I, 11, 5v: "Stricte autem illud dico solum nomen secundae intentionis quod praecise significat intentiones animae quae sunt naturalia signa, et sic accipiendo nullum nomen secundae intentionis est nomen secundae impositionis. . . . Nomina autem primae intentionis vocantur omnia alia a praedicta, quae verum significant aliquas res quae non sunt signa nec consequentia talia signa, cuiusmodi sunt omnia talia: 'homo,' 'animal,' 'Socrates,' 'Plato,' 'albedo,' 'album,' 'bonum,' 'verum,' et huiusmodi; quorum aliqua significant praecise res quae non sunt signa nata supponere pro illis, aliqua vero significant talia signa et simul cum hoc alias res. . . . Ex quibus omnibus colligi potest quod quaedam nomina significant praecise signa ad placitum instituta et non nisi dum sunt signa. Quaedam autem praecise significant signa sed tam ad placitum instituta quam signa naturalia" (these two groups are, respectively, words of second imposition, and terms of second intention). "Quaedam vero significant praecise res quae non sunt signa talia quae sunt partes propositionis" (terms of first intention); "quaedam vero significant tales res quae non sunt partes propositionis vel orationis, et etiam signa talia, cuiusmodi sunt talia nomina: res, ens, aliquid, et huiusmodi . . ." (these are the transcendentals, which are predicable significatively of both the terms of first and of second intention, since they stand for any or every thing that is, whether it be a term or what is not a term).

nature—substances and the qualitative contraries. Such analysis is itself possible, however, only insofar as we maintain the unequivocal distinction between the indivisible concepts which are not produced by the synthetic operations of reason, and those forms of discourse whose unity and being are functions of human modes of apprehension or of expression.

Unless it is possible to analyse the discursive structure of a science purely as a discursive structure, and thus to differentiate between the character of a science insofar as it is a science, and the character of a science insofar as it is the science *of* such or such kinds of *things or natures*, it will be impossible to distinguish that which exists by nature from that which exists by the voluntary operations of reason or by the contingent circumstances of human modes of apprehension. To confuse terms of second intention with terms of first intention, or even to say that terms of second intention signify really or formally distinct parts *in* the things signified by terms of first intention, is to break down the distinction between logic and real science, or between forms of discourse and the things discourse is about. From Ockham's point of view, such a confusion entails the destruction of all demonstrative science, and of the whole philosophy of Aristotle, through substituting dialectic (or the art of synthesizing opinions through analogy and generalization) for metaphysics, natural science, and logic, which in Aristotle are distinct.[1]

What a concept or intention is, considered as a psychological event or state, is as irrelevant to logic and to real science as the question concerning the nature of the ink used in writing.

[1] Ockham's views on this subject (i.e., the disastrous results of confusing signs with what they signify) are expressed with considerable fervour in Exp. aur., III, 2, 90r: "Una (opinio) est quod res extra concepta sive intellecta est passio animae isto modo quo ponunt aliqui quod praeter res singulares sunt res universales et quod res particulares conceptae sunt subiecta propositionum singularium, et quod res universales sunt partes propositionum universalium. Sed opinionem istam (quantum ad hoc quod ponit aliquas res esse extra praeter singulares existentes in eis) reputo absurdam et destruentem totam philosophiam Aristotelis et omnem scientiam et veritatem et rationem, et est pessimus error in philosophia et reprobatur ab Aristotele 7. Met., et tenentes eam sunt inhabiles ad scientiam capescendam."

The fact that terms are significant is presupposed by every inquiry and by every act of understanding, and we cannot, by thought or reasoning, show how signification or thought is possible as such. Whether a concept is something existing in the mind distinct from it, and all disputes as to how, in the first instance, things can be understood by the mind, are extraneous to logic and to real science. All that is required, for logic or by the scientist, is terms or intentions which signify things and which can stand for them in discourse. No matter what the concept is in itself, and no matter what sort of thing it may be likened to or imagined as, it will be that which, as a part of a proposition entertained in the mind, stands for things which it means.

The act of understanding—whether or not it involves an image or an "intelligible species" really existent in the mind and distinct from it—is presupposed by every theory concerning the nature of the act of understanding. But since the act of understanding, or the *habitus* consequent on it, can fulfil the function of being a sign of things for which it can stand in thought, the scientist and the logician need not burden themselves with the unnecessary task of trying to understand how there can be such a thing as understanding.[1]

In his commentary on Aristotle's *De interpretatione*, commenting on the statement that "written words are signs of the passions which are in the soul," Ockham reviews several opinions concerning the nature of the concept or intention, considered in itself. The opinion that it is something outside the soul, so that propositions would be composed of things and not of terms or signs of things, is rejected as absurd and

[1] Intelligence and the intelligible are signified by correlatives of the type discussed by Aristotle (Cat. 7, 7b 15–8a 12) in which an order of prior and posterior is found. Intelligence exists actually only when something is actually understood. Since there can be no science of what is not actual, or of what is not measured by the actual, there can be no science of the *act* of understanding other than the science of the things which are actually understood, nor of the intelligence as a faculty or potentiality of understanding, other than the science of things potentially understood (i.e., of things intelligible). For a compact and difficult, but most illuminating, discussion of this, see R. McKeon, "De Anima: Psychology and Science," in the *Journal of Philosophy*, vol. XXVII, No. 25, Dec. 4, 1930.

THE LOGIC OF TERMS

contrary to Aristotle.[1] Three other opinions are mentioned by
Ockham as probable: (1) The opinion, attributed to Avicenna,
that the concept or intention is a quality really existing in
the soul and distinct from it, as heat is distinct from that
which is hot. (2) The opinion, held by Petrus Aureolus and
others, that the intention has no being of its own distinct from
the being of the object understood by it. According to this
theory the concept is the object itself appearing to the mind;
it is said to possess *esse apparens* or *esse obiectivum*, and to be in
itself nothing real, but only a fiction or figment resulting from
the compresence of the intellect and the thing understood.
(3) The opinion, preferred by Ockham, that the intention
or concept is nothing other than the act of understanding.

The first opinion, that the concept is a quality distinct from
the mind and produced in it by the act of understanding, is much
preferred to the second theory of the concept as a figment
having only "objective" being. The ground for Ockham's
preference of the third theory is his famous principle of economy
—all the theories presuppose the act of understanding, and
the act of understanding is sufficient to fulfill the functions of
the term, both for logic and for the sciences. Therefore the
positing of a third entity besides the act of understanding, and
the thing understood, is useless.[2]

But what, in the soul, is this thing which is a sign? It must
be said that with regard to this there are various opinions. For
some say that it is nothing but a certain fiction produced by the
soul. Others say that it is a certain quality existing subjectively
in the soul, distinct from the act of understanding. Others say
that it is the act of understanding. And in favour of these there
is this to be said: what can be explained on fewer principles is
explained needlessly by more (*frustra fit per plura quod potest fieri
per pauciora*). Everything, however, which is explained through
positing something distinct from the act of understanding can be
explained without positing such a distinct thing. For to stand

[1] Exp. aur., III, 2, 90v–91v; cited above, p. 47, Note 1.
[2] Exp. aur., III, 2, 88r–91r, gives a long discussion of these opinions, and a
fairly rigorous criticism of the theory of "esse obiectivum" and of the concept
as a "figmentum." Ockham's own preference, as indicated by his manner of
referring to the "universal in the soul" at various places throughout his logical

for something and to signify something can belong just as well
to the act of understanding as to this fictive entity; therefore one
ought not to posit anything else beyond the act of understanding.[1]

One advantage of the theory that the intention is nothing
but the act of understanding, is that it helps to dispose of the
temptation, never far away from the scholastic who has been
nurtured on augustinian exemplarism and on the *Liber de
causis* or equivalent works, to think of the object of the act of
understanding as something other than the individual things
for which the intention or term, in a proposition of science,
stands. If, however, we talk about a *species intelligibilis* existing
in the mind, and produced by the mind when it apprehends
individual things existing *in re*, as a kind of representation of
them to itself, we run the risk of forgetting that the act of
understanding the individuals outside the mind is prior to the
production of the *species intelligibilis* in the mind *by* this act of
understanding. And if we forget this, we are likely to make
the object of science separated forms produced (by reminiscence,
by illumination from within or above, or even by sheer mental
creation) by the mind, instead of things which can exist *per
se* as individuals, independently of the operations of the mind.[2]

works, seems to be this: In the first instance the concept is the act of understanding
the things signified by it, and regarded in this way, as an *actus* rather than as a
habitus, it is nothing other than the soul actually intelligent in determinate
manner; but if we talk about the concept as a *habitus intelligendi*, as it is *qua* part
of the abstract and universal propositions of the sciences insofar as these are
known as necessary and *per se*, then the concept is something real "established"
in the soul—i.e., as a real quality which has been acquired and which is possessed,
equivalent to the *species intelligibilis* as this term is generally used by Aquinas. A
briefer survey of these opinions is given in S. tot. log., I, 12, 6r; and also in Quodl.
IV, Qu. 19 (McKeon's Selections, vol. II, p. 386–391).

[1] S. tot. log., I, 12, 6r. ·
[2] The question at issue here, which divides aristotelianism from platonism, is
well appreciated by St. Thomas Aquinas, who, though he regards the *species
intelligibilis* as something distinct both from the act of understanding and from the
individuals *in re* which are the things science is about, is in full agreement with
Ockham as to the importance of distinguishing between the concept as *product*
of the act of understanding, and the individual things outside the mind which
are the direct object of the act of understanding (which is the act of abstraction).
Indeed, it is hard to see how Ockham's theory differs in any important respects
from that of Aquinas—for Ockham too allows that the *habitus* produced by the
act of understanding things *in re*, is a real quality in the mind distinct from the
mind itself and from the things outside the mind, and Aquinas, like Ockham,

The point at issue, here as elsewhere, is the maintenance
of the distinction between logic and real science. Propositions
are true or false of that for which their terms stand, and which
their terms signify. If the terms of universal propositions

denies emphatically that the object of understanding is the concept *by* which
understanding takes place. The *species intelligibilis*, in the words of Aquinas, is not
id quod intelligitur, but is *id quo intelligitur*. Cf. Aquinas, S. theol., I, Qu. 85, art. 2:—
"Respondeo dicendum quod quidam posuerunt quod vires quae sunt in nobis
cognoscitivae, nihil cognoscunt nisi proprias passiones, puta quod sensus non
sentit nisi passionem sui organi. Et secundum hoc intellectus nihil intelligit
nisi suam passionem, scilicet speciem intelligibilem in se receptam; et secundum
hoc species huiusmodi est ipsum quod intelligitur.—Sed haec opinio manifeste
apparet falsa ex duobus: primo quidem quia eadem sunt quae intelligimus, et
de quibus sunt scientiae. Si igitur ea quae intelligimus, essent solum species quae
sunt in anima, sequeretur quod scientiae omnes non essent de rebus quae sunt
extra animam, sed solum de speciebus intelligibilibus, quae sunt in anima; sicut
secundum Platonicos omnes scientiae sunt de ideis, quas ponebant esse intellectas
in actu. Secundo quia sequeretur error antiquorum dicentium omne quod
videtur, esse verum; et similiter quod contradictoriae essent simul verae. Si
enim potentia non cognoscit nisi propriam passionem, de ea solum judicat. Sic
autem videtur aliquid secundum quod potentia cognoscitiva afficitur. Semper
ergo judicium potentiae cognoscitivae erit de eo quod judicat, scilicet de propria
passione, secundum quod est; et ita omne judicium erit verum; puta si gustus
non sentit nisi propriam passionem, cum aliquis habens sanum gustum judicat
mel esse dulce, vere judicabit; et similiter si ille qui habet gustum infectum,
judicat mel esse amarum, vere judicabit; uterque enim judicabit secundum
quod gustus eius afficitur. Et sic sequitur quod omnis opinio aequaliter erit vera,
et universaliter omnis acceptio. Et ideo dicendum est quod species intelligibilis
se habet ad intellectum ut quo intelligit intellectus; . . . species intellecta secundario est id quod intelligitur;—sed id quod intelligitur primo, est res, cuius species
intelligibilis est similitudo. . . ." Cf. also S. theol. I, Qu. 76, art. 2, ad. 4:
"Id enim quod intelligitur, non est in intellectu secundum se, sed secundum suam
similitudinem; lapis enim non est in anima, sed species lapidis, ut dicitur in 3. de
Anima, text. 38, et tamen lapis est id quod intelligitur, non autem species lapidis,
nisi per reflexionem intellectus supra seipsum; alioquin scientiae non essent de
rebus, sed de speciebus intelligibilibus."
    What Aquinas calls the "reflection of the intellect on its own act," Ockham
calls the "act of understanding a term or concept of first intention by a term or
concept of second intention." What Aquinas calls the "act of abstracting the
species intelligibilis in apprehending the particular," Ockham calls the "act of
understanding"—i.e., the act of apprehending, through a concept of first intention,
an individual *such* as can be understood through that concept. The object of
understanding, for both Ockham and Aquinas, is *that which is individual in nature ;*
the occasion of contingent intuition by sense perception, is *particular fact.* Only
a universal concept that is an absolute term, signifies precisely *that which is individual
in nature ;* connotative terms which stand for individuals by indicating a fact or
qualification, indicate *particular facts,*—it is the principles of the definition of
connotative terms, which are absolute terms, that signify what is individual or
undivided in nature. Hence it is the grasp of a connotative term by its defining
principles, or by absolute terms, that is, in Ockham's system, the act of abstraction
from particular existence—but it is not abstraction *from* individuality, but from
particular fact (which is always con-tingent or a function of two or more
individuals) *to* the grasp of individuals *per se*, by their undivided nature.

stand for entities produced by the mind, and not for the individual things which exist independently of our thought and which we come to know through sense perception, then all sciences will be of states of mind, or of particular acts of particular human beings, and logic, natural science, and metaphysics will lose their distinction and become merged in a single discipline which seeks to discover the object of thought in the processes and movement of thought itself, as in the platonic, or in the hegelian, dialectic.

The questions so far touched on, concerning the distinctions between logic and the real sciences, between the significative and non-significative use of terms, and between terms of first intention and terms of second intention, reveal in rather a striking fashion the fact that Ockham's nominalistic treatment of logic is rooted in, and necessitated by, a thoroughly realistic metaphysics. Logic, for Ockham, is not a speculative science, for it is not concerned with *being* as such, nor with any determinate kind of being as such. The reason for this is precisely the fact that for one who is a realist in metaphysics *being* is prior to, and independent of, the processes and products of discursive thought, as the measure of truth is prior to the truth measured by it. Realism in metaphysics entails nominalism in logic. The alternative is to efface the distinction between logic and metaphysics by locating the measure of truth, and the principles of being and of reality, in the processes and products of human thinking itself. And when this is done, all science is of the processes and forms of human thinking, and is a metaphysical dialectic. Such a dialectic, insofar as it makes thought the measure of its own truth, can be called a nominalistic metaphysics; and insofar as it seeks by analysis of the processes of thinking, to discover the principles of being and of reality, it can be called a realistic logic.

That Ockham is unalterably opposed to such a confusion between logic and metaphysics, is obvious from his emphasis on the necessity of maintaining without equivocation the distinction between the concept, or act of understanding, and the things understood and signified by it. Knowledge, for Ockham, is relative to what is known; but nothing is relative to itself; therefore knowledge is of things that are not that knowledge. Hence the discipline (logic) which treats of knowledge *as such*, does not treat of that which is distinct from knowledge—namely, the things which exist independently of human acts of signification, and to which knowledge is relative and posterior. Nor is logic concerned with the nature of the human soul, though all human acts of signification come into existence by reason of human intelligence. Logic, for Ockham, is not a science of nature, nor of being as such—for it is not a speculative discipline. Rather it is an "ostensive practical science" which deals with modes of signification—with the ways in which we can use written, spoken, or mental signs, to signify things which can exist independently of our acts of understanding, and to signify them as they are. Unless we can distinguish modes of signification and forms of discourse from the things signified in discourse, and thus have a logic of terms that is not a science of things that are not terms, we will be unable to distinguish the things our discourse is about from discourse itself, and thus will be unable to have any *real sciences* at all. Ockham, in emphasizing and making explicit the nominalism of aristotelian logic, is everywhere actuated by the concern to preserve and to make evident the realism of aristotelian metaphysics.

III

While Ockham, as we have seen, states that logic is principally concerned with such forms of discourse as can be exhibited as "fabrications" of the mind, this way of characterizing the subject matter of logic involves the recognition of elements of discourse that are not fabrications, but starting points or *principles* of discursive knowledge and signification. If there were no such indivisible elements or principles of discursive signification and of scientific knowledge, then it could not be said that logic was concerned with "fabrications" of the mind, but on the contrary, it would then be concerned with *creations* of the mind *ex nihilo*. If the meaning of all terms, or the truth of every true proposition, were evident immediately and *per se*, demonstration and definition would be impossible or superfluous. Likewise, if the meanings of all terms, or the truth of every true proposition, were knowable only *per aliud* and never *per se*, so that there were definable terms and demonstrable propositions but no principles of definition and no primary premises of demonstration, demonstration and definition would also be impossible. Aristotle's *Posterior Analytics* is largely devoted to establishing the fact that the existence of knowledge involves not only the existence of definable terms and of demonstrable propositions, but also the existence of determinate concepts that are principles of definition and that yield indemonstrable and evident premises of demonstration.[1]

For demonstration, and scientific knowledge, to be recognized as such, there must be some way in which an immediate premise can be distinguished from a demonstrable or non-immediate proposition. Such a distinction cannot be found in the form of affirmation or denial as such, but it is a function of the meanings of the terms of which such propositions are composed. Hence the distinction between elements of discourse which can be exhibited as products of synthesis by the human mind, and the elements which cannot be exhibited as "fabrications," is exhibited by Ockham by means of a distinction between two kinds of terms—namely, absolute terms and connotative terms.

Absolute terms are described as those which do not signify one thing primarily and another thing, or the same thing,

---

[1] Arist., An. Post., I, 1, 71a 1–2: "All instruction given or received by way of argument proceeds from pre-existent knowledge." Ibid., 3, 72b 18: "Our own doctrine is that not all knowledge is demonstrative: on the contrary, knowledge of the immediate premises is independent of demonstration. (The necessity of this is obvious; for since we must know the prior premises from which the demonstration is drawn, and since the regress must end in immediate truths, those truths must be indemonstrable.) Such, then, is our doctrine, and in addition we maintain that besides scientific knowledge there is its originative source which enables us to recognize the definitions." Ibid., II, 19, 100b 13: "demonstration cannot be the originative source of demonstration, nor, consequently, scientific knowledge of scientific knowledge. If, therefore, it is the only other kind of true thinking except scientific knowing, intuition will be the originative source of scientific knowledge."

secondarily or obliquely; but whatever things are signified
or in any way indicated by such a term, are signified equally
and by a single indivisible intention of the mind. For example,
"animal" signifies individual men, horses, cows, etc., indifferently and by a single intention, and it does not stand for
such individuals through indicating some determination,
fact, circumstance, or part, attributable to them or discernible
in them, in common. In other words, an absolute term
means precisely the things which it can be used to denote,
and hence it can be used as a sign of the things which it
means without involving, implicitly or otherwise, the truth
of any proposition or the existence of any fact, circumstance,
or temporal or spatial determination such as might be involved
in any particular experience of such individuals.[1]

A *connotative term* is said to be one which signifies one kind of
thing primarily, and a different kind of thing secondarily or
obliquely. It stands for one kind of thing by connoting something distinct from it contingently connected with it, or by
connoting a determinate part of it as if separated or separable
from it. Thus the connotative term "hot" stands for things
in which heat can be present, by connoting the quality *heat*—
but it does not stand for heat, nor can the word "heat"
stand for anything denoted by the term "hot." In the same
way, the word "two-footed," or the word "rational," stands
for men; but that which they connote or consignify (namely,
"two feet" and "reason") are not the men which they can
denote, but parts of them considered in separation from men
taken as complete individual beings.[2]

All connotative terms have "nominal definitions," one of
whose parts does not signify precisely the same things that
the word defined is a sign of. It is by this character of the
definition, that a connotative term can always be distinguished

---

[1] S. tot. log., I, 10, 5r: "Mere autem absoluta sunt illa quae non significant
aliquid principaliter et aliud vel idem secundario, sed quicquid significatur per
tale nomen aeque primo significatur."

[2] S. tot. log., I, 10, 5r: "Nomen autem connotativum est illud quod significat
aliquid primario et aliud secundario; et tale nomen proprie habet diffinitionem
exprimentem quid nominis, et frequenter oportet ponere aliquid illius diffinitionis
in recto et aliud in obliquo."

from an absolute term. Absolute terms have "real definitions," whose parts can stand for precisely the individual things for which the term defined can stand; thus "man" is defined as "rational animal," and it is true to say that every man is an animal, and also that every man is rational. But the term "father," which is connotative, has only a nominal definition, one of whose parts cannot stand for that which is denoted by the term itself—for the thing that is said to be a father, is something which *has* a son or daughter—it is not itself the son or daughter which it is said to have.

Thus, whenever the parts of the definition of a term cannot stand for precisely the same individual things that the term defined can stand for, then the term defined is a connotative term, and is said to have a nominal definition. But where the parts of the definition each signify precisely the individual things for which the term defined can stand, then the term defined is an absolute term, and has a "real definition"—for in such a case the definition of the term is likewise the definition of the things for which the term can stand.

Absolute terms are of two kinds, namely, the terms in the category of substance (except for essential differentiæ which are connotative), and the abstract forms of certain terms in the category of quality, such as the qualitative contraries which are principles of sense perception. Now in sense experience we apprehend things by their changes or their perceptible affections; we do not experience heat in abstraction from things that are hot, nor do we experience substances in abstraction from contingent determinations. Hence as things are apprehended by us in sense experience, they are signified first, in the order of coming to know, by concrete connotative terms. All such terms are, however, capable of analysis or of definition, whereby their meaning is exhibited as a function of elements or principles signified by absolute terms. Where we are able to state both parts of the nominal definition of a connotative term determinately (e.g., to define "the calefactible" not merely as "*something* in which heat can exist" but as "a *body* determinable with respect to heat"), we achieve at the same time a complete analysis of the meaning of the connotative term, through reduction to absolute terms, and also a commensurately universal *per se* proposition, by which the attribute "calefactible" may be demonstrated of any individual things for which the absolute term "body" can stand. Thus Aristotle, in discussing definition and demonstration, states that although essential nature (i.e., that which is signified by an absolute term) cannot be demonstrated *a priori*, demonstration is nevertheless an exhibition of essential nature.[1]

The significance, for the whole aristotelian theory of demonstrative science, of Ockham's distinction between connotative and absolute terms, and of his distinction between absolute terms which are concrete (those in the category of substance) and absolute terms which are abstract (qualities), can easily be seen. If connotative terms could not be defined, or analysed, into functions of absolute terms, we would either have no means of demonstration, or else demonstration would involve infinite regress or circularity. Again, if there were no absolute terms by which the subjects of accidental determination, apprehended in experience, could be signified *per se* and independently of questions of contingent fact or present existence, the same consequence would follow. For if all terms were connotative, or if the only non-connotative terms were proper names and abstract common names (as J. S. Mill contended), univocal definition and demonstration would be impossible, since the commensurate subject of a connotative term could not be signified univocally or *per se,* but would always be another connotative term which in turn would require analysis, and so on *ad infinitum.*[2]

The fact that terms in the category of substance, concrete in form, have abstract counterparts, thus resembling con-

---

[1] Arist., An. Post., II, 8, 93b 15–20. The more complete discussion of the relation between definition and demonstration, and between the order of coming to know, and the order of knowing, will be taken up when we come to Ockham's treatise on demonstration.

[2] J. S. Mill, *System of Logic* (London 1892), p. 25, rightly appreciates the *importance* of the distinction between connotative and non-connotative terms, though his classification of concrete general names as connotative in every case, is, from the aristotelian point of view, destructive of the possibility of science,

notative terms, led many of Ockham's predecessors and contemporaries (and indeed many of his successors in the history
of logic) to treat absolute terms in the category of substance
as if they were, in some sense at least, connotative. Thus,
since a white thing is said to be white by reason of whiteness
existing in it, a man was said to be a man by reason of humanity
being present in him. The question naturally arises, when
such a statement is made, as to whether a man's humanity
is something distinct from him, and if so, the further question
arises as to what the man is insofar as he is something distinct
from his humanity. It may also be asked what the
differentiating principle is, by which the individual man is
essentially distinguished from his humanity. The whole set
of problems centering around the so-called "problem of
universals" and the so-called "problem of individuation,"
with which so many mediæval writers were concerned, can
be stated in terms of whether the distinction between concrete
general names and their abstract counterparts is in any sense
equivalent to the distinction between connotative and absolute
terms. Ockham's discussion of the distinction between concrete
and abstract terms is, therefore, worth considering in some detail.

Abstract and concrete names are said to be those which
have the same root, but different endings, such as "white"
(concrete) and "whiteness" (abstract). Properly speaking,

---

since it leaves no means of signifying, by a univocal middle term, the essential
nature of what is signified by the attribute. The result is, consequently, that the
only middle term of affirmative demonstration remaining, is the proper name,
and hence the only propositions which can serve as primary premises of scientific
knowledge are singular or particular propositions. To be sure, we can use as
middle term, signifying the things for which our universal attribute stands, the
transcendental term "being" or "something," and thus demonstrate the conclusion of "something". But this is not rightly demonstration, because the
possibility of the attribute standing for "something" is already recognized prior
to the demonstration, in the mere grasp of the attribute as a term or predicate of
first intention. Mill's thesis, that concrete general names are always connotative,
not only gives rise to the difficulties which modern logicians experience in attempt-
ing to avoid circularity or infinite regress in proof—a difficulty usually met by
an espousal of circularity or infinite regress—but it underlies also the difficulties
encountered in the "problem of universals." Mill's point of view was not new,
and goes back at least as far as Porphyry; it was, in all essentials, the viewpoint
of those mediæval logicians criticized by Ockham—i.e., those who sought to make
a real distinction between the individual and its essential nature.

only connotative terms can have abstract forms which signify
things really distinct from what their concrete forms signify;
according to Ockham, the concrete and abstract forms of
absolute terms in the category of substance, are synonyms.
Only when a concrete noun signifies something for which it
can stand in a proposition, which its abstract counterpart
does not signify and for which it cannot stand, is there a
distinction in *meaning* (as against *usage*) between the concrete
and abstract form.[1]

Among terms where the concrete and abstract forms are not
synonyms, we may distinguish three types. (1) The concrete
term may stand for a substance in which an accidental form
(in the physical sense, of quality), which its abstract counterpart signifies absolutely, is present. Thus the term "hot"
can stand for a stove, or for any other substance in which
heat happens to be present; but it cannot stand for what the
abstract term "heat" signifies, nor can the term "heat"
stand for a stove. (2) There are many cases where the concrete
term stands for a part of a thing, while its abstract counterpart stands for the whole, or *vice versa*. For example, in the
proposition "the soul is human," the term "human" stands
for a part of what its abstract counterpart "humanity"
signifies. Or the differentia "rational," in the proposition
"Every man is rational," stands for individual men, while
its abstract counterpart "rationality" signifies only their
souls. (3) The third type is where the concrete term stands
for something distinct from the abstract term, the things for
which they stand being related neither as part to whole nor
as accident to subject. Examples of this type are found where

---

[1] S. tot. log., I, 5, 3r: "concretum et abstractum sunt nomina consimile
principium secundum vocem habentia, sed non consimiliter terminanda. . . .
Nominum autem abstractorum et concretorum multi sunt modi, quandoque
enim concretum aliquam rem significat . . . pro quo etiam supponit, quam
abstractum nullo modo significat nec aliquo modo supponit pro eadem—ut
iustus et iustitia, et similia, nam 'iustus' vere supponit pro homine quando dico
'iustus est virtuosus,' non enim potest supponere pro iustitia, quia iustitia quamvis
sit virtus non tamen est virtuosa; et hoc nomen 'iustitia' supponit pro qualitate
et non pro homine, et propter hoc accidit quod praedicatio talis concreti de abstracto
est impossibilis, quia semper tale concretum et abstractum pro distinctis rebus
supponunt."

the concrete term stands for something whose efficient or final cause is signified by the abstract term, as when we call a house a "human" product, being caused by what is signified by humanity (which according to Ockham signifies nothing other than what is signified by "man" or by "all men"). Or if we call something divine not because it is God, but because of an analogy or resemblance to what the term "divinity," which stands only for God, signifies, we again have an example of this third type.[1]

Other concrete and abstract terms are held by Ockham to be synonyms, in the sense that the concrete term signifies nothing, either directly or obliquely, distinct from what its abstract counterpart signifies, and *vice versa*, even though the terms may differ in the way in which they can be used in discourse.[2] In this sense Ockham maintains that the abstract counterparts of absolute terms in the category of substance, and the abstract forms of terms in the categories of quantity and relation (and indeed in all accidental categories other than that of quality), are usually synonyms of their concrete counterparts. Thus "divinity" can stand for nothing distinct from what the term "divine," if used literally, signifies; "humanity" for nothing other than what "man" signifies; and the terms "quantum" and "quantity" denote nothing

---

[1] S. tot. log., I, 5, 3r: "Sunt autem ad praesens talium nominum tres differentiae, quasi tres species inferiores. Prima est quando abstractum supponit pro accidente vel forma quacumque realiter inhaerente subiecto, et concretum supponit pro subiecto eiusdem accidentis vel formae, vel econverso. . . . Secunda . . . est quod concretum supponit pro partibus et abstractum pro toto, vel econverso. . . . Tertia est quando concretum et abstractum supponit pro distinctis, quorum tamen neutrus est subiectum nec pars alterius, et hoc contingit multis modis. Nam tales termini quandoque se habent sicut causa et effectus . . . quandoque sicut signum et signatum quandoque sicut locus et locatum, sicut dicimus quod ille est anglicus et non Anglia."

[2] S. tot. log., I, 6, 3v: "nomen concretum et abstractum quandoque sunt nomina sinonima. Sed ne in equivoce procedatur sciendum est quod hoc nomen 'sinonima' dupliciter accipitur, stricte et large. Stricte dicuntur illa sinonima quibus omnes utentes intendunt simpliciter uti pro eodem et sic non loquor hic de sinonimis. Large dicuntur illa sinonima quae simpliciter idem significant omnibus modis, ita quod nihil significatur aliquo modo per unum quin per reliquum eodem modo significetur, quamvis non omnes utentes credant illa idem significare, sed decepti existimant aliquid significari per unum quod non significatur per reliquum, sicut si aliquis existimaret quod hoc nomen 'deus' importaret unum totum et 'deitas' partem eius."

distinct *in re*, while "father" and "fatherhood" are synonyms in the same sense.[1]

The principle underlying this analysis is one which is fundamental to Ockham's understanding of Aristotle—namely, that in nature there are only two kinds of unities of elements of diverse character (*alterius et alterius rationis*), the *per se* unity of the material and formal principles of changeable substances, and the contingent unity of a qualitative form with a substantial subject. To recognize a real distinction between "man" and "humanity" is to deny the unity or individuality of the nature signified by "man." And to make a real distinction between "quantum" and "quantity" is to suppose that quantity is something really distinct from substance such as can, in a literal sense, be acquired or lost by a substance. Indeed, when the accidental categories other than that of quality are analysed as predicates which indicate the inherence of a distinct accidental form in substance, so that their abstract forms signify abstract accidents, the only effect is to make the nine accidental categories subdivisions of the category of quality—for such a procedure is nothing but a characterization of all accidental predicates as signs of distinct forms of qualification.

The obvious objection to Ockham's position is that if "man" signifies precisely the same things that "humanity" signifies, we ought to be able to affirm truly the proposition "humanity

[1] S. tot. log., I, 6, 3v: "sicut apud antiquos illa nomina sunt sinonima, 'calor caliditas,' 'frigus, frigiditas,' ita illa essent sinonima apud eos: 'equus, equinitas,' 'homo, humanitas,' nec in talibus curabant distinguere inter nomina concreta et abstracta quantum ad significationem quamvis unum illorum haberet plures sillabas et formam abstractorum primo modo dictorum, nec tali diversitate talium nominum utebantur nisi causa ornatae locutionis vel aliqua alia causa accidentale, sicut nec nominibus sinonimis. Sub hoc etiam modo nominum concretorum et abstractorum secundum intentionem Philosophi et Commentatoris comprehenduntur omnia nomina substantiarum et abstracta ficta ab eis, quae nec pro accidente nec pro parte nec pro aliqua re disparata ab eo supponunt, cuiusmodi sunt haec nomina secundum eos: 'animalitas, asinitas, equinitas,' et huiusmodi. Non enim animalitas stat pro aliquo accidente animalis nec pro parte nec pro aliquo toto cuius pars sit animal, nec pro re aliqua extrinseca totaliter ab animali distincta." Similarly concrete terms in the categories of quantity and relation are synonymous with their abstract counterparts, in the sense that they stand for nothing distinct *in re* from what can be signified by the term "substance" or the term "quality." This is a distinctive position of Ockham, which will be discussed more fully in connection with his exposition of Aristotle's *Categoriae*.

runs," if Socrates, who is a man, is running. Ockham therefore sets out to prove, first, that the term "humanity" signifies nothing really distinct from what the term "man" signifies, and secondly, that the falsity of such propositions as "humanity is running" can be accounted for without altering this basic thesis.

If the term "humanity" signifies anything really distinct from what the term "man" signifies, it will, says Ockham, signify either an accidental form present in man, or else a part of the essence of man, *scil.* his body or soul. Obviously it cannot signify an accident, nor does it, as some seemed to think, signify the soul in separation from the body. For if that were the case we could truly affirm that "Humanity is thinking," if the soul of Socrates were thinking, which is quite as inconvenient as the example on which the objection against Ockham's view was founded.

Does "humanity," then, signify the *specific* nature of man, as something distinct from what a man is *qua* individual? Such was the scotist contention, for the scotists held that it is not the nature signified by the *infima species* that constitutes a thing as an individual distinct from other individuals of the same species, but that a distinct individuating form is added to the specific nature, contracting it to individual existence. From this point of view, then, that which "humanity" signifies is something that an individual man is, insofar as he is *not* individual, whereas the concrete term "man" signifies what he is, but also connotes the contraction of his essence by a distinct formal principle of individuation. This scotist distinction, against which Ockham argues constantly in his logical treatises, is here stated to be contrary to the intentions of Aristotle, and contrary to reason, since it involves a contradiction. It is conceded by the scotists that "humanity" signifies the essential nature of individual men. But the essence is what a thing is; hence, if Socrates is an individual and cannot be anything at all without being individual, and if "humanity" signifies what is essential to the nature of Socrates, then it signifies what is *per se* individual. According to the strict usage of language, therefore, a proposition such as "Man *has* humanity," or "Humanity is *in* man," is false, for a thing cannot be said to have itself, nor to be in itself.[1]

Why, then, if "man" and "humanity" signify precisely the same individual things, are such propositions as "Humanity is walking" not true if, for example, it is true that Socrates, who is a man, is taking a walk? The reason is, says Ockham, that the term "humanity" is used as equivalent to the reduplicative phrase "man insofar as he is a man," and when a reduplicative phrase appears in a proposition, it is exponible, being equivalent to several distinct propositions, of which at least one is of universal character. For the proposition "Socrates *qua* man is walking" to be true, the following propositions would have to be true: (1) Socrates is walking; (2) Socrates is a man; (3) Every man is walking; and (4) If anything is a man, it is walking. In other words, "humanity" signifies individual men conjunctively, while "man" signifies them disjunctively. Nevertheless, it remains a fact that "humanity," or the phrase "man *qua* man," signifies nothing *in re* distinct from what is signified by the concrete term "man." And this is the point that is important from Ockham's point of view.[2]

Duns Scotus cites Avicenna in support of his contention that the essence or nature of a thing is prior to, and formally distinct from, its determinate modes of being, outside the mind (as individual) and in the mind (as universal). To this indeterminate nature singularity is added by the creation of it as an

---

[1] S. tot. log., I, 7, 3v: "Haec valet cavillatio aliquorum dicentium quod 'humanitas' significat tantum naturam specificam, 'homo' autem addit ultra naturam individualem. Nam hoc inferius ostendetur esse falsum et contra intentionem Aristotelis." Cf. Arist., Met. Z, 6, 1032a 5: "Clearly, then, each primary and self-subsistent thing is one and the same as its essence." We can abstract from the *this* by leaving accidental differences out of consideration, but if we state that the essential nature of a thing is not indivdidual, then either it is not the essential nature of an individual from the conditions of whose apprehension it was abstracted, or else the same thing will be individual and not-individual at the same time and in the same respect. Cf. S. tot. log., I, 7, 4r: "omnes tales propositiones de virtute sermonis, hoc est secundum proprietatem sermonis, falsae sunt: 'omnis homo habet humanitatem,' 'omnis humanitas est in homine,' . . . quia . . . nihil habeat se nec aliquid sit in se. . . ."

[2] S. tot. log., I, 8, 4r. For Ockham's analysis of reduplicative propositions, cf. *Post*, ch. v., pp. 202–4 The same principle allows us to say that 'substance' stands for the same things *in re* as the term 'quantity' stands for, even though it is false to say "substance is quantity," though true to say "every quantum is a substance." In the same way, Ockham holds that "intellect," "will," and "soul"

existent thing, and universality is added to it by the combined agencies of the phantasm (produced in the soul by the individual affecting the sense organs) and the active intellect. From this point of view, consequently, the object of understanding, and the primary subject of predication, is not the nature which is individual and which is apprehended in sense experience as the subject of particular changes or affections, but rather it is an abstract or "separated" form according to which existence is given to the individual, and by turning to which the mind grasps its true and proper object of understanding, on the *occasion* of sense experience of such individuals. Despite many qualifications, the augustinian and platonic tendencies of Duns Scotus' position are manifest in his distinction of what the abstract substantial term signifies, from what its concrete counterpart signifies.[1]

Ockham gives a very different interpretation to Avicenna's words, which, while scarcely accurate as an interpretation of the arab philosopher's own point of view (which was better interpreted by Duns Scotus), is thoroughly in keeping with Ockham's way of understanding Aristotle.

So it is in this way that Avicenna, in the fifth book of his Metaphysics, is to be understood, where he says: "Horseness (*equinitas*)

(i.e., human or rational soul) stand for the same things *in re*; but "intellect" is equivalent to "soul insofar as it can understand," and "will" is equivalent to "soul insofar as it is capable of desiring or of loving something." Hence these terms, though they signify nothing distinct *in re* from what "soul" signifies, cannot be predicated of each other, since they are equivalent to reduplicative expressions.

[1] Duns Scotus, Met. VII, Qu. 18, n. 8: "Est ergo natura in potentia remota ad determinationem singularitatis, et ad indeterminationem universalis; et sicut a producente coniungitur singularitati, ita a re agente, et simul ab intellectu agente, coniungitur universalitati. Et isto modo bene intelligitur illud dictum Avicennae, V. Met., c. 1, quod natura de se non est universalis, nec particularis, sed tantum natura." Cf. Duns Scotus. Op. Oxon., II, Dist. III, Qu. 1, n. 234: "et secundum istam unitatem propriam naturae, ut natura est, est indifferens ad unitatem singularem; non ergo de se est sic una unitate illa, *scil.* unitate singularitatis, etc. . . . " Duns Scotus conceives the "particularity" in which an individual substance is contingently involved, as in some sense internal to the substance—and he calls it "singularity" and opposes it to the unity of the essential nature signified by the infima species. Ockham, however, does not consider that the "external relations" in which individual natures are contingently involved, are internal to their essential being in any sense, and hence for him "particularity" is precisely contingent fact—the "being together" of distinct individual substances or qualities, indicated by a contingent proposition. Most of the difficulties concerning the "problem of universals," are due to confusion between "individual" and "particular."

is nothing other than plain horseness (*equinitas tantum*); for it is of itself neither one nor many, nor existing in these sensible things, nor in the soul." He intended here to say nothing other than that a horse is not defined in terms of one, nor of many, nor by its existence in the soul, nor by its existence in things outside, so that none of these terms enters into its definition; and hence he meant that this term "horseness," in the sense in which he was then using it, was equivalent to a complex expression, whether stated as a unity, or with verb and copula. Wherefore he did not understand that horseness is something and that nevertheless it is not really or actually either one or many, and neither outside the mind nor in the mind, for this is impossible and absurd; but he understood that no such terms ought to be placed in the definition of it.[1]

The difference in approach between Ockham and Duns Scotus is shown here clearly enough. For Ockham, logic is an instrument of discursive science, and the possibility of discursive science is dependent on the possibility of determinate and finite signification of substances—of the individual concrete substances which are involved in the changes and events apprehended through sense perception. If the substantial term signifies not the individual natures of the things for which it stands, but stands for them by connoting a form or exemplary cause distinct from these individual natures, then the substantial term will not signify changeable things *per se*, nor will it be an appropriate middle term for demonstrating attributes (which indicate ways in which things are *essentially* changeable) of subjects.

As Aristotle remarks, the possibility of science does not depend on there being a One beside a Many (such as an exemplary form prior to the individual existing things), but it does depend on the possibility of signifying many individuals *per se* and unequivocally, by a single term or intention. It is Ockham's literal and careful adherence to this aristotelian principle that underlies his analysis of terms, and which leads him to criticize those who sought to qualify and restate the aristotelian logic in such manner as to make room for augustinian exemplarism and for an illumination theory of knowledge.[2]

[1] S. tot. log., I, 8, 4v.   [2] Arist., An. Post. I, 11, 77a 5–9.

CHAPTER THREE

PORPHYRY AND THE PROBLEM OF UNIVERSALS

I

THE first part of Ockham's *Golden Exposition* is a commentary on Porphyry's treatise on the five predicables. It is chiefly devoted to the rather difficult task of "interpreting" Porphyry's text in such manner that the treatise will not, as its author intended, be taken as an introduction to Aristotle's *Categories*. Had Ockham lived in more recent times, it is probable that he would have written not an exposition of Porphyry, but a devastating criticism of what the neo-platonist philosopher had done in his treatise. In Ockham's day, however, it was not fashionable to treat the ancients with anything but respect. Where one of them seemed to have erred, the proper procedure was to make every effort to interpret his words in such manner that the error would disappear, and be attributable not to the author's intention, but to unfortunate modes of expression. This procedure frequently resulted in rather forced "interpretations," and in the present instance especially so. Ockham, indeed, after making heroic efforts to "save" Porphyry's text, finally concludes that Porphyry's treatise was perhaps not intended by its author to be a discussion of the five predicables, but rather a treatise on five equivocal words.[1]

[1] Exp. aur., I, 29v: "Sciendum quod nec hic nec in aliquo loco huius libri invenitur quod auctor dicat se velle de praedictis quinque determinare tanquam de quinque universalibus et ideo non semper quando determinat de proprio et accidente determinat de illo quod est unum quinque universalium, sed determinatio sua principalis est de quinque vocabulis equivocis. . . ."

In view of the fact that Aristotle's discussion of the ways in which predicates can be asserted of their subjects—as genus, definition, property, or accident—is relegated, in the *Organon*, to his treatise on topical or dialectical argumentation, Porphyry's idea of using the predicables as an introduction to the *Categories* of Aristotle, stands as a master stroke, though probably an unconscious one, in the struggle to restore to dialectic the primacy that Plato had claimed for it, and that Aristotle had denied. Aristotle had sought to find a basis for demonstration and for science which would be distinct from, and prior to, the synthetic operations of discursive thinking. Hence he exhibited demonstration, and our knowledge of necessary and universal principles, as functions of meaning or signification. In the development of the *Organon*, consequently, the analysis of modes of signification contained in the *Categories* was prior to, and presupposed by, the analysis of modes of predication dealt with in the *Topics*.

But Porphyry insisted that Aristotle's analysis of modes of signification could only be understood in the light of his analysis of the ways in which one term can be related to another in predication. Thus he reversed the aristotelian order, bringing the very instrument of Aristotle's criticism of Plato into the service of the platonic dialectic. The effectiveness of the porphyrian strategy is attested by the entire history of aristotelianism. Of the innumerable writers—modern as well as mediæval—who have expounded the logic of Aristotle, extremely few can be said to have escaped the consequences of Porphyry's use of the predicables as a means of understanding Aristotle's *Categories*.[1]

---

[1] Porphyry's assumption, that the ten categories cannot be understood except as orderings of elements according to the ways in which they can be predicated of each other and of individuals, seems to have gone unquestioned, with few exceptions, from Boethius to George Grote, W. Windelband, and most of the neo-scholastics themselves. Cf. Boethius (Migne PL 64, cl. 77), where Porphyry's text is given in Latin, stating that it is necessary to know what a genus, species, etc., is, in order to understand Aristotle's doctrine of the categories; and cl. 78 D, where Boethius makes the same statement more diffusely.

A good instance of the unquestioned assumption of Porphyry's point of view, in mediæval times, is found in Pseudo-Thomas, *Summa totius logicae*, Proem.

The significance of Porphyry's reversal of the aristotelian order, and the consequences of this reversal in reducing demonstrative science to a dialectical metaphysics, can best be appreciated if we consider at the outset the difference between Aristotle's analysis of terms in the *Categories*, and his discussion of the predicables in the *Topics*.

In the *Categories* Aristotle is concerned with terms as incomplex modes of signification, considered in abstraction from questions of existence or fact, and from the truth or falsity of any propositions such as can, by the voluntary act of judgment, be formed through the synthesis of such terms. The division of terms of first intention into the ten categories is based on differences in the way in which terms signify things that are not terms—it is not a classification of terms according to the different ways in which they can be truly *predicated* of each other. To make signification a function of judgment, or to confuse it with predication, as Porphyry constantly does throughout his treatise, is to make the form

---

(Lethielleux ed., Aquinas, Opuscula omnia, vol. V, p. 1; Paris 1927): "Et quia predicamentum ut hic sumitur, nihil aliud est quam ordinatio predicabilium in ordine predicamentali, ideo, ad cognoscendum predicamenta, oportet prae-cognoscere predicabilia."

Grote: *Aristotle*, vol. I, p. 155 (London, 1872), likewise holds that the book of Categories is concerned with terms as elements of propositions, rather than as incomplex modes of signifying things, distinguishable independently of the truth or falsity of propositions: "The whole classification of the Categories rests on the assumption of the proposition with its constituent parts, and on the different relations borne by each of the nine genera of predicates towards their common Subject." Ibid., p. 117: "We thus see that all the predicates, not only under the Category which Aristotle terms *Ad aliquid*, but also under all the last nine Categories, are relative. Indeed the work of predication is always relative."

W. Windelband, *Hist. of Ancient Philosophy* (Cushman's transl., 3rd ed., N.Y., 1899), is a good modern representative of Porphyry's notion of the Categories: "The possible kinds of predicates, the Categories, are the highest class-concepts for logical investigation, and are irreducible. They represent the different points of view under which the different concepts can be made elements of a proposition or judgment by virtue of the factual relations of their contents." It is only a step from this notion of the *Categories*, to the "propositional function" of symbolic logic; but to make the distinctions between terms, dealt with in the *Categories*, a function of *factual relations*, is against both the letter and the spirit of Aristotle's treatise.

Another excellent modern porphyrian, from neo-scholastic circles, is Father G. H. Joyce, S.J., whose *Principles of Logic* is throughout concerned to refer distinctions among terms and forms of discourse to parallel, and all but indistinguishable, "internal relations" in Being.

of judgment the measure of the truth of judgment, instead of making the truth of a judgment a function of the being of the things signified by its terms.[1]

In the *Topics* Aristotle deals with dialectical argumentation —i.e., with reasoning from opinions generally accepted. The primary elements of dialectical argumentation, therefore, are propositions—these are taken to be true, but are not known to be true in the unqualified sense, because the middle term signifying the essential nature or being of the things of which the proposition is true, is not known. In the *Topics* the discussion of genus, definition, property, and accident, is a discussion of the ways in which a given term may, by the manner in which it is predicated of various subjects in propositions conceded by the opponent, be exhibited as predicable necessarily (or be shown not to be predicable necessarily), of the subject term of the proposition or "thesis" being defended or attacked. Aristotle here deals with terms not in their intentional character as determinate ways in which things can be signified or recognized, but he deals with them as elements of propositions believed or conceded to be true *as a matter of fact*—i.e., in extension.[2]

---

[1] Arist., Cat. 4, 2a 4: "No one of these terms, in and by itself, involves an affirmation; it is only by the combination of such terms that positive or negative statements arise." Ibid., 4, 1 b 25: "Expressions which are in no way composite signify substance, quantity, etc. . . ." But Aristotle had previously distinguished simple from composite expressions as follows (Cat. 2, 1a 16): "Forms of speech are either simple or composite. Examples of the latter are such expressions as 'the man runs,' 'the man wins'; of the former, 'man,' 'ox,' 'runs,' 'wins.'" It is obvious from these statements that Aristotle, in the *Categories*, is concerned with terms as incomplex signs of things, and not as elements of propositions or as parts of complex signs.

[2] Arist., *Topics* I, 1, 100a 18: "Our treatise proposes to find a line of inquiry whereby we shall be able to reason from opinions that are generally accepted about every problem propounded to us, and also shall ourselves, when standing up to an argument, avoid saying anything that will obstruct us." Ibid., I, 4, 101b 11–37: "First, then, we must see of what parts our inquiry consists. Now if we were to grasp (a) with reference to how many, and what kind of, things arguments take place, and with what materials they start, and (b) how we are to become well supplied with these, we should have sufficiently won our goal. Now the materials with which arguments start are equal in number, and are identical, with the subjects on which reasonings take place. For arguments start with 'propositions,' while the subjects on which reasonings take place are 'problems.' Now every proposition and every problem indicates either a genus or a peculiarity or an accident . . ." etc. There follows the enumeration of

What is the consequence of using the classification of terms according to the ways in which they are assertible of a subject, as the basis for the division and ordering of terms in the ten categories? It is to destroy the possibility of identifying the things of which a given proposition is said to be true or false, without presupposing the truth of some proposition which determines the denotation of the terms. The proposition to be verified will be true or false of that which is signified by its terms. But if the signification of terms cannot be determined independently of the truth of propositions into which they can enter, the verification of a proposition will presuppose knowledge of the truth of other propositions which determine the meaning of the terms, and the verification of these propositions in turn will presuppose knowledge of the truth of still other propositions for the same reason. The grasp of meaning, and knowledge of any truth of determinate character, will therefore presuppose an infinite system of propositions. Since an infinite regress is not actually traversed, postulates or definitions are assumed or laid down as starting points for the construction of a symbolic system.

Porphyry's failure to distinguish between meaning and attribution, or between *things* and *facts*, renders determinate definition impossible—and, by the same token, literal truth as well. Every term is a sign of "something" of which the propositions into which it can enter are verifiable; but this "something" cannot be grasped by the mind determinately, or apart from an infinite whole such as is potentially exemplifiable in the unity of an infinite system of mutually implicated

---

the four modes of predication. It appears from the above that dialectical arguments are, in Aristotle's view, about terms and propositions as instances of forms of discursive signification. In dialectic we do not discuss kinds of things (for we do not know essential nature by opinion) nor kinds of discourse, in their universality (as in pure science or in pure logic), but we introduce terms of first intention as instances of kinds of terms signified by terms of second intention, as when we argue as to whether or not "virtue" is a *property* of "man." We must either state it this way, or do what Ockham does in his *Consequentiae*, where he exhibits all topical reasoning as enthymematic, the logical relation between subject and predicate (which takes the place of the middle term), or between antecedent and consequent, being an "extrinsic" middle or way of knowing the truth of the consequence.

propositions. The consistent development of the point of view involved in Porphyry's failure to distinguish between signification and predication, and between things and facts, yields a metaphysics of internal relations which can be expressed as a cosmology, a system of symbolic logic, a system of mathematics, or as a mystical theology. Where such consistent development takes place, finite signification and literal propositions are abandoned, or reduced to the status of conventional symbols or postulates incidental to the process of developing the system. Apparent contradiction or apparent externality, is the signal not for a distinction or definition, but for a generalization; and the final or supreme generalization, hovering always in the background, is that whereby the distinction between truth and falsity, affirmation and negation, and between terms and relations, is transcended in the incommunicable intuition of the infinite.[1]

Such is the metaphysics involved in Porphyry's treatise on the predicables. Unfortunately he injected this metaphysical point of view into the subject matter with which he was dealing, without giving it any such consistent development or expression. Had he done so, it would have been apparent that the aristotelian distinctions between essential and accidental predication, and between definitions and properties, are, if taken literally, unintelligible when placed against such a metaphysical background. It was, perhaps, because Porphyry wanted to take an aristotelian point of view in

[1] This metaphysics of internal relations, which Porphyry presents in muddled form because he seeks at the same time to preserve the aristotelian distinctions between essential and accidental predication, receives what is perhaps its best modern statement in A. N. Whitehead's works, especially *Process and Reality*. Whitehead is one of the few who appreciate the affinity between platonic metaphysical and cosmological ideas, and their exemplification in modern mathematical and cosmological theory. If students of mediæval philosophy could bring themselves to study St. Bonaventura or Duns Scotus, to mention only the most prominent, with the same appreciation of the philosophical (and not merely the religious) character of mediæval platonism, and without seeking to make aristotelians and thomists out of these philosophers, their efforts would be rewarded—for the metaphysics which was only half present in Porphyry's treatise, and which was neither a good platonism or a genuine aristotelianism, was developed in consistent and relatively pure form, by the greater scholastics of augustinian leanings, into coherent and impressive statements of the metaphysics of internal relations.

expounding Aristotle, that he submerged his own viewpoint as far as was within his power—but what made his treatise so insidious as a mediæval "secondary source" for the study of Aristotle, was the fact that he was unable to lose this viewpoint, and unwilling to make overt and systematic use of it. What was submerged was not Porphyry's metaphysics of internal relations, but only the aristotelian distinction between meaning and truth, and between things and contingent facts.

We may here indicate one or two particulars in Porphyry's discussion, which reveal his metaphysical viewpoint, and which have never ceased to affect subsequent interpretations of aristotelian logic and metaphysics. One departure from Aristotle which has often noted by historians—though rarely with sufficient appreciation of its importance—is the statement by Porphyry that the *infima species* is predicable *per se* and *in quid* of individuals.[1]

Now if we were to restate this as meaning that the specific term *signifies* individuals essentially, without connoting or implying any contingent fact or circumstance, we would have a thoroughly aristotelian statement. But Porphyry uses the word "predicable" to express the relation between the species and individuals, which indicates that the species is *attributable* to individuals by an act of judgment—and

---

[1] Porphyry (Boethius comm., Migne PL 64, cl. 101 A): "species est quae de pluribus et differentibus numero in eo quod quid sit praedicatur."

W. D. Ross, *Aristotle* (2nd ed., London, 1930), p. 57, shows some appreciation of the wreckage of aristotelian logic wrought by Porphyry's "fifth predicable," as follows: "This is Aristotle's classification of predicables which Porphyry later muddled hopelessly by reckoning *species* as a fifth predicable."

But cf. Father Joyce, *Principles of Logic* (3rd ed., Longmans, 1929), p. 121: "The account of the Predicables given by the Scholastic philosophers, is derived from the *Isagoge* of Porphyry. Porphyry's treatment of the subject differs from that of Aristotle in one or two details. . . . It is, however, as it explicitly professes to be, in full accord with the principles of his philosophy."

Cf. also De Wulf, *Hist. of Med. Phil.*, vol. II, p. 75: "The *Isagoge* studies the five predicables or ways in which the predicate of a judgment can be related to a subject (genus, species, specific difference, property, and accident); it served as an introduction to the *Categories* of Aristotle. Porphyry in the *Isagoge* did not get beyond this logical aspect of the predicables. He scarcely noticed the problem of the objectivity of universal ideas, and his statement of the question became the starting point of the controversy concerning the Universals."

hence it is not of itself a sign of individuals, but stands for them only through a human act of attribution or synthesis. If we then seek to determine what Porphyry means by "individual," we discover that he means that which is the *occasion* of accidental determination—i.e., an individual, for Porphyry, is a "this" which is constituted by the togetherness of contingent elements of fact. Thus he says that "the species is predicable only of individuals; but the individual is predicated of one particular only," and illustrates what he means by an "individual" through mentioning the following terms: "Socrates," "this white thing," or "the son of Sophroniscus coming this way."[1] These indeed are individuals in the sense of being terms that can be subjects only of singular propositions, and it is true that the specific term can be predicated of such singular subjects. But for Aristotle such predication is indirect or "unnatural" predication, and in any case it is contingent and accidental, and consequently not *per se* or *in quid*.[2] But Porphyry states that the species is predicated of such terms *essentially*—and this is the destruction of the distinction between essential and accidental predication, and of the distinction between necessary and contingent propositions.

Porphyry's point of view, when reduced to its simplest presuppositions, makes the primary subject of all predication, and hence the object of science, infinite and incapable of being comprehended or signified in determinate manner.

---

[1] Porphyry (Migne PL 64, cl. 112 D): "solum autem species de omnibus individuis (dicitur); individuum autem predicatur de uno solo particulari. Individuum autem dicitur Socrates, et hoc album, et hic veniens Sophronisci filius, si solus sit ei Socrates filius." Ibid., cl. 114 B: "Individua autem dicuntur huiusmodi; quoniam ex proprietatibus consistit unumquodque eorum, quarum collectio nunquam in alio quolibet eadem erit."

[2] Arist., An. Post., 1, 22, 82b 36–83a 23. Cf. also 83b 10: "Nor . . . can a *quale* be reciprocally predicated of a *quale*, nor any term belonging to an adjectival category of another such term, except by accidental predication; for all such predicates are coincidents and are predicated of substances." The reason why such predication is accidental is, as Ockham states it, because the terms are connotative, signifying something extrinsic to the things for which they can stand. But Porphyry, and all who reduce genera and species of substance to the status of connotative terms which stand for individuals by signifying abstract or universal elements or "parts," make the category of substance into an adjectival category, and thus transform all predication whatsoever into accidental predication.

For every term, insofar as it is predicable of a subject, is exhibited by Porphyry as a connotative term—the species or genus of substance is predicated essentially of a term like "this white thing," but the term "white" is predicated only accidentally of "this thing." Hence the subject of predication, in both cases, is no more determinate than the word "thing" or the word "something." It is that in which forms, connoted by concrete universal terms and signified directly by their abstract counterparts, *inhere*, as parts in a whole. The term "man," being predicable *in quid* of the "something that happens to be white," stands for this "something" by connoting the *fact* that "humanity" *inheres* in it, or that "humanity" is a part of it, of which "animality" and "risibility" and "whiteness" and "rationality" are other parts. In short, every universal term is an attribute, predicable of "something" indicated only by other attributes—no determinate concept, but only the indeterminate concept, "thing" or "something" or "being," is the primary subject of attribution.[1]

Thus Porphyry's point of view erases the distinction between metaphysics and science, through recognizing as the primary subject of all predication only the transcendental terms of metaphysics. No term, according to Porphyry's point of view, means or signifies precisely the individual natures of finite things. All terms indicate abstract forms or "ideas" by which *something*, that is not a form or idea, is posited. "Man" stands for "something *in* which humanity inheres," and this "something" is held to be distinct from that which is signified by the abstract term "humanity"—distinct either as a whole is to a part, or as a part is to a whole. The only primary subject of knowledge, and the only thing by which propositions are true, is that which is indicated by the term "something." If we take this something to be God, then science is of the subsistence of ideas in God; and if we take it

---

[1] Cf. *Ante*, ch. ii, pp. 57–65, on Ockham's criticism of those who construe all concrete universal terms as connotative, through making a metaphysical distinction between what is indicated by their abstract forms and what is denoted by their concrete forms.

to be a substratum of existence, or principle of individuation, distinct from God, then science is of the ingression or inherence of ideas in this indeterminate substratum. The net result of Porphyry's point of view, whereby all determinate terms are *attributable* to the indeterminate, is to make all terms attributes of a single subject-genus, so that there is only one science, whose subject is "being as such."[1]

Ockham, as has already been indicated, criticizes Porphyry chiefly for equivocal forms of expression, and seeks to "interpret" his statements in such manner that they will not have metaphysical implications. After all, Porphyry explicitly states that he is not concerned in his treatise with the "loftier questions" of metaphysics, but with five ways in which terms can be predicated of a subject term. In his commentary on Porphyry, therefore, Ockham seeks to do what Porphyry said he intended to do—namely, to discuss the predicables, and to keep the discussion of them clear of metaphysical

---

[1] Since, in a philosophy of internal relations, the indeterminate whole cannot be signified *per se* but only as that *in* which the ideas achieve relatedness and actuality, the only materials for discourse, or the only terms, appear as attributes or properties of Space-Time, or of God, or of Infinite Matter, or of Infinite Number—but merely to attribute them to this indeterminate receptacle, as in the proposition "Triangularity is in Space-Time," etc., is insufficient for generating connected discourse. It is equivalent to collecting a multitude of propositions such as "Something is a man," "Something is a tree," etc. To form a discursive structure, therefore, such propositions have to be connected—and thus we find symbolic logic, and other modern logical systems based on relations as constitutive of fact, exhibiting all discourse as built up through hypothetical propositions, the constituents of which are elementary propositions which assert the existence of a quality or of a relation. Since that to which the quality or relation is referred, in these elementary propositions, is indeterminate ("x"), it makes little or no difference whether we conceive it as an infinite homogeneous "receptacle" like Space-Time, or as an infinite multitude of atomic "points of reference." In either case, science is exhibited as a potentially infinite system of relations, of first order, second order, etc., between the elementary existence propositions, and between propositions which express relations between relations, etc. It need not be added that in such an infinite system, every proposition or equation has a place, so that falsity is only a function of misplaced reference, which tends always to elicit further expansion of the system in which it may finally be absorbed. The analogy is close, in all such systems, with the augustinian dialectic of redemption—with original sin (a misplaced reference called Pride) generating the restlessness which never ends (infinite regress) until the misplaced reference is abandoned, absorbed, and redeemed, through recognition of the actually infinite as an omnipresent Principle, to be found in any instance of existence or of truth, and which is not added to by our dialectical regress, but only made manifest to us.

implications. His method is comparatively simple. After stating that a "universal," as used in logic, is nothing but a term or concept predicable of many other terms or concepts, he points out that the terms "universal," "genus," "species," etc., are terms of second intention, and cannot therefore mean things *in re*, or parts of things *in re*, but only kinds of terms or concepts. Since, however, a sign is posterior, *qua* sign, to that which it signifies, and since terms of second intention are signs of terms of first intention, it follows that the understanding of the predicables is posterior to the understanding of the distinctions between terms of first intention made in the *Categories*. In this way Ockham reverses Porphyry's reversal of the aristotelian order, and restores the priority of forms of incomplex signification, over modes of predication. Truth and scientific knowledge are to be exhibited as functions of the grasp of meaning—of acts of understanding *what it is to be* such or such an individual thing. But such grasp of essential individual nature, is only possible if some determinate concepts are "absolute" and not connotative.[1]

In his discussion of the problem of universals raised by Porphyry, Ockham seeks to establish the priority of acts of signification over modes of predication, by showing that the term "universal," and the names of the predicables, are terms of second intention which stand for terms and not for things *in re* nor for parts of things *in re*. After showing, by this method, that the word "universal" is not a metaphysical term but only a logical term, Ockham follows

---

[1] Porphyry's statement that the species is predicated *in quid* of individuals is "interpreted" by Ockham to mean that it signifies or means individual (undivided) essential natures. Exp. aur., I, 14r: "Notandum est hic quod species predicatur in quid de individuis *quia exprimit vel significat totum individuum* et non plus unam partem quam aliam, neque aliquid extrinsecum . . ." (italics mine). In another place Ockham indicates explicitly that the specific term is not predicable essentially of anything, if we take "predicari" in its strict sense and not merely as equivalent to "significare". S. tot. log., II, cap. 11, 35r: "intelligendum est quod proprie et stricte accipiendo 'predicari per se et in quid,' quod scilicet est necessario predicabile, sic nulla talis species 'homo,' 'asinus,' 'numerus' et huiusmodi predicatur in quid et dicitur per se de aliquo, maxime in propositione de inesse et de praesenti; et hoc quia nulla talis est necessaria, 'Sortes est homo, 'iste asinus est asinus,' 'iste numerus est numerus,' 'iste motus est motus,' et huiusmodi."

Porphyry's discussion of each of the predicables, distinguishing in each case the sign from what it signifies, and eliminating the metaphysical implications of Porphyry's language. In the *Sum of All Logic*, the same subjects are dealt with, and a number of other terms of second intention, such as "definition," "description," "subject," "predicate," "signify," and "attribute," are analysed and defined. In the present chapter we will examine Ockham's discussion of the problem of universals, of the predicables themselves, and of these other terms of second intention, in this way clearing the ground for Ockham's own interpretation of the *Categories*, which in all fundamentals is exactly the opposite of the porphyrian point of view.

II

The problem of universals is raised by Porphyry in the second sentence of his treatise, in the form of three questions concerning the relation between genera and species of substance and the individuals which we apprehend through sense perception. He asks (1) whether genera and species subsist outside the mind, or exist only in the mind; (2) whether, assuming that they subsist outside the mind, they are corporeal or incorporeal; and (3) whether, if they subsist outside the mind, they are separated from sensible things or exist *in* sensible things.[1] Porphyry declines to discuss the possible solutions to these questions, stating that they belong to a loftier part of philosophy—presumably metaphysics. But his own treatment of logic, and his own notion of what the categories are, involve this metaphysical problem at every point. For if universal concepts of substance are related to individual sensible things not as signs to things signified nor as acts of understanding to things understood, as Ockham holds, but rather as predicates to subjects, as indicated by Porphyry—then a distinction inevitably arises between what the universal term signifies, and the things denoted by any subject term of which it is predicable.

[1] Porphyry's text is given in Migne PL 64, cl. 82 A (Boethius' transl.).

The problem of universals, according to Ockham's analysis, is a consequence of Porphyry's confusion of signification with predication, or of meaning with attribution. For Ockham, who holds that individual things are understood by generic and specific concepts precisely because such concepts are natural signs (acts or habits of understanding) of such individual things, there can be no problem of a *relation* between that which is signified or understood by a generic or specific concept, and the individuals *in re* for which it can stand. But for Porphyry, who holds that genera and species are attributable to individuals by an act of judgment which is a synthesis of distinct elements, a distinction between the individual, and the essential nature attributed to it, corresponding to the distinction between a subject and a predicate, becomes inevitable. From this distinction between individual things, and their essential natures, arises the problem of universals and the corresponding problem of individuation.[1]

Ockham, commenting on the passage in which Porphyry raises his three questions, agrees that such questions do not pertain to logic, but to metaphysics. He adds, however, that metaphysical errors on these questions have led so many *moderni* to manifold errors in logic, that it is not out of place to deal with them. His discussion of this "problem of universals," in the commentary on Porphyry, is rather brief, a more detailed analysis being given in the *Sum of All Logic*. It is this more detailed discussion that will, for the most part, be followed here.[2]

Ockham's discussion deals principally with Porphyry's first question, since the answers to the others follow without difficulty from his solution of the first. Do genera and species subsist *per se* outside the mind, or do they exist only in the

---

[1] For Ockham's theory of the concept as a natural sign, or act of understanding, of individuals *in re*, see ch. ii, pp. 39-40, 44, 47-52.

[2] Exp. aur., I, 8v: "Quamvis praedictae quaestiones et consimiles non ad logicam sed ad metaphysicam sint pertinentes, quia tamen ex earum ignorantia multi moderni in multiplices errores in logica sunt elapsi, ideo de ipsis breviter quid sit secundum sententiam Aristotelis et secundum veritatem dicendum est docendum, quia de eis aliubi diffusius est tractatum" (i.e., in the Summa totius logicae).

mind as acts of understanding or as forms or "intelligible species" produced in the mind by its act of understanding? Most mediæval writers conceded that genera and species do exist in the mind; what Ockham argues against is the notion that genera and species, or "universal things " corresponding to them, exist outside the mind as *parts* of individual substances, in such manner that substances are "individuated" by something distinct from the essential nature signified by the universal substantial term. If generic and specific terms or concepts signify substances, they signify individual substances, because a substance is precisely a thing that exists and is one *per se*, as distinguished from an accident (in the physical sense) which exists, and is particular, *per aliud* or by reason of the existence of substances. A substance is an individual thing, and an accident a particular fact—facts occur, and are particular, by reason of the individual substances which give rise to them. There is no cause of individual existence, no principle of individuation, except substances.

It must be maintained undoubtedly that anything imaginable whatsoever, which subsists by itself, is without any addition to it a singular thing and one in number, so that no imaginable thing is singular through having something added to it, but this (*scil.* being singular) is an attribute belonging immediately to every thing, because every thing is *per se* identical or diverse from others. . . . Secondly it must be said that no universal is really existent outside the soul in individual substances, nor is it a part of the substance nor of its being, but in every case it is merely in the soul, or else it is universal by convention, as this spoken word "animal" or "man" is universal because it is predicable of many, not (standing) for itself but for the things which it signifies. The first conclusion can be proved both by reason and authority, by reason as follows: If there be anything which is not *per se* a singular thing, then, since anything you please can be given a name, let it be called "a." Then I ask whether it contains essentially several things or whether it is precisely one thing. If the first answer be given, then I ask concerning those things which are included essentially in it, whether they are of a definite number or not; it cannot be said that they are not of a definite number, because then they would be actually infinite which is impossible. If they are of a definite number, then each of them is one in number, and consequently the resulting total is one number. If the answer is given that the thing is not several things and does not contain several things essentially, then the question is conceded, because whenever there is something which does not include a multiplicity of distinct things, that thing is one in number, and consequently singular.

Further, I take this universal thing called "a," and then I ask whether "a " and Socrates are several things or one. If one, and if Socrates is a singular thing, then "a" also is singular. If they are more than one thing and are not infinite, then they are finite, and consequently they are of some determinate number; and it cannot be said that they are more than two, hence they are two things. But where there are just two things each of them is one in number, and therefore this universal thing ("a") is one in number and consequently it is singular.

Nor can it be said that this thing is universal although not several things, and this on the ground that it is in several things and of the being of several, as "humanity" or "man" is (said to be) in all men and of the being of all men. This does not hold, because such a thing is either varied so that it is other and other in these many things, or it is unvaried so that it is not other and other. If the first answer be given, then necessarily each of these things is singular and consequently, since there is no other thing outside of these things, it follows that each thing is singular. If the second answer be given, the question is conceded, because that thing, however much it may be (said to be) *in* many things, will be singular from the fact that it is one and not many.[1]

The above argument is a dialectical proof of the indemonstrable metaphysical principle of the convertibility of *ens* and *unum*. Since it is a primary principle of first philosophy, it cannot be demonstrated from any principles prior to it. But it can be shown to be presupposed in all discourse, in the manner in which Aristotle proves dialectically, in the *Metaphysics*, that the law of non-contradiction is presupposed by any affirmation or denial. It is rather interesting, in view of what was said about Porphyry's submerged metaphysics of internal relations, to see how Ockham's argument hinges on the impossibility of human comprehension of the indeterminate or of the actually infinite. What cannot be conceived cannot be signified, and hence it cannot be the primary

[1] Exp. aur., I, fol. 8v.

subject of significant discourse—such is Ockham's contention, which rests on the impossibility of comprehending the indeterminate. In Duns Scotus we find a consistent statement of the opposite point of view—for Duns, the true object of science is indeterminate with respect to individuality, but for him also, the infinite is known implicitly in every act of discursive thought. [1]

Every thing that is, according to Ockham, and consequently every thing that can be called a universal as well as every thing that can be signified by a universal, is, by the fact that *ens* and *unum* are convertible, an individual thing in the sense that it is one and not many. How, then, does the term "universal" differ in meaning from the term "individual?" Ockham answers the question by distinguishing between two uses of the word "individual." As a transcendental term, equivalent to *unum*, it is predicable of the term "universal" as well as of every other term; for each thing that can be called a universal is *a* universal and not many universals, and hence it is an individual thing. Similarly, if we distinguish between a universal and what it signifies, it must be said that each and every thing that can be signified by any universal term, or conceived by any universal concept, is, by the very fact that it is a *thing*, individual and numerically one and distinct from other things—*res et unum convertuntur*. Taking the word "individual" in this sense, therefore, as that which is one and not many, nothing can exist, either outside the mind or in the mind, which is not individual. [2]

---

[1] Cf. Duns Scotus, Op. Oxon., I, Dist. II, Qu. 1 and 2; and Dist. III, Qu. 4, especially art. 5.

[2] S. tot. log., I, 14, 6v: "Est igitur primo tractandum de terminis secundae intentionis . . . et ideo de illis quae ponuntur quinque universalia est modo dicendum. . . . Primo tamen dicendum est de hoc communi 'universale,' quia predicatur de omni universali, et etiam de singulari sibi opposito. Est autem sciendum quod 'singulare' potest sumi dupliciter. Unomodo hoc nomen 'singulare' significat illud quod est unum et non plura. Et hoc modo tenentes quod universale est quaedam qualitas mentis predicabilis de pluribus non tamen pro se, sed pro illis pluribus, dicere habent quod quodlibet universale est vere et realiter singulare, quia sicut quaelibet vox quantumcumque communis per institutionem est vere et realiter singularis et una numero, quia est una vox et non plures, ita quodlibet universale est singulare . . . unde vocando universale aliquod quod non est unum numero, quam acceptionem multi attribuunt universali, dico quod nihil est universale. . . ."

But the word "individual" can be taken also as a term of second intention, meaning any thing that is a *sign* of one individual thing only. In this sense, the term "individual" is equivalent to the expression "discrete term," and is divided into three kinds—proper names, demonstrative pronouns, and demonstrative pronouns plus a common name. If we use the term "individual" in this sense, then no individual is a universal, and no universal is an individual—for since a universal is by definition something that is a sign of many, it obviously cannot be individual in the sense of being a sign of one thing only. The *opposition* between "individual" and "universal," therefore, is intelligible only as an opposition between two different kinds of *signs;* it cannot be an opposition between two kinds of things that are not signs, for nothing that is not a sign of many can be called universal, and every thing, *qua* thing and not *qua* sign, is individual by the fact that it is a thing. A universal, therefore, is in itself an individual thing, and it is universal only because it is, either by nature or by convention, a sign of many individuals for which it can stand in discourse.[1]

If only what is a sign of many can be called a universal, can it be said that universals exist outside the mind? The word "sign," as stated by Ockham in the very beginning

[1] S. tot. log., I, 14, 6v: "Aliter accipitur hoc nomen 'singulare' pro omni eo quod est unum et non plura, et est signum alicuius singularis primo modo accipiendo 'singulare'; hoc est, natum esse signum unius. Et sic nullum universale est singulare quia quodlibet universale natum est esse signum plurium et natum est predicari de pluribus; unde vocando universale aliquod quod non est unum numero, quam acceptionem multi attribuunt 'universali,' dico quod nihil est universale. . . . Dicendum est igitur quod quodlibet universale est una res singularis, et ideo non est (universale) nisi per significationem quia est signum plurium. Et hoc est quod Avicenna dicit quinto metaphysicae: 'Una forma apud intellectum est relata ad multitudinem, et secundum hunc respectum est universale, quia ipsa est intentio in intellectu cuius operatio non variatur ad quodcumque aspexeris. Et sequitur haec forma, quamvis in comparatione individuorum sit universalis, tamen in comparatione animae singularis in qua imprimitur, est individua; ipsa enim est una ex formis quae sunt in intellectu'—vult dicere (*scil.* Avicenna) quod universale est una intentio singularis ipsius animae, nata predicari de pluribus non pro se sed pro ipsis rebus. . . . sic intentio animae dicitur universalis, quia est signum predicabile de pluribus, et dicitur singularis quia est una res et non plures. . . . tale universale non est nisi intentio animae, ita quod nulla substantia extra animam nec aliquod accidens extra animam est tale universale."

of his *Sum of all Logic*, has two senses, distinguished as "natural sign" and "conventional sign." A natural sign is that by which something distinct from it is understood to be, in the first instance, and which without any voluntary act of attribution or of imposition, is capable of being used to stand, in thought, for the things which can be understood by it. A conventional sign is something that *reminds* someone of something already known to him in some other way, as a piece of string on the finger reminds one of an errand, or as a written or spoken word reminds one of something which he is able to remember or think of.

In the case of the natural sign, or concept, the significative relation is immediate. That is to say, the concept is an act or habit of understanding *what something is* or *what it can be*, such that no third thing, beyond the understanding (i.e., the mind) and the things understood, is required or presupposed. In the case of the conventional sign, however, the significative relation is mediate, and involves as a third element the concept or act of understanding by which the meaning of the word is established, and by which the things that the word can stand for are identified and distinguished from other things. The existence of a conventional sign, *qua* sign, involves and presupposes the existence of a concept or act of understanding, in some intelligence, by which the significative relation is established and, when established, recognized.[1]

The above analysis of signification makes possible a formulation of the problem of universals (or of "ideas") in which the position upheld in mediæval times by Ockham (and, in all essentials, by St. Thomas before him) is seen to differ fundamentally, in aim as well as in method, from the positions of Averroes, Avicenna, and the scholastics of augustinian tendencies. The relation of signification between a conventional sign and the things it is used to denote presupposes, for its establishment and maintenance, a concept or act of understanding in some intelligence; further, the recognition

---

[1] The distinction between these two senses of the word "sign" is made by Ockham in the S. tot. log., I, 1, iv, cited ch. ii, p. 40, Note 2.

of the symbol as a conventional sign of such things, is possible
only to the intelligence which possesses the concept by which
its signification is established.

If now we ask, concerning the unspoken words which form
the inner discourse of the soul, whether these are concepts
or acts of understanding in the sense that they are *natural*
signs of the individual perceptible things for which they
stand in discourse, or whether, like conventional signs, their
capacity to stand for individuals *in re* is a function of some
third element distinct both from the human mind and from
the perceptible things signified—if we ask this question, the
difference between the position upheld by Ockham and St.
Thomas, and that of the augustinians and arabs, will be
clearly indicated by the two ways of answering it.

Let us first state the answer given by Ockham and by St.
Thomas. For them, nothing is required for the act of understanding beyond individual material substances perceptible
to sense, and individual human minds capable of understanding them. For Ockham and Aquinas, equally, the act
of understanding is a function of individual human minds,
and of individual perceptible things *in re*. Both elements are
required, and no other element is required. The "inner
discourse of the soul" is, for both Ockham and Aquinas,
made up of concepts which are either identical with, or
immediately formed by, acts of understanding—acts of
individual human beings. These concepts are immediate
or natural signs of the individual perceptible things *in re* for
which they can stand in the propositions of discursive science,
and no third element is needed or presupposed for establishing
or for maintaining the significative character of such concepts
as signs of individual things.[1]

---

[1] Ockham, Sent. II, Qu. 24, quoted by Federhofer, *Phil. Jahrbuch*, XXXIX,
p. 274. Cf. Aquinas, S. theol. I, Qu. 85, art. 2, cited ch. ii, p. 50, Note 2, on
distinction between *id quo intelligitur* and *id quod intelligitur*. St. Thomas makes a
real distinction, in the human soul, between an active intellect *by* which the act
of understanding takes place, and a possible intellect *in* which things are understood.
Ockham does not make this real distinction, considering it as merely a way of
expressing, by analogy with material things, the being of a substance which,
not being material, cannot be understood literally in terms of the principles of

Let us now examine the position of Averroes on this same question. For him, concepts, insofar as they are formed by individual human souls and insofar as they exist in individual human minds, are merely phantasms or images, produced not by an act of understanding but by sense affections and imagination. As such, they are not signs of many and hence are not universals. According to Averroes, these phantasms acquire universality through being illumined by a separated and eternal Intelligence to which, in the act of understanding, the individual human soul is in some way conjoined.[1]

St. Thomas' criticism of Averroes on this question is well known. As Aquinas points out, either it is the individual

---

change in material substances—*scil*. in terms of matter and form, or of the reception of a form in it. This difference between Ockham and Thomas, however, is of slight moment in comparison to the important point on which they agree, and which differentiates them equally from the position of the arabs and augustinians. Indeed, when Thomas talks about a "real distinction" between the faculties or powers of the soul, with respect to the soul itself and to each other, it is hard to see how he can mean a metaphysical distinction, such as his modern expositors attribute to him. As Aquinas insists, it is the individual man who knows or who desires, or who acts—and if to understand is an essential or natural act of man, then the power of understanding is not something conjoined to individual human nature, but it *is* individual human nature. The other view would lean towards the averroist doctrine of knowledge by conjunction with a separated Intelligence —a view strenuously combated by St. Thomas.

It cannot be denied that Averroes, and those who interpret the laconic reference to the active and possible intellect, in Aristotle's *De anima* III, 5, in the averroist manner, can with much plausibility claim to be closer to the thought of Aristotle than Aquinas or Ockham, concerning the sense in which intellect is eternal and "separated." Yet when the averroist interpretation is developed on this basis, it gives rise to a neo-platonic metaphysics that seems entirely against the normal point of view of Aristotle; the same applies to those scholastic interpretations which, though insisting that each man has his own intellectual powers, make a metaphysical distinction *within* the human soul between essential "parts" and potentialities—for this also generates a discursive metaphysics of internal relations.

The best reason for doubting the accuracy of the averroist manner of interpreting Aristotle's *De anima*, on this point, is the fact that Aristotle's reference to this "eternal" and "impassible" part of the soul is so laconic. This would indicate that discursive knowledge of it is not to be had, because it is a *simple* and noncomposite substance; but the neo-platonic interpretation makes the comprehension of such pure and unconditioned being the very task of discursive thinking, the *unconditioned* being (as for Porphyry) the only true and primary subject of science.

[1] Cf. Aquinas, Contra Gentiles II, c. 73: "Secundum enim dictam positionem (*scil*. Averrois), nihil ad intellectum pertinens remanebit numeratum secundum multitudinem hominum, nisi solum phantasma," etc.

human being that understands, or it is not. If it is, then he understands by and in his own personal intelligence, and consequently needs no separated Intelligence to make perceptible things intelligible to him. But if it is not the individual human being who understands, then conjunction with a separated Intelligence, or illumination of his phantasms, will not make the individual man understand, but will only make that individual man's phantasms intelligible to the separated Intelligence.[1]

It can easily be seen that on Averroes' position, the "unspoken words" formed by the human soul in itself (which for him are only phantasms or sense images) are related to the perceptible things that they are used to denote, as *conventional* signs. They are symbols *attributable* to the things they stand for, by reason of a third element which establishes the significative relation and maintains it—this third element being a separated and eternal Intelligence distinct from the individual man. Averroes' position is thus equated to that which is implicitly involved in Porphyry's notion of the indeterminate particular occasion, as that to which all universal terms are referred—for according to this, no term is universal by determinate signification, but only *qua* predicable of a subject, the connection between predicate and subject being established and maintained by what is not a determinate

---

[1] Aquinas, Contra Gentiles II, c. 59 and c. 76. Aquinas, in the *Summa contra Gentiles*, gives a very fine analysis of Averroes' position, showing a keen appreciation of its consistent character and of its relation to platonism and hence to augustinian exemplarism and the illumination theory of knowledge. The affinity of Averroes' position with augustinism is well illustrated in William of Auvergne, who has merely to identify the separated Intelligence with God, to reconcile Averroes with augustinism. The reconciliation tends to break down, however, at just the point which most distinctively divides the theology of Islam from that of Christianity—i.e., the question of free creation, and of conditioned freedom (proper causal being) of created things.

Ockham uses Averroes' argument, that the existence of a single concept of many implies the singularity of the intellect which has the concept, to support his point that a concept is of itself a singular thing and is many only through signification. Exp. aur., I, 8v: "Similiter secundum intentionem Commentatoris tertio de Anima, comm. 5 et aliubi pluries, quia non est alius intellectus in me et in te, tamen secundum eum est unus numero, ita quod generaliter esse cum diversis vel in diversis vel sub diversis, nihil facit, quia illud sit unum numero, dummodo non sit aliud et aliud; et ita omnis res quae non est plures necessario est una res secundum numerum et per consequens est singularis."

human act of understanding. For Porphyry the connection between terms, whereby a true proposition is formed, is mediated by indeterminate contingent existence; for Averroes the connection is mediated by the act of the separated Intelligence contemplating itself, and thereby creating the actual occasions which move the senses. Thus the parallelism is extremely close between Averroes' reference of terms and of the truth of discourse to internal relations within the eternal creative Intelligence (which is the cause and unity of the world of change) and the metaphysics of internal relations implied in Porphyry's treatise.

Aquinas' arguments against the averroist doctrine—that individual human beings understand not by their own intellectual power but by conjunction with a separated and eternal Intelligence—are quite as destructive of the augustinian illumination theory of knowledge, as they are of Averroes' doctrine. Whether there are exemplars in the divine intellect, prior to created things, is irrelevant to the question at issue. The question at issue is a question concerning *human* knowledge —can we, or can we not, understand the being and nature of perceptible things by our own intellectual powers? If so, then we do not understand by means of exemplars or *universalia ante rem*, and the human act of understanding involves no third element beyond individual things understood, and the human intellect in which and by which they are understood. Stated another way, the relation between human concepts and perceptible things signified by them, is immediate; the unspoken word which goes to form the inner discourse of the soul is a *natural* sign of the perceptible individuals for which it stands, and not, like the spoken or written symbol, a conventional sign.

From the above analysis it will be observed that Averroes, on the one hand, and Ockham and Aquinas on the other, are not talking about quite the same thing when they discuss the nature of the universal, so that their positions are, in one sense, not incompatible with each other. This is well illustrated in the works of St. Thomas, who, by interpreting the *universale ante rem* with which Averroes is concerned as the exemplar of creation in the divine essence, and by distinguishing between the problem of creation or of divine understanding, and the problem of human knowledge, leaves room for the averroist point of view (or for an augustinian version of it) in theology, while removing it from philosophy and from his theory of science.

The opposition between Aquinas and Averroes, and that between Ockham and the *moderni* whom he criticizes, centres not on the question of whether or not created things are imitations of God or of exemplary forms internal to the divine Wisdom, but on the question of whether or not the things that have been created, and that exist in the past, present, or future and in particular places, can be understood by individual human minds to be the things that they are, and to be distinct from each other *per se*, by what they are. Ockham and Aquinas criticize the arabs and augustinians not because they hold that the divine intellect is prior to created things and therefore prior to the human intellect which is measured by created things, but because they seek to deny the possibility of any kind of knowledge other than that which is proper to the Creator. Stated in more modern language, it is not a question of holding that a metaphysics of internal relations, in which the part exemplifies the whole and is referred to the whole, is "wrong"—rather the question at issue is whether or not a science of finite things is possible to finite human beings.

In opposing those who hold that a third element is needed, besides the human understanding and the individual things understood, to establish and maintain the significative relation between human concepts and perceptible things, Ockham and Aquinas are opposing a position which would reduce all concepts to the status of spoken or written words. Such a position reduces concepts to conventional signs, or mere symbols, which, though attributed to *that which is*, do not make known to the human mind *what* it is that they stand for. If the effort to reduce all determinate concepts to the status of conventional signs, is characteristic of nominalism, then Ockham, far from being a nominalist, is, with the possible exception of Aquinas, the most thorough-going critic of nominalism that the Middle Ages produced.

The doctrine of Avicenna, which appears to have played an important part in the formation of Duns Scotus' theory of knowledge and of the universal, differs from that of Averroes, as well as from that of Ockham or Aquinas, by identifying the "possible intellect" *in* which concepts exist, with individual human minds, and the "active intellect," *by* which concepts are formed, with the separated Intelligence. According to Avicenna, the human soul is that which understands, but it does not understand by its own act; the work of abstraction is not the work of the human intellect, but of a separated Intelligence which illumines and universalizes the phantasms.

In other words, the human soul *receives* forms, or "intelligible species," which are produced neither by itself in the act of understanding perceptible things, nor by perceptible things themselves, but by the separated Intelligence. The immediate object of human understanding, therefore, in the real sciences, is a form that is, *qua* intelligible, distinct from and prior to the human mind and to individuals *in re*, though *qua* existent it is *in* human minds and attributed to individuals outside the mind. It is neither a concept formed by the mind in itself, nor the kind of thing that can exist independently of an act of understanding. It is neither a second intention nor a first intention, neither a universal (in the sense of a natural sign of many) nor an individual, but something prior both to existence *in re* as individual, and to existence in the mind as a universal concept (in the sense of a predicable). It is what Avicenna, and Duns Scotus after him, conceive to be the true object of scientific knowledge—an "absolute nature" which is *per se* neither individual nor universal, neither in the human mind nor apart from it, but which acquires individuality through having existence added to it, and which acquires universality, or existence in the human mind, by the combined agency of the human sense faculties which produce the phantasm, and the separated active intellect which illumines it.

Duns Scotus, while discarding Avicenna's theory of the separated active intellect, retained the notion of the object of understanding as something indeterminate with respect to existence either in the mind or outside the mind, and as something that is *per se* neither one nor many. While it could be understood as an equivalent of the aristotelian doctrine of abstract signification, it could also be harmonized with the older augustinian theory of knowledge, according to which the objects of human understanding are not the perishable things apprehended in sense experience, but possible forms of exemplification of Being (or of God), prior to the existence of sensible things, prior to the soul in which they are understood, but posterior to God and distinct from Him. These absolute natures, according to Duns Scotus, are signified only connotatively by concrete general names: "man," for instance, appearing as subject of a universal proposition, signifies the absolute nature (*scil.* "humanity") but connotes its contraction to individual existence by an individuating form "formally distinct in the thing."[1]

The scotist doctrine of the "absolute nature" that is neither one nor many, was criticized by Ockham in his discussion

---

[1] Cf. ch. ii, p. 64, Note 1, for Duns Scotus' doctrine of the absolute nature indeterminate with respect to existence as individual or as universal. Cf. also Duns Scotus, Qu. in metaph. VII, 18 (Wadding, vol. IV, p. 723 A), where he distinguishes, following Avicenna, three senses of the term "universal": "Universale sumi potest tripliciter: Pro intentione secunda, quae est quaedam relatio rationis in predicabili ad illud de quo est predicabile. . . . Alio modo accipitur pro illo quod denominatur ab illa intentione, quod est aliqua res primae intentionis; nam secundae intentiones applicantur primis. Et sic accipi potest dupliciter: Uno modo pro illo, quod quasi ut subiectum remotum dicitur natura absolute sumpta universale, quia non est de se haec; secundo modo non est universale nisi sit actu indeterminatum ita quod unum intelligibile numero sit dicibile de omni supposito." That Duns Scotus is a good porphyrian in considering that modes of signification presuppose modes of predication, rather than *vice versa*, and that second intentions are in some way prior to, or at least co-ordinate with, first intentions, is nicely indicated in his statement: "Alio modo accipitur (universale) pro illo quod denominatur ab illa intentione, quod est aliqua res primae intentionis, nam secundae intentiones applicantur primis."

of concrete and abstract terms.[1] The theory of the contraction of such an absolute nature to individuality by an individuating differentia, in such manner that two individuals of the same species are essentially identical, *qua* absolute nature, and essentially diverse, through their individuating *differentiae*, by a "formal distinction in the thing," is criticized by Ockham as follows:

Although it is clear to many that the universal is not any substance existing outside the mind in individual things, and really distinct from them; nevertheless it appears to some that the universal is in some way outside the mind and in individual things, not, however, really distinct from them, but only formally so. Whence they say that in Socrates is human nature, which is contracted to Socrates through an individuating differentia which is not distinguished really from that (human) nature, but formally, so that there are not two things, though one is not formally the other. But this opinion seems to be unreasonable: because in created things there cannot be any distinction of any sort outside the mind, except where there are distinct things. That it is necessary that there be such things really distinct, I prove thus by syllogism: "This nature is not formally distinct from this nature; this individuating differentia is distinct formally from this nature; therefore this individuating differentia is not this nature." Further, the same thing is not both common and peculiar; but according to them the individuating differentia is peculiar, while the universal is common; therefore the universal and the (individuating) differentia are not the same thing. . . .

Again, anything you please is distinguished from whatever it is distinguished from by itself and not through another. But the humanity of Socrates is one, and that of Plato another, whereby they are distinct from each other; therefore they are distinct not through added differentiae. Further, I take that individuating differentia, and the nature which it contracts, and ask whether between them there is a greater distinction than between two individuals, or a less distinction. Not a greater, because they do not differ really, while individuals do differ really; nor a less, because then they would be one in definition (*eiusdem rationis*) as two individuals are one in definition, and consequently if one (i.e., the individuating differentia) is of itself one in number, then the other (i.e., the specific or absolute nature) will be one in number.[2]

[1] Cf. ch. ii, pp. 57–65.

[2] S. tot. log., I, 16, 7r–v. The theory here criticized is explicitly referred by Ockham to Duns Scotus, and subjected to a detailed analysis and criticism, in

Duns Scotus' "formal distinction in the thing," whereby two things are said to be one while remaining two, apart from the human mind, again reveals the important part played by the notion of infinity, in the metaphysical point of view criticized by Ockham. The scotist distinction, from Ockham's viewpoint, is all right for theology, and especially for statements about the Trinity or about the dual nature of Christ, since theological truths are statements about what is actually infinite, and are composed of terms which, being finite signs of what is infinite, are to be understood analogically. But for natural philosophy, whose object is created or finite things, the scotist distinction is an unintelligible contradiction in terms, involving a confusion of things known with human ways of knowing things—an attempt to find a mean between signs and things signified.

It may be noted that the solution of the problem of universals preferred by Avicenna, and taken over by Duns Scotus, constitutes, quite as much as the more consistent solution of Averroes, a denial that the human mind is capable of the act of understanding things outside the mind. According to Avicenna, things which exist *in re* as individual sensible substances, are signified by concepts in the human mind only mediately, through a third element which is called the "absolute nature" prior alike to existent things and to the concept. The concept, therefore, is related to individuals *in re*, for which it stands in the propositions of real science, as a conventional sign and not as a natural sign; its significative function is established and maintained by an act of

---

his Comm. in Sent. I, Dist. II, Qu. 6 B (partly quoted by Abbagnano, p. 80 et seq.). Ockham's point is that the term "this man" has not a more determinate concept (act of understanding) corresponding to it, and giving it its meaning, than the term "man." The word "this" is demonstrative, not significative. It is in this same sense that St. Thomas says that the intellect does not understand particulars directly. Thus, while a univocal universal concept signifies individuals, so that the things understood by the concept "man" are individual men, we do not understand individuals by any distinct or formal individuating principle, precisely because the circumstance of an individual happening to be present to us in such manner that we can point to him and call him "this man" instead of "a man," is not a part of the reason of the being of the individual. Though everything is *per se* one and individual, nothing is *per se* pointed to.

understanding other than a human act of understanding—
for the "absolute nature," prior to existence either in the
human mind or in the world of changing things, fills
the place occupied in older statements of augustinism by
the exemplars subsisting in the thought of the Creator.

Porphyry's questions thus receive a clear-cut answer from
Ockham. Insofar as human knowledge is concerned, there
is only one kind of thing that can be called universal. Such
are concepts formed in the human mind by human acts of
understanding, which are natural or immediate signs of
individual things for which they can stand in discourse.
Whether or not there are also *universalia ante rem*, or exemplars
in the divine intellect, is irrelevant, since they can be of no
more help in explaining *human* knowledge of sensible things,
than is the separated Intelligence of Averroes.

As for *universalia in re*, there is no literal sense in which such
a phrase is intelligible; for if we mean by the phrase *"in re"*
the same thing as "outside of any mind," then we mean
something which is not a natural sign of many and which
is not predicable of many. If by *"in re"* we mean outside
of the human mind though not outside of the divine Intelligence, then there is no distinction between *universalia in re*
and *universalia ante rem*.

The point of Ockham's discussion is that every attempt
to found the characteristics of discursive thought in discursive thought, as when we attempt to refer universal
concepts to universal "things," or abstract signs to abstract
things, involves infinite regress as a principle, and hence
involves the actually infinite as that to which all discourse is
to be referred.[1]

---

[1] The metaphysical principle of the convertibility of *ens* and *unum* remains
unshaken, whether our metaphysics is dialectical or not. The difference is,
that for Aristotle the object of each discursive science is that which can exist
only in conditioned manner, while for the philosophy of internal relations the
object of understanding is the unconditioned whole, and the means by which
this object is revealed is the exemplification of the unconditioned whole through
conditioned (or hypothetical) discursive systems. The aristotelian point of view
allows unconditioned (actual) knowledge of the conditioned (the potential, as
limited cause); platonism permits conditioned (potential or hypothetical)
knowledge of the unconditioned (the absolutely actual, which is existence as

It remains, therefore, that the universal which is a principle of finite human knowledge, and which alone concerns the philosopher as such (if philosophy is to be distinguished from theology, and science from dialectic), is the *universale post rem*. This is the concept or act of understanding which is proper to individual human minds, and which is a natural or immediate sign of the finite causes of change with which the science of nature is concerned. Porphyry's questions, consequently, receive the following answers: (1) Universals exist only in the mind. (2) Being acts of the understanding, which is incorporeal, they are incorporeal. (3) Being acts of the understanding, which is not a sensible or material thing, they cannot be said to be *in* sensible things nor of the being of sensible things.[1]

---

such and as a unity). The two points of view are different in end and in method, but are proportioned in such manner that every concept that appears in one philosophy appears, at a different and usually opposite place, in the other. Thus chance, or accidental conjunctions (such as one man being both white and musical) appear in Aristotle's Physics, as consequent on the plurality of conditioned causes (i.e., limited potentialities, which are substances); in the metaphysics of internal relations, it appears as that which accounts for the internal movement or plurification of the changeless whole—or, in theological terms, it is the first motive of creation, by which the One posits the Other.

[1] Exp. aur., I, 9r: "Ex praedictis patet solutio praedictarum quaestionum. Nam quantum ad primam quaestionem tenendum est quod genera et species non sunt substantiae extra animam sed tantum sunt in intellectu quia non sunt nisi quaedam intentiones vel conceptus formati per intellectum exprimentes esse rerum et significantes eas, et non sunt ipsae res, sicut signum non est suum significatum; nec sunt partes rerum non plus quam vox est pars significati sui; sed sunt quaedam predicabilia de rebus non pro se, quia quando genus predicatur de specie, genus et species non supponunt pro se sed pro suis significatis quae sunt res singulares; sed illa genera et species predicantur de rebus pro ipsismet rebus quas significant. . . . Ex istis patet solutio secundae quaestionis, quia (non loquendo de vocali) tenendum est quod genera et species et universaliter omnia talia universalia non sunt corporalia quia non sunt nisi in mente in qua non est aliquod corporale. Solutio etiam tertiae quastionis patet, quia universalia non sunt in sensibilibus nec de esse sensibilium nec partes eorum, dicente Commentatore 7 Met., comm. 47, quod impossibile est quod universalia sint partes substantiarum existentium per se, et comm. 45, dicit quod impossibile est quod aliquod eorum quae sunt universalia sint substantia alicuius rei etsi declarent substantiam rerum. Ecce quomodo manifeste Commentator vult quod universalia non sint partes substantiarum nec sunt de esse substantiarum sed tantum determinant vel declarant substantias rerum sicut signum declaret sua significata, et ideo non sunt ipsa, quia inter signum et significatum debet esse distinctio." It is interesting to notice how neatly the arguments of Averroes can be transposed from the setting which they have in the averroist system, and used in support of what is, in fundamentals, the opposite of the averroist point of view. Averroes

III

Turning now to the division of terms according to the ways in which they can be said to be *predicable* of many, Ockham enumerates them in very much the same language used by Aristotle in the *Topics*, and used, indeed, by Porphyry himself. While Ockham makes note of the fact that for Aristotle only four predicables, or four ways in which a predicate may be asserted of a subject, are of importance in the kind of topical discussions whose aim is to establish or overthrow general propositions, he includes the *species* as a fifth predicable, following Porphyry. Ockham differs from Porphyry, however, by holding that the specific and generic terms signify precisely the individual things for which they can stand, *per se* and non-connotatively. Consequently his inclusion of the species as a fifth predicable does not alter the aristotelian thesis that the individuals of which a scientific proposition is true, and for which its terms stand, are signified *per se* and absolutely by the generic or specific term, independently of particular fact and of the truth of contingent propositions. The species is a predicable, because it can be predicate in many singular propositions—but it cannot be predicated *per se* or necessarily of any subject, nor is it properly speaking a predicate in direct or "natural" predication. For Ockham, as for Aristotle, the primary subject of all necessary and scientifically known propositions, is the universal term, which is a genus or species.[1]

---

can say that no universal is a substance, but that all universals reveal (*declarant*) substance, meaning that they reveal *the* substance of all sensible things, which is the creative separated Intelligence; Spinoza gives a fine statement of this point of view. Ockham can use the same statements to support his contention that each distinct substantial term or concept signifies individual substances *per se*, distinct from substances signified by other such terms.

[1] S. tot. log., I, 31, 12r; "Tertio modo dicitur predicatum illud quod predicatur de aliquo subiecto predicatione directa, de quo subiecto potest esse scientia proprie dicta, et sic philosophus accipit predicatum primo Topicorum, ubi distinguit quattuor predicata, *scil.* genus, diffinitionem, et accidens. Et sub genus comprehendit differentiam, ubi non enumerat speciem, quia quamvis species predicatur de individuo, quia tamen individua non possunt esse subiecta in propositionibus scitis scientia proprie dicta, ideo inter illa predicata non enumeratur species." It is perhaps unnecessary to note that Ockham here uses

The way in which Aristotle states the distinctions between the modes of predicability, and which indeed is used by Porphyry as well, indicates very clearly that the division of terms according to modes of predicability *presupposes* the distinctions between modes of signification established in the *Categories*, and not, as Porphyry held, *vice versa*. *Genera*, *differentiæ*, and *properties* are all predicated necessarily rather than contingently of their subjects; their distinction rests not on the way in which they are predicable of their subjects, but on the way in which they *signify* the things signified *by* their subjects. A genus, for example, signifies the things for which it can stand, *per se* and non-connotatively; an essential differentia signifies the things for which it can stand, *per se* but connotatively, by indicating what they are only partly; a property, finally, signifies the things it can stand for, *per aliud* and connotatively, through connoting something extrinsic to them as potentially existent by reason of their individual nature.

Thus, contrary to Porphyry's notion that the categories cannot be understood unless modes of predication are first distinguished, Ockham makes evident the priority of the distinction between terms as modes of signifying individuals in abstraction from contingent fact, over the relations which terms have to each other in true propositions. In this, Ockham has the full support of the aristotelian text; for Aristotle likewise distinguishes between genus, definition, and property, by the fact that a genus or definition signifies the things it can stand for by their essential nature (or *per se*), while a property signifies the things for which it can stand by something other than their essential nature (*per aliud*).[1]

the term "individuum" as a term of second intention, equivalent to "discrete term." Concerning the fact that the species is not predicated *in quid* or *per se* of singular terms, cf. *Ante*, p. 76, Note 1. In the strict sense, no term can be a subject with respect to an *infima species*, at least in propositions of which scientific knowledge can be had; cf. S. tot. log., I, 30, 12r: "stricte . . . dicitur subiectum quod subiicitur alteri in predicatione directa . . . strictius, pro illo quod est subiectum in conclusione demonstrata quae scitur vel est nata sciri. . . ."

[1] Arist., Topics I, 4, 101b 17–23. Ockham, S. tot. log., I, 18, 8r: "Omne universale est de multis predicabile, aut igitur predicatur de illis multis in quid,

Terms are predicable of many as genus or as species when they signify precisely the things for which they can stand in any proposition, without signifying or connoting anything extrinsic to the essential or individual being of what they can stand for, and without signifying such individuals through indicating a part of their nature in abstraction from their undivided being. Such terms are said to be predicable of a subject term *in quid*, being appropriate answers to the question, "What is this?" pointing to something. In a loose sense, terms in the accidental categories are also used in answer to such questions, as when we point to a black object and say, "What is the black?" and receive the answer "It is the coloured." Only in this improper sense do we call "coloured" the genus of which "white," "blue," etc., are species. Absolute terms in the category of quality, however, like "whiteness," are in the strict sense species of qualitative genera, such as "colour."[1]

---

aut non; si in quid, ita quod convenienter contingit respondere ad interrogationem factam per quid de aliquo, hoc contingit dupliciter, quia aut illa multa de quibus predicatur sunt omnino similia, ita quod omnia quae uni conveniunt aequaliter conveniunt unicuique nisi forte unum componatur ex pluribus aeque similibus, et sic est species specialissima. Aut non omnia de quibus predicatur praedicto modo conveniunt sed contingit reperire aliqua duo quae secundum se tota vel secundum suas partes, si habeant partes, sunt dissimilia, sic est genus. . . . Si autem tale predicabile non predicatur in quid, vel hoc est quia exprimit partem rei unam et non aliam, nihil extrinsecus exprimendo, et sic est differentia; sicut 'rationale' si sit differentia hominis exprimit partem hominis, *scil.* animam, id est formam et non materiam. Vel exprimit aliquid quod non est pars rei, et tunc vel predicatur contingenter vel necessario; si contingenter tunc vocatur accidens, si necessario tunc vocatur proprium."

[1] S. tot. log., I, 18, 8v: "Verumtamen sciendum est quod tam genus quam species dupliciter accipitur, large et stricte. Stricte autem vocatur genus illud per quod convenienter respondetur ad quaestionem factam per quid de aliqua re per pronomen demonstrans illam rem, sicut si quaeretur 'quid est hoc,' demonstrando Sortem, convenienter respondetur quod est animal vel homo et sic de aliis generibus et speciebus. Large autem dicitur genus vel species illud per quod convenienter respondetur ad quaestionem factam per quid per pronomen connotativum quod non est mere absolutum, sicut si quaeretur ' quid est album?' convenienter respondetur quod est 'coloratum,' et tamen si quaeretur 'quid est hoc?' nunquam convenienter responderetur per 'coloratum' . . ."
Predication *in quid* is distinguished from predication *in quale quid* and from predication *in quale*, as follows, the basis of the distinction being the difference between three modes of *signification—scil.*, essential and absolute, essential and connotative, and connotative and non-essential. Exp. aur., I, 10v–11r: "notandum quod predicari in quid de aliquo est predicari vere de aliquo et non importare

The classic definition of a genus is "that which is predicated *in quid* of many differing in species." Ockham remarks, first, that this is not a real definition, but a description or "nominal definition," since only substances that exist *per se* and independently of the operations of the mind, have "real definitions." Secondly, he notes that a genus is not anything *in re* which is predicated of many, but it is a term or intention of the mind predicable of such other terms (which may be common or discrete terms) as signify and stand for individuals of which the generic term is a natural sign. When a genus is predicated of a species, it is not asserted that the subject term *is* the predicate term, nor that the species *is* the genus or a part of the genus—but what is asserted is that each of the individuals of which the specific term is a sign, is signified also by the generic term. The terms of such propositions do not signify classes, nor anything distinct from the individuals for which they can stand, nor do they signify or connote something that is a part of these individuals. But both a genus and a species signify the whole individual ("undivided") nature of individual

---

aliquod extrinsecum competens illi de quo praedicatur, nec significare determinatum partem illius de quo verificatur. Per primam particulam excluditur quod 'asinus' non predicatur in quid de 'homine,' nec econverso. Per secundam particulam excluditur omnis predicatio passionis et importantis aliquid extrinsecum illi pro quo subiectum supponit, sicut 'risibile' importat actum ridendi qui nec est homo nec pars hominis. Per tertiam particulam excluditur differentia, quia omnis differentia essentialis importat determinate unam partem illius pro quo supponit et non aliam, sicut 'rationale,' quod supponit pro Socrate et Platone, quando ponitur in propositione, importat determinate animam intellectivam, nec sic 'animal' importat aliquam partem correspondentem; et ideo illud quod importat totum et non importat partem, nec aliquid extrinsecum, predicatur in quid; quia quaerendo quid sit aliquid, puta Sortes, convenienter respondetur quod est animal, et non quod habet animalitatem, sed quod est animal. Sed per differentiam non convenit sic respondere, quia quaerendo quid est Sortes, non convenienter respondetur ad interrogationem illam, quod est rationalis, quia 'rationale' non dicit principaliter totum Sortem, sed dicit primo partem, illo modo quo concretum dicit illud quod importatur per abstractum sibi correspondentem. Est igitur differentia inter genus et differentia, quia genus importat totum, propter quod 'animal' non importat partem, quia 'animalitas' non est pars hominis sed est homo. Differentia autem dicit partem primo, et ideo abstractum sibi correspondens importat praecise partem; unde si 'rationale' sit differentia 'hominis,' 'rationalitas' importabit idem quod 'anima intellectiva,' et rationalitas est anima intellectiva, etiam sicut 'materiale' quod est differentia primo importat partem illius cuius materia est pars."

things, in abstraction from contingent circumstances under which they might happen to have been apprehended in sense experience.[1]

The description of species is "that which is predicated *in quid* of many differing in number." This is to be understood in the sense that the specific term *signifies* the whole individual nature of the individuals for which it can stand, without connoting anything as a part of such individuals, nor anything distinct from them. It is not to be understood as though the *infima species* could be predicated of any singular term, essentially or necessarily, for this is not the case—even a proposition such as "This man is a man" is not an instance of essential predication in the strict sense, for it is not a necessary proposition.[2]

All that applies to the genus applies to the species, except that the terms of which the genus is essentially predicable may differ with respect to other terms essentially predicable of them, whereas this is not true of the species. The species is not, and does not signify, something that is a part of individuals for which it stands, any more than the genus signifies or is a part of the species, or of the individuals signified by the specific term.

Porphyry's language, in his exposition of the predicamental order whereby species are subordinate to genera, and "superior" to individuals, etc., is such that this predicamental order is frequently taken as an order of things, or of metaphysical "parts" of things, outside the mind, instead of as an order of terms or intentions that are merely signs of individual things. For example, the statement so often made that the species is "part" of the genus, or that the genus is "part"

---

[1] Exp. aur., I, 10r: "Genus est quod praedicatur de pluribus differentibus specie in eo quod quid, sicut 'animal'." "Notandum est quod haec diffinitio non est diffinitio proprie dicta . . . et ideo haec est quaedam descriptio notificans et faciens cognosci an aliquid sit genus aut non." S. tot. log., I, 20, 9r: "notandum est quod genus non est aliquae res extra animam existens de essentia illorum de quibus predicatur, sed est quaedam intentio animae predicabilis de multis non quidem pro se sed pro rebus quas significat . . . et ita quando genus predicatur de specie non denotatur quod subiectum sit predicatum nec quod predicatum realiter conveniat subiecto in esse reali; sed denotatur quod illud quod importatur per predicatum sit illud quod importatur per subiectum."

[2] Cf. *Ante*, p. 76, Note 1.

of the species, cannot be understood in any literal sense, either as applying to terms, or to things that are not terms. The term "man" is not a part of the term "animal," nor *vice versa*. Similarly the individuals signified by "man,"—Socrates, Plato, etc.—are not parts of the things signified by "animal," nor the other way around; for "animal" signifies Socrates, Plato, and any other individual man, and so does the term "man," but we cannot say that an individual thing is a part of itself. If it be said that the genus is a part of the definition of the species, and that the definition is the same as what it defines, and that therefore the genus is a part of the species, Ockham replies that the minor premise is false. It is not true that a definition is the same as what it defines, except metaphorically; they are the same only in the sense that the definition is a sign of the same things that the term defined is a sign of.[1]

The statement that the genus "contains" the species, and that the species is "contained" by the genus, must also be taken as a metaphorical statement. The only sense in which the genus contains the species is this, that the genus is predicable of any term of which the species is predicable, but not *vice versa*. Similarly, if it be said that the species contains individuals it is meant either that the species is a *sign* of many individuals *in re*, or else that the species is *predicable* of many terms that cannot stand for the same things, or which are not predicable of each other.[2]

[1] Exp. aur., I, 14r: "sicut genus non est de esse speciei nec pars eius, ita species non est de esse individui sed est quaedam intentio in anima significans ipsa individua et est predicabilis de eis non pro se sed pro ipsis individuis . . ." S. tot. log., I, 20, 9r: "Ex quo sequitur quod genus non est pars speciei, et non solum hoc sed etiam quod nec genus importat materiam et non formam, proprie loquendo de importare sive significare. . . . Et si dicas, genus est pars diffinitionis et diffinitio est eadem cum diffinito, igitur genus est pars diffiniti, dicendum est quod de virtute sermonis illa est simpliciter falsa 'diffinitio est eadem realiter cum diffinito,' sed illa est simpliciter vera 'diffinitio et diffinitum significant unum sive idem'; nec aliud intendunt auctores." Ibid., I, 21, 9r: "proprie loquendo nec genus est pars speciei, nec species est pars generis, sed in hoc differunt, quia species est communis ad pauciora quam genus ita quod genus est signum plurium et species pauciorum."

[2] S. tot. log., I, 22, 9v: "Alia autem differentia ponitur, *scil.* quod genus continet speciem, species autem non continet genus; quod sic est intelligendum. quod genus est natum predicari de pluribus, hoc enim vocatur 'continere,' species autem non potest predicari de pluribus quam suum genus." Exp. aur.,

With respect to the statement that the genus is "naturally prior" to the species, Ockham remarks that this can only mean that the genus is predicable of more terms than the species—i.e., of all the terms of which the species is predicable, and also of all the terms of which other co-ordinate species are predicable. It cannot be prior in the sense that the existence of the intention which is a species, in the mind, presupposes the existence in the same mind of the intention which is the genus; for we may very well have in mind the concept "man" without the concept "animal." Likewise, the statement that the destruction of the genus entails the destruction of the species, cannot be taken literally; it can only be understood as a kind of "logical destruction," in the sense that if the genus is truly denied of a subject term, its subordinate species cannot be truly affirmed of the same subject.[1]

Ockham's entire discussion of these ways of comparing genus and species is directed against the tendency, common enough among mediæval interpreters of Porphyry, to regard the predicamental order known as the "Tree of Porphyry" as a metaphysical order. It is, according to Ockham, purely a logical order, whose elements are not things *in re* nor parts of such things, but intentions of the mind that are signs of individuals. It is not because the generic term "animal" signifies something *in* Socrates and *in* Plato distinct from

---

I, 14v: "Notandum est quod ordo predicamentalis non componitur ex rebus extra animam, sed componitur ex conceptibus sive intentionibus in anima, quae non habent aliquem ordinem nisi quod unum est communius et dicitur de pluribus, et illud vocatur superius, et aliud est minus commune et dicitur de paucioribus et istud est inferius."

[1] S. tot. log., I, 22, 9v: "Alia differentia ponitur, quod genus est naturaliter prius quam species, quae non est intelligenda sicut sonat quasi prius natura sit illa intentio quae est genus quam illa intentio quae est species, quia illa intentio quae est species potest esse in anima sine illa intentione quae est genus, sicut econverso. . . . Sed per illam propositionem 'genus est prius natura quam species,' nihil aliud intendunt auctores nisi quod genus communius est quam species. . . . Alia differentia ponitur quae est 'quod interemptis generibus interimuntur species,' quae non est intelligenda de interemptione reali. . . . Sed praedicta differentia intelligenda est de interemptione logicali, hoc est, quod a negatione generis ad negationem speciei est bona consequentia. . . . " Practically every one of these properties and ways of comparing genus and species, which Ockham states and then interprets, are taken word for word from Porphyry, though in the S. tot. log. they are usually attributed to the "auctores" in general.

what the specific term "man" signifies, that the one term is related to the other as genus to species. On the contrary, it is because "animal" signifies, as an individual or undivided nature, each thing that "man" signifies as an individual nature, that "animal" is predicable universally of "man," and is a genus of "man." The order of genus and species presupposes the predication of terms in true universal propositions; but true universal predication presupposes the existence of terms, or acts of understanding, that are univocal signs of many self-identical individuals distinct from the terms by which they are signified. Predication presupposes signification. The determination of how one term can stand for the same things that another term can stand for, presupposes the possibility of determining, independently of knowledge of the truth or falsity of such predicative relations, what the terms *can* stand for—and that is to define their meaning through the grasp of essential or undivided nature.[1]

The term "differentia" is used in a broad sense to denote any term by which one kind of thing is signified as different from another kind of thing, and in this sense a property, or a peculiar collection of accidental terms, is called by Porphyry a "differentia." But the term "differentia," as one of the five predicables, is properly distinguished as a term which stands for those terms which are predicated of a subject *in quale quid*—i.e., in such manner that they connote nothing extrinsic to the essential or undivided nature of the things they can stand for, but signify such individuals through indicating their being or nature *per modum partis*. Thus the specific differentia "rational" is predicated *in quale quid* of the term "man"; for it does not connote anything distinct from the undivided nature signified by "man," but signifies that which is *per se* one and undivided, by a part conceived in abstraction from the undivided whole. In this case,

[1] That scientific knowledge of the truth of propositions is a function of the grasp of essential nature *in* the demonstration, is the point of Book II of Aristotle's Posterior Analytics, and especially of the first ten chapters where the relation between demonstration and definition is discussed. Cf. *post*, ch. vi, III, on Ockham's treatment of demonstration and definition.

"rational" signifies man by connoting the intellective soul signified abstractly by the term "rationality." This is expressed in the nominal definition of the term "rational," which is: "something having an intellective soul."[1]

Because the differentia usually signifies the things for which it can stand, by connoting the formal principle of their individuality (as "rational" connotes the soul or the intelligence by which an individual man is just such an individual as he is), many *moderni* make the mistake of confusing the essential differentia, which is the formal part of the definition of a substantial term, with the form of the thing signified by the substantial term, and of confusing the genus, which is the material part of the definition, with the material principle of the thing signified by the definition. Ockham, citing the authority of Averroes, denies: (1) that the differentia *is* the formal element of anything that can exist outside the mind, or the genus the material element (for what is predicable as genus, or as differentia, is a term or concept, and things *in re* are not composed of terms and concepts, but are only signified by them); and (2) he denies that the differentia always connotes or determinately signifies the form of the things for which it can stand, or that the genus signifies the matter of the things it can stand for, any more than their form. The use of the terms "matter" and "form" in describing the relation between the parts of the definition is purely analogical; for in a literal sense both genus and

---

[1] S. tot. log., I, 23, 9v: "Stricte dicitur differentia quae per se primo modo predicatur de aliquo et non indicat aliquod extrinsecum rei pro qua supponit illud de quo predicatur, et sic est unum de quinque universalium de quo in hac parte est loquendum. . . . Et est intelligendum quod differentia non est de essentia rei sed est intentio animae predicabilis de contentis non in quid sed in quale; quae ideo dicitur differentia quia potest esse medium concludendi negativam in qua negatur illud cuius est differentia ab alio, sicut 'rationale' est medium concludendi negativam quae negat hominem ab asino. . . . " *Quale quid* is explained as follows: Exp. aur., I, 24r: "notandum quod ad rationem differentiae non sufficit predicari in quale praecise, sic enim accidens predicatur in quale, sed simul cum hoc requiritur quod non exprimat aliquid extrinsecum illi pro quo supponit. Tertio sciendum est quod ideo differentia predicatur in quale, quia non exprimit primo totum, sed suum abstractum significat unam partem rei et non aliam." Cf. *Ante*, p. 100, Note 1, where the difference in mode of signification between a genus or species, and a differentia, is discussed in detail.

differentia are accidental forms (*scil.* acts of understanding), and it is only because they signify, when combined in the real definition, things that are *per se* one or undivided, that the *per se* unity of matter and form that is the individuality of finite changeable things, is attributed to them by analogy.[1]

A term predicable as a "property," in the strict and proper sense, is any term or intention predicable of a subject convertibly and *in quale*, such that it signifies the things for which it can stand (and which the subject signifies *per se*), by connoting, either affirmatively or negatively, something extrinsic to the essential nature of the individuals for which it can stand. It is not always the case that the extrinsic element indicated by the nominal definition of the property, is a thing or quality existing *in re*, but it may very well be something that exists only potentially, or it may be a fact or circumstance indicated by a proposition in the mode of possibility. Thus the term "risible," which is predicable convertibly of "man" as a property, stands for whatever things the term "man" stands for, but consignifies the act of laughing—not as actually taking place, but as an act of which

---

[1] Exp. aur., I, 24r: "Item ex praedictis patet quod non est bene dictum quod genus est materia rei, et differentia forma, quia genus non est in re, cum in re non sit nisi materia et forma particularis secundum Commentatorem 7 Met., comm. 44. Nec est bene dictum quod genus importat materiam, quia non plus importat materiam quam formam, patet etiam de genere generalissimo substantiae quod non accipitur a materia, quia tunc in omni contento sub eo esset materia, quod est falsum quia in substantiis separatis a materia non est materia, et tamen sunt in genere substantiae." Ibid., 24r: "notandum quod aliqui errantes ex ista littera (*scil.* Porphyry's statement, Migne PL 64 cl. 118 A, that "animali enim rationalis differentia adveniens aliud facit, et speciem animalis facit") accipiunt quod omnis species componitur ex genere et differentia quod est manifeste falsum. . . ." Cf. Walter Burleigh, Exp. sup. art. vet. (cited by Prantl, p. 304, Anm. 603): "Species de genere substantiae componitur ex genere et differentia et ex omnibus superioribus ad ipsum. . . ." Ockham, ibid., 24r, continues: "Sed intentio sua (*scil.* Porphyry) est quod genus et differentia componant diffinitionem convertibilem cum specie, et quod exprimit explicite quod species importat implicite; vult etiam quod sicut in rebus compositis aliquid est materia et aliquid est forma, vel aliquid est loco materiae et aliquid est loco formae, ita in diffinitione genus est loco materiae respectu differentiae . . . quia scilicet sicut materia est prior natura ipsa forma et forma advenit materiae, ita in diffinitione genus quod est quaedam intentio sive conceptus in anima praecedit differentiam et differentia advenit sibi, et ita differentia ponitur in diffinitione loco formae, et hoc sive differentia illa principaliter significat materiam sive formam, quia nihil refert quantum ad hoc."

individual men are essentially capable. Another way of stating this is to say that all propositions in which terms are predicated of a subject as property, are equivalent to propositions in the modality of possibility predicating an accidental determination of the subject. Thus, "every man is necessarily risible" is equivalent to "every man is possibly laughing" or to "every man is a potentiality of laughter."[1]

A term predicable as "accident" is any term predicable of many which is predicated contingently of its subject in such manner that it may be affirmed or denied of the subject with the latter standing for the same individual thing or things. "Accident" as a term in logic (i.e., as one of the predicables), is to be carefully distinguished from "accident" as a term in physics. In physics it is used as a term of first intention signifying a qualitative form contingently determining a substance but really distinct from it, as heat qualifies a hot stove, and yet is not a stove. In logic, "accident" means any *term* predicated contingently of a subject in direct predication, whether the term connotes a form, or the privation of a form, or some circumstance or fact indicated by a proposition.

Porphyry's language, as usual, is equivocal, for his statement that an accident is that which may be present or absent from its subject without the subject being destroyed, seems to refer more to "accident" in the physical sense than to the "accident" which is one of the five predicables and a

---

[1] S. tot. log. I, 24, 10v: "dicendum est quod proprium . . . est quaedam intentio animae predicabilis adequate et convertibiliter in quale connotans affirmative vel negative aliquid extrinsecum illi quod importatur per subiectum; non tamen oportet quod illud extrinsecum semper sit aliquae res extra animam existens realiter in rerum natura, sed forte aliquando sufficit quod sit aliquod potentiale in rerum natura potentiale, vel forte aliquae propositio existens vel potens existere in mente." Exp. aur., I, 27v: "proprium non est aliquae res realiter illi cuius est proprium formaliter inhaerens . . . sed est unum predicabile de eo supponens in propositione pro omni eodem pro quo supponit id cuius est proprium. Nono notandum est quod proprium isto modo dictum frequenter non significat rem aliquam formaliter inhaerentem illi cuius est proprium quando de eo predicatur, . . . nam quamvis verum sit dicere omnis homo est risibilis, non tamen oportet quod aliqua res importata per 'risibile' sit in homine formaliter, sed sufficit quod possit inesse; nam idem est dicere 'omnis homo est risibile' et 'omnis homo potest ridere.'"

term used by the logician. Ockham, by an heroic effort, seeks to "save" Porphyry's text by stating that Porphyry is using "to be present" (adesse) and "to be absent" (abesse) as equivalent to "to be affirmed" and "to be denied." Thus the porphyrian description of "accident" is, according to Ockham, to be understood as follows: "An accident is what may be present in (i.e., may be predicated of) a subject, or may be absent from (i.e., truly denied of) the same subject, without the subject being destroyed: i.e., without the thing of which the subject was first verified, being destroyed."[1]

IV

Apart from the five predicables, certain other terms of second intention, constantly used in the analysis of discourse, and also used equivocally by Porphyry in his little treatise, require precise definition. Among these are such terms as: *definition, description, subject, predicate, signify, opposite,* and *attribute* (passio).

The term "definition" is used in two ways, distinguished as "real definition" (*diffinitio quid rei*) and "nominal definition" (*diffinitio quid nominis*). A real definition is a compact expression stating the individual or undivided nature of a thing without connoting anything distinct from it. A real definition may be stated in two forms, as (a) a "natural definition," or (b) a "metaphysical definition." In a natural definition are included words, in oblique cases, which signify the essential parts of the individuals for which the term defined can stand, as when "man" is defined as "a substance composed of a body and of an intellective soul."[2]

[1] Exp. aur., I, 28v : "accidens dupliciter accipitur, uno modo pro aliquo reali alteri tanquam subiecto realiter inhaerente sicut albedo, nigredo, calor, et sic de ceteris; et isto modo communiter accidens accipitur. Alio modo vocatur accidens aliquod predicabile contingenter de alio. . . . Si autem accidens accipiatur secundo modo tunc debet intelligi descriptio (*scil.* Porphyrii) : Accidens est quod adest (i.e., predicatur de) aliquo, et abest (id est, vere potest negari ab aliquo) praeter subiecti corruptionem; hoc est, non destructo illo de quo primo verificabatur. . . . Et ita in proposito, 'adesse' et 'abesse' accipiuntur pro 'affirmari' et 'negari.'"
[2] S. tot. log., I, 26, 11r: "Diffinitio autem dupliciter accipitur, quia quaedam est diffinitio exprimens quid rei et quaedam quid nominis. . . . Diffinitio

In a metaphysical definition, on the other hand, the parts do not stand for essential *parts* of the things signified by the *definiendum*, but they stand for these things as individuals which are *per se* one. Such a definition contains no terms in oblique cases, and is composed of genus and essential differentiæ, the genus signifying precisely the things for which the *definiendum* can stand, and the differentia signifying these same individual natures—not "absolutely" as the generic term does, but connotatively, by consignifying a determinate essential part such as could be signified directly by its abstract counterpart. If, for example, the definition of "man" is "rational, sensitive, living substance," each differentia, though it connotes an essential principle of the being of that which is a man, does not stand for what it connotes, but rather for the undivided nature signified by the term "man." The abstract counterparts of the differentiæ, such as "rationality," "sensitivity," and "animation," *denote* the essential principles *connoted* by the differentiæ, in abstraction from the concrete whole which is the individual man. Hence, while every essential differentia is a concrete connotative term, with an abstract counterpart included obliquely in its nominal definition, no essential differentia is an abstract term and no abstract term can be an essential differentia.[1]

Ockham's distinction between the two forms of a real

exprimens quid rei . . . stricte . . . est sermo compendiosus exprimens totam naturam rei nec aliquid extrinsecus rei declarens. . . . Nam quandoque in tali sermone ponuntur casus obliqui exprimentes partes rei essentiales, sicut si diffiniam 'hominem' sic dicendo: 'homo est substantia composita ex corpore et anima intellectiva'. . . . Et illa potest vocari diffinitio naturalis. . . ."

[1] S. tot. log., I, 26, 11r: "Alia est diffinitio in qua nullus casus obliquus ponitur, sed ponitur genus in recto et similiter differentia, vel ponuntur termini plures exprimentes partes rei diffinitae, ad modum quo album exprimit albedinem. Et ideo sicut album quamvis exprimat albedinem non tamen supponit pro albedine sed pro subiecto albedinis, ita differentiae illae quamvis exprimant partes rei non tamen supponunt pro partibus rei sed praecise pro toto composito ex illis partibus; talis est illa diffinitio hominis 'animal rationale,' vel illa, 'substantia animata sensibilis rationalis.' Nam illae differentiae 'animatum, rationale, sensibile,' supponunt pro homine quia homo est animatus, sensibilis, rationalis; tamen important partem hominis, sicut abstracta eis correspondentia, quia abstracta eis correspondentia important partes vel partem hominis quamvis non eodem modo. Et ita potest vocari metaphysicalis, quia sic diffinit metaphysicus hominem. . . ."

definition—"natural" and "metaphysical"—is rather inter-esting. It indicates his strict adherence to the aristotelian thesis expressed in the *Metaphysics* (Book N, ch. i, 1087b, 1–4), that the principles of first philosophy are not contraries. The principles of the sciences of nature are substances and the contraries; the attributes which physical sciences demonstrate of their subjects, signify substances by connoting pairs of contraries with respect to which such substances are change-able. Insofar as we signify a substance as *subject of change*, we necessarily distinguish what it is actually from what it can become (what it is potentially)—hence act and potentiality, or matter and form, are principles of the science of changeable things, *scil* physics. It is for this reason that a physical or "natural" definition of a substance signifies what is actually undivided (or actually individual) *as if* it were composed of distinct parts. But metaphysics, not being concerned with things qua subjects of change, does not consider substances by way of the distinction between substance as form and substance as matter—but metaphysics considers the *actual being* of sub-stances, and consequently the "metaphysical definition" of a substance signifies the individual or undivided nature by a compact expression forming a single undivided act of understanding. The physicist speaks of *man* as if he were a synthesis of soul *and* body—but if we seek to state what a man actually is, insofar as he is a thing, and not insofar as he is changeable with respect to other things, then we say that he is a "rational animal", and in our definition we do not place conjunctions, prepositions, or verbs.

By way of indicating Ockham's aristotelianism through contrasting it with the platonist alternative, it may be added that the platonist invariably regards the "natural" and "metaphysical" definitions as equivalent. For the platonist, the first principles of metaphysics are contraries, and hence every finite thing is, metaphysically, a synthesis of a form or idea, *and* recalcitrant matter. For Plato, consequently, the "natural definition" would be the most proper form. For Ockham, who follows Aristotle in distinguishing physics from metaphysics, it is not the *ultimately* proper form, but is appropriate only for discursive science, which is of the changeable.

Ockham states that although a real definition, or an element of it, is predicable significatively of any term of which the term defined is predicable significatively, and *vice versa*, nevertheless such predication does not, as some seemed to think, yield a necessary assertoric proposition of present time. For if no man is now existent, the statement "man is a rational animal" or "every man is rational," is not true as a proposition of present time, though it is necessarily true of that which *can* exist at *some* time. This qualification is brought up again in connection with Ockham's discussion of the meaning of the term "necessarily true," as applied to the propositions of demonstrative science. It is not a denial of necessary universal truths, in the sense in which Aristotle states that scientific propositions are necessary and universal; but it is Ockham's way of making evident the fact that science is of necessary and eternal *truths* and not of necessary or eternal *things*. For the things known through sense perception are perishable, and yet they are the things of which scientific demonstrations are true—the necessity and eternity of scientific propositions, consequently, rests on the fact that their terms do not stand for what happens to exist at the present time or at any determinate time, but for what *can* exist in time. Such a proposition must, in Aristotle's words, be "true in every instance . . . and at all times, not at this or that time only."[1]

Real definitions are predicable significatively of any term of which the term defined is predicable significatively. Hence the definition of a term, if it be a real definition, is also a state-

---

[1] S. tot. log., I, 26, 11r: "Est autem sciendum quod quamvis de quocunque, significative sumpto, predicatur diffinitio, et diffinitum predicatur significative sumptum et econverso, et quamvis propositiones cathegoricae de possibilibus equivalentes tali et similiter conditionalis, ex diffinitione et diffinito composita, sint necessariae . . . tamen nulla propositio talis affirmativa de inesse et mere de praesenti est necessaria. Unde illa est simpliciter contingens, 'homo est animal rationale' . . . et hoc, quia si nullus homo esset, quaelibet talis esset falsa. . . . Verumtamen Aristoteles qui ponit quod tales sunt necessariae, 'homo est animal,' 'asinus est animal,' poneret quod tales sunt necessariae secundum sensum iam dictum." Cf. Arist., An. Post., I, 4, 73a 27–33. Cf. also ch. vi, I, where this question is discussed.

ment of the essential nature of each thing for which the term can stand. But *nominal definitions* merely state explicitly what the term defined connotes implicitly. Connotative terms (other than essential differentiæ) stand for individual things which they do not signify *per se*, but which they signify through indicating circumstances or ways in which the existence of individuals for which they can stand, may come to be apprehended. It is these circumstances, qualities, or contingent determinations indicated by the connotative term, that are explicitly distinguished and exhibited by the nominal definition.

While only terms in the category of substance can have real definitions by genus and essential differentiæ, the connotative terms in the accidental categories can, and do, have nominal definitions, including those accidental terms which do not signify anything that can exist *per se*, but which are equivalent to complex expressions or which connote negative propositions. Thus the term "chimera," though it signifies nothing *in re* of which being can be predicated, may be defined as "equivalent to the expression *something composed of goat, lion, and cow.*" The more typical instance of a nominal definition is that of "the white," defined as "something in which whiteness is present," where the form or principle by which a substance is contingently qualified, is connoted obliquely by the concrete term that is being defined, and is denoted by the abstract counterpart ("whiteness") which appears in the nominal definition. A fully determinate nominal definition, which was sometimes called the "real definition" of a connotative term, states not only what is connoted by the term defined, but also the proximate subject of the accidental determination thus connoted. For example, "the white" is determinately defined, through the essential nature of the things for which it can stand, as "*a body* in which whiteness exists."[1]

[1] S. tot. log., I, 26, 11v: "Diffinitio autem exprimens quid nominis est oratio explicite declarans quicquid per unam dictionem importatur implicite, sicut significans volens alium docere quid significat hoc nomen 'album,' dicat quod significat idem quod haec oratio 'aliquid habens albedinem.' Et haec diffinitio non solum est nominum de quibus vere affirmatur esse in rerum natura, sed etiam aliorum de quibus talis predicatio est impossibilis. Et sic hoc nomen 'vacuum,' 'non ens,' 'impossibile,' 'chimaera,' et huiusmodi habent diffinitiones. Nam

While nominal definitions may include a genus, and do so when they are partially or fully determinate, *descriptions* are composed only of properties and accidents. In a loose sense we may call the phrase "white musician" a description; strictly, however, a description is a compact expression composed only of properties, for only then is it peculiar to the subject and convertible with it. Thus the phrase "what can learn grammar and can laugh" is a strict description of "man," such that it can be used in place of a real definition, where we do not possess the latter, to determine the extension of the subject genus in empirical inquiry, and in dialectical argumentation.[1]

What does a definition define, or a description describe? This may be answered in two ways; for we may say that the *definiendum* of a real definition is that whose essential parts are signified by the definition, in which case what is defined are the individual things for which the terms stand. Or we may say that the *definiendum* is a term convertible with the definition, of which the definition is predicable essentially and convertibly. In this case it is not the individual that is defined, but the generic or specific term or concept. Aristotle and many other authors, says Ockham, speak both ways on the subject at various times, sometimes saying that definitions are of individuals and sometimes saying that they are of species. Their

istis nominibus correspondent aliquae orationes significantes idem quod illae dictiones. Ex quo sequitur quod, sic accipiendo diffinitionem, aliquando predicatio diffinitionis de diffinito, utroque significative sumpto, est impossibilis; sicut haec est impossibilis 'chimaera est animal compositum ex capra, leone et bove'; illa tamen propositio in qua isti termini materialiter supponunt, 'chimaera idem significat quod hoc totum: aliquod compositum ex capra, leone, et bove,' vera est." As concerns the determinate form of a nominal definition, in which the things for which the term defined can stand, are signified *per se* by a genus or species functioning as material part of the definition, Ockham shows, in his treatment of demonstration (cf. *post*, ch. vi), that the determination of the commensurate and immediate subject of an attribute with a nominal definition, depends on experience and on the intuitive grasp of essential nature *in* a demonstration; once grasped, the connection is known as immediate, *per se*, and necessary.

[1] S. tot. log., I, 27, 11v: "Descriptio est sermo compendiosus compositus ex accidentibus et propriis. Unde dicit Damascenus in logica sua, cap. VIII, 'Descriptio ex accidentibus componitur, id est, proprio et accidentibus'. . . . Ex verbis huius auctoris patet quod in descriptione nihil debet poni quod predicatur in quid vel per se primo modo de descripto, et in hoc differt descriptio a diffinitione. . . ."

words are intelligible only in the light of the above distinction. The same rule of interpretation applies with respect to descriptions and to that of which they are said to be descriptions.[1]

The term *subject*, as a logical term of second intention, is distinguished from the term of first intention used in the real sciences. The latter signifies individuals such as exist by reason of their own nature, and which, in Aristotle's words, "have no cause of their essential being other than themselves." But "subject," as used in logic, signifies any *term* of which some other term is predicated. In a broad sense, the term that precedes the copula in any proposition, true or false, is called a subject; more strictly it is a term preceding the copula in direct predication, and in this sense "man" is a subject with respect to "animal," or with respect to "musical," but not *vice versa*. Still more strictly, a subject is a term which precedes the copula in the conclusion of a demonstration, and in this sense the term "this man" is not a subject with respect to "man" or to any universal term. Still more strictly, a subject is said to be that which is prior in perfection, or in predication, or otherwise, among subjects of demonstration.[2]

The term *predicate*, similarly, means any term that follows the copula or that includes it equivalently. More strictly, it is any term predicated universally, and in direct predication, of a subject of which there can be science in the strict sense. This, Ockham adds, is the way in which Aristotle understands the term "predicate" or "predicable" in the *Topics*, where he enumerates as kinds of predicates, with respect to a subject significant *per se*, genus, definition, property, and accident,

---

[1] S. tot. log., I, 29, 11v: "diffinitum dupliciter accipitur. Uno modo pro illo cuius partes vel essentia per diffinitionem exprimitur, et sic diffinitio est ipsarum rerum singularium sicut illa diffinitio 'animal rationale' est diffinitio omnium hominum, quia omnium hominum essentia per illam diffinitionem importatur, unde per illam diffinitionem nullius rei essentia importatur nisi hominis particularis, quia nulla res est quae sit animal rationale nisi ille homo vel ille, et sic de singulis. . . . Alio modo accipitur diffinitum pro aliquo convertibile cum diffinitione de quo diffinitio adequate predicatur . . . et illo modo non diffinitur singulare, sed praecise species. . . . Et per istam distinctionem possunt glosari multae auctores, Aristoteles et Commentator, quarúm aliquae dicunt quod diffinitiones sunt singularium et aliquae quod non sunt nisi specierum. . . ."

[2] S. tot. log., I, 30, 12r.

but omits from his list the species, since the species, being predicable only of discrete terms, cannot be a predicate in universal propositions of demonstrative science.[1]

The word *signify* has four senses, two of which are applicable both to absolute and to connotative terms, while the other two are applicable only to connotative terms. (1) A term may signify the things it stands for in such manner that it can be truly predicated of a demonstrative pronoun that "points" to what it stands for. It is in this sense that a term is significant when it is subject or predicate of a proposition of present time. In this sense, also, the signification of a term may be said to change, so that it ceases to signify something it previously signified, or begins to signify something it previously did not signify, solely by reason of a change or movement *ex parte rei*—as when the individual denoted by the term "this man," or "the white thing," walks away or turns another colour, so that the proposition "This is a man," or "This is white" is no longer true.

(2) The second sense of *signify*, is when a term is said to signify not only the things it can stand for in propositions of present time, as in the first sense already mentioned, but also in propositions of past or future time, or in propositions whose terms stand for *what can be*. In this sense—which is the sense in which a universal concept is a univocal sign of many independently of questions of contingent fact or circumstance— a universal term (or the concept which determines its meaning) cannot cease to signify anything that it previously signified, nor begin to signify what it did not previously signify. In other words, a term is significant in this sense when it is taken as standing for every individual that could, not only now but at any time, and not only here but in any place, be signified by it in the first sense of the word "signify."

(3) The third sense of *signify* is equivalent to the sense in which a connotative term consignifies something present in the thing or things for which it stands, or to the sense in which a connotative

---

[1] S. tot. log., I, 31, 12r: cited *Ante*, p. 95, Note 1. Such expressions as "inhere," "be present in," etc., when used in logic, should be taken as synonyms of the word "to be predicated of"; and the term "participate," in logic, is to be understood as synonymous with "to be subject of" (subiicere).

term indicates a determinate part of the being of the things for which it stands. Thus "hot," in the proposition "This stove is hot," signifies "heat" in this sense; and "rational," in the proposition "This animal is rational," signifies the intellective soul as the principle of the individual being of an existent man.

(4) The fourth sense of *signify* applies to all other connotative terms, which are said to signify something for which they do not stand, though what is thus signified is neither a determinate part or principle of the essential nature of what they can stand for, nor a qualitative form really distinct from it and existing in it. That is to say, all connotative terms other than those included in (3) above, are said to be significant in this sense, whether what they connote is something that exists actually or only potentially, and whether what is connoted be a proposition, a privative term, or something of that sort. In this sense the term "blind" is said to signify "blindness", though "blindness" does not denote anything that can exist *per se* as a thing; rather the "blindness" connoted by the concrete term is equivalent to these two propositions: "something is by nature able to see but cannot actually see." Likewise, privative terms such as "nothing," "vacuum," "non-being," etc., are said to be significant in this sense.[1]

Every universal term, according to Ockham, is significant

[1] S. tot. log., I, 33, 12r: "Nam unomodo dicitur signum aliquid significare quando supponit vel natum est pro aliquo supponere, ita scilicet quod de pronomine demonstrante illud mediante hoc verbo 'est,' idem nomen predicatur. . . . Aliter accipitur 'significare' quando illud signum in aliqua propositione de praeterito vel praesenti vel futuro, vel in alia propositione vera de modo, potest pro illo supponere, et sic 'album' non tantum significat illud quod est album nunc, sed etiam illud quod potest esse album. . . . Accipiendo 'significare' primo modo et signum sibi correspondens, per solam mutationem rei frequenter vox et etiam conceptus cadunt a suo significato; sed secundo modo accipiendo 'significare' et signum sibi correspondens, vox vel conceptus per solam mutationem rei non cadit a suo significato. . . . Aliter accipitur 'significare' quando scil. illud dicitur significari a quo ipsa vox imponitur, vel primo modo significatur per conceptum principalem vel vocem principalem, et sic dicimus quod 'album' significat albedinem, quia 'albedo' significat albedinem pro qua tamen non supponit hoc signum 'album'; sic etiam 'rationale' (si sit differentia hominis) significat animam intellectivam hominis. . . . Quarto modo accipitur 'significare' communissime quando scil. aliquod signum . . . aliquid importat sive principaliter sive secundario, sive in recto sive in obliquo, sive dat intelligere illud, vel quocunque modo significat illud, sive affirmative sive negative—quomodo hoc nomen 'caecus' significat visum quia negative, et hoc nomen 'nihil' sive 'non aliquid' significat aliquid negative, de quo modo significandi loquitur Anselmus de casu diaboli."

in the first two senses which we have distinguished, and genera and species (being absolute and not connotative terms) are significant only in these two senses. The other universals are significant in either the third or fourth sense as well as in the first or second.[1]

The term *opposite* may be used either as a term of first intention or as a term of second intention. In its use as a term of first intention, it is a synonym of the term "contrary" (taken also as of first intention), since the only opposites *in rerum natura* are the qualitative contraries which are formal principles of change—substance being the opposite of nothing. As a term of second intention, "opposite" has many senses, and applies not only to terms but also to propositions. Propositions are, as Aristotle states in the *De interpretatione*, opposed as contradictories or as contraries; or, Ockham adds, they may be opposed in the sense that they imply contradictories, though they are not themselves contradictories or contraries.[2]

Terms may be opposed as contraries, as positive and privative, as relative and correlative, and as affirmative and negative. A term which signifies something negatively cannot be called the contrary of its opposite; it is rather a privative term opposed to a positive term. Further, while terms opposed as contraries may signify things opposed as contraries (*scil.* the accidental forms that are principles of change in substances), privative terms signify nothing privative *in re*, but signify something that is or that can be, by connoting a negation. Thus the term "matter" signifies only what is a substance and a form, connoting the proposition that some other form, accidental

---

[1] S. tot. log., I, 33, 12v: "Omne enim universale vel significat plura primo modo vel secundo modo, quia omne universale predicatur de pluribus vel in propositione de inesse de praesenti, de praeterito, vel de futuro, vel de modo. Ex quo patet quod errant illi qui dicunt quod haec vox 'homo' non significat omnes homines, cum enim hoc universale 'homo' . . . significat plura et non significat plures res quae non sunt homines, oportet quod significat plures homines, et non plus unum quam alius significat, igitur omnes homines; sed universale quod est genus vel species quod predicatur de pronomine demonstrante rem quam significat in quid, significat plura primo modo vel secundo modo accipiendo 'significare.' Alia vero universalia significant plura tertio vel quarto modo accipiendo 'significare,' quia talia significant aliquid in recto et aliquid in obliquo sicut patet de 'rationali,' 'risibili,' 'albo,' et de consimilibus."

[2] S. tot. log., I, 36, 12v–13r.

or substantial, is not present in it or not identical with it. We can, however, use the term of second intention "privative," significantly of a *term*, for the term itself is something positive (being a term), and it is a privative term because its nominal definition includes a negation.[1]

The term *attribute* (passio) is, as used by the logician, a term of second intention distinct from the term of first intention that is the *summum genus* (in the loose sense of the word genus) of one of the accidental categories. As a term of second intention, it signifies any term or intention predicable *per se* and necessarily of the subject of which it is said to be the attribute —*per se* not in the sense that the attribute is an element in the real definition of the subject (*primo modo dicendi per se*), but in the sense that the subject term is an element in the determinate nominal definition of the attribute (*per se secundo modo*).

Since genera and differentiæ are predicable of a subject as elements in its real definition, they are not *attributes* of their subjects. And since accidents are not predicable *per se* or necessarily of any subject, but only contingently, they are not attributes in the conclusions of demonstration. Since, also, the predication of a specific term of an individual or discrete term, is not universal predication, and does not yield a necessary proposition, it follows that a species is not an attribute. It remains, therefore, that only terms which are predicable as property, of a term that is their first subject, are attributes in the strict sense. And since affirmative demonstration is of the universal predicability of an attribute of some subject, demonstration is discourse which exhibits the reason for the universal truth of the conclusion of a syllogism, by a middle term which defines the subject (as its genus) and which defines the attribute as its commensurate subject.[2]

---

[1] S. tot. log., I, 36, 13r. While Ockham's analysis of such terms as "opposite" and "contrary" is of interest and by no means unimportant, especially in relation to the analysis of motion and change proper to physics, it seems unnecessary to discuss it in detail here, since his thoroughness, and his method, of dealing with terms of second intention and of distinguishing them from terms of first intention, has been already exhibited in other connections. As concerns the logical opposites, Ockham's exposition is faithful to Aristotle's discussions, and introduces no innovations or departures.

[2] S. tot. log., I, 37, 13v: "secundum quod logici loquuntur de passione, sciendum est quod passio non est aliqua res extra animam inhaerens alicui cuius

Such are the ways in which Ockham distinguishes the principal terms used by the logician—always, as in the case of the predicables, guarding against the confusion between modes of signification and things signified, or between discourse and the things discourse is about. Ockham's discussion of Porphyry's treatise on the predicables is, in its own way, an introduction to the *Categories* of Aristotle. For though Aristotle himself seemed not to think an introduction to his treatise on terms a necessity, but seemed rather to look upon the book of *Categories* as the starting point of his logic, the tradition inaugurated by Porphyry, and kept alive ever since, gave Ockham a good excuse for dealing with the material of Porphyry's treatise in such manner as to offset the porphyrian tradition and the porphyrian metaphysical orientation with respect to Aristotle's analysis of terms. Ockham, in short, seeks to clear the ground of a dialectical and metaphysical point of view which would reduce all finite or *determinate* signification to conventional signification, and which would reduce all *determinate* principles of knowledge to hypotheses incidental to the development of a metaphysical system, without speculative value of their own. If we keep in mind Ockham's critique of the porphyrian implications, and his view of the universal concept as an act or habit of understanding *that which is individual in nature*, his own interpretation of the book of *Categories* will be seen to follow a path which in every important respect is the direct antithesis of the path indicated by Porphyry, and which may lay a fair claim to being an accurate and thoroughly philosophic statement of aristotelianism.

---

dicitur passio, sed passio est quoddam predicabile mentale, vocale, vel scriptum, predicabile per se secundo modo de subiecto cuius dicitur esse passio . . . generaliter verum est quod subiectum et sua passio non sunt idem realiter quamvis supponunt pro eodem et quamvis predicatio unius de alio sit necessaria." The attribute can stand only for the things that its commensurate subject signifies *per se* or *in quid*, but the *per se* proposition is not a tautology, since the two terms signify the things they stand for, in different ways—the *passio* connotatively, through the pair of contraries or potential accidental determination made explicit in its nominal definition, and the subject signifying the things it stands for nonconnotatively or absolutely, because it means precisely *such individual things*.

CHAPTER FOUR

THE CATEGORIES OF ARISTOTLE

I

THE terms with which Aristotle is concerned in the book of *Categories*, according to Ockham, are the terms of first intention of which the propositions of the real sciences are composed—terms which signify things that are not signs. In the *Sum of All Logic*, Ockham prefaces his discussion of these terms of first intention with a brief consideration of the transcendental terms *ens* and *unum*. These, being significative not only of things that are not signs but also of things that are signs, are, together with the other four transcendentals, the only concepts of absolute universality, and consequently the only terms which properly belong to metaphysics.

"Being" (*ens*), and the transcendental terms convertible with it, cannot, as Aristotle proves, be a genus or in a genus.[1] From this two consequences may be drawn. The first is that metaphysics cannot be a demonstrative science, and the second is, that the principles of the demonstrative sciences are not demonstrated by metaphysics. The first conclusion follows from the fact that every demonstrative science demonstrates attributes of its subject through middle terms that are prior, in the sense of being more universal than, its subject. But the subject of metaphysics is "being," and there is no term or concept prior to, or more universal than, "being." Furthermore, there are no metaphysical "conclusions" distinct from metaphysical principles; for metaphysics is the science of first principles as such, and first principles, by the very fact that they are first, are indemonstrable.

[1] Arist., Met. B, 3, 998b 22–7.

The second consequence, that the principles of the demonstrative sciences are not demonstrated by metaphysics, so that the discursive sciences are not related to metaphysics as subalternate to subalternant, is likewise obvious from the character of the subject of metaphysics. First, a science that is non-demonstrative cannot demonstrate the principles of another science; and secondly, since "being" and the other metaphysical terms are not genera nor included under a genus, they cannot be middle terms of any demonstration *in* a discursive science. Demonstrative sciences show how *things that are* differ in their being; but *being as such*, with which metaphysics is concerned, cannot be a principle of demonstrating differences in being, and hence metaphysics cannot yield the principles of any demonstrative science. On the other hand, since every speculative science is concerned with *things that are*, the principles and terms of every such science must exemplify metaphysical concepts and metaphysical truth; and since metaphysics is the science of first principles *as such*, the recognition by the demonstrative scientist of the "firstness" of his first principles will involve the recognition of the metaphysical principles as exemplified and exhibited in the subject genus of his science.

Metaphysics, consequently, is neither a glorified cosmology nor a transcendental logic, because it is not a discursive science. It is concerned neither with the ways in which things come to be thus or thus qualified from not having been so qualified, nor with the ways in which truths come to be known from not having been known—in these respects differing, by its subject, from natural philosophy and logic. It is a speculative science and not an art, because it is concerned with *that which is*, considered for its own sake, and not with means of producing something or of attaining an end. It is concerned neither with natural processes or movements, nor with the processes of discursive thought, and it is not itself a process, any more than the act of recognition, or the actual grasp of a truth, is, *qua* actual, a process. Metaphysics is, rather, a kind of Wisdom, as Aristotle often calls it—it is the actuality of intelligence, as such, by which *being* in the unqualified sense, is grasped through the attributes which belong to it in the unqualified sense, and not, as in discursive sciences, through the attributes which belong to it insofar as it is thus or thus determinable.[1]

The way in which metaphysics is related to discursive science, and hence the way in which the transcendental terms, of which it consists, are related to the terms of limited universality of which the propositions of the discursive sciences are composed, is indicated by Ockham, as by many other

[1] Arist., Met. Gamma, 1, 1003a 18–20: "There is a science which investigates being as being and the attributes which belong to this in virtue of its own nature." Ibid., 2, 1005a 12–5: "Obviously then it is the work of one science to examine being *qua* being, and the attributes which belong to it *qua* being. . . . ."
That Aristotle conceived the first philosophy to be a non-discursive and non-demonstrative science, is indicated frequently in the *Metaphysics*, as in the following passages: Met. K, 1, 1059a 16–8: "That Wisdom is a science of first principles is evident . . ."; and 29–34: "Further, does it deal with substances only or also with their attributes? If in the case of attributes demonstration is possible, in that of substances it is not. . . . If we think of it as demonstrative, the science of the attributes is Wisdom, but if as dealing with what is primary, the science of substances claims the title." Met. Lambda, 1, 1069a 18: "The subject of our inquiry is substance; for the principles and the causes we are seeking are those of substances."
Substance is *that which is* "in the unqualified sense" (cf. for example Arist., An. Post. II, 2, 90a 8); metaphysics, which considers being in the unqualified sense, *qua* being, can therefore be called the science of substance.
The transcendental attributes of *ens* are not demonstrable of it, since there cannot "be" a middle term distinct from being, by which an attribute might be demonstrated of being. And this is why dialectic, when conceived as a discursive metaphysics, has to make use of Non-being as a principle—for discourse requires distinct things, and hence, if *being as such* is taken as one thing (the subject of discursive signification), *non-being* is all that remains to serve as the other principle.
While the transcendental terms are convertible with, though not demonstrable of, "being," there are no other attributes predicable of being *as such*, since all other attributes are of limited universality, and can be predicated commensurately and *per se* only of terms that signify determinate kinds of beings, as in the natural sciences or in mathematics. Hence metaphysics, since it deals with being *qua* being and with the attributes of being *qua* being, cannot be a demonstrative nor a discursive science—consequently it consists simply in the grasp of *ens* and its commensurate attributes, which make up the six transcendental terms or concepts.
Metaphysics, understood in this way, is the intelligence of the indemonstrable, for being as *such* is indemonstrable. The first principles and primary concepts of a natural science are indemonstrable principles of *that* science; and hence, though they cannot be demonstrated by metaphysics (because they are indemonstrable and because metaphysics is not a demonstrative science), it is by metaphysics that they are recognized or "seen" as *first* principles. This is why metaphysics is called the science of first principles—i.e., of first principles *qua* first principles, and not *qua* middle terms of demonstration, as in the discursive sciences.

mediæval writers, in the statement that "being" and the transcendental terms convertible with it, are predicated equivocally of the terms in the ten categories. The term "being," in itself, is not an equivocal name, for the meaning of the word is referred to a single concept or act of understanding—and the distinction between equivocal and univocal names is a matter of the relation between the conventional sign and the singleness or diversity of concepts by which its use in discourse is determined.[1]

But "being" is predicated of a term that signifies individual things disjunctively (*divisim*) in a different sense from the way in which it is predicated of a term that stands for individuals conjunctively (*coniunctim*). Thus the term "animal," though it is a sign of many, can stand for individual animals taken individually or *divisim;* but the term "similarity," though it stands for real things in such a proposition as "There is a similarity between this white thing and that white thing," cannot stand for any single individual taken by itself, but only for two or more distinct things *considered together* by the mind. Likewise, the term "motion" stands for *that which is*, in the proposition "Motion is with respect to contraries," but it stands neither for the mover or the moved, taken alone, nor for anything other than the mover and the moved; hence it must stand for the mover and the moved conjunctively, or taken together. The being which is signified by such a term is not distinct from the being of individuals such as can be signified by concepts of individual nature, but it is a function of the co-existence of individual things or causes; similarly, the significative unity of such a term is a function of the unity of the act of apprehension or of judgment by which two

---

[1] Ockham, S. tot. log., I, 38, 13v: "Dicto de terminis quibusdam secundae intentionis et etiam de quibusdam secundae impositionis, videndum est de terminis primae intentionis. Primo tamen dicendum est de quibusdam communibus omnibus, sive sint res quae non sunt signa, sive sint res quae sunt signa, cuiusmodi sunt ly 'ens' et 'unum.' Unomodo accipitur hoc nomen 'ens' secundum quod sibi correspondet unus conceptus omnibus rebus predicabilis in quid primo modo, quomodo transcendens potest predicari in quid. . . . Nam de omni ente vel de pronomine demonstrante quodcumque ens potest idem conceptus predicari, sicut eadem vox vere potest de quolibet predicari."

or more discriminated individuals are understood to be together.[1]

The distinction between *ens per se* and *ens per aliud*, or between substance and accident, is not a metaphysical distinction—not a distinction between two ultimate kinds of entities. It is rather a distinction between two ways in which individual things (which are what they are *per se* or by their individual nature) are apprehended or signified in discursive thought. For we sometimes signify individual things by absolute terms, which connote nothing but which mean precisely the individual ("undivided") nature of the things for which they can stand disjunctively; and such terms signify what can exist *per se*, by a mode of signification which is absolute and not relative or connotative. But we also signify such individual things connotatively or relatively, by reference to something distinct from them by which their existence can come to be apprehended; and such terms signify *ens, per aliud*.

A corresponding account is to be given of the distinction between *ens in potentia* and *ens in actu*. This also is not a metaphysical distinction, because that which is said to be something potentially is, insofar as it is, something actual; but metaphysics considers being *qua* being, and not the relative privation of being indicated by the expression *ens in potentia*. This distinction, according to Ockham, is a distinction between two ways in which a term may stand for things of which it is a natural sign. It may stand for individuals of which it

[1] S. tot. log., I, 38, 13v: "Tamen non obstante quod sic sit unus conceptus communis omni ente, hoc nomen 'ens' est equivocum, quia non predicatur de omnibus sibi subiicibilibus quando significative sumitur secundum unum conceptum sed sibi diversi conceptus correspondent sicut super Porphyrium declaravi." Cf. Exp. aur., I 16r: "Sed de dicto auctoris (*scil.* Porphyrii) hic quomodo debet intelligi, dico breviter, quod intentio sua et etiam Aristotelis est quod ens non dicitur univoce de decem predicamenta sed equivoce. Cuius ratio est, quia aliqua predicamenta significant res pro quibus non tantum coniunctim sed divisim supponunt, ita quod quando ponuntur in propositione denotatur quod predicatum dicatur vere de contento sub eo, non tantum cum alio, sed etiam per se sumpto. . . . Sed aliqua predicamenta sic res significant quod non significant alias res quam facient alia predicamenta, sed magis significant tales diversas res coniunctim, ut non possit verificari quod aliqua una res sit talis, vel talis, sed magis quod plures res simul sumptae recipiunt predicationem talis predicati; sicut non possum dicere quod hoc album est similitudo vel illud album sit similitudo, sed possum aliquo modo dicere quod haec duo alba sunt similitudo."

is a sign, in a proposition of present time and of assertoric form, in which case it is said to signify something that is actual. Or it may stand for individuals of which it is a natural sign, in a proposition *de possibili*, in which case it is said to signify *that which can be* or *ens in potentia*. But the notion of the accidental, of the material, and of the potential, is proper only to discursive thought, and applies only to the analysis of change through reduction to finite causes or principles. The transcendental terms of metaphysics, being of absolute universality, cannot signify *being* through excluding any kind of being, or through connoting privation or contrariety— each of the terms convertible with *ens* involves a double negation, like the term "one" which, *qua* transcendental, signifies *that which is* by connoting *indivision*.[1]

[1] If *ens* were predicated univocally of terms whose meaning determines their supposition (i.e., terms which mean precisely the individual things for which they can stand), and of terms whose supposition is indeterminate (as is the case with connotative terms taken alone, so that what they stand for is indicated only by the word "something" placed in their nominal definition), then the distinction between *ens in actu* and *ens in potentia*, and between *ens per se* and *ens per aliud*, would be shifted from the realm of discursive science into the realm of things discourse is about, and in that case all science would imply a metaphysics whose first principles were contraries—as actual and potential are contraries. For Ockham the principles of act and potentiality, or of form and matter, are principles of physics (which deals with changeable things, change being between contraries), but not of metaphysics. Hence, to avoid making the distinction between matter and form metaphysical, which would involve the augustinian and neo-platonist position of regarding *materia prima* as something absolute (like the "void") and as a first principle of metaphysics, Ockham insists that *ens* is predicated equivocally of terms which signify individuals *divisim*, and of terms which signify things which are *per se* diverse, *coniunctim*, as if they were parts of a single thing.

Cf. Ockham, S. tot. log., I, 38, 13v–14r: "Quae divisio (*scil.* between *ens per se* and *ens per accidens*) non est intelligenda quod aliquid ens sit per se et aliud secundum accidens; sed ostendit ibi diversum modum predicandi unius de alio mediante hoc verbo 'est'. . . . Similiter philosophus dividit ens 7 Met. in ens in potentia et ens in actu, quod non est intelligendum quod aliquid quod non est in rerum natura sed potest esse sit vere ens, et aliquid quod est in rerum natura sit etiam ens; sed intelligendum est quod hoc nomen 'ens' predicatur de aliquo mediante hoc verbo 'est' mere de praesenti, non equivalenti propositioni de possibili, dicendo sic, 'Sortes est ens,' 'albedo est ens'; de aliquo autem in propositione de possibili vel equivalenti propositione de possibili, sic dicendo, 'Antichristos potest esse ens,' sive 'Antichristos est ens in potentia' . . ."

Cf. also Aristotle, Met. N, I, 1087b 1–4: "All contraries, then, are always predicable of a subject, and none can exist apart, but just as appearances suggest that there is nothing contrary to substance, argument confirms this. No contrary, then, is the first principle of all things in the full sense; the first principle is something different." It follows from this that the principles of act and potency,

The term "one," (*unum*) is convertible with "being," and is therefore predicable of the terms in the categories in the same senses in which "being" is predicable of them. Ockham takes exception to the statement of the scotists that specific unity is prior, *in re*, to numerical unity; for the unity of the species, as a single concept significative of many individuals, presupposes the numerical unity of each of these many individuals, and not the other way around. It is impossible, says Ockham, that there should be any nature or essence which is one in species or in genus, and yet neither one thing, nor many distinct things, numerically.[1]

The foregoing discussion of the relation of metaphysics, and of the transcendental terms, to discursive science and to the terms in the categories, indicates the basis of Ockham's

---

which are contraries, cannot from Aristotle's point of view be metaphysical principles in the strict sense, though in an analogical sense perhaps they may be applied to *being as such*, or to immaterial things like the intellective soul. Further, since discursive science is knowledge by contraries—i.e., knowledge of substances as determinable with respect to contraries—the science which deals with discursive knowledge as such (logic) will not deal with metaphysics as such, or be an instrument of metaphysics, because metaphysics is not, according to Aristotle, knowledge by contraries.

[1] S. tot. log., I, 39, 14r: "*Unum* autem est passio entis quia est predicabilis de *ente* per se secundo modo; et hoc quia significat aliquid quod non eodem modo significatur per *ens*, quamvis aliquo modo significatur per *ens*. . . . Et quamvis philosophus 5 Metaph. ponat multiplices modos unius per se, tamen ad praesens sufficit ponere tres modos unius quibus logicai utuntur frequenter." " . . . nihil est unum specie nisi sit unum numero, et ideo impossibile est quod sit aliqua natura quae sit una specie et non sit una numero vel plures res numero; similiter impossibile est quod sit aliqua natura una genere nisi illa sit specie una vel specie plura." Cf. Duns Scotus, Op. Oxon. II, Dist. III, Qu. I, (Quaracchi ed., 1914, p. 227, 233 f), for argument against ranking numerical unity as prior to, or co-ordinate with, specific unity. Ockham's reply to this argument is to be found in his Sent., I, Dist. 2, Qu. 6 EE (cited by Prantl, p. 359, Anm. 813).

As concerns the differences in the mode of signification between the six transcendental terms, *ens* being absolute and the other five connotative, cf. Aquinas, De veritate I, art. 1, who distinguishes them by the same method as does Ockham, though in more detail. Ockham indicates their manner of distinction in S. tot. log., I, 37, 13v: "Est autem sciendum quod passio semper supponit pro illo eodem pro quo subiectum supponit: quamvis aliquid aliud ab illo significat aliquo modo, *scil.* in recto vel in obliquo, affirmative vel negative; unde etiam quaedam passiones vocantur positivae et quaedam negativae. Ex praedictis potest patere quomodo ly 'unum' est passio 'entis,' et distinguitur ab illo *ente* cuius est passio, *scil.* a communi conceptu entis, et tamen significat idem quod ille conceptus licet alio modo; sicut patet per diffinitionem exprimentem quid nominis."

treatment of Aristotle's analysis of modes of finite signification. The book of *Categories* is not, in Ockham's view, a discussion of the kinds of things that can exist *per se* or by nature (for then it would be indistinguishable from the whole body of natural sciences), nor is it a discussion of *being as such* (for "being" is not a genus nor defined by a genus). It is, rather, a discussion of the different ways in which things that are not parts of discourse, can be apprehended, signified, or *said to be*.[1]

The distinction between univocal and equivocal names, made by Aristotle at the beginning of the *Categories*, is applicable, strictly, only to written or spoken signs, and not to concepts or acts of understanding. If a word whose meaning has been established by one concept comes to be used also to mean the things understood by a different concept, the word is said to be equivocal in meaning. An univocal term is any conventional sign whose signification is a function of a single concept or intention. Definitions reveal whether or not the same word is understood univocally or equivocally by different people using it, for definitions reduce connotative terms to absolute terms. But absolute terms (or the concepts corresponding to them) are such that if they are understood at all, they are understood by the things that they mean and

---

[1] Exp. aur., II, 37r: "Circa primum sequendo Boetium in commento suo dicendum est quod in hoc opere haec intentio est de primis rerum nominibus et de vocibus significantibus disputare, non in eo quod secundum aliquam proprietatem figuramque formantur (i.e., not from the grammatical point of view), sed in eo quod significantes sunt. . . . Verumtamen non obstante quod philosophus inferius tractet de vocibus, tractat simul cum hoc de rebus; hoc est, multas propositiones ponit et accipit in quibus termini non pro vocibus sed pro rebus supponunt, et haec est intentio Boetii dicentis quod 'de significativis vocibus et de rebus quoque est aliquatenus tractaturus, res etenim et rerum significatio est unita, sed principalior erit illa disputatio quae de sermonibus est.' . . . Et ignorantia intentionis Aristotelis in hoc libro facit multos modernos errare, credentes multa hic dicta pro rebus quae tamen pro solis vocibus et proportionabiliter pro intentionibus seu conceptibus in anima vult intelligi."

"Utilitas istius libri est scire quae nomina quas res significant, et hoc est multum necessarium ad omnem disputationem, cum omnis disputatio significata vocabulorum praesupponit; est autem scientia ista specialiter utilis ad notitiam fallaciae figurae dictionis, cuius ignorantia multos involvit, nam cum aliquae voces aliquas res absolutas significant, et aliquae significant res in comparatione ad alias, ideo arguere a primis vocibus ad secundas . . . est facere fallaciam figurae dictionis." E.g., to argue that because that which begins to be hot acquires heat, therefore what begins to be equal acquires equality, is to commit the fallacy of figure of speech.

which exist *per se* and *divisim*, independently of human ways of thinking about them and independently of human operations of synthesis. Through definitions the meanings of words can be determinately referred to concepts that are the same for all men, as the things signified by them are public property and the same for all. The book of *Categories*, as Ockham understands it, is chiefly concerned with the ways in which the meanings of words can be made evident and determinate, through reduction to defining formulae composed of absolute terms.

Denominative terms are, in the broad sense, the terms which Ockham calls connotative. In the strict sense, however, only a concrete connotative term whose abstract counterpart signifies a qualitative form that is an indivisible or indefinable principle of intuitive apprehension (as in sense perception), is a denominative term. Such terms indicate the things for which they can stand not by the absolute or *per se* nature of such things, but by what is absolute in our ways of coming to know—i.e., by what are principles or starting points of knowledge, with respect to human perceptual powers.

It is to be noted, finally, that every term, whether denominative or not, is predicated either equivocally or univocally of any subject of which it is predicated; for every term when used in discourse is either understood determinately through a single concept convertible with a single definition, or it is not. There is no mean, in demonstrative science or in discursive knowledge generally, between univocal and equivocal predication.[1]

---

[1] S. tot. log., I, 13, 6r: "Est autem illa vox equivoca quae significans plura non est signum subordinatum uni conceptui. . . . Univocum autem dicitur omne illud quod est subordinatum uni conceptui, sive significat plura sive non." Exp. aur., II, 39v: "Strictissime dicitur denominativum cui correspondet aliquod abstractum importans accidens alteri inhaerens formaliter. . . . Notandum quod etiam predicatio denominativa non est aliquid simpliciter distinctum a predicatione univoca et equivoca. . . . cuius ratio est, nam omne nomen predicabile de multis aut habet quid nominis convertibile cum nomine . . . vel habet aliquem conceptum correspondentem in anima, aut non habet tale. . . . Si primo modo, sic est univocum, nam nomen est idem et ratio subest eadem. Si secundo modo, sic est equivocum." Aquinas, though allowing analogical predication in theology, excludes it from demonstrative science of finite things; cf. S. theol., I, Qu. 13, art. 5.

Aristotle's statement that "Forms of speech are either simple or composite" serves to distinguish the subject matter of the book of *Categories* from that of the *De interpretatione*, and indicates, as Boethius also observed, that both treatises are concerned with forms of discourse rather than with kinds of things *in rerum natura*.[1] The next distinction made by Aristotle, between (1) what is predicable of a subject, (2) what is present in a subject, (3) what is both present in, and predicable of, a subject, and (4) what is neither predicable of, nor present in, a subject, shows quite clearly, according to Ockham, that Aristotle is here distinguishing between kinds of terms or intentions, and not between kinds of things *in re* such as the real sciences are concerned with.

Boethius had stated that this was a division of things into universal substances, universal accidents, particular substances, and particular accidents. If these terms are taken as terms of first intention, the distinction is false and impossible; but since such "things" may be understood to be terms, Boethius' restatement can be understood in accordance with the truth and with the principles of Aristotle. Only terms or concepts can be called universal, and nothing but what is a term or concept can be said to be "predicable of a subject." Hence it is obvious that Aristotle is here making a distinction between kinds of terms and not between kinds of things that are not terms.[2]

---

[1] Arist., Cat. 2, 1a, 17. Boethius, In Cat. Arist. I (Migne PL 64, cl. 169 A–B).

[2] Arist., Cat. 2, 1a, 20–1b, 9. Ockham, Exp. aur., II, 40v: "Intelligendum est primo quod ista non est divisio rerum extra animam, quia res extra animam non predicatur de pluribus, non enim predicatur nisi vox, vel conceptus vel aliquod signum ad placitum institutum. . . . Et si dicatur quod ista expositio est contra mentem Boetii dicentis quod ista est divisio rerum, quae est in substantiam universalem et particularem, et accidens universale et accidens particulare. . . . Istis non obstantibus dicendum est simpliciter quod nulla est substantia realiter extra animam nisi solum substantia particularis, et quod ista est divisio incomplexorum ex quibus componuntur propositiones, et ex quibus lineae predicamentalis componuntur. Et hoc potest probari. Nam sicut secundum Boetium, haec substantia nullo modo potest fieri accidens nec econverso, igitur secundum eum, sicut substantia et accidens non sunt idem realiter, ita nec particulare et universale, igitur si utrunque sit res erunt duae res extra animam distinctae realiter. Tunc sic, sicut accidens particulare est subiective in substantia particulari, ita accidens universale est subiective in substantia universali; sed hoc est impossibile, quia sequeretur quod contraria essent realiter simul in subiecto

The division is to be understood as follows: (1) "Things predicable of a subject" are any universal terms predicable of *infimae species* of substance, or of singular terms standing for individuals signified by such *infimae species;* and taken in this way, Aristotle's division of predicables as given in the *Topics*, is exhaustive and coincides with this first division; (2) "Things present in a subject" are not, as Boethius' restatement might indicate, all terms other than those *essentially* predicable of a subject; rather they are the absolute terms of abstract form which are principles of the definition of concrete connotative terms, but which cannot be unequivocally predicated of a subject in direct predication—such are terms like "whiteness," "heat," etc. (3) "Things predicable of a subject and present in a subject" are the abstract terms which are predicable as *genera* of the terms "present in a subject" just mentioned, as "colour" is predicable of "whiteness" and in this sense is present in that which happens to be white. (4) "Things neither predicable of, nor present in, a subject," are absolute terms which are not elements in the definition (either real or nominal) of any term. While it might be held that this last group consists only of singular or "discrete" terms, and hence does not consist of *infimae species* of substance, this interpretation implies that the primary subject of science is the singular term (which cannot be a subject in a necessary or *per se* proposition), and not the specific term (which can be a subject of necessary predication, since it signifies individuals disjunctively and without connoting contingent determinations or particular facts). Since Aristotle's analysis of terms is intended as an essential part of his theory

---

primo. Probatio istius ultimae consequentiae: Nam ponatur quod solus homo sit albus, et solus homo sit niger, ita quod omnia alia corpora vel non sint colorata, vel sint colorata mediis coloribus. Tunc albedo universalis, cum sit accidens per propositum, erit in aliquo subiecto et non erit primo in homine particulari, quia in illo est primo albedo particularis; ergo primo est in homine universali, et eadem ratione in homine universali erit primo nigredo universalis; ergo in eodem subiecto primo sunt albedo universalis et nigredo universalis. . . . Ideo dicendum est absolute quod quaelibet res imaginabilis ita est particularis sicut Sortes vel Plato, vel haec materia vel haec forma." Cf. Boethius, In Cat. Arist., I, (Migne PL 64, cl. 170 B).

of demonstration, and since the subjects of demonstrative science are held by Aristotle to be universal terms, the above notion of what is meant by a "thing neither predicable of, nor present in, a subject," would seem to be more in accordance with aristotelian principles than the usual interpretation which, in porphyrian manner, understands by the term "subject" *merely* the singular term, which can be a subject only of a contingent proposition.[1]

The above interpretation overcomes a difficulty with respect to the *dictum de omni*, as stated in the *Categories*. Aristotle says: "When one thing is predicated of another, all that which is predicable of the predicate will be predicable also of the subject." Boethius restricts Aristotle's expression "predicable of a subject" to universal substantial terms with respect to

---

[1] Exp. aur., II, 40v: "sed ista est divisio vocum, sive conceptus, sive intentionum in anima, et tunc est intelligenda sic talis divisio; scil., eorum quae sunt, id est eorum vocum vel intentionum in anima importantium res extra, quae sunt quaedam incomplexa—hoc est, incomplexorum quaedam de subiecto dicuntur, in subiecto vero non sunt; hoc est, de eis vere dicitur predicari de subiecto, sicut de hoc incomplexo 'homo' vere dicitur quod predicatur de 'Socrate,' et tamen de incomplexo illo supponente personaliter non verificatur esse in subiecto, quia haec est simpliciter falsa, 'homo est in subiecto,' quia nullus homo est in subiecto. . . ."

Ibid., 46v: "sciendum est hic quod cuiuslibet accidentis existentis in subiecto sunt duo nomina; quorum unum est abstractum et aliud concretum. Et est differentia inter illa duo nomina, quia nomen abstractum significat praecise illam rem existentem in subiecto et pro ea supponit in propositione; sicut hoc nomen 'albedo' significat praecise illam qualitatem quae informat corpus et pro ea supponit in propositione; et propter hoc tale nomen non praedicatur de subiecto nec de aliquo quod supponit pro subiecto; quia universaliter ad hoc quod propositio mere in recto sit vera, oportet quod subiectum et predicatum pro eodem supponant; et ideo haec est falsa 'homo est albedo. . . .' *Album* vero quod est eius concretum significat illam eandem rem quam significat abstractum connotando tamen subiectum et propter talem specialem connotationem in diffinitione exprimente quid nominis ipsius concreti debet poni subiectum vel nomen supponens pro subiecto, ut si diffiniatur quid est album debet dici quod est corpus habens albedinem. Et propter istam rationem tale nomen concretum supponit pro subiecto accidentis, et ideo vere dicitur de subiecto ut sic vere dicatur: 'homo est albus.'"

In the broadest sense, the *infima species* of substance belongs in the group of "things predicable of a subject," while only proper names and the other discrete terms belong in the group of terms "neither predicable of nor present in a subject." But elsewhere Ockham makes the point that for scientific purposes, the *infima species* is the subject of universal direct predication and is not in this sense predicable of a subject. Cf. ch. iii, p. 76, Note 1, where Ockham points out that the species is not predicable, in any necessary or scientific propositions, of a singular subject. Cf. also, ch. iii, p. 95, Note 1, where Ockham indicates that for Aristotle the *species* is not a "predicable" in scientific discourse.

particular substantial terms, and to universal accidents with respect to particular accidents, so that it is only terms which are elements of the definition of the subject, that are said to be "predicable of a subject." Hence he takes the *dictum de omni* as applicable only to essential predication. He gives as an instance of the accidental predication to which the *dictum de omni* does not apply, a case which, according to Ockham, is fallacious not because the predication is accidental, but because the terms have equivocal supposition. This instance is: "Socrates is a man; man is a species; therefore Socrates is a species."[1]

Ockham concedes that Boethius' restriction, in the sense in which it ought to be understood, is justified. But he adds that the *dictum de omni* can, and indeed must, be understood as applicable to predication *in quale* as well as to predication *in quid*. Otherwise demonstration would be confined to elements of the essential definition of the subject, and there would be no demonstration of properties of substances. Instead of emasculating the *dictum de omni* in order to avoid such fallacies as that mentioned by Boethius, Ockham substitutes the following qualifications: (1) the terms must be used significatively or with personal supposition; (2) the middle term must be distributed, unless it is a singular or discrete term, standing for one individual only. These conditions exclude the instance of equivocal supposition mentioned by Boethius, and exclude the fallacy of "undistributed middle," while retaining, as terms predicable of a subject in scientific demonstration, attributes which are not elements in the definition of the subject.[2]

---

[1] Arist., Cat. 3, 1b 10–1. Boethius, In Cat. Arist., I (Migne PL 64, cl. 176 A–B). Ockham, Exp. aur., II, 41r: "Sciendum est hic quod Boethius intelligit istam regulam quando predicatum predicatur de subiecto in quid, unde dicit 'illa sola de subiecto predicari dicuntur quaecunque in cuiuslibet rei substantia et diffinitione ponuntur,' et per hoc excludit illas instantias quod 'homo' predicatur de 'Sorte' et 'species' predicatur de 'homine,' et tamen 'species' non predicatur de 'Sorte'. . . ."

[2] Exp. aur., II, 41r–41v: "quamvis dictum Boetii bene intellectum sit verum, tamen regula Aristotelis generalius intelligi potest, ut non tantum regula est vera quando predicatum predicatur in quid, sed etiam quando aliquid non in quid sed alio modo predicatur de aliquo. Sed tunc debet intelligi quod omnes

Those who, like Walter Burleigh, considered the ten categories to be a distinction or classification of ten kinds of things
per se distinct outside the mind, receive uncompromising
criticism from Ockham.[1]   The only "real distinction"
involved in the analysis of terms of first intention, is the distinction between the things signified by terms "predicable
of a subject and not present in a subject," and the things
signified by terms "present in a subject." This distinction,
moreover, which is the distinction between substances and
the qualitative contraries which are principles of the analysis
of change, is not a metaphysical distinction, but rather a
distinction involved in discursive signification of things which
are, in themselves, individual substances. "Substance" and
"quality" are distinct kinds of absolute terms only for discursive
science, and not terms which express an absolute distinction
in *being as such*. These, however, are the only distinct *kinds* of
absolute terms required for discursive science; all other terms
signify things that are signified *per se* by absolute terms of these
two kinds, though they differ in their mode of signification,
some standing for such things through connoting other such
things, and some standing for different kinds of things taken
together: or conjunctively.

It should be understood that these categories are not things
outside the mind really distinct from each other; and it should

termini propositionum acceptarum supponant personaliter. Et per hoc excluduntur instantiae de genere et specie. . . . Requiritur etiam quod quodlibet
predicatum predicatur de subiecto suo universaliter, nisi forte subiectum sit
singulare, et ita oportet quod omnes propositiones sint universales vel singulares;
et ideo quamvis 'coloratum' predicatur de 'homine' sic dicendo, 'homo est
coloratus,' et 'lapis' predicatur de 'colorato' sic dicendo, 'coloratum est lapis,'
non tamen lapis predicatur de homine, et hoc quia haec non est universaliter
vera: 'omne coloratum est lapis'; si tamen quaelibet illarum est universalis et
vera, ex his posset sequi conclusio necessario in primo primae figurae."

[1] Burleigh, Exp. sup. artem veterem, 16r A (cited by Prantl, p. 302, Anm.
593): "Dicit Boethius, quod in hoc libro intentio est philosophi, de primis
rerum nominibus et de vocibus significantibus res disputare. . . . Alia est
opinio Avicennae et Averrois, quam credo veriorem, quod in hoc libro determinatur de rebus principaliter et ex consequenti et secundario de vocibus. . . ."
Burleigh holds the view, much criticized by Ockham, that propositions can be
composed of things outside the mind—outside *materialiter* and inside *formaliter*.
Cf. Prantl, p. 303, Anm. 598.

not be imagined that just as man, ass, and whiteness are three
things outside the soul entirely distinct . . . that it is the same
with substance, quantity, relation, and so on, or that substance,
quantity, and relation are three things really distinct such that
nothing that is a substance or part of a substance is a quantity
or part of a quantity, and similarly that quantity is a thing really
and entirely distinct from substance, relation, and quality. . . .
But it is to be understood and imagined that these are three distinct
words and distinct intentions of the mind, or concepts, signifying
things outside. It is not however to be said that just as these
intentions or words are distinct from each other, because one is
not the other, that there are as many distinct things corresponding
to them. For not always is there a corresponding distinction
between significant words and mental intentions, and the things
signified. But this is to be said: that these categories are distinct,
but the things signified by these categories are not correspondingly
distinguished, but that the same thing (at least sometimes) is
signified by diverse predicaments, although not in the same manner.
For some times the same thing is signified by one of the predicaments without connotation of any other thing, or of several things,
and without connoting that it is itself another thing or not another
thing, and in general without any connotation or consignification
of several things. For example, the predicament of substance is
a sign of this man, as of any other substance you please, and it
connotes nothing. When however I say "father," this predicate
"father" which is one of the terms included in the category of
relation, stands for that man who is a father, by connoting his
son—for it is impossible to understand that he is a father unless
it is understood that he has a son; and thus it is with the various
predicaments.

That the predicaments are not things outside the soul and of
the essence of the things contained by them has often been shown,
and the opposite (*scil.* that they are not things outside the soul)
can be proved of the accidental categories one by one. For if
that which is the genus of quality is a real thing outside the mind,
and of the being of whatever quality is inferior to it (i.e., contained
in the category of quality), then of the essence of "this whiteness"
there are at the very least "universal whiteness," "universal colour,"
and "quality," which is the *genus generalissimum*. But this is
impossible, for I ask: either these universals are the same really,
or they are really distinct. If they are the same in reality, then
one is not more universal than the other, and hence "whiteness"
is a *genus generalissimum* and common to all qualities, which is
impossible. If they are really distinct and form a *per se* unity and

yet are of different character (*alterius rationis*), then one of them must be matter and the other truly a form, which is false and against Aristotle 9 Met., where he gives to understand that accidents do not have matter *ex qua* (i.e., as an intrinsic principle) but merely *in qua* (i.e., as the extrinsic subject in which they exist).[1]

The terms in the categories are, as Ockham never tires of stating, signs of things and consequently distinct from the things of which they are signs. Some of these terms are nouns, some verbs, some adverbs. This is why not all the predicaments have an order of more inclusive and less inclusive in the same way that terms in the category of substance have. The predicament "when," or *quando*, is not divided by essential differentiae, yielding definitions of co-ordinate species, as is the case with the predicament "substance." Those who attempt to make every category an order of terms such as is found in the category of substance, by changing the adverbial predicaments to nouns (e.g., "when" to "whenness"), and by taking them as elements in essential definitions of ten distinct kinds of things, succeed only in erasing the distinctions, in mode of signification, by which terms are divided among the ten categories; their attempt is to reduce all terms to species of substance or of hypostatized qualities.[2]

The term "predicament" is used in two senses: (1) to signify the whole order of terms in a category (which is the sense in which "category" is generally used in English), or (2) to

[1] Exp. aur., II, 42r. The reference to Aristotle is probably to Met. Theta, 7, 1049a 27–36.

[2] Exp. aur., II, 42v: "Tertio est sciendum, quod expresse patet per exempla Aristotelis, quod aliqua predicamenta sunt nomina, et aliqua verba, et aliqua adverbia . . . et ideo non est consimilis co-ordinatio positorum in linea predicamentali in omnibus predicamentis, nam ordinata in aliquibus predicamentis sic se habent quod semper superius predicatur de suo inferiori, ut patet in predicamento substantiae . . . non autem sic est de omnibus predicamentis, nam in predicamento 'quando,' non est sic, non enim bene dicitur 'omne heri est quando,' et sic de aliis multis. . . . Et ratio istius diversitatis est, quia quamvis omnia predicamenta veras res important, non tamen eodem modo ipsas important, et ideo non eodem modo de se invicem predicantur, nec eodem modo secundum superius et inferius ordinantur." In contrast to Boethius (Migne PL 64, cl. 180 b) who says "hac enim enumeratione major non potest inveniri," Ockham says (Exp. aur., II, 42v): "sciendum circa numerum et sufficientiam predicamentorum quod difficile est probare numerum et sufficientiam eorum, scil. quod sint tantum decem predicamenta."

signify the *genus generalissimum* of one of these categorical orders.
In the first sense the word "predicament" or "category" is
a word of second imposition, similar to "declension" or to a
purely grammatical term. In the second sense, it is a term
of second intention which stands for terms of first intention;
for if by "predicament" we mean the terms "substance,"
"quality," "relation," etc., then "predicament" is a term
that signifies and stands for terms.[1]

For a thing to "be *in* a predicament" may also be taken
in two senses. If we mean by those things which are "in a
category," the *things signified* by the terms ordered under the
genus generalissimum of that category, then nothing is in a
category except individual substances or individual qualities.
But the more usual sense of "being in a category" is this:
that of which the *genus generalissimum* of any category is predicable, in a proposition whose terms are taken significatively,
is a term in that category. In this sense, it is not the things
signified by terms of first intention that are in the categories,
but it is the *terms* of first intention that are in the categories
—and in this sense genera and species can be said to be substances, because such terms are in the category of substance.[2]

The division of terms of first intention into the ten categories
—ten ways in which things may be *said to be*—, is a division
determined by the kinds of question concerning substances,

[1] S. tot. log., I, 40, 14r: "Hoc nomen predicamentum est nomen secundae
impositionis vel intentionis . . . quamvis illa de quibus predicatur sint incomplexae primae intentionis. . . . Unomodo (accipitur 'predicamentum')
pro toto ordine aliquorum ordinatorum secundum superius et inferius . . .
aliomodo accipitur pro primo et communissime in tali ordine. . . . Et hoc
secundo modo accipiendo predicamentum, quodlibet predicamentum est unum
incomplexum primae intentionis, et hoc quia significat res quae non sunt signa."

[2] S. tot. log., I, 40, 14v: "dicendum est quod aliquid esse in predicamento
dupliciter accipitur. Uno modo pro illo quod sic est in predicamento quod de
pronomine demonstrante ipsum predicatur primum illius predicamenti sumptum
significative, et sic accipiendo esse in predicamento, nihil est in genere substantiae
nisi substantia particularis, quia nihil est substantia nisi substantia particularis.
Et sic accipiendo esse in predicamento, omnia universalia quae important praecise
substantias sunt in predicamento 'qualitas,' quia quodlibet universale est qualitas
(*scil.* animae). Aliter accipitur esse in predicamento pro illo de quo significative
sumpto predicatur primum illius predicamenti significative sumptum, et sic
quaedam universalia sunt in genere substantiae, quia de quibusdam universalibus
significative sumptis predicatur 'substantia' quando sumitur significative, sic
dicendo 'omnis lapis est substantia,' 'omnis homo est substantia'. . . ."

to which the terms can be intelligible and appropriate answers. As long as we are talking about *things* that are not terms, the ten different sorts of question that may be asked are irreducible to one another; for though the *term* "place" has a nominal definition (such as that given by Aristotle, Physics IV, 4, 212a 6–7), this definition is of the term, and is not an answer to the question "Where is this thing?"[1]

We may now state Ockham's ways of answering two questions pertinent to the analysis of the terms with which Aristotle's *Categories* is concerned. (1) Are the ten predicaments distinct and irreducible because they signify ten distinct and irreducible kinds of "real" entities? Ockham's answer is no—they are ten distinct ways of signifying individuals in abstraction from the contingent circumstances of their existence, and from the truth or falsity of judgments about them. The analysis of these modes of signification presupposes, as principles of signification and of definition only the distinction between the two kinds of elements involved in discursive signification as such—namely, between substances and the qualitative contraries, signified disjunctively by the two kinds of absolute terms. (2) Is the order of more and less universal, within the different categories, based on a corresponding hierarchy of elements or "parts" of individual things *in re*? The answer is no—generic terms signify the same individuals that specific terms signify, and the difference is in the mode of signification. The "Tree of Porphyry" is an order of terms according to predication, not according to any order of universal parts *in* individual things.

In his analysis of each category, Ockham applies this point of view, with precision and consistency, to the questions discussed by Aristotle, and seeks to show how those terms which signify individuals conjunctively (e.g. "similarity"), or

---

[1] S. tot. log., I, 40, 15r: "Et sufficiat scire quod omne incomplexum per quod convenienter responderi potest ad aliquam quaestionem factam de substantia est in aliquo predicamento, sive illud sit adverbium, sive verbum, sive nomen, sive prepositio cum suo casuali. Alia autem incomplexa non sunt in aliquo predicamento, propter quod coniunctiones et syncathegoreumata in nullo predicamento reponuntur, per talia enim ad nullam quaestionem respondetur."

connotatively (e.g. "similar"), differ as forms of signification, reducible in every case to the principles of signification and of definition which are the absolute terms. Ockham's analysis, both from the standpoint of logic and from that of physics and mathematics, constitutes an illuminating and significant contribution to the aristotelian tradition, offering an alternative to the porphyrian interpretation which has, in the history of aristotelianism, enjoyed such unbroken immortality.

II

The term "substance," in the strict sense, is a term of first intention that is the most general answer appropriate to the question "What is this?" pointing to something. As such, it is the *summum genus* of a category of terms which signify individual things by what they are, in the unqualified sense of the word "is." The "predicamental line" is the order of these terms according to greater or less universality in predication, such that whatever things the inferior term signifies, are also signified by the superior term.

Aristotle's distinction between first and second substances is a distinction between two kinds of terms included in the category of substance, and it is not a distinction between two kinds of things signified by these terms. For all terms in the category of substance signify *things that are* in the unqualified sense of "is," but since, taken in itself, that which is something is *per se* one thing, it follows that all terms in the category of substance signify things which are individual. That this is the case is easily shown from Aristotle's statement, in the *Metaphysics*, that no universal is a substance; it can also be demonstrated from the *dictum de omni et de nullo*, as follows: Whatever is denied of every discrete term of which a common term is predicable significatively, is denied universally of the common term; but the term "second substance" is denied of every discrete term of which the common term *substance* is significatively predicable; therefore the term "second substance" is denied universally of the term "substance."

Consequently, it is impossible that any second substance should be a substance, if the term "substance" be taken significatively as standing for things outside the mind. The distinction, therefore, between first and second substances is intelligible only as a distinction between two kinds of *terms* that signify individual substances—namely, first substances are those terms which can stand for one individual substance only (like "Socrates," "this man,"), and second substances are those terms which can stand for many individual substances understood by a single univocal concept. But whether the term be a first substance or a second substance, it must stand for individuals of which the term "substance" is a sign, without connoting or consignifying anything distinct from the individual natures of the things for which it can stand.[1]

Though Aristotle sometimes uses the term "first substance" as a term of first intention, this use is improper, and is to be understood metaphorically—i.e., because first substances are *signs* proper to a single individual, the name of the sign is

---

[1] S. tot. log., I, 42, 15r: "Aliter dicitur substantia strictissime de illo quod nec est accidens alteri inhaerens, nec est pars essentialis alicuius; et illo modo substantia ponitur genus generalissimum quod secundum Aristotelem dividitur in substantias primas et secundas, sed non est intelligendum quod sit divisio alicuius communis predicabilis de suis dividentibus per se, sive de pronominibus demonstrantibus illa dividentia. Nam demonstrando quaecumque substantiam secundam, haec est falsa, 'hoc est substantia,' imo haec est vera, 'nulla substantia est substantia secunda.' . . ." "Item secundum doctrinam Aristotelis, quicquid negatur ab omnibus contentis sub aliquo communi negatur universaliter ab illo communi; sed substantia secunda negatur universaliter ab omni contento sub substantia; ergo negatur universaliter a substantia." Exp. aur., II, 45r: "omnis substantia quae est vera res contenta in genere substantiae est simpliciter substantia prima, et individua, et singularis, ita quod genera et species et ipsummet genus generalissimum non sunt substantiae verae extra animam, nec sunt de essentia substantiarum particularium, quia sunt quaedam intentiones, extra animam nullo modo existentes, vel voces, vel alia signa importantia veras substantias. . . . Causa autem quare Aristoteles sic dividit substantiam est ista, quia philosophus principaliter in isto libro determinat de incomplexis ex quibus fiunt propositiones et sillogismi, et quia magna differentia est inter nomen vel incomplexum importans praecise unam rem, et inter nomen vel incomplexum importans plures res, et quaedam incomplexa contenta sub generalissimo important plures res et quaedam non, ideo necesse fuit distinguere talia posita in linea predicamentali, et aliqua vocavit substantias primas, et aliqua substantias secundas, non tamen quia sint verae substantiae, sed quia important substantias multas. . . . Quod autem secundae substantiae non sint verae substantiae extra et de essentia primarum substantiarum potest probari per philosophum primo Met. . . ." Cf. Arist., Met. A, 990b 9—991b 8; Z, 1038b 15–6; H, 1042a 22.

applied metaphorically to what it signifies. Aristotle, as Ockham occasionally points out, often uses his terms somewhat loosely, though the sense in which he is using them is in most cases easily determined. In the present instance we need only refer to his statement that "All substance appears to *signify* that which is individual," and that "in the case of first substances this is indisputably true," to see that first and second substances are distinguished as two kinds of signs of, or ways of signifying, individuals.[1]

The statement that of secondary substances the specific term is more truly substance than the genus, means only that the species signifies individual substances more determinately than the genus. The statement that "it is a common characteristic of all substance that it is never present in a subject," must be understood only of substance in the sense of substances outside the mind; for substantial *terms*, *qua* parts of propositions or of complex signs, can be said to be present in a subject, as parts are present in a whole, or as genus and differentiae are present in a single definition.[2]

Second substances are differentiated from first substances in that they are said to be predicable univocally, which is not true of first substances, since only what is predicable of terms signifying numerically distinct individuals can be said to be predicable univocally. This distinction is taken to show that universals (or "second substances") do not, in Aristotle's opinion, signify a common nature primarily, and individuals

---

[1] Arist., Cat. 5, 3b 10-1. Ockham, Exp. aur., II, 45v: "Intelligendum est tamen quod equivoce accipit philosophus 'substantias primas,' quia aliquando vocat substantias primas ipsas res extra animam, et aliquando vocat primas substantias nomina ipsarum rerum extra animam. . . . Ex illa auctoritate patet quod illa quae significant *hoc aliquid* appellat substantias primas, dicens quia de primis quidem substantiis indubitabile et verum est quod *hoc aliquid* significant. Sed illa quae significant non sunt substantiae, quia res substantiales significantur sed non significant, igitur illa quae in rei veritate non sunt substantiae vocat substantias. . . ."

[2] Exp. aur., II, 47r: "dicendum est absolute quod nunquam fuit intentio philosophi quod genera et species essent vere substantiae extra animam, nec quod essent de essentia individuorum, et ideo species non est magis substantia realis quam genus, nec econverso. Sed magis substantiam vocat illud quod expressius et distinctius et determinatius ipsam rem significat, *scil.* istam substantiam individuam." Cf. Arist., Cat. 5, 3a 6; and Ockham, S. tot. log., I, 43, 15v.

only secondarily *by* this common nature. For if that were so, second substances would be signs of one thing, primarily, and hence could not be differentiated from first substances on the ground of being predicable univocally—at least not in the unqualified sense in which Aristotle states the distinction.[1]

While primary substances (i.e., discrete terms) signify one thing and not many, secondary substances (genera and species) signify many things *aeque primo*, by a single intention or act of understanding. Thus it is said that while primary substances signify *hoc aliquid* ("this somewhat") second substances signify *quale quid* (the "such"). Three ways are distinguished by Ockham in which *quale quid*, or the "such," is signified: (1) accidentally, by a term which stands for individual substances by connoting something extrinsic to their individual nature; (2) essentially but connotatively, by a term which stands for individual substances by indicating a determinate part of their essential or undivided nature—thus the essential differentia stands for individual substances by indicating that by which they are understood to differ *per se* from other individual substances signified by the same proximate genus; and (3) essentially and absolutely, or non-connotatively, by a term which signifies many individuals, not as one thing, but disjunctively, in such manner that each individual signified by the term is understood to be, *per se*, just *such* an individual as each of the other individuals signified by the term.[2]

---

[1] S. tot. log., I, 43, 16r: "Secunda proprietas substantiae est quod omnibus substantiis secundis et etiam differentiis convenit univoce predicari, quamvis illa proprietas non conveniat primis substantiis." Ibid.: "hoc enim nomen 'homo' non significat primo unam naturam communem omnibus hominibus sicut multi errantes imaginantur, sed significat primo omnes homines particulares. . . . Ille enim qui primo imposuit hanc vocem 'homo' ad significandum, videns aliquam hominem particularem, instituit hanc vocem 'homo' ad significandum illum hominem et quamlibet talem substantiam qualis est homo ille," i.e., if the generic or specific term were a function of the act of understanding one individual only, or of understanding one nature distinct from individuals, it would signify *hoc aliquid*, and not *quale quid*—but Aristotle says that such terms signify *quale quid* and not *hoc aliquid*.

[2] Exp. aur., II, 51v–52r: "concreta accidentium significant *quale quid* quia significant qualitates quae sunt extra essentiam ipsarum pro quibus predicantur. Differentiae vero dicuntur significare *quale quid* quia significant partem rei quae non est tota essentia rei. Sed secundae substantiae dicuntur significare *quale*

Thus Aristotle's statement, that "species and genus determine the quality with reference to a substance," should not be taken to mean that genera and species signify individual substances by indicating a form or quality distinct from these individuals—such a view would destroy the middle term of demonstration, which must be a term that is a univocal and essential sign of many. Rather Aristotle's statement means that a generic or specific term, though it signifies nothing other than the individual things for which it can stand, does not signify any one of them by distinguishing it from the others, but rather by indicating it to be *such* an individual as the others are. Thus, if it were known that some individual was *a* man, it would not thereby be known that it was this man rather than that man; but it would be known that whatever individual was intended, was an individual *such as* this man or that man is. Hence discrete terms signify *hoc aliquid*, but universals, because they signify many individuals by a single intention, are said to signify *quale quid*.[1]

---

quid quia non significant praecise unum numero, sed multa; et hoc satis innuit Aristoteles (Cat. 5, 3b 15) quando dicit non tamen verum est, *scil.* quod secunda substantia significat *hoc aliquid* sed magis *quale quid* significat, nec enim unum numero est quod subiectum est quemadmodum prima substantia; sed de pluribus 'homo' et 'animal' dicuntur."

[1] Exp. aur., II, 51v–52r: "Ecce manifeste quod per hoc quod 'homo' significat multa et predicatur de multis, probat philosophus quod significat quale quid, et ita quicquid multa significat, quale quid significat; quia scilicet significat unum et aliquid aliud. Unde sciendum quod quando dicit philosophus quod genus et species circa substantiam qualitatem determinat (Cat. 5, 3b 18–20), non est intelligendum quod significant aliud a substantia individua, et (quod) ideo dicuntur determinare circa substantiam qualitatem; sed ideo dicuntur circa substantiam qualitatem determinare, quia scilicet, cognito de aliquo quod est homo vel animal, non propter hoc habetur distincta cognitio quod est hoc aliquid et non illud aliud (demonstrando aliud individuum); sed habetur cognitio per hoc quod est unum tale quale est aliud individuum, et ideo quasi videtur importare quale quid. Verbi gratia, si videam aliquod animal a remotis, si cognosco quod est animal, adhuc tamen non cognosco quod est Socrates vel Plato, sed cognosco quod est unum tale quale est Socrates. Similiter si cognoscam quod est homo non cognosco propter hoc quod est Socrates, sed cognosco quod est unum tale quale est Socrates; et ideo tam 'homo' quam 'animal' videntur significare unum quid tale quale est Socrates, et ita significant quale quid, quia hoc et non aliud est significare quale quid. Et propter hoc quod 'animal' significat plura quam 'homo,' magis appropinquat ad quale, quia per hoc minus cognoscitur quod est hoc et non aliud, demonstrando aliud individuum determinatum, *scil.* Socratem."

A further property of substance mentioned by Aristotle is that substance has no contrary. This characteristic, as applied to *terms* in the category of substance, is revealed by the definition of contrary terms—i.e., terms are contraries when they cannot be predicated of the same individual subject, or singular term, simultaneously, though they can successively. But every subject of which contrary terms are predicable, stands for something for which the term "substance" can stand; and since contrary terms cannot be predicated of each other, it follows that every substantial term, though it can be a subject of contrary predicates, is itself the contrary of no predicate. It is true, likewise, that substances *in re* have no contraries (which is probably what Aristotle had chiefly in mind); for the individual is *per se* one, and every substantial term signifies individuals *per se*, so that co-ordinate species of substance cannot signify a single identical thing either at the same time or successively.

That substances, according to Aristotle, are not distinguished from each other as contraries, shows that the principles of matter and form are strictly and literally principles of substance only *qua* changeable, and not *qua* beings, in the unqualified or metaphysical sense. In other words, there is no "prime matter" to be a subject of contrary *substantial* determinations, for if there were, substances would be differentiated as contraries. So the use of the antithesis of matter and form, or of potentiality and act, as principles by which being in the unqualified sense can be explained, is purely analogical; were this not the case, we would be positing diverse principles prior to being, so that metaphysics would no longer be first philosophy, but would be identified with physics, or with discursive science of the changeable. [1]

[1] S. tot. log., I, 43, 16r: "Quarta proprietas substantiae est quod substantiae nihil est contrarius." As applied to things *in re*, contraries are defined as follows: "Stricte dicuntur illae res contrariae quae in eodem subiecto mutuo se expellunt et partabiliter in eodem subiecto acquiruntur vel acquiri possunt, saltem naturaliter; et illo modo nulla substantia contrariatur alteri." Though it was often said that two substantial forms are contrary because they cannot both inform the same matter, Ockham, who recognized no "prime matter" absolutely and really distinct from form, but considered "matter" to be a term that signifies substance

That substance does not admit of variation of degree means, according to Ockham, that of no subject can any universal term of the category of substance be truly predicated in combination with the adverb "more" or "less." We cannot say that Socrates is more man now than he was before, except in a metaphorical sense, nor that he is more man than Plato, if Plato be a man.[1]

An important consequence of the chief property of substance —namely, that it *alone* is said to be capable of receiving contrary determinations successively, is that only substances are the subjects of accidental determinations. Hence the thesis upheld, in Ockham's time, by *multi moderni*, and which in modern philosophy became very widely accepted, that qualities are attributable to substances by reason of quantitative determinations of the substance, is shown to be against the principles of Aristotle. Since only substance is subject of contrary determination or of change, it follows that that which is changeable or potential, is that which is a substance, and not any accident or property, or potentiality, distinct from it. From this it follows that, according to Aristotle, there is no distinction *in re* between an individual substance and its potentiality of change, or, for example, between the soul and its faculties, if the soul is a substance.[2]

---

privatively or as determinable with respect to accidental contraries, denies that such a position is attributable to Aristotle. The philosophical consequences of regarding substances as determinations of a common substratum in itself indeterminate, are fundamental; the platonist notion of space as the "receptacle" or "mother of forms," as well as the atomist doctrine of the "void," are forms of this position, which received frequent criticism from Aristotle. To make matter and form causes of the being of substances, in the unqualified sense of being, constitutes an identification of physics with metaphysics, which at the same time changes physics from a demonstrative science to a dialectic.

[1] S. tot. log., I, 43, 16r: "Quinta proprietas substantiae est quod substantia non suscipit magis et minus, quae sic intelligenda est quod de nulla una substantia numero potest verificari aliquod commune de genere substantiae cum hoc adverbio 'magis,' et postea cum hoc adverbio 'minus'; nec econverso." Exp. aur. II, 52r: "Sed hoc est sic intelligendum. . . quod nulla una substantia est magis substantia quam alia una substantia eiusdem rationis."

[2] S. tot. log., I, 43, 16v–16r: "Aliud sequitur esse de mente Aristotelis quod nullum accidens est subiectum alterius accidentis, saltem accidentis habentis contrarium. Ex quo sequitur quod est extra mentem philosophi dicere quod intellectus et voluntas sunt quaedam accidentia ipsius animae intellectivae, in

III

While the terms in the category of substance are such that any terms of which they are predicable significatively, always and without exception stand for individual things *in re* which can be called substances, the terms in the other nine categories, with the exception of the abstract qualitative contraries, do not signify *per se* the individual things outside the mind for which they can stand. They are not, in other words, appropriate answers to the question "What *is* this thing?" pointing to something. For although we may denote Socrates by the term "six feet tall," or by the term "teacher of Plato," or by the term "learned," such terms signify the thing that is the man Socrates, through indicating one or more substances or qualities really distinct from what is signified by the term "this man," applied to Socrates.[1]

---

quibus primo recipiuntur intentiones et volitiones, et tales actus et habitus. Et eodem modo potentiae sensitivae secundum eum non sunt quaedam accidentia recipientia aliqua alia accidentia. Sequitur etiam secundum eum quod relationes non sunt quaedam res distinctae realiter a substantia, realiter existentes in quantitate et qualitate quae sunt accidentia realiter existentia in substantia. Unde intentio Aristotelis est quod omne accidens est immediate existens in substantia ita quod inter substantiam et quodcumque accidens suum, nihil est medium in ratione subiecti."

De Wulf, *Hist. of Med. Phil.*, II, p. 183, Note 4, states that for Ockham quantity or extension is identical with the essence of bodies, "as in the system of Descartes." This is scarcely the case, since for Descartes bodies were defined as *res extensae;* for Ockham a "body" is defined by the definition signifying it through its essential principles, i.e., "material (or changeable) substance," and no quantitative terms can enter into its real definition. For Descartes the quantitative term signified material substance essentially, but for Ockham it signifies substances accidentally or only in contingent propositions.

[1] Exp. aur., II, 64v: "Secundum intentionem Aristotelis nulla res extra quae non est signum nec nomen nec intentio animae, est per se in quocunque genere nisi tantum in genere substantiae vel qualitatis; quia de nulla re quae non est nomen vel signum aliquid aliud predicamentum per se predicatur, sed omne aliud predicamentum aliquid extrinsecum tali rei importatae vel consignificat vel connotat, et ideo de nulla tali predicatur in quid. . . ." e.g., when we ask "How much?" or "How many?" we do not mean "How much quantity?" or "How many numbers?" but rather "How much of this or that substance?" or "How many individual substances or qualities such as are signified by this or that substantial or qualitative term?" In the S. tot. log., I, 53, 22r,

In the book of *Categories* Aristotle, after discussing substance, takes up quantitative predicates. He starts out by making two general divisions of such terms, according to whether they signify (*a*) discrete quantities or continuous quantities, and (*b*) quantities consisting of parts which have relative position to each other, or quantities consisting of parts which do not have relative position to each other though they may have an order of prior and posterior. Number and speech are given as instances of discrete quantities; lines, surfaces, solids, and, besides these, time and place, are instances of continuous quantity. Aristotle distinguishes between the discrete and the continuous by stating that the parts of a discrete quantity have no common boundary at which they join, whereas the parts of a continuum have such a common

---

in discussing the predicament *ad aliquid* (relation), Ockham says: "Et quod distinctio predicamentorum non sumitur ex distinctione rerum importarum, sed potius ex distinctione interrogationum de individuis substantiae, ut docet Commentator VII Met., non enim putandum est decem genera esse decem res extra animam aut significare decem res quarum nulla significatur nisi per unum illorum, sed doctrina peripateticorum assignat decem genera fore decem terminos easdem res aliter et aliter importantes, quemadmodum enim partes orationis possunt esse distinctae et tamen significare idem, ut 'album,' 'albescens'; sic cum distinctio entis per absolutum et respectivum non est entis inquantum ens, sed terminorum . . . cum nulla res proprie dicatur absoluta aut respectiva. . . ."

The above indicates clearly Ockham's view that the book of *Categories* is not a book of metaphysics, and that neither logic nor the discursive real sciences deal with being *qua* being, or with the transcendental terms which signify being *qua* being. Even the qualitative contraries which are first principles, together with substances, for physics, and which are signified by terms that are called "absolute" by the fact that they are principles of the definition of the attributes demonstrated of substances, are first and "absolute" principles only for discursive science, and not for metaphysics. Why they should be first principles of physics is explicable by the fact that physics is the science of substances *qua* changeable and *qua* perceptible, and the qualitative contraries are indispensable starting points of perception and of the analysis of change; the science of things *qua* perceptible and *qua* changeable, therefore, involves an act of abstraction whereby that which changes and which is perceived to be, is differentiated from the contraries with respect to which it changes and by which it has been perceived to be. But since the middle term of affirmative demonstration in physics, or in any real science, is always a genus which signifies substances without connoting any determinate contraries, the differentiation of substance and the contraries (or of matter and form) is offset by its integration through such a middle term. Science is of propositions, but every proposition involves a differentiation of subject and attribute; yet the act of understanding by which a proposition is evidently known to be true, is not the act of understanding this differentiation, but of understanding the being and unity of the *substances* for which the terms stand.

boundary. For example, the parts of a line have as common boundary the point dividing it into parts.[1]

According to Ockham, it was generally held by the *moderni* that terms in the category of quantity signify something really distinct from substances or qualities, so that concrete quantitative terms, and the abstract terms corresponding to them, stand for entirely distinct things. Thus "length" was said to stand for something distinct from that which is long, but present in it—just as "heat" stands for something distinct from that which is hot, but present in it. Against this view, which amounts to holding that the term "quantity" signifies real accidental forms, so that the different kinds of quantity are just so many species of quality, Ockham devotes many pages of detailed argument, not only in his logical works, but also in his *De sacramento altaris*, which discusses the same problem in connection with the theological dogma of transsubstantiation.[2]

If quantitative terms, in general, signify something really distinct from substances or qualities, then the terms "point," "line," "surface," etc., will indicate something positive and really distinct from anything that can be called a substance or a quality. That this is not the case is shown by the following argument.

First therefore it must be shown that a point is not something other than a substance or a quality, or than the other things which

[1] Arist., Cat. 6, 4b 20–5a 14. Ockham, Exp. aur., II, 54r: "Illud est quantitas continua cuius partes ad unum communem terminum copulantur; sed 'linea,' 'corpus,' 'superficies,' 'tempus,' et 'locus' sunt huius modi; igitur etc.; major est manifesta, minorem probat quantum ad quamlibet sui partem. Nam partes lineae copulantur ad aliquem communem terminum, *scil.* ad punctum, et partes superficiei ad lineam, et corporis partes ad superficiem; et partes temporis, praeteritum scilicet et futurum, ad praesens; et partes loci copulantur ad unum terminum communem, quia partes corporis occupant locum sed partes corporis copulantur ad aliquem communem terminum, igitur similiter partes loci ad eundem communem terminum copulantur. Ad evidentiam totius praecedentis et istius capituli est intelligendum quod non est intentio Aristotelis quod quantitas sit quoddam praedicamentum importans rem absolutam realiter et totaliter distinctam a rebus in genere substantiae et in genere qualitatis, sicut communiter tenetur, sed est intentio sua quod nulla res importatur per genus quantitatis quin sit realiter substantia vel qualitas."

[2] Cf. T. B. Birch, *The De Sacramento Altaris of William of Ockham*, published by The Lutheran Literary Board, Burlington, Ia., 1930, which gives the text and a translation.

are commonly called quantities by the moderns; for if a point is any such distinct thing, it will be distinct from a line, but this is false. For if a point were anything distinct from a line, I ask, either it would be part of a line or not. It cannot be said that it is, for according to the philosopher, Physics VI, no line is composed of points. . . . If however the point is not a part of the line, it is likewise obvious that the line is not part of the point; and thus they are two things totally distinct, of which neither is a part of the other; and it is plain that if the point is not part of the line, *a fortiori* it is not a part of anything else. From this I argue thus: whenever there is some absolute and positive entity which is neither an essential part of another thing, nor a first thing (i.e., a transcendental first principle), that thing is *per se* in some predicament, and not merely accidentally so or by reduction; but "point" is not in any predicament *per se*, therefore it is not such a thing. The major is plain, because it is by this that matter and form are not *per se* in the genus of substance, since they are essential parts of something which is *per se* in the genus of substance; nor can any other reason be given why one thing is *per se* in one genus rather than in another. The minor is also obvious, because the point is not in the predicament of substance, as is plain, nor is it in the predicament of quantity (scil. *per se*), for then it would be a quantity (for according to those who hold this view, every genus is predicable *in quid* of anything *per se* contained under that genus). Nor is it in the predicament of quality, as is plain, nor in any other accidental category, and therefore it is not *per se* in any category, nor is it in any through reduction, as has been shown (i.e., where it was shown that it is not an essential part of anything that is *per se* in a category), and therefore it is not any such distinct entity.[1]

The point is not a magnitude nor a multitude, and hence it is not *per se* a quantity; rather the term "point" is an intention of the mind signifying a substance as limited with respect to length. It is not by anything extrinsic to itself that a given line is limited in length—a line is not finite by anything other than itself, for if it were not of itself determinate as a length, it would not be a line. Similarly, "line" is a term signifying something as determinate with respect to length (or as limited *qua* surface); but length is not something distinct from that which is long, since any substance having parts with relative position to one another, can merely through motion of these

[1] Exp. aur., II, 54v.

parts become longer or shorter, without anything being added to it or subtracted from it. In the same way "surface" and "solid" signify nothing distinct *in re* added to, or formally inhering in, a substance; but they are ways of signifying a substance as determinate with respect to two, or three, ways of measuring it.[1]

Time, in the same way, is not a distinct entity added to, or inhering in, substances or qualities; for a thing cannot be a subject in which something else inheres, unless that which inheres in it actually exists. But the parts of time do not actually exist (since the present is not a part, but a division, of time—a division into two parts, past and future); therefore neither time as a whole, nor any part of time, is anything really distinct from individual things which endure.[2]

That discrete quantities, such as number, do not signify things really distinct from substances or qualities numbered, is easily shown. If a number were an accidental form really inhering in a subject, both the number and its subject being distinct individual things, it would follow necessarily that the number, and any subject in which it inhered, would be *per se* one. But if we had a trio of dogs, and if it were asked whether "threeness" was present, in its *per se* unity as a "real" number, in each dog, or whether one part of it was present in one, another part in another, and the third part in the third dog, both alternatives would be impossible. For it could not be present as a whole in each dog, since the same self-identical

---

[1] Exp. aur., II, 54v: "punctus est nomen vel intentio importans non ulteriorem pertransitionem secundum longitudinem . . . et ideo linea nunquam finitur alia re sed se ipsa finitur formaliter . . . unde circumscripta omni alia re, adhuc linea esset finita. . . . Linea . . . est notans aliquid esse longum, nam si substantia realiter habeat partes distinctas, possibile est quod illae partes longiori corpori coexistant et breviori, quantumcumque corpori aeque lato coexistant, sicut patet in rarefactione et condensatione, et ita ista substantia non erit longa propter aliquam rem absolutam sibi advenientem, sed ex hoc solum quod partes eius corpori longo coexistunt, vel coexistere possunt, ipsis non mutatis."

[2] Exp. aur., II, 55r: "Praeterea quod tempus non sit aliqua res talis alia ostendo, quia omnis res per se una habens partes distantes realiter, si sit accidens, est in aliquo subiective tam secundum se quam secundum partes suas. Sed tempus non est in aliquo subiective tanquam unum accidens ipsius, quia subiectum non est subiectum alicuius nisi quod actualiter existit, sed partes temporis non existunt secundum istos. . . . Praeterea, nulla pars temporis est, quia nec praeterita nec futura, igitur nec ipsum tempus est aliqua res distincta totaliter ab aliis rebus."

accident cannot be present in diverse subjects. But if *threeness* is present in the three dogs by its parts, then, since accidents are diverse by the diversity of their subjects, it is not a single distinct thing, and hence it is nothing *in re*. By the same argument it can be shown that the parts of spoken discourse, which is a discrete quantity in that it is composed of parts (syllables) that have no common boundary, are not anything really distinct from the sounds (which *per se* are qualities) numbered.[1]

Hence no species of quantity, either continuous or discrete, signifies anything *in re* distinct from substances or qualities; and therefore the term "quantity" is predicable *per se* of no absolute terms such as signify precisely individual things outside the mind, but it is predicable *per se* only of quantitative *terms*—i.e., terms which signify substances or qualities through connoting divisions into parts, or which signify them as taken together (as a multitude).[2]

One objection against Ockham's position might be based

[1] Exp. aur., II, 55r: "Item de quantitate discreta probo quod non sit talis res; et primo de numero, quia si sit accidens per se unum, oportet quod habeat subiectum per se unum. Sed nullum tale potest dari, quia accipio trinitatem trium canum, et quaero aut illa trinitas est subiective in quolibet illorum trium canum secundum se totam, aut una pars est in uno et alia in alio. Primum non potest dari, quia tunc idem accidens numero esset in diversis subiectis. Si detur secundum, igitur sicut subiectum diversarum partium non faciunt per se unum, ita nec accidentia existentia in eis facient per se unum." Cf. with Ockham's argument against the scotist thesis that numerical unity is posterior to specific unity; *ante*, p. 124, Note 2.

[2] Exp. aur., II, 55v: "Ex praedictis patet satis quod non est verum nec est intentio philosophi ponere quantitatem esse aliam rem absolutam et per se unam et totaliter distinctam ab aliis rebus. Sed intentio philosophi fuit assignare differentiam nominum et predicabilium intentionum quae non predicatur nisi de aliquo habente diversas partes, vel de rebus diversis et distinctis coniunctim sumptis. Et tunc potest fieri divisio talis, quia predicabile aut predicatur de aliquo per se uno composito ex partibus per se unum facientibus, aut predicatur de aliquibus simul sumptis et de nullo separatim. Si primo modo, sic accipitur divisio philosophi quando dicit quod aliqua habent positionem, et aliqua non habent. . . . Non sic autem est de numero quia ad hoc quod numerus predicatur de aliquibus simul sumptis nihil refert quod illa distant loco et situ vel non distent loco et situ. . . ." 56r: "Ex praedictis patere potest quod omne predicabile quod non predicatur nisi pro aliquo habente multas partes, vel nisi pro aliquibus multis simul sumptis et non pro aliquo illorum sumpto per se, est in genere quantitatis." Since a number signifies a multitude of individuals *simul sumptis* or *coniunctim*, and since any universal concept can determine such a multitude, a number, taken in itself, is, for Ockham as for many modern mathematicians, a "class of classes similar to a given class."

on Aristotle's statement that the parts of a continuous quantity have a common boundary; e.g., the parts of a line are joined by the point as by a common boundary. But since they are not joined by nothing, therefore the point is something. To this Ockham responds with several arguments to show the impossible consequences of holding the point to be something positive and actual in itself, distinct from the line. One such consequence is that in every line there would be an actual infinity of distinct positive entities joining its parts, a consequence which is in opposition to a fundamental aristotelian principle. Aristotle's words about the point as a common boundary should be interpreted not as if they meant that points are positive entities distinct from lines, but only in the sense that the term "point" signifies the absence of anything between the parts of a continuum—i.e., it signifies the line to be a continuum through negating any interposed entity by which it would be discontinuous.[1]

Another objection to Ockham's position is this. If "line," "surface," and "body" signify nothing distinct from substance they need not signify distinct things. But since distinct species in any genus are distinct because they denote distinct things, it would follow that "line," "surface," etc., are not distinct species of continuous quantity. To this Ockham replies that only species which are uniformly significative of the things

---

[1] Exp. aur., II, 56v: "Sed contra ista videntur esse multae auctoritates Aristotelis, quae sonare videntur quod quantitas est alia res a substantia et qualitate . . . nam dicit hic quod partes quantitatis continuae ad aliquem communem terminum copulantur . . . sed non copulantur ad nihil nec copulantur ad se ipsas, igitur punctus est alia res a partibus lineae, etc. . . . ; dicendum est quod intentio philosophi est dare differentiam inter continua et discreta, quae non est per hoc quod aliqua una res totaliter distincta liget eas partes adinvicem, sed quod illae sine omni intermedio imaginabili adinvicem extenduntur ita quod unum illorum vere extenditur ad aliud et econverso, et nisi ita extendantur ad invicem non sunt continua, et hoc vocat Aristoteles 'terminum communem,' scil., hoc ad illud extendi, et econverso; quasi si esset unum commune ad quod utrunque extenditur et non ultra." The continuum does not presuppose the divisions that can be made in it, but rather the divisions (points) presuppose the continuum. The concept "between," involved negatively in t'e concept of "point," is involved positively in the concept of "motion" or of "change." To be *between* is to be determinable by contraries, while the contraries are themselves understood to be, only through substance which has no contrary and is not a contrary.

for which they can stand, signify distinct things. But "line," "surface," and "body" are not uniformly significative of the substances for which they can stand, for when a substance is condensed it is less in quantity (i.e., in volume, surface, length, etc.) than when it is rarified, and yet nothing has thereby been generated or destroyed in it, but the substance remains essentially what it was. Consequently quantitative terms, which vary when that which they signify remains the same essentially, do not signify things by their specific nature, and they themselves are called species of quantity not because they signify distinct kinds of things, but because they are distinct kinds of quantitative terms.[1]

Since, according to Ockham, nothing is signified *per se* by a term in the category of quantity, and since quantitative terms are predicated contingently when the terms stand significatively for individual substances, how is it that mathematical propositions are necessary and universal? The answer lies in the distinction in mode of signification which is implicit in the use of the abstract quantitative term, in contrast to its concrete form. For though "quantity" and "quantum," like "man" and "humanity", are strictly synonymous when taken as standing for individual things with personal supposition, we do nevertheless use the concrete and abstract forms of such terms in different ways. For example, "quantum" is used to stand for any individual substance that is a quantum, without any further qualification; but "quantity" is used as equivalent to an expression containing a syncategorematic word, *scil.*, as equivalent to "quantum insofar as it is a quantum." Such a restriction, implicit in the abstract form of

---

[1] Exp. aur., II, 55r: "Et si quaeratur tunc quomodo 'linea,' 'superficies,' 'corpus' sunt distinctae species quantitatis, cum species distinctae distinctas importent res; dicendum est ad hoc quod omnes species quae uniformiter predicantur de rebus, ipsis manentibus, quarum quaelibet est per se una, important res distinctas. Sed tales species non sunt 'linea,' 'superficies,' 'corpus,' nam corpus non semper uniformiter predicatur de substantia, ipsa substantia manente, nam quando substantia densatur tunc est minus corpus, et quando rarefit tunc est maius corpus, et tamen nulla est rei absolutae corruptio nec rei absolutae generatio, sed tantum illa substantia maiori corpori extenditur nunc quam prius." Cf. Arist., *Physica* IV, 9, 217a 20–217b 11, on rarefaction and condensation, and the fact that it is not generation or corruption, but merely accidental change.

the term, implies that propositions whose subjects are abstract quantitative terms, are equivalent to hypothetical propositions; thus the proposition "Every triangle has internal angles equal to two right angles," or the proposition "The triangle as such has internal angles, etc.," is equivalent to the conditional proposition "If anything is a triangle, it has internal angles equal to two right angles."

An important difference between propositions with abstract quantitative terms as subjects, and those with abstract forms of substantial terms as subject, is that the mathematical propositions are demonstrable through elements of the *nominal definitions* of their terms, whereas a proposition like "Humanity (taken as 'man *qua* man') is capable of searching for food," is demonstrable through a middle term signifying essential nature—i.e., through "animal." This brings out the sense of the aristotelian statement that the objects of mathematics are distinct from physical substances only by the fact that the mathematical sciences consider the quantitative determinations of substance in abstraction from substances quantitatively determinate. Thus "the snub" is defined by the physicist as "a concave nose," by the pure mathematician as "concavity," and by applied mathematics as "nasal concavity."[1]

---

[1] Exp. aur., II, 58v: "quamvis quantitas non sit alia res a substantia et qualitate, tamen contingenter predicatur de substantia. . . ." Ibid., 56r: "Et si quaeratur an haec de virtute sermonis est concedenda, 'substantia est linea,' similiter talis, 'substantia est superficies,' . . . potest dici quod de virtute sermonis, si predicata praecise supponant pro rebus et non pro aliquo conceptu vel nomine, tales propositiones sunt concedendae, quia in talibus non videtur concreta et abstracta posse supponere pro diversis. . . . Intelligendum est etiam quod frequenter quando philosophus ponit talia abstracta non vult quod supponunt pro rebus, sed quod supponunt pro ipsis intentionibus animae quae sunt species." S. tot. log., I, 45, 18r: Referring to Aristotle's statement (Cat. 6, 5a 38—5b 10) that "album" is a quantum only per accidens, Ockham says that this does not imply that anything *in re* is a quantum per se, but it means merely that the term "quantity" is predicable universally and *per se primo modo* only of those terms in whose nominal definitions it is included. And though it is true to say that "omne album est quantum" (because any substance that can be white is signifiable by the term "surface"), this is because the middle term "surface" is included in the nominal definition of the *term* album, though it is not included in the essential definition of anything that the term "album" can stand for or denote. This is why quantitative terms, though they cannot denote anything *in re* which is not *per se* a substance or a quality, are nevertheless predicable contingently of sub-

WILLIAM OF OCKHAM

Aristotle's second manner of dividing quantities, into those which consist of parts having relative position to one another, and those consisting of parts which do not have relative position, brings up the question of the precise sense in which the word "part" is, in each case, to be understood. In the strict sense, only what is *per se one* can be said to have parts, and in this sense only such quantities as are divisible into co-existent continua, can be said to have parts—and it is only such quantities (namely "line," "surface," and "solid") that have parts with relative position to one another.

In a looser sense, the word "part" may signify any one of a number of things *taken together in predication*, even though these things do not form a *per se* unity; and in this broad sense Socrates and Plato may be said to be "parts" of what is signified by the word "couple," or this white thing and that white thing may be called parts of what is signified by the term "similarity." In the same sense we may speak of time or of speech, as having parts, as well as of number. Thus all discrete quantities, and continuous quantities, like time, which are not divisible into co-existent parts, can be said to have parts in this second sense; and these are the quantities which are said to have parts that do not have relative position, though they may have an order of prior and posterior. Accidentally it might happen that the things signified by a number, which in the loose sense are called "parts" of the number, had relative position to each other—but they would still not

---

stantial and qualitative terms. Hence it is a great mistake to hold, as De Wulf does, that Ockham identifies substance, quantity, and quality, in the sense that substances are essentially quantities, or in the sense that quantity defines substance. Cf. De Wulf, *Hist. of Med. Phil.*, II, p. 183, Note 4: "These (*scil.* quantity and extension) accordingly become identical with the essence of bodies, as in the system of Descartes." Ibid., p. 183, in the text: "Qualities in their turn are confounded with substances." Ockham's repeated assertion that the only "real distinction" between things signified by the ten predicaments is that between individual substances and individual qualities, shows the groundless character of M. De Wulf's statement.

On the ways of defining "snub," and the difference between the objects of physics and of mathematics, cf. Aristotle, Met. E, 1, 1025b 18–1026a 33. Cf. also Met. M, ch. 1–3, 1076a 8–1078b 6, which gives very direct and complete support to Ockham's analysis of quantitative terms and of their significative relation to substance.

be signifiable by a quantitative term of the first kind, because their relative position would not be between parts of a continuum, or of something *per se* one.[1]

Quantities which have parts that do not have relative position to each other, and which only have parts in the broader sense of the word "part," do nevertheless exhibit an order among these parts. Thus the parts of time are ordered as prior and posterior, as are also the parts of spoken discourse, or of number. The order of things numbered is, however, accidental, and attributable to the inability of the human soul, which numbers things, to do so except with an order of prior and posterior, as in counting. Hence the order in which things are counted is accidental to their signification as a multitude, by the number arrived at on the completion of the count.[2]

Since Aristotle uses the word "part" in the broad sense, as signifying any one of several things *considered together*, Ockham states that the division between quantities whose parts have position, and those whose parts do not have position, may be understood so as to include a kind of quantity not explicitly mentioned by Aristotle. This third species of quantity would consist of terms which signify a multitude of things taken together, as having determinate relative position *or* order, but which are not predicable distributively of terms that signify the individuals which compose the multitude.

[1] Exp. aur., II, 57v: "Postquam philosophus determinavit de una divisione quantitatis, in ista parte (Cat. 5a 15-37) exequitur de secunda dicens quod aliquae quantitates constant ex partibus habentibus positionem, et aliquae ex partibus non habentibus positionem . . . quantitates constantes ex partibus non habentibus positionem sunt tempus, et oratio, et numerus. . . . Sciendum est hic primo quod philosophus non accipit hic 'partem' stricte, pro illa scilicet quae facit per se unum cum alio, nam numerus tales partes non habet, nec similiter tempus, nec oratio; sed accipit hic 'partem' large, pro illo quod cum alio potest recipere predicationem alicuius predicabilis, et non per se sumptum, sicut Sortes et Plato sunt 'partes' binarii, quia scilicet de Sorte et Platone predicatur hoc predicabile 'duo' vel 'binarius,' et de neutro per se sumpto verificatur." Ibid., 57v: "partes numeri aliquando vere habent positionem, nam accipiendo duo corpora vere contingit assignare ubi situm est unum et ubi aliud, nec philosophus intendit hoc negare, sed intendit dicere quod accidit partibus numeri quod partes sint in distinctos situs, nihil minus 'numerus' predicaretur de eis. . . . "
[2] Exp. aur., II, 57v: "Sciendum est tertio quod partibus numeri accidit ordo, quamvis anima, quae debet ipsas numerare, secundum ordinem oportet quod procedat ab uno ad aliud. . . . "

Included in this kind of quantity are such terms as (1) "army," "populace"; (2) the abstract forms of universal terms when these are taken not as synonyms of their concrete forms but as "class names"; and (3) the names of artificial things, whose parts are not signified disjunctively by the name, and yet do not form a *per se* unity. In the strict and most proper sense of the words "part" and "number," neither this third kind of quantitative term, nor the term "number," can be said to signify things that are parts of what is by nature (or *per se*) one. Nor do they signify any one real thing (such as a subsistent form or "ideal number") of which the individual things numbered, or collectively signified, are parts.[1]

That Aristotle in his discussion of quantities is talking chiefly about terms, and not about things that are not terms, is

---

[1] Exp. aur., II, 56r: "Sciendum est tamen quod illud praedictum de divisione quantitatis per quantitatem habentem positionem et non habentem positionem, potest largius intelligi quam sit ibi dictum, ut dicatur omnis quantitas habere positionem quae requirit certam positionem et ordinem partium secundum situm distinctarum, sive illae partes faciant per se unum, ut dictum est ibidem, sive non; et isto modo potest dici 'civitas,' 'exercitus,' et huiusmodi, quantitas habens positionem." Ibid., 57r: "Ultimo sciendum quod ex ista littera (i.e., Cat. 5a 37–5b 10) non potest haberi quod non sint plures species quantitatis quam illae quas enumerat philosophus . . . et ideo in nullo est contra Aristotelem ponere aliquae species ibidem non enumeratas, sicut forte 'civitas,' 'regnum,' 'exercitus,' et huiusmodi habent aliquod genus contentum sub 'quantitate' predicabile de eis, quod non est aliquod illorum enumeratorum; et ita potest dici de artificialibus, qualiter tamen exponetur illud dictum Aristotelis 'naturalia non sunt artificialia vel non sunt in genere per se,' alibi patebit. Quod autem multa talia possint poni per se in genere quantitatis videtur manifeste, quia non apparet quod minorem unitatem habeant talia nec minus faciunt unum, quam numerus; sed numerus ponitur in genere quantitatis, igitur et talia eadem ratione." Ibid., 56r: "stricte sumendo numerum, numerus non predicatur nisi de illis quae non faciunt per se unum, et isto modo materia et forma in composito non sunt duae res, nec plures partes corporis sunt plures res. Large accipitur 'numerus' pro omnibus illis quorum unum non est aliud, sive faciant per se unum sive non, tamen accidit omnibus talibus quod faciant per se unum. Per istum modum talia predicabilia 'populus,' 'civitas,' . . . et universaliter omnia predicabilia quae non supponunt nisi pro multis simul acceptis et pro nullo illorum divisim sumpto, possunt poni in genere quantitatis, ut sic, quod non sit inter ea aliquis ordo . . . praeter illum ordinem qui est illorum quae sunt partes alicuius per se unius (quod dico propter materiam et formam in genere substantiae) quae non in alio predicamento per se continentur." In the strict sense, therefore, no number signifies a continuum, for a continuum, though divisible, is *per se* undivided. Ockham would not approve of the modern practice of signifying a continuum by an infinite number, unless the qualification were made that the infinite number is merely a sign of a potentially infinite number of successive operations applicable to the continuum.

indicated by his statement that quantities have no contraries. For if the quantitative terms "one cubic foot" and "two cubic feet" are predicated at different times of the term "gas" taken significatively, then these quantitative terms *do* stand for a substance by signifying contraries; i.e., in the case where the gas, without being added to or substracted from, has altered, by rarefaction, from the smaller to the larger volume. Hence, if "quantity" were understood as a term of first intention, Aristotle's statement that quantities have no contraries would be false. Indeed, one of the contrarieties between which change takes place, is described by Aristotle in the *Physics* (Book V, 2, 226a 23–33) as a contrariety with respect to quantity, between which increase and diminution takes place. Therefore the meaning of Aristotle's statement is that no quantitative *terms* are contrary to each other in such manner that they always signify contrary determinations of substance.[1]

That quantities do not admit of variation in degree means, for Ockham, that no quantitative term can be predicated significatively of anything with the adverb "more" or "less" added to it. Here again Aristotle is speaking of terms when he uses the word "quantities," and not of the things *in re* which they signify; for quantitative terms may very well stand for *things* which are more or less such and such, as when something three feet long is whiter than it was when it was two feet long.[2]

The distinctive or commensurate property assigned by Aristotle to quantity, that one quantity is said to be equal or unequal to another, applies to terms as signs either of things measured or divisible into parts, or of discrete things taken together as a multitude; but it does not apply *per se* to the individual things thus signified, for no substance is of itself

---

[1] S. tot. log., I, 47, 19r: "Dicendum est ergo quod intentio Aristotelis est quod haec est vera: 'quantitas quantitati contrariatur si termini supponant pro re extra'; tamen haec est vera 'nulli termini per se contenti in genere quantitatis contrariantur sic quod semper important res contrarias,' et illam propositionem intendit Aristoteles quando dicit quod quantitati nihil est contrarium."

[2] S. tot. log., I, 47, 19r: "quantitas non suscipit magis et minus; hoc est, nullum contentum in genere quantitatis predicatur de aliquo aliquando cum hoc adverbio 'magis,' aliquando cum hoc adverbio 'minus.'"

equal to another, nor is one substance equal to another by
any form or thing really distinct from it—rather it is equal
to the other insofar as it is signifiable by a term connoting
an operation of division, or of enumeration of parts, applicable
to the other.[1]

IV

In the case of the category of relation (*ad aliquid*), as in that
of quantity, Ockham insists that the individual things for
which relative terms can stand when taken significatively,
are not of themselves "relations," but are either individual
substances or individual qualities. Thus "similar," which
is a relative term, can stand for Socrates in the proposition
"Socrates is similar to Plato," but it does not signify or connote
or in any way indicate the existence of anything distinct
from the individual substances which are Socrates and Plato
—or from some qualitative determinations of them, with
respect to which they are said to be similar. In other words,
Socrates is not similar to Plato by reason of a third thing called
"similarity," but by reason of being a man just as Plato is,
or by reason of being white just as Plato is white—in short,
by reason of *quale quid* or *quale*, which are signified *per se*
only by terms in the categories of substance or of quality.[2]

[1] Exp. aur., II, 60r: "quantitati convenit secundum se esse aequale vel
inaequale, nam de omni quantitate vere predicatur quod est alteri quantitati
aequalis vel inaequalis, nam omne corpus est alteri corpori aequale vel inaequale,
et similiter omnis numerus alteri numero est aequalis vel inaequalis, et omne
tempus est alii aequale vel inaequale."

[2] Exp. aur., II, 64v: "secundum intentionem Aristotelis nulla res quae non
est signum nec nomen nec intentio animae est per se in quocunque genere nisi
tantum in genere substantiae vel qualitatis . . . ille homo ex hoc ipso quod genuit,
et posito filio, sine omni re adveniente sibi, dicitur vere pater, non propter aliquam
rem advenientem sibi, sed propter hoc solum quod ille homo incipit esse qui
dicitur filius eius. Similiter album dicitur simile de novo alteri propter hoc solum
quia illud aliud incipit esse album, et non propter aliquam rem sibi advenientem.
. . . Hic tamen est intelligendum quod philosophus . . . intendit quod relatio
advenit per predicationem; hoc est, de novo vere predicatur de aliquo propter
solam mutationem in alio, quia Sortem esse similem Platoni non est aliud quam
Sortem esse album et Platonem esse album, vel habere qualitates eiusdem rationis,
et ita . . . relatio non importat aliquam rem quae non sit de genere substantiae
vel qualitatis, et tamen de nulla re predicatur in quid; sicut 'simile' non predicatur
in quid nec de homine nec de albedine, et hoc quia connotat plus quam illud de
quo predicatur, et sicut est de quantitate et relatione ita est de omnibus sex
generibus aliis."

A problem arises, in connection with the word "relation" or "relative" itself, and in connection with the abstract forms of relative terms, as to whether they are terms of first intention, and if so, as to what things *in re* they can stand for. The term "similar" or "father" can stand for an individual substance, but of no individual substance or quality is it true to say "This is similarity" or "This is paternity." Likewise, "mover" and "moved," which are correlatives, can each stand for individual substances; but for what individual substance can "motion" stand? It cannot stand for any individual substance taken alone, says Ockham, and it does not signify any "universal thing" distinct both from concepts of the mind and from individuals *in re*; hence, if it is a term of first intention, it stands conjunctively for the two individuals, that are signifiable disjunctively by the concrete terms "mover" and "moved." The only remaining alternative is to regard such terms as "relation" or "motion" or "paternity," etc., as terms of second intention which stand for acts of the mind by which two individuals are signified as contingently together.

The word "relation," and even its concrete form "relative," presents a more difficult problem. The only two things for which the term "relation" could stand, or which it could be said to signify together (in the manner that "motion" is said to signify mover and moved together), would be things signified by the terms "relative" and "correlative." But nothing except what is a term is *per se* signified by the term "relative" or by the term "correlative," so that it is hard to see how the term "relation" or the term "relative" is a term of first intention. The terms ordered under it, which are called "relative terms" or "relations," *are* terms of first intention—in their concrete form undoubtedly so, and in their abstract form also, in the sense in which "motion" is said to signify the mover and the moved taken together, though it signifies neither of them taken alone.[1]

[1] Exp. aur., II, 65v: "manifeste patet quod relativa de quibus loquitur Aristoteles principaliter hic, sunt nomina et non res extra quae non sunt signa, sicut moderni dicunt." S. tot. log., I, 49, 20r: "Et ideo secundum opinionem Aristotelis, ut existimo, sive 'ad aliquid,' sive 'relatio' sive 'relativum' est nomen

Relatives, according to Aristotle, are things which are said to be "of something else," and practically all commentators illustrate this by adding that relatives are things which include an implicit reference to something in an oblique case, either genitive, dative, or ablative. But obviously only terms, and not anything *in re* signified by them, can be said to include a reference to something in an oblique case. The term "teacher," for example, which may stand for Socrates, includes the connotation "of a pupil" (let us say, Plato); thus we may say, pointing to Socrates, "This is a teacher of Plato," but we cannot say that he is "Socrates of Plato," or "a man of Plato." A further indication that relations were regarded by Aristotle as terms, and not as distinct entities *in re*, may be found in the *Physics*, Book III, where it is said that not every mover is moved. But if relations were entities distinct from substances and qualities, really existent *in* them, then every mover would in moving something else receive a new relation ("motion") and would thereby be itself changed, which Aristotle denies.[1]

---

secundae intentionis sive impositionis, et non nomen primae impositionis sive intentionis . . . debet concedi quod hoc nomen 'pater' est relativum, et non ille qui est pater."

Cf. Doncoeur, "Le nominalisme de G. Occam: la theorie de la relation," in *Revue Neo-scolastique*, 1921, pp. 5-25, on the question of whether or not Ockham considered the term "relation" or "relative" to be a term of second intention or of first intention. Doncoeur cites the following passage from Ockham's Comm. in Sent., I, Dist. 30, Qu. 1, Q: "dico quod relatio non est fundamentum, sed tantum intentio vel conceptus in anima importans plura absoluta, vel est plura absoluta, sicut populus est plures homines et nullus homo est populus. . . . Similitudo, sic in abstracto posita, non potest stare nisi pro intentione in anima, vel pro pluribus quorum quodlibet est simile." Doncoeur concludes that the S. tot. log., and the Comm. in Sent., are later works than the Exp. aur., because Ockham's views on relative terms seems firmer in them than in the Exp. aur. If any difference is to be found, however, it is slight—the solution of the problem of what terms like "similitudo" signify rests firmly on Ockham's way of distinguishing between the two senses in which *ens* is predicated of the terms in the categories, *divisim* or *coniunctim*, and Ockham's views on this subject are even more definitely and fully expressed in the Exp. aur. than in the S. tot. log.

[1] S. tot. log., I, 49, 20r: "*Ad aliquid* talia dicuntur quaecunque hoc ipsum quod sunt aliorum dicuntur vel quolibet aliter ad aliud" (says Aristotle in Cat. 7, 6a 36-7); "et exemplificat quomodo aliquid dicitur ad aliud diversimode, quia aliquid sub habitudine casus genitivi, dativi, vel ablativi. Ex quo arguo sic: nihil dicitur alterius sub habitudine casus genitivi vel sub alio casu nisi nomen; sed omne 'ad aliquid' dicitur ad aliud sub aliqua tali habitudine casuali; ergo

Finally, if relations were such distinct entities *in re*, it would follow that in any existing thing there would exist an actual infinity of such entities, since in any material substance there would be an infinity of relative positions of its parts. It is to be concluded, therefore, that the only things which are *per se* in the category of relation are terms—namely, any term which cannot be verified of anything for which it can stand without reference to some other term connected with it by a preposition or by an oblique case-ending, this other term being called its correlative.[1]

Some relatives, according to Aristotle, have contraries. This means, in Ockham's view, that relative terms may be *signs* of contrary qualities. Thus "knowledge," which is a relative term (since knowledge is knowledge *of* something), signifies a quality in the mind whose contrary is the relative term "error" (for error is error concerning something). Some relatives do not signify true contraries, as for example "double" and "half," because these may be true of the same thing at the same time, with respect to diverse things to which it is related. Hence two conditions are required for relative terms to be contraries: (1) they must signify contrary qualities, and (2) they must not be verifiable of the same thing at the same time.[2]

---

omne 'ad aliquid' est nomen ... relinquit ergo secundum philosophum quod 'ad aliquid' est nomen importans suum significatum sic quod non potest pro eo supponere nisi convenienter sibi posset addi aliquis casus obliquus." Exp. aur., II, 64r: "Praeterea philosophus III Physicis habet pro inconvenienti quod omne movens moveatur, . . . et per consequens si tales relationes essent res distinctae a rebus absolutis, omne movens moveatur quia reciperet talem respectum, quod est falsum." Cf. Arist., *Physics* III, 3, 202b 5–23; and *Phys.* VIII, 5, 258b 4–9.

[1] Exp. aur., II, 64r: "Praeterea si relationes essent tales res distinctae realiter, sequeretur quod in quocunque essent res infinitae distinctae realiter. . . . Ex istis patet quod omnia talia nomina quae non possunt verificari de aliquo nisi aliquo nomine expresso in certo casu vel sub intellectu, sunt ad aliquid et in predicamento relationis."

[2] Exp. aur., II, 65r: "in proposito aliqua nomina relativa dicuntur contraria quia sunt signa contrariorum, et hoc propter istam similitudinem, quia sicut illae res importatae non possunt eidem competere realiter, ita ipsa non possunt eidem competere per veram predicationem; et ita potest dici quod duo requiruntur ad hoc quod aliqua nomina . . . dicuntur contraria, *scil.* quod important vera contraria, et quod non possint vere dici de aliquo eodem simul. . . ."

Some relative terms admit of variation of degree, in the sense that they may be predicated with the adverbs "more" and "less" added to them, as when we say that Socrates is more like Plato than Cicero. But the variation signified by these adverbs does not involve a variation in degree of the relativity of the terms to each other, but only of the qualities compared. According to Ockham, only with respect to qualities *in re* can there be said to be variation in degree in the sense that a thing can become more or less something by addition or by loss without change of place or position. One thing does not become more similar to another with respect to similarity, nor with respect to its essential nature, but only with respect to qualitative determination.[1]

The distinctive property of relative terms is that every relative term has a single correlative, and is reciprocally connected with it. That the correlation is between terms, and not between things outside the mind for which the terms can stand, is indicated by Aristotle when he says that "The term slave, if defined as related, not to a master, but to a man, or a biped, or anything of that sort, is not reciprocally connected with that in relation to which it is defined, for the statement is not exact."[2] Nor will it do, adds Ockham, to say that although the things signified by the related terms are not reciprocally connected, yet the relation "founded in" those things is reciprocally connected with its correlative relation. For it is not true that "paternity" is reciprocally connected with "filiation," since we cannot say that "paternity is the paternity of filiation," though we can say that a father is father of a son. One man is not related to another by some

---

[1] Exp. aur., II, 65r: "Intelligendum quod aliquid dicitur suscipere magis et minus dupliciter; vel quia est vere augmentabile per additionem partis ad partem in eodem loco et situ, et isto modo nihil suscipit magis et minus secundum intentionem philosophi nisi sola qualitas, quia illa sola est augmentabilis isto modo; et ideo si 'relatio' non supponat nisi pro nominibus relativis, dicendum est quod relativa non suscipiunt magis et minus. Aliter dicitur aliquid suscipere magis et minus quod est verum predicabile cum hoc adverbio 'magis' et 'minus' . . . et isto modo multa nomina relativa suscipiunt magis et minus, nam Sortes est magis simile Platoni quam Cicero, et Cicero minus consimile Platoni quam Sortes, et isto modo loquitur Aristoteles in proposito."

[2] Arist., Cat. 7, 7a 28–30.

entity called "fatherhood," but a man comes to be called a father when another human being, generated by him, begins to exist.[1]

V

In the category of *quality* are included those terms, other than essential differentiæ of substance, which constitute appropriate answers to questions concerning the character (*quale*) of things. As Aristotle says, "Quality is a term that is used in many senses," and hence there is no single concept or meaning corresponding to the *summum genus* "quality," that is univocally predicable of all four of the species of quality enumerated by Aristotle. [2]

[1] Exp. aur., II, 67r: "Et si dicitur quod verum est quod res absoluta in qua fundatur relatio non dicitur ad convertentiam, sed illa relatio in re absoluta fundata dicitur ad convertentiam; hoc non valet, quia secundum istos 'paternitas' est relatio, sed illa paternitas non dicitur ad filiationem, non enim dicitur quod paternitas est filiationis paternitas . . . igitur remanet quod tantum nomen vel signum rei dicitur ad convertentiam, et ita cum philosophus dicat relativa dici ad convertentiam patet manifeste quod ipse per relativa vel relationes vel ad aliquid intelligit ipsa nomina vel signa rerum, et ita nomina relativa in isto capitulo describit et eorum proprietates assignat." Cf. S. tot. log., I, 49, 20r, where Ockham quotes Priscian as follows: "Ad aliquid dictum est quod sine intellectu illius ad quod dicitur proferri non potest." In discussing the reciprocal connection of relatives with their correlatives, in S. tot. log., I, 52, 21v, Ockham distinguishes between symmetrical and asymmetrical correlations as follows: "Sciendum est tamen quod aliquando idem nomen ponitur in recto et in obliquo, et ista vocantur relativa similium nominum, sive relationes aequiparantiae, ut 'simile' est simili simile, et aequale est aequali aequale. . . ." Others, such as "father" (for a father need not be a father of a father), "vocantur nomina relativa dissimilium nominum, sive disquiparantiae."

The two senses in which *ens* is predicable of the terms in the categories, i.e., predicable in one sense of terms which signify individual things *divisim*, and in another sense of terms which signify individuals *coniunctim* only, is nicely illustrated in the case of the category of relation. Nothing that can be understood to be *per se* one, or an individual thing, can be called a relation of similarity, because the concept "similarity" is an act of understanding two really distinct things, together; hence "similarity" can be said to stand for real things *coniunctim*, but not *divisim*.

[2] Arist., Cat. 8, 8b 26. Ockham, Exp. aur. II, 71v: "omne illud per quod respondetur ad quaestionem factam per quale, quod non est differentia essentialis, ponitur in predicamento qualitatis. . . . Philosophus in principio istius capituli dicit quod qualitas est unum eorum quae multipliciter dicuntur, volens quod non eodem modo predicatur de omnibus suis contentis." The differences between the mode of signification of each of the four species of qualitative terms, is briefly summed up as follows: "Aliqua de predicamento qualitatis important res simplices mere absolutas sine omni connotatione, ita scilicet quod quodlibet istorum de una re potest verificari" (such compose the first species of qualitative terms); "aliqua autem non sic important sed important plures res nec de una

The first kind of qualitative term signifies, according to Aristotle, habits or dispositions, habit differing from disposition in that it is with difficulty acquired or lost, while disposition is easily acquired or lost. Now what can be said to be acquired or lost by a substance must be something really distinct from the substance which is said to acquire it or to lose it; consequently in this species of quality are included all those qualities which Ockham calls "absolute," such as are signified by abstract terms that can stand disjunctively for individual things *in re*, and which yet do not stand for the individual things for which their concrete counterparts can stand. Both the concrete and abstract forms of such terms are included in this species of qualitative term; but whereas the concrete form signifies a substance by connoting a particular quality really present in, and distinct from, the substance, the abstract form (which appears in the nominal definition of the concrete term) signifies and denotes precisely the particular quality without connoting or indicating its presence in a substance. In the sense in which the terms "habit" and "disposition" are used here, they include not only qualities such as may be present in the soul, but also any qualities really distinct from substances, such as the contraries (or their intermediates) which are principles of alteration in sensible substances— e.g., heat and the privation of heat (frigidity).[1]

---

aliqua re possunt predicari" (this gives the second species of qualitative terms); "Aliqua autem important unam rem aliam connotando" (such are the third and fourth kinds of qualitative terms).

[1] Exp. aur., II, 71v: "si quaeratur qualis est homo, convenienter respondetur quod est albus vel niger, calidus vel frigidus; et tamen 'calor' quod est abstractum 'calidi,' de una re simplici verificatur, nam haec est vera: 'haec res est calor' et sic de aliis. Et quando ita est tunc res pro qua supponit illud abstractum est in genere qualitatis quod non est de genere substantiae, et tale concretum et abstractum sibi correspondens simpliciter pro diversis supponunt, sicut 'calidum' supponit pro subiecto, et 'calor' pro qualitate informante ipsum subiectum. . . ." Ibid., 72r: "Philosophus non ponit hic praecise in prima specie qualitatis dispositiones et habitus ipsius animae, sed omnis qualitas quae est per se una collocatur in ista specie qualitatis, quia omnis talis res vel est de facili mobilis vel de difficili mobilis, et ita omnes qualitates sensibiles et omnis potentia naturalis vel impotentia, quae est res per se una, continetur sub prima specie qualitatis. . . . In ista specie continetur omnis actus et passio animae, et universaliter omnis res alia per se una a substantia. . . ."

In view of the fact that Ockham calls abstract qualitative terms of this first kind, "absolute" terms, verifiable of individual things outside the mind which are *per se one* and distinct from individual substances, it might seem that Ockham was making the contraries *entia per se*, and thus positing them as absolute principles distinct from substances, such that the first principles of metaphysics would include contraries. Such an interpretation, however, overlooks the important fact that logic, and especially the book of *Categories*, is for Ockham, as for Aristotle, concerned with the terms and concepts used by the discursive sciences, which signify things *qua* changeable. The *Categories* is not concerned with terms that signify things purely as beings, in the unqualified sense of *ens*. Logic is the instrument of physics; but physics is concerned with substances, not *qua* instances of being in the absolute sense, but *qua* changeable or sensible things. Hence it uses terms that signify substances not merely as *things which are* and which are *per se one*, but as things without which something else cannot be said to be. The "something else" is being in the qualified and equivocal sense, i.e., the *ens per aliud* which is a function of the conjunction or co-existence of two or more things which, considered separately, are beings in the unqualified sense. Thus the term "moveable" stands for some *thing* that exists *per se* in the absolute sense, though *qua* moveable it signifies it as capable of being what it actually is not.

Genera and species of substance are absolute terms only for the science that is concerned with changeable things— i.e., with things which are in no instance actually all that they can become. Absolute substantial terms signify changeable things *per se* and absolutely only in the sense that they connote no *determinate* contraries with respect to which they are changeable. Similarly, the abstract qualitative terms which Ockham calls "absolute," are absolute only in the sense that they signify forms of existence which substances acquire and lose *per aliud* (and which are *per se* the forms of nothing signified by absolute substantial terms), without connoting any *determinate* subject in which or by which such forms can come to be.

Hence both kinds of "absolute terms," are absolute only for the science which analyses change and its forms. Every concrete connotative term signifies individual substances as determined, or as determinable, with respect to contrary forms of existence; and according to Ockham, all forms of change can be exhibited as functions of qualitative change. Things qualified are apprehended by us through sense perception, which is qualitative change in us; through memory, experience, and abstraction, as Aristotle describes it in the *Posterior Analytics*, we come to define the concrete connotative terms by terms which signify substances in abstraction from any determinate qualitative determinations, and by abstract qualitative terms which signify the contraries in abstraction from that which changes with respect to them. And thus we arrive at both kinds of "absolute terms" by the act of abstraction—and neither kind of absolute term signifies the individual things which are, by all that they actually are, but both kinds of absolute terms signify them through abstraction from their being in the sense in which it is signified by the other kind of absolute term.

Thus discursive science, which begins with facts whose actuality is certified by sense experience, and which discovers principles or causes by abstraction and analysis, exhibits, in demonstration, the facts from which it starts as functions of causes or principles which can be understood to be *per se*. The material and efficient causes of change can be referred to the formal nature of things signified essentially by absolute substantial terms, and in this respect the regress is finite, and demonstration is possible. But the formal causes of *change* (i.e., the contraries with respect to which changes take place) cannot be referred to any determinate subject through which they exist *per se* and whose essential nature they are, because no substance can be a contrary. Consequently the attempt to discover the primary cause of things being not merely determinable with respect to contraries, but actually determined (which is the attempt to discover why things which can be or not be, *in fact are*), involves infinite regress, among contingent facts, and justifies, according to one form of *a posteriori* proof, the inference that if any changeable thing actually changes, a Prime Mover, who is unmoved, exists.[1]

The second kind of qualitative term includes all those which are habits, in the sense in which qualities signified by the first kind of qualitative term are habits, and which in addition are inborn principles of doing or of resisting something easily. It is in virtue of a quality of this kind that a man

---

[1] For further discussion of the kinds of principles, and of the way in which abstract qualitative terms are principles of demonstrative science, without entering (in their abstract forms) into any premises of demonstration, cf. *post*, ch. vi. The distinction between substance and quality, or in any case between the potential and the actual, is absolutely necessary for the analysis of change, if undertaken against the background of aristotelian principles. The reason of this necessity, and for the fact that no such distinction is, or can be, a truly *metaphysical* distinction, lies in the fact that things can be identified and determinately signified, in thought and in discourse, only by acts of understanding many (*quale quid*), which, precisely insofar as they are determinate and accurate, and insofar as they make known the nature of the things they signify, signify things privatively. Thus, in the category of substance, the most determinate terms are those in whose definitions are the greatest number of differentiae—but an essential differentia makes known what a thing is by distinguishing it from the kinds of things it is not, as is indicated by the fact that the differentia is a middle term only in negative universal demonstration. Similarly, the more knowledge we have of a given genus or species of substance, the more commensurate properties we know to belong to it—but a property signifies *that which is* actually, by what it is potentially, which is to say, by what it actually is not.

If we could know individual things in their complete actuality, without negative connotation or the notion of the potential, the things so known would not be changeable things—for changeable things are precisely those which *per se* are not all that they can be. Only if we, like God, could have immediate awareness of the actual determinate being of every individual thing at every time, and in a single unchanging intuitive act, could we know the individual things which are signified by terms in the category of substance, by their complete actuality, without abstraction and without the concept of potentiality. Such would be the divine metaphysics which, as a kind of absolute ideal, is the Eros of metaphysical dialectic, by which the negation which is inevitably involved in discursive thought is ideally negated, in an absolute sense, and practically negated by substituting a different antithesis, in itself, like all others, temporary and such that it must be overcome. The notion of metaphysics as a non-discursive science, consisting simply in the recognition of unconditioned being signified by the six transcendentals, does not reject the "divine persuasion" but merely concludes, on the ground that a lifetime of dialectical pursuit of the infinite is still infinitely removed from its goal, that unconditioned knowledge of conditioned being gives us more of a taste of *that which is*, than the endless occupation of pursuing that which cannot be caught —the actually infinite, comprehended by the actually infinite.

may be called a naturally good runner or boxer. Further, a term of this kind cannot have, or is not, an abstract form that signifies a distinct "real quality" that is *per se* one, as in the case of the first species of qualitative term. Thus "health" does not signify any one quality really distinct from substance and from other qualities, but rather it signifies a group of qualities of the body—each of which is a single quality such as is signified by some abstract term of the first species of quality—signifying them however conjunctively, as well ordered or proportioned. In this property of signifying many individual things taken together, as ordered in some manner which is accidental to any one of them, it resembles those terms which Ockham places in the category of quantity, such as "populace," "army," etc., on the ground that they signify a multitude of things which are *per se* distinct and form no real unity *in re*, as if they were parts of a whole—a mode of signification which Aristotle seems to attribute to numbers, when he calls the things numbered "parts" which do not have relative position, though they have an order.[1]

The third kind of qualitative term is composed of those terms which signify qualities, or things qualified, through connoting the pleasure or pain consequent on their apprehension through sense perception. These are what Aristotle calls the affective qualities (*passibiles qualitates*); things are not signified by these terms because they cause sensation in the sense organs, for in that case colours and such things would have to be included. But in that case we would not be able to distinguish the third species of quality from the first,

---

[1] Exp. aur., II, 72v: "omnis qualitas quae est principium agendi faciliter vel resistendi alicui agenti, et de difficili mobilis, vocatur potentia naturalis, sicut patet manifeste ex littera Aristotelis" (Cat., 9a 13–27); "si quaeratur qualis est homo, convenienter respondetur quod est sanus, vel eger, vel bene complexionatus, vel male, et sic de aliis; puta quod est pulcher, vel turpis; et tamen nullum abstractum correspondens alicui istorum praecise significat unam rem ita quod sit predicabilis de una re simplici et per se una; nam sanitas nec est aliqua qualitas una distincta ab aliis qualitatibus, quia non est nisi debita vel determinata proportio humorum, ita quod ultra ipsos humores et qualitates eorum, abstractum nihil absolutum dicit, et ita de nulla una qualitate vere predicatur . . . et ita est de multis aliis quae ponuntur in predicamento qualitatis, quod nullum eorum significat unam rem de quo possit vere predicari, sed multas, ad modum quo dictum est de aliquibus in genere quantitatis. . . ."

since no distinction can be made between a quality as principle of alteration in a body outside, and as principle of
alteration in the sense organ (which is also a body). Hence
affective qualities are so called because of the connotation of
pleasure or *distaste* following on perception of them—as in the
case of the term "hateful," or of the term "delightful,"
which are applied to things though nothing is *per se* hateful
or delightful.[1]

The fourth kind of qualitative term is that which signifies
a substance by connoting a determinate order among its
parts, instances of such terms being "form," "figure,"
"straightness," "curvature," etc. Such terms do not signify
anything *in re* distinct from substances or qualities for which
they stand, for a thing may cease to be signifiable as straight,
merely through local motion of its parts, and without losing
any entity such as might be called "straightness." The only
straightness it loses is the possibility of the term "straight"
being truly predicated of any term standing for it.[2]

According to Aristotle, all concrete terms signifying things
as *such* or *such*, are derivatives of the abstract forms—i.e.,
they name things which are not qualities, by qualities present
in them.[3] While Ockham concedes that nothing is called
quale except because of some quality, he denies that it is
Aristotle's intention to assert that a thing is signified as a
such, *always* because of some qualitative form signified *per se*
by the abstract form of the concrete term. This is the case only
with the first two species of qualitative term, where the abstract

---

[1] Exp. aur., II, 73r: "in proposito (i.e., Cat. 9a 28–10a 10) accipitur passio
pro delectatione vel tristitia consequente apprehensionem sensitivam, et isto
modo tales qualitates non inferunt passiones subiectis in quibus sunt . . . sed
istae qualitates inferunt passiones tales sensibus. . . . Et propter hoc illae qualitates
et huiusmodi dicuntur passibiles qualitates non quia causent sensationem in sensu,
quia tunc colores et huiusmodi dicerentur passibiles qualitates, . . . sed dicuntur
passibiles qualitates quia delectationem vel tristitiam causant mediante cognitione
sensitiva."

[2] Exp. aur., 74r: "Notandum quod ista 'forma,' 'figura,' 'rectitudo,' et
'curvitas' non important aliquas alias res absolutas a substantia et quantitate et
qualitatibus aliis (si quantitas sit alia res a substantia et qualitate, quod tamen non
est verum secundum intentionem philosophi), sed illa dicunt substantias connotando certum et determinatum ordinem partium."

[3] Arist., Cat. 10a 27–32.

term is verifiable of something distinct from the substance for which its concrete counterpart stands, and which is really present in it; or, in the case of the second species of quality, where the abstract form signifies a number of such really distinct individual qualities taken together, though it signifies no one of them taken alone.

But in the case of the third and fourth species of qualitative term, and in the case of all other accidental terms that are said to be predicable *in quale* of their subjects, no accidental form really distinct from substance or from the qualities signified *per se* by the first species of qualitative term, is signified by the abstract form of the term. In all these cases the abstract form is either a synonym of its concrete counterpart, but used differently because it is taken to include implicitly a syn-categorematic word (as "humanity" is a synonym of "man," but used as equivalent to "man *qua* man," so that it is restricted to necessary propositions and is equivalent to "every man"); or else the abstract term can be said to stand for a multitude of individual substances or qualities taken together, no one of which it signifies when taken alone, as in the case of "populace," or as "triangularity" may be said to signify all triangles taken together, but no one of them taken alone.[1]

One quality may be the contrary of another; and of qualities alone is it true to say that they signify things which are *per se* contraries, in the sense that they may be acquired or lost by a substance through change, but cannot both be present in

---

[1] Exp. aur., II, 76r: "Sciendum est hic quod nunquam dicitur aliqua res 'qualis' nisi propter aliquam rem quae potest aliquo modo qualitas nominari. Sed aliquando illa res propter quam dicitur aliquid 'quale,' est realiter differens ab illo quod est quale, et informans ipsum, sicut 'homo' dicitur 'albus' et 'qualis' propter albedinem quae realiter distinguitur ab homine et quae est in homine subiective. Aliquando autem hoc non contingit, sed nulla est talis res in eo quod dicitur 'quale,' sed propter hoc quod ipse se habet aliter ad aliquid extrinsecum vel quantum ad partes suas intrinsecas . . . et in isto casu de virtute sermonis loquendo abstractum impositum tali qualitati et concretum debent esse nomina sinonima, sicut secundum Aristotelem 'homo' et 'humanitas'. . . . Aliter potest contingere quod aliquid dicitur 'quale' non propter unam rem praecise sed propter multas res (*scil.* simul sumptas), sicut est de pulcro, aegro, sano, sapiente, et huiusmodi . . . et in isto casu abstractum et concretum non sunt nomina sinonima, sed de virtute sermonis concretum predicatur de subiecto, et abstractum de illis pluribus rebus simul sumptis et de nulla illarum separatim sumpta. . . . "

the same subject at the same time. Qualities are contraries
in the strictest sense only when they are the extreme limits of
some kind of change; in this sense "whiteness" and "blackness" are contraries, but the intermediate colours are not,
even though they cannot qualify the same subject simultaneously. In a broader sense, the intermediate values of a qualitative contrariety may be called contraries of each other and
of the extremes. Not only the qualities which are limits of
change in material substances are contraries, but also the
qualities of the soul, such as justice and injustice, knowledge
of some one truth, and error with respect to the same
truth.[1]

Though Aristotle says that qualities admit of variation in
degree, this may be understood in two ways. Insofar as the
reference is to qualitative terms, we may say that many qualitative terms can be predicated of other terms with the adverbs
"more" or "less" added to them. If the reference is to things
signified by qualitative terms, it may be said that the substances signified by concrete qualitative terms may come to
have more of a certain quality than before, though it cannot
be said that the qualities themselves become more or less
what they are. Only in this sense can that which is signified
by a qualitative term be said to become more qualified with
respect to the same quality; for in the use of the word "more"
or "less," a comparison is involved, and consequently the
qualitative term with "more" or "less" added to it does not

---

[1] Exp. aur., II, 76r: "contrarietas vere convenit multis qualitatibus quae sunt
res de genere qualitatis, quia multae tales res sunt mutuo se expellentes et per
motum acquisibiles . . . et isto modo albedo et nigredo vere sunt contraria. Et
isto modo album et nigrum non contrariantur." Ibid., 76v: "stricte sunt illa
(contraria) quae mutuo se expellunt de eodem subiecto, et per motum acquisibiles,
ita tamen quod nullo modo sint compossibiles, et sic colores medii sunt contrarii.
Strictissime dicuntur contraria illa quae habent praedictas conditiones, et praeter
hoc sunt summe distantia in illo genere, et isto modo colores medii non sunt
contrarii. . . . Tertio notandum quod ex ista littera patet quod qualitates animae
vere contrariantur sicut qualitates corporis, quia iustitia et iniustitia non sunt
nisi qualitates animae et tamen vere contrariantur." Cf. Arist., Cat. 10b 11–2.
"Album" and "nigrum" are contrary *terms* because they cannot stand for the
same thing *in re* at the same time but can successively; but they do not stand
for contraries, but merely consignify them; "albedo" and "nigredo" however
stand for contrary qualities *per se*.

signify precisely one thing, but signifies one thing (*scilicet* a substance) with respect to a quality.[1]

Of qualities alone are the relative terms "like" or "unlike" predicable. Ockham uses this statement of Aristotle to prove his previous contention, that relations are not things really distinct from substances or qualities, but are terms or intentions which signify things that are *per se* either in the genus of substance or in that of quality. For we cannot signify any individual thing, taken by itself, by the term "likeness"; and hence, as Aristotle's statement indicates, it is only by qualities that two things can be said to be similar or dissimilar, and not by anything distinct called "similarity." Again, Aristotle's statement that the determinate kinds of habits and dispositions are signified by qualitative terms that are not relative, though their genera may be signified by relative terms, indicates that relations, for Aristotle, are at least in some cases terms of second intention—for if they signify genera in the category of quality, they signify things that are terms or concepts.[2]

[1] Exp. aur., II, 76v: "Philosophus principaliter loquitur hic de nominibus, intendens quod aliquibus concretis potest convenienter addi illud adverbium 'magis' et 'minus' respectu illorum de quibus predicantur, ut convenienter dicatur quod Sortes est magis album quam Plato . . . sed si sint aliquae abstracta quae non recipiunt comparationem (i.e., in the grammatical sense of "comparison") ideo non suscipiunt magis et minus." Ibid., 77r: "quamvis philosophus non intendit hic quod res extra suscipiunt magis et minus, tamen res extra est augmentabilis ita quod res eiusdem rationis potest addi alteri rei eiusdem rationis, et propter hoc contingit quod nomen rei suscipit magis et minus. . . . Et ita est de albedine quod quando aliquid fit magis album una pars albedinis advenit subiecto eidem in quo fuit albedo et facit per se unum cum albedine prima, et ideo dicitur magis album."

[2] Exp. aur., II, 77v: (with reference to Arist., Cat. 11a 15–40): "Notandum est hic quod hic habetur illud quod dictum est in capitulo de 'ad aliquid,' *scil.* quod signum vel nomen est ad aliquid et tamen res quaecunque importata per se una, non est ad aliquid, sed est in genere alio; et ideo de nullo termino supponente praecise pro rebus predicatur in quid et per se primo modo 'ad aliquid' quando supponit mere personaliter. Et ideo ista est sententia Aristotelis quod genus relationis et huiusmodi non continet aliquem rem de qua predicatur quando supponunt mere personaliter quin illa sit de aliquo predicamento (alio). Secundo notandum est hic quod non tantum est verum de habitu et dispositione quod genera sunt ad aliquid et singularia sunt qualitates, sed hoc est verum de omni genere et omni specie in predicamento relationis, et omni singulari de quo predicatur aliqua genus vel aliqua species predicamenti relationis in quid, quod singularia quae sunt res importatae per talia nomina de quibus predicantur, quando mere supponunt pro rebus et personaliter, sunt qualitates vel substantiae secundum intentionem philosophi."

Of the other categories little need be said, for Ockham's characteristic method of analysis of those terms which do not signify individual substances or qualities *per se*, but which are different modes of signifying individual substances and qualities either conjunctively or connotatively, has been sufficiently illustrated in the discussion of quantity, relation, and quality. In the case of time and place, his arguments against the "moderns," who apparently held time and place to be distinct entities inhering in substances, are of some interest. Since a thing is signified by a temporal term through connoting one or more divisions or instants of time, the thesis that time inheres in things, such that at each instant a thing acquires a distinct entity or a "new time," leads to the consequence that anything that has endured through any period of time will have acquired (and retained as its "past") an infinite number of such entities. For any period of time, however small, is divisible into parts *ad infinitum*.[1]

If place, likewise, were an actual entity distinct from substance or quality, it would follow by the same reasoning that distance and togetherness were such distinct things. But if this were so, then in each thing that is in place there would be an infinite number of distinct entities; for any part of any continuum has potentially an infinite number of relations of distance to the other parts of the continuum, and therefore, if these distances were distinct *actualities*, any part of any continuum would be actually infinite or would contain an actual infinity. But according to Aristotle the human mind cannot understand anything to be actually infinite, because we understand things by distinguishing them from things which they are not—which is the same as saying that whatever we understand to be, we understand to be finite. Consequently, if we are to follow the principles of Aristotle, we must say that for a body to be in a place is nothing other than for it not to be separated from the body or surrounding medium that is said

---

[1] Exp. aur., II, 78v: "*quando* non dicat rem talem aliam . . . quia sic necessario derelinquitur ex tempore in re, sed hoc est impossibile, nam tunc in illa re quae fuit in infinitis instantibus essent tales res infinitae. . . ."

to be its place—i.e., so that no other body is between it and that which is its place. Just as "in place" signifies two bodies by negating their separation by a third body, so "distant" signifies two bodies as separated by a third body which is said to be "between" them.[1]

As with these, so with action and passion, position and state; they are modes of signifying individual substances or qualities either conjunctively or connotatively, and they signify nothing *per se* distinct from individual substances or qualities.

Ockham's treatment of the *Categories* of Aristotle is guided by two concerns: first, he seeks to preserve the distinctions between the categories as *forms or modes of signification*, from the combination of which affirmative and negative statements arise, through denying that terms are placed in distinct categories because they signify really distinct things. Secondly, he seeks to preserve the distinction between terms, and the individual things signifiable by them, by insisting on the fact that "being" is predicated equivocally of the terms in the categories, so that no term of first intention, when taken alone, signifies *that which is* by its complete and actual being, whereas every term in a category signifies *that which is*, in one of its senses, by abstracting from the signification of it in another of its senses. In other words, Ockham's whole aim is to preserve the relativity of knowledge to being, without destroying the distinction between knowledge and what is known.

---

[1] Exp. aur., II, 78v: "Item de 'ubi' patet, quia si 'ubi' diceret talem rem aliam, eadem ratione 'distantia' et 'propinquitas' diceret talem rem aliam, sed hoc est impossibile, quia tunc in eodem essent infinitae res, quia quaelibet pars alicuius continui habet infinitos respectus ad omnes partes alias alterius continui, quae sunt infinitae. . . . Ideo non est intentio philosophi quod 'ubi' sit aliqua res distincta realiter a loco, et locato, sed corpus esse propinquum loco non est aliud quam corpus non distare a loco, hoc est, quod non sit aliquod medium inter corpus et locum, et ideo 'propinquitas' non dicit nisi quod inter hoc et hoc non est corpus medium, et hoc posito quod hoc sit et illud sit et sint simul, et posito quod nullum aliud corpus sit medium inter ea, tunc unum est vere propinquum alteri omni alia re circumscripta." Cf. Arist., *Physics* V, 3, 226b 24–6: "That which a changing thing, if it changes continuously in a natural manner, naturally reaches before it reaches that to which it changes last, is *between*." Local motion is change with respect to place; and place is intelligible in terms of substance and contrariety; but the primary kind of contrariety, by which all others are definable and by which all change is apprehended through the senses, is qualitative contrariety.

Ockham's effort to show that none of the terms in the categories signifies things that are really distinct from substances or qualities, preserves the possibility of signifying the same individuals in diverse ways—i.e., it preserves the possibility of true affirmative predication. For if the accidental categories signified distinct things *in re*, there would be no difference between them and qualitative terms with respect to mode of signification, and thus the different genera of accidental categories would differ only as one qualitative term differs from another—*scil.* through indicating a different quality. In that case there would be no more reason for putting "quantity" and "relation" in different categories, than for putting "colour" and "heat" in different categories. Or if "quantity" and "relation" constitute distinct categories because they signify distinct things, then co-ordinate species in the category of substance, or in that of quality, should constitute distinct categories by reason of the fact that they signify really distinct things. In short, the effort, so much criticized by Ockham, to interpret the categories as a division of terms according to distinctions between entities signified by them, instead of according to differences in mode of signification, can only result, when carried out consistently, in the destruction of the very idea of the categories.

On the fact that "being" is predicated equivocally of the terms that are in the categories, depends the possibility of distinguishing between signs and things signified, and also the possibility of adequating signs to *that which is*, through true propositions. The distinction between the categories is a distinction between different forms by which finite causes of change can be understood or apprehended; hence, while every term in the categories is a form by which individuals can be apprehended, no single term signifies any individual by all that it is. That is to say, every term in the categories abstracts from something by which the individuals for which it can stand exist actually under particular conditions. Every term in the categories stands either for substances or for qualities, either disjunctively, conjunctively, or connotatively; and hence every such term abstracts either from qualities (some or all) by which a substance can be apprehended to exist, or from substances by which a quality can be understood to exist. In short, no term in the categories is an adequate sign of the existence of any particular individual, and yet it is not the sign of any existence other than that of individuals—for "to be" is to be individual.

From this we can see how terms combined in propositions, or with the verb "is" or its equivalent added to them, are alone adequate signs of individual existing things. We can see why no single term, and no definition, is either true or false, and why a term is said to be a sign *capable* of standing for individuals, but does not by itself stand for any individuals. Which is perhaps the reason why every term in the categories is of determinate significative character only *qua* universal, and the reason, also, why no term of first intention can *stand* for anything other than individual things.

As a form of signification, every term that is *per se* in a category is universal because it is potentially a factor in the knowledge (through propositions) of individuals really distinct and different from each other. But precisely because one individual actually existent, being *per se* distinct in its existence from other individuals, cannot *of itself* be a factor in knowledge of other individuals, it follows that nothing for which any term of first intention *can stand*, is universal.

A consequence of this analysis is that the only things that can be said to be "individuated" are universal terms. The "principle of individuation" is the verb or copula consignifying time, which, when applied to a term that stands only potentially for individuals, forms a complex sign (proposition) which affirms that something is or is not. The very word "individuate" indicates the character of predication—it is the act of "un-dividing," an act applicable only to what has been divided, and which therefore presupposes an act of dividing elements that exist together (i.e., "con-tingently"). All finite terms of first intention are elements abstracted either directly, or through the parts of their definitions, from experience of contingent or undivided existence; until this abstraction is offset by an affirmation or negation which re-introduces the indication of "being together" in time, supplied by the verb "is" taken as of present tense, a term is not adequated to that which actually is, and hence is not true or false of actual existence. The abstraction is offset in another manner by propositions *de possibili*, by which terms are formed into adequate signs of *that which can be*, as is the case with universal propositions. But every term, taken alone, is only a form by which individuals can, *in* an act of affirmation or negation, be indicated or apprehended as actually or potentially existent; it is not itself an indication or an apprehension of the existence of individuals.

That terms can be analysed and distinguished as forms by which individual being or nature can be *recognized and signified*, independently of affirmations of existence involving these terms, is what makes the analysis of terms given in the *Categories* a "formal" analysis. Though the analysis presupposes the existence of propositions (since terms are significant only *qua* potential elements of propositions), it does not presuppose knowledge of the truth or falsity of any propositions about things which the terms in the categories signify. Hence it provides us with a means of defining terms independently of questions of truth or falsity, and with a means of understanding *what* is affirmed or denied by a proposition independently of the determination of its truth or falsity.

The possibility of evident and determinate knowledge of the truth or falsity of a universal proposition, on which depends the possibility of demonstrative science, depends on the possibility of defining terms independently of prior knowledge of the truth or falsity of universal propositions in which such terms are involved. Ockham's underlying concern, throughout his analysis of the *Categories*, is to show how this can be done, and thereby to preserve Aristotle's foundation for a science of nature distinct from a discursive or dialectical metaphysics.

CHAPTER FIVE

FORMS OF COMPLEX SIGNIFICATION

I.

Just as Ockham's analysis of terms of first intention, and their distinction as of different categories, proceeds independently of the consideration of the forms of affirmation or denial by which such terms become subjects or predicates of propositions, so the analysis of propositional forms, in the second part of the *Sum of All Logic*, abstracts from the consideration of differences between terms, and only presupposes that there *are* terms which can function as subjects or as predicates of propositions. Both the *Categories* and the *De interpretatione*, as Ockham understands them, are concerned with forms of speech and of thought which come into existence when true or false statements are made about things *in re;* and yet neither of these treatises is concerned with the truth or falsity of any statement about things *in re.* This formal treatment is achieved by analysing kinds of terms in abstraction from forms of affirmation and denial, and by analysing propositional forms in abstraction from the consideration of distinctions between terms.

That Aristotle, in his *De interpretatione*, is concerned with forms of statement and not with things outside the mind, is indicated at the very beginning of the treatise, where he proposes to define such terms of second intention as "noun," "verb," "denial," "affirmation," "sentence," and "proposition." Hence Ockham says of the *De interpretatione*, as he said of the *Categories*, that it is principally concerned with kinds of signs, and not, except incidentally, with things outside the mind or extraneous to spoken or written discourse.[1]

---

[1] Arist., De int., 1, 16a 1–3. Ockham, Exp. aur., 88r: "Postquam philosophus in libro predicamentorum de incomplexis doctrinam tradidit, in isto libro qui

While Ockham, in Part II of the *Sum of All Logic*, confines himself rigorously to the differentiation of propositional forms, in his commentary on Aristotle he devotes a number of pages to the discussion of certain preliminary considerations mentioned in the first chapter of the *De interpretatione*, wherein Aristotle distinguishes the subject he is about to discuss from the subjects which he discusses elsewhere. The question of the *relation* of the spoken or written sign to the thoughts that are in the mind, and the problem of what a concept or intention is—questions which Aristotle refers to his *De anima*—are treated in some detail in Ockham's commentary: but since they have already been sufficiently dealt with, the discussion may here be passed over.[1] The indication, in Aristotle's treatise, of the difference between terms and propositions, and between the kinds of intellectual acts (apprehension and judgment) to which they are referred, gives Ockham occasion to make a few rather important distinctions.

Aristotle seeks to indicate the difference between terms and propositions, as distinct forms of expression, by referring them to two kinds of intellectual acts, or to the habits of the soul generated by these two kinds of acts. The act of apprehension or understanding, which is, or which produces at its *habitus*, the concept, is simple and cannot be said to be true or false. But the act of judgment, which is, or which produces as its *habitus*, knowledge or opinion, is complex. Its object may be things in the act of existence, apprehended intuitively as the actual unity of substance and quality, and assented to immediately through recognition of the present actuality; and such intuitive judgments yield, as their expression, *evident* contingent propositions. Or the object of judgment may be the meaning of a term, as the unity of the elements of its definition; and such judgments, depending on the kind of term which is the object of judgment, or on the kind of definition it can have, yield indemonstrable

dicitur liber Perihermenias de propositionibus et complexis intendit dare notitiam. . . . Intelligendum est hic primo quod philosophus hic loquitur principaliter de vocibus supponentibus pro vocibus, quamvis forte incidenter determinat de vocibus supponentibus pro rebus."

[1] Cf. *ante*, ch. ii, pp. 39–40, and pp. 47–52.

and self-evident ˌpropositions of various kinds, such as are discussed in the *Posterior Analytics* as indemonstrable premises of
demonstration. Or, finally, the object which is judged may
be a proposition, and it is with complexes of this kind, *qua*
objects of judgment, that the logician is chiefly concerned; for
science, both demonstrative and topical, is of propositions
assented to as true.[1]

[1] Arist., De int., 1, 16a 9–18. Ockham, Exp. aur., III, 91r: "intellectus (hoc
est, intellectio) aliquando est vera, aliquando falsa, aliquando nec est vera nec
falsa. Secundo notandum quod raro a philosopho invenitur quod ponat aliquem
veritatem vel falsitatem nisi in propositione, et ideo consequenter philosophus
non vocat aliquid verum vel falsum nisi propositionem."

The distinction between apprehension and judgment, and between their
objects, is dealt with at length in Ockham's *Quodlibeta*, of which the more important
passages are translated, with very literal accuracy, by R. McKeon, *Selections from
Mediæval Philosophers*, vol. II (Scribners, N.Y., 1930). See especially the selection
from Quodl. IV, Qu. 17, on pp. 383–4, where the distinction is made between
two kinds of assent: assent to things or to terms which is not assent to a proposition,
and assent to a proposition whereby it is judged to be true. Thus (p. 384): "the
act of assenting is of two sorts: one by which I assent that something is or is not,
as I assent that *God is three and one*, and that *God is not the devil*. Whence by the
power of word I assent by the latter act to nothing, yet by the same act I apprehend
God and the devil, because every act of assenting is an act of apprehending and
not conversely. Another kind is the act of assenting by which I assent to something so that the act of assenting is referred to something by assenting or dissenting
to a complex, as by assenting to this proposition, *man is an animal*, because I consider
that it is true, and I assent (preferably 'I assent also') not only to this proposition,
this proposition man is an animal is a true proposition, in which this proposition, *man is
an animal*, is subject, but I assent to this proposition, *man is an animal*, in itself
and absolutely; and this is so because I know that as it is in fact, so it is conveyed
by this proposition. Concerning the second I say in general that the first assent
never presupposes necessarily the apprehension of a complex, because this assent
is not in respect of a complex as object, but it presupposes the apprehension of
individual things, although the understanding may not assent to the individual
things. But the second assent, naturally speaking, presupposes necessarily the
apprehension of a complex, and this indifferently, whether that complex is
compounded of conceptions of (individual) things or not."

Knowledge involves assent and something apprehended, but if the assent is of
the first kind distinguished above, we may say that although it is known that
something is white or that something is not another thing, the knowledge has as
object neither "something" nor "white," but rather the existence from which, by
a single act, these two intentions are abstracted. Intuitive knowledge is of this
kind; scientific knowledge, however, is of propositions assented to as true. Cf.
Quodl. III, 6 (quoted by Prantl, p. 333, Anm. 752): "Actus assentiendi est
duplex sicut actus sciendi; unus quo aliquid scitur esse vel non esse, sicut scio,
quod lapis non est asinus et tamen nec scio lapidem nec asinum; . . . alius est
actus, quo aliquid scitur de aliquo, de quo habetur scientia. . . . Loquendo de
ipso assensu dico, quod ille actus non habet pro obiecto complexum. . . .
Loquendo vero de actu secundo sciendi vel assentiendi dico, quod ille actus est
proprie complexivus . . . quia ille actus est, quo aliquid verum scitur, sed res
extra non scitur, non enim scio lapidem vel asinum." Cf. Sent. I, Dist. II, Qu. 4,
M (Prantl, p. 354, Anm. 797): "Scientia quaelibet, sive sit realis sive rationalis,

Every act of judgment presupposes an act of apprehension, whether the judgment is of a proposition already formed, or is itself the act of forming an evident proposition. Where the act of judgment has a proposition for its object, both the proposition, as a single affirmation or denial, must be apprehended, and also its terms must be apprehended or understood. But where the act of judgment is not *of* a proposition, but is the act of forming an evident proposition, the only apprehension presupposed is the apprehension in a single act of what the terms stand for (in evident contingent judgments), or of what they *can* stand for (in evident universal judgments).[1]

That the act of apprehending a proposition is distinct from the act of judging it, is manifest from the fact that we can form any proposition in our minds without assenting or dissenting to it. Even a self-evident proposition can be apprehended and yet not be assented to; and the reason for this is that every act of assent or dissent is the act of forming a proposition, and the will is free to form or not to form a proposition. But in the case of self-evident propositions, the apprehension of them and of their terms, *plus* an act of the will whereby it wills to form a proposition with the proposition apprehended as subject, and with either "true" or "false" as predicate, causes necessarily the judgment that the proposition apprehended is true.[2]

---

est tantum de propositionibus tanquam de illis, quae sciuntur, quia solae propositiones sciuntur. . . ." This indicates Ockham's use of the aristotelian distinction between "scientific knowledge" ($\epsilon\pi\iota\sigma\tau\eta\mu\eta$) and intuition ($\nu o\hat{u}\varsigma$); science is knowledge of that which is true, but only propositions can, strictly speaking, be called true. Aquinas takes the same position, holding that truth is found only in the mind which judges, and not in things outside the mind to which the judgment is said to be adequated; cf. De veritate, Qu. 1, art. 3.

[1] Quodl. V, Qu. 6 (McKeon's *Selections*, vol. II, pp. 380–3).
[2] Exp. aur., 91r: "tam scientia habitualis quam actualis distinguitur a propositione, quia . . . ipsa potest esse in mente modo sibi convenienti ante omnem actum sciendi. . . ." Sent. II, Qu. 25, K (Abbagnano, p. 137, Note 2): "Ideo dico quod causa quare plus formatur propositio vera vel falsa, affirmativa vel negativa, est voluntas; quia voluntas vult formare unam et non aliam, et ideo actus, quo apprehenditur post complexum, formatur a notitiis incomplexis terminorum illius propositionis et ab actu illius voluntatis. Et hoc generaliter, quia posito actu voluntatis quo vult tale complexum formari, et positis notitiis incomplexis terminorum, sequitur actum apprehendi sive formandi illud complexum, sicut effectus sequitur necessario ad suam causam."

Although the act of apprehending a proposition in the mind involves the formation of it in the mind, this act is not the same as that of knowledge, or belief, or doubt. Every act of assent or dissent is an act of forming a proposition in the mind, but not every act of forming a proposition in the mind is an act of assent or dissent. Thus to ask the question "Is it true that every surface can be coloured?" we have to form the proposition "every surface can be coloured," and yet we do not by that act answer the question.

It is generally said that the terms "true" and "false" are predicable, in the sense in which these terms are opposed, only of propositions, and that anything that is a proposition is either true or false. If now we apply Ockham's method of analysing terms, to the terms "true" and "false," we may ask whether these are absolute or connotative terms, and if connotative, whether that which is connoted by them (and which is signified directly by their abstract counterparts "truth" and "falsity") is distinguished from the things for which they can stand (propositions) as essential part, as a "real" quality inhering in them, or as something distinct from them that is neither an essential nor an accidental part. In other words, is a proposition said to be true (1) in the sense in which a man is said to be an animal, or (2) in the sense in which a man is said to be rational, or (3) in the sense that a surface is said to be white, or (4) in some other way?

That "true" and "false" are not absolute terms is obvious, for an absolute term cannot cease to signify a thing that it can stand for, except through the destruction of the thing; but contingent propositions may first be true and then false, the proposition remaining unchanged. For the same reason, "true" and "false" cannot be connotative terms of the type that indicates an essential part of what it stands for, nor of the type that indicates the presence of a real quality *in* that for which it stands.

It remains, therefore, that "true" and "false" signify propositions by connoting the actual or potential existence of things which do not depend for their existence on the being of the propositions which are called true or false, but by whose existence the truth or falsity of such propositions can be known. Connotative terms of this type may connote a fact, another term, or a proposition. And as a matter of fact it would seem to be through reference to the existence of these three kinds of things, that propositions are known or believed to be true or false. For if we wish to show that a proposition is true, or that it is false, we will, where possible, point to the fact before our eyes; or we may appeal to the meanings of the terms; or we may seek to find some other proposition conceded to be true by our opponent, from which, by a recognized rule of inference, the proposition at issue follows, or by which it is contradicted.

Since the third method of ascertaining the truth or falsity of a proposition gives us determinate knowledge of its truth or falsity only if the regress terminates with a proposition known by the first or second method, the meaning of the terms "true" and "false" is established by the first two ways of understanding propositions to be true or false. But in these senses, "true" and "false" stand for propositions by indicating the actual or potential existence of the thing or things signified by the terms of the proposition; or, if the proposition is a negation, by indicating that the thing or things signified by the terms do not, or cannot, exist in the manner indicated. "True" or "false," therefore, stand for human acts by which existence is, in some determinate way, affirmed or denied, and "true" connotes the existence of that which is affirmed to be, as existing (actually or potentially) in the manner affirmed, while "false" connotes the existence of something by which the contradictory of the proposition is true.[1]

[1] Exp. aur., 91v: "Ultimo notandum est quod veritas et falsitas propositionis non sunt quaedam qualitates inhaerentes ipsi propositioni illo modo quo albedo inhaeret parieti. Quia sine omni mutatione a parte propositionis potest eadem propositio esse primo vera et postea falsa propter solam mutationem a parte rei; sicut ista 'Sortes sedet,' ipso sedente, est vera, et postea, ipso surgente, sine omni mutatione propositionis, est falsa. Sed veritas et falsitas sunt quaedam predicabilia de propositione importantia quod est ita vel non est ita a parte significati sicut denotatur per propositionem quae est signum, unde propositionem esse

While the terms "true" and "false," in the sense in which they are opposites, are terms of second intention which can stand only for what is a proposition, the term "true" is also used in another sense, as a transcendental term which can stand for anything that is, by connoting the act of the intellective soul by which its being can be affirmed. Thus "true," in this sense, is predicable of the term "false," connoting that act of understanding by which the mind can know that a false proposition is, in truth, a false proposition. Similarly, "true" in this sense signifies that *by* which a proposition is false; for a proposition is false by reason of the existence of something which can be signified truly by its contradictory —the reason of the falsity, as of the truth of propositions, is *that which is* (*ens*), and *that which is* can be truly understood to be.[1]

Since "true" and "false" are predicated of propositions by reason of the existence of something that is neither identical with, nor a part of, the propositions of which these terms are predicated, it follows that the proposition *as such* can only be analysed through abstracting from the consideration of propositions *qua* true or *qua* false, and through differentiation

---

veram, est ita esse in re sicut significatur per eam, et propositionem esse falsam est aliter esse in re sicut significatur per eam, et eodem modo dicendum est de aliis propositionibus secundun alios modos ut alibi ostendetur." Cf. Aquinas, De veritate, Qu. 1, art 3, for a lucid discussion of the *ratio* of the truth of propositions.

[1] Aquinas, De veritate, Qu. 1, art. 1, gives the nominal definitions of the five connotative transcendentals convertible with *ens*. "Si autem modus entis accipiatur . . . secundum ordinem unius ad alterum; hoc potest esse dupliciter. Uno modo secundum divisionem unius ab altero"—(which is the way in which *aliquid* signifies *ens—scil.*, "quasi *aliud quid*")—"Alio modo secundum convenientiam unius entis ad aliud; et hoc quidem non potest esse nisi accipiatur aliquid quod natum sit convenire cum omni ente. Hoc autem est anima, quae quodammodo est omnia, sicut dicitur in III de Anima (text. 37). In anima autem est vis cognitiva et appetitiva. Convenientiam ergo entis ad appetitum exprimit hoc nomen *bonum*. . . . Convenientiam vero entis ad intellectum exprimit hoc nomen *verum*." The rest of this article, and also arts. 2 and 3 of the De veritate, illuminate the questions touched on by Ockham at this point, and in all essentials conform to Ockham's own position. Obviously, the term "true" could just as well be said to stand for that *by* which a proposition is true, connoting the proposition, as to stand for the proposition through connoting that by which it is true. St. Thomas expounds both ways, but, like Ockham, considers the second analysis more appropriate for logic and science.

of them as different forms of affirmation and denial—different possible ways in which two terms can be joined together by a copula, through various temporal or modal qualifications, or through quantitative restrictions whereby the terms are indicated to stand not for all the things which they *can* stand for, but for one of them, or for some.

The analysis of the proposition as such, consequently, is an analysis of the different ways in which a complex sign can be "fabricated" from two incomplex signs, by forms of affirmation or denial, modified in various ways with respect to modality and time reference, or through quantitative exponents—these forms of affirmation or denial being indications that the two terms do or do not stand for the same individual thing or things. An affirmation does not, Ockham reminds us, affirm that one thing outside the mind is some other thing outside the mind—for that would be to affirm a contradiction. Nor does it affirm that the subject of the proposition *is* the predicate, for the same reason. Nor does it affirm that the predicate stands for something that inheres in what the subject stands for (for we affirm not that "this surface is whiteness," but that "this surface is white"). Nor does it affirm that the predicate is predicated of the subject, for if that were the case, every affirmation would affirm an infinite regress in predication. But an affirmation affirms that the predicate term stands, in the way indicated by the form of the proposition, for one, some, or all of the individuals that can be signified by the subject term.[1]

[1] S. tot. log., II, 2, 31r: "ad veritatem propositionis singularis quae non equivalet multis propositionibus, non requiritur quod subiectum et predicatum sint idem realiter, nec quod predicatum a parte rei sit in subiecto . . . nec quod uniatur ipsi subiecto a parte rei extra animam . . . sed sufficit et requiritur quod subiectum et predicatum supponant pro eodem." The same fundamental condition, with the requisite modifications, applies to indefinite, particular, and universal propositions, both assertoric and modal.

What is nowadays called the "subject-predicate theory" of the proposition, and which is criticized by contemporary writers not on the ground that it is erroneous, but on the ground that it is too narrow, is explicitly rejected by Ockham, who is surely on good aristotelian ground on this point. According to the "subject-predicate theory," a proposition is true if something corresponding to the predicate is combined with something corresponding to the subject, by a "real" inherence-relation, or existential togetherness, corresponding to the predicative relation constituting the *form* of affirmation. Cf. Stebbing, *A Modern Introduction to Logic*,

Since propositions are formed out of pre-existent elements (terms) by an act of will, they do not have being or unity *per se*, but only in the sense in which artificial products have being or unity. They are, quite literally, fabrications; hence their analysis is not through essential parts, but through enumeration of material parts and of modes of putting them together. The parts required for fabricating a proposition are a subject, a copula, and a predicate, or, as the minimum, a subject and a verb. Aristotle, in the first part of the *De interpretatione*, differentiates the minimum parts required for a proposition as "noun" and "verb," stating that the verb consignifies time, while the noun does not. Thus any one term can, in combination with "is" or some tense of it, form a proposition; for "is," when added to any significant term, indicates the existence, at the present time, of something for which the term can stand. Such words as "not-man" are not, strictly speaking, nouns or adequate subjects of predication; to be a *term*, a word must have a definite or proper meaning, such that it can "terminate" a question.[1]

(N.Y., 1930), pp. 36–8. Also Eaton, *Symbolism and Truth* (Cambridge, 1925), p. 42, where the metaphysical hypostasis of the form of predication is carried beyond the confining limits of the "inherence-relation," and generalized to cover, by the same method of hypostatic union, two-, three-, and multiple-term relations: "The phrase or sentence reproduces the logical relations of the elements in the fact by similar logical relations among the symbols." Such a statement would surely make William of Ockham turn in his grave, for though his mediæval contemporaries often asserted that relations are distinct real entities outside the mind, they did not at the same time insist that they should be called "logical" relations—being outside the mind (i.e., not produced by acts of thinking) was usually considered to be sufficient reason for honouring them with the title "metaphysical"; perhaps Duns Scotus' *distinctio formalis a parte rei* is the nearest mediæval approach to the notion of logical form *in re;* but Duns did not consider it a disgrace to call a metaphysical distinction a metaphysical distinction.

It might also be noted that the inability to exhibit two- and three-term relations, attributed to the subject-predicate form of the proposition, applies only to the subject-predicate proposition *if its terms are taken as non-significant.* In Aristotle, who states that a proposition, *qua* sentence, is a sign composed of parts with independent meaning, the constituents of a fact, whether they be two, three, or four, are revealed not by analysis of the form of statement, but by analysis of the meaning of its terms.

[1] Cf. Arist., De int., 3, 16b 6–12. Ockham, Exp. aur., 93r: "accipitur (*scil.* 'nomen') stricte pro illo quod imponitur primario ad significandum aliqua, et sic nomina infinita non sunt nomina." He also gives a lengthy discussion, with reference to "infinite verbs," of the two causes of falsity in affirmative propositions

The fact that Aristotle uses the words "noun" and "verb" to signify the minimum parts required to form a proposition, instead of signifying these parts as "substances," "quantities," "relatives," etc., indicates the extent to which the analysis of the proposition as such, abstracts from the consideration of the meanings of terms, while presupposing the existence of terms which *can* stand for things which are, or which were, or which can be. It presupposes that terms have the *capacity* for signifying existing and therefore individual things, not as signs *that* something exists at a determinate time, but as signs of *what* something can be understood to be, when, as, and if it exists. The differentiation of these "whats," however, according to the principles of abstract signification exhibited in the *Categories*, plays no part in the analysis of propositional forms, with which Aristotle is primarily concerned in the *De interpretatione*.

II

As Prantl has pointed out, there is a striking difference between Ockham's commentary on the *De interpretatione*, and his analysis of the proposition in Part II of the *Sum of All Logic*.[1] The commentary on Aristotle follows the text closely, introducing relatively little material or terminology not found in Aristotle or in the ancient commentators. But in his own logical treatise, Ockham makes partial use of the technique of expression developed by the terminist logicians of the late thirteenth and early fourteenth centuries, to give a systematic statement of the kinds of propositional forms, of the manner in which these forms condition the procedure of verification, and of the manner in which propositions of these different forms convert. The discussion of the relations

---

—i.e., either what is affirmed to exist in a certain way does not exist in that way, though it exists, or else what is affirmed to exist does not exist at all within the time indicated by verb or copula. Cf. also Exp. aur., 97v: "Intelligendum est hic quod propositio est quoddam compositum non tanquam per se unum, sed tanquam aggregatum ex subiecto, predicato, et copula, quae quasi simul iungit subiectum cum predicato," i.e., propositions are "fabrications."

[1] Cf. Prantl, pp. 379–80.

of opposition between propositions, found in the *De interpretatione* and in Ockham's commentary on it, is not found in Part II of the *Sum of All Logic* at all, but in Part I, where the different senses of the term *opposita*, which is a term of second intention, are discussed. Similarly, the discussion of the law of excluded middle and of the problem of future contingent propositions, included in Aristotle's treatise and in Ockham's commentary on it, is absent from his analysis of propositional forms in the *Sum of All Logic*.

The significance of these differences is not, as Prantl appears to have thought, that Ockham in his *Sum of All Logic* was abandoning Aristotle's analysis of the proposition entirely, in favour of a new theory whereby truth and falsity are exhibited as consequences of the properties of terms, considered merely as words. Rather Ockham is seeking to exclude from his treatise, as irrelevant to its proper subject matter and to its purpose, the discussion of those grounds of truth or falsity which lie outside of the proposition itself considered as a *form* of affirmation or denial. The truth of a proposition is primarily a function of the actual or potential existence of things signified by its terms; but it is also conditioned, at least in a negative or restrictive manner, by the tense or mood of the copula and by syncategorematic words modifying the copula or the terms. It is not with the truth and falsity of propositions, but with these conditioning factors of verification involved in the form of the proposition itself, that Ockham is concerned here. And to state these conditioning factors, he makes use of the technique of expression developed by William Shyreswood, Lambert of Auxerre, Peter of Spain, and other "modern" logicians of the time, at least to a degree adequate for his purpose. Certainly it is true that Ockham here uses a language, and a method of analysis, which Aristotle did not use. But it by no means follows from this that he was using this language and method in an un-aristotelian manner or in support of an un-aristotelian theory of predication.[1]

---

[1] Prantl, p. 380, says: "Nur hat die Supposition . . . hier im Urtheile eine andere Function, als bei den Kategorien, indem bezüglich der Satzverbindung

The difference between Aristotle's method of exhibiting distinctions in propositional forms, and the method used by the terminist logicians, may be expressed by an analogy. If we were interested in making an exhaustive classification of the ways in which different kinds of houses could be constructed out of different kinds of materials, two methods might be* used. (1) We might make a tour of inspection among all the houses that had been constructed from such materials, noting the differences in their construction, and giving to each distinct type of house a name. (2) We might try out the various combinations of materials, by building houses out of them, and, in addition to giving names to the different kinds of houses, also give names, or assign properties, to the materials, according to the way in which their presence in a house, in combination with the other materials, affects its construction. In general, it may be said that Aristotle finds the first method sufficient for his purposes, in the analysis of propositional forms, though of course he does to some extent use the second method also. Thus he talks about universal and particular, assertoric and modal, *propositions*, giving examples to illustrate what he means; he does not, as

---

die Worte nicht so fast für die Dinge supponiren, sondern überwiegend für Worte, d. h. insoferne aus denselben als Worten Wahrheit oder Falschheit hervorgeht." Prantl, as shown by the two citations which he gives in support of this statement, seems to have confused two distinct questions. The first citation (Exp. aur., Predicament., Proem.) is concerned with the difference between the analysis of terms in the *Categories*, and the discussion (of the kinds of words from which propositions can be constructed), given in the *De interpretatione*— these kinds of words being differentiated not by their meanings, as in the *Categories*, but by the effects which they have on the conditions of verification of propositions. Thus Ockham says: "In libro vero Predicamentorum determinatur de vocibus, quales res significant ostendendo. Sed in libro Periherm. determinatur de vocibus secundum quod veritatem vel falsitatem propositionis sunt causativae." The other citation given by Prantl (from the Exp. aur., Perih. Proem.) is concerned with the fact that Aristotle, in the *De interpretatione*, discusses the meanings of terms of second intention, such as "noun," "verb," "proposition," etc., rather than the meanings of terms which can stand for things *in re*, such as "man," "substance," "quality," "horse," etc.: "Philosophus hic loquitur principaliter de vocibus supponentibus pro vocibus. . . ." Prantl, confusing these two distinct subjects of statement in Ockham, concludes erroneously that terms of second intention are the only ones that can have supposition in propositions, and that therefore the terms of all propositions stand only for words *as* words, so that the *only* cause of truth or falsity is words, *qua* words and not through things signifiable by them.

a rule, talk about distributive signs, or about the "ampliative"
property of the verb or copula, or about modal signs used as
modifiers either of the copula or of the proposition as a whole.
But the terminist logicians, whose effort was toward making
their analysis of propositional forms independent, as far as
possible, of the use of examples and illustrations, followed and
developed this second method. Ockham makes some use of
the terminology which they developed, but only to a limited
extent, and only insofar as the analysis could be simplified,
rather than made more complicated, by such use. The logical
writings attributed to Duns Scotus, as well as the logical
treatises of the *moderni* who were Ockham's contemporaries,
are much more affected by the terminist innovations than is
William of Ockham; furthermore, Ockham carefully avoids
a habit which became very fashionable in his time, as for
example in the logical *Summa* of the pseudo-Thomas, of treating
terms like substances, with essential parts and matter and
form.[1]

[1] The distinctions between the *proprietates terminorum*, such as *suppositio, copulatio,
restrictio, ampliatio, appellatio, distributio*, and *relatio*, as made by William Shyreswood, Lambert of Auxerre, and Peter of Spain, are covered in Prantl, pp. 17–9,
31–2, and 51–68. The criticism so often made of Ockham, that he was interested
in making distinctions among forms of speech for the mere purpose of exhibiting
dialectical skill, might be justified if applied to these ealier *moderni* and to their
studies of the properties of terms. The invention of separate names to express
the "restrictibility" of a term by the addition to it of a modifying adjective, or
to express its "amplifiability" by an expanded time reference in the verb or
copula, etc., was a favourite occupation among Ockham's contemporaries and
many of his predecessors. In the pseudo-Thomas, and in most of the minor
thomists and scotists of the early fourteenth century, we find terms and forms
of speech treated like substances, with formal and material causes, etc., so that
a metaphysical nominalism (or logical realism) came to be developed with a
different emphasis, though similar principles, as compared with earlier forms
of dialectical philosophy. Porphyry, for example, and the arab and augustinian
philosophers who developed his neo-platonist interpretation of Aristotle, attributed
the characteristics of discursive signification or of forms of discursive synthesis,
to "things" outside the mind; these *moderni* achieved a similar result by attributing
the characteristics of changeable substances, as exhibited in the aristotelian
physics, to words or ideas in the mind, and to their properties *qua* parts of
propositions. The metaphysical treatment of terms, so popular among the *moderni*, was
criticized by Ockham constantly, and it was against just this tendency that his
"razor" was employed. Ockham took no part in the multiplication of terms
of second intention, and went against the fashion of his day by declining to use
most of the terms and distinctions with which his contemporaries were occupied.
Thus he declines to make use of the distinction between *suppositio* and *appellatio*,

The one terminist distinction which Ockham does use constantly, is that between signification and supposition, and between the different modes of supposition of terms. This, however, is an ancient and honourable distinction, which is aristotelian in motive even if not in name; for the possibility of univocal predication, wherein a concept whose *signification* is single, can *stand* for many individuals signifiable by concepts of diverse signification of which it is predicable, depends on it. Ockham's analysis of the kinds of supposition that terms can have, which he includes at the end of his treatment of terms in Part I of the *Sum of All Logic*, serves as a transition from the analysis of terms to that of propositions—for though it is the term which has supposition, it has it only *qua* subject or predicate of a proposition.

The most general division of kinds of *suppositio personalis*, attributable to a term *qua* subject or predicate of a proposition that is either true or false of something signified by its terms, is between "discrete" and "common" supposition. The former is had by a proper name or a demonstrative pronoun, and always yields a singular proposition. "Common supposition" is had by a universal term when it is subject or predicate of a proposition.[1]

The fact that Ockham attributes "discrete supposition" only to proper names and demonstrative pronouns, and omits terms formed from a demonstrative pronoun plus a universal term, indicates that it is only by such terms (e.g., "Socrates"

S. tot. log., I, 63, 24v: "Large accepta (suppositio) non distinguitur contra appellationem, sed appellatio est unum contentum sub suppositione. Aliter accipitur stricte secundum quod distinguitur contra appellationem, sed sic non intendo loqui de suppositione, sed primo modo tantum, et sic tam subiectum quam predicatum supponit, et universaliter quicquid (quod) potest esse subiectum propositionis vel predicatum supponit. . . ." The other current distinctions, such as *ampliatio, restrictio, copulatio*, etc., he does not even mention.

[1] S. tot. log., I, 70, 26r: "Suppositio autem personalis potest dividi primo in suppositionem discretam et communem. Suppositio discreta est in quo supponit nomen proprium alicuius, vel pronomen demonstrativum significative sumptum, et talis suppositio reddit propositio singularis, sicut hic 'Sortes est homo,' 'ille est homo,' et sic de aliis. . . . Suppositio personalis communis est quando terminus communis supponit, sicut 'hic homo currit,' 'omnis homo est animal.' . . ."

or "this") that a single individual can be denoted to the exclusion of all other individuals. Hence it indicates that a term such as "this man" has discrete supposition only if the proposition "This is a man," accompanied by pointing, is true. From this it follows that the term "man," and every other universal term, is *per se* capable of standing for individuals that can be indicated by a demonstrative pronoun, and consequently does not acquire its *capacity* for signifying many individuals, as a consequence of the truth of singular propositions. In other words, although the proposition "Man is an animal" affirms the existence of something to which we could point, saying, "This is a man and it is an animal," it is not equivalent to any such singular proposition and is not an affirmation of the truth of singular propositions. Similarly, "Every man is an animal" affirms the actual or potential existence of individual things concerning which true singular propositions could be formed; and yet the universal proposition is not an affirmation of the truth of any or of all of these singular propositions, nor is it equivalent to all such singular propositions taken together. Universal propositions have terms which stand for many individual things, and such propositions are true by reason of the actual or potential existence of the many things for which their terms stand; but it is not the case that universal propositions are true of the many for which their terms stand, by reason of the truth of many singular propositions about these things.

"Common supposition" is divided into "confused" and "determinate" supposition. A universal term has determinate supposition when it is possible to descend disjunctively to singular propositions; e.g., in the proposition "man runs," the subject term has determinate supposition, because that by which the proposition is true is something by which a disjunctive set of singular propositions, *scil.* "This man runs *or* this man runs *or* this man runs, etc.," can be verified. "*Confused* supposition" is of two kinds, *confusa tantum* and *confusa et distributiva*. The former kind ("merely confused") is had by a universal term where reduction to singularity is not effected through a disjunctive set of propositions, but through disjunction of the predicate only; thus in the statement "Every man is an animal," the *predicate* has "merely confused supposition," for we cannot infer that "Every man is this animal *or* every man is this animal, etc.," but only that "Every man is either this animal or that animal or that other animal, etc." "Confused and distributive supposition," on the other hand, is had by the *subject* of universal affirmative propositions, and is described as the case where the subject of the universal proposition can be subject in a conjunctive set of singular propositions implied by it; thus in the statement "Every man is an animal," the subject has "confused and distributive" supposition, because it stands for the things it can signify in such manner that the conjunctive set "This man is an animal *and* this man is an animal, etc.," prolonged indefinitely, is true of whatever individuals, *such* as can be signified by the terms of the universal proposition, happen at any time to exist.[1]

Various rules are given for identifying these different kinds

---

[1] S. tot. log., I, 70, 26r–26v: "Suppositio personalis communis dividitur in suppositionem confusam et determinatam. Suppositio determinata est quando contingit descendere per aliquam disiunctivam ad singularia. Sicut bene sequitur, 'homo currit, ergo ille homo currit vel ille homo currit . . .' et sic de singulis. Et ideo dicitur suppositio determinata quia per talem propositionem denotatur quod talis propositio sit vera pro aliquo singulari determinata, et quaelibet singularis sufficit ad verificandum talem propositionem. . . . Suppositio personalis confusa est suppositio personalis termini communis quae non est determinata, et illa dividitur, quia quaedam est suppositio confusa tantum, et quaedam est confusa et distributiva. Suppositio confusa tantum est quando terminus communis supponit personaliter et non contingit descendere ad singularia per disiunctivam, nulla variatione facta a parte alterius extremi, sed per propositionem de disiuncto extremo, et contingit eam inferri ex quaecunque singulari. . . . Suppositio confusa et distributiva est quando contingit aliquo modo descendere copulative si terminus communis habeat multa contenta, et ex nullo uno formaliter infertur. . . ." It is not *because* disjunctive and copulative sets of singular propositions may (Ockham says "contingit descendere") be equated to the general propositions, that the terms of the general proposition have such or such supposition, but rather the other way round. If we do in fact identify the supposition of a general term, by trying out these different ways of using it in sets of singular propositions, our procedure is *a posteriori*; and in the case of *suppositio confusa et distributiva*, as Ockham points out, our *a posteriori* verification can never (except through an infinite experience) constitute a demonstration, in the strict sense, of the supposition of the term of the general proposition. The disjunctive and conjunctive sets of singulars are, as Aristotle might say, "prior and better known with respect to us," so that our apprehension of them together *elicits* or *induces* a prior grasp of the universal.

of personal supposition, with respect to terms functioning as subject or predicate in various kinds of propositions. Thus in all universal categorical propositions, the subject has "confused and distributive" supposition, while in affirmative universal propositions (but not negative), the predicate always has "merely confused" supposition.[1]

The significance of this analysis of kinds of personal supposition is not to be found in its utility, which is rather slight, but in the fact that it is an effort to show that a general proposition affirms or denies a *single* fact about things which are individual. For although the truth of the general proposition is involved in the truth of one or many singular propositions, nevertheless the general proposition is not to be understood as a statement of many particular facts, or as an ambiguous expression equivalent to the set of singular propositions which imply it. There is quite a difference between saying "Every man is an animal," and saying "Every 'this man is an animal' is true." It is this difference that is made evident through exhibiting universality as a function of the capacity of a single term to stand univocally for many individuals, so that a universal proposition is the statement of a single truth about individuals which may exist in an indefinite number of instances, and not a single statement of an indefinite number of contingent truths.

In Part II of the *Sum of All Logic*, Ockham confines himself to three tasks. (1) The enumeration of the ways in which propositions are distinguishable and classifiable by their form. (2) The statement of the way in which the supposition of the terms of a proposition, and consequently the conditions of its truth, are affected by syncategorematic words, modal terms, and the time-reference of the copula or verb, which introduced in various combinations in propositions, generate the different *forms* of affirmation and denial. (3) The statement of the rules for the conversion of various types of proposition.

The most general division of propositions is into categorical

[1] S. tot. log., I, 73–4, 28r–28v.

and hypothetical, the latter being subdivided into five kinds: copulative, disjunctive, conditional, causal, and temporal. Apart from a brief description of these kinds of hypothetical propositions, given at the end of his analysis of categorical propositions, Ockham's treatment of the hypothetical proposition is postponed to the part of his logical *Summa* entitled *Consequentiae*, which is concerned with topical reasoning.[1]

Of categorical propositions some are assertoric (*de inesse*) and others are modal. A proposition is called modal not because a modal term can be truly predicated of it (for all propositions are modal in this sense), but only when it explicitly contains a modal term either as a noun following the copula, or as an adverb modifying the copula. The kinds of modal propositions that can be formed are as many as the kinds of modal terms; apart from the four discussed by Aristotle, terms such as "true," "false," "doubted," "believed," etc., can generate modal propositions.[2]

Categorical propositions may also be divided into (1) those which are equivalent to a hypothetical proposition, these being called "exponible propositions," and (2) those not equivalent to hypothetical propositions. The *exponibilia* include reduplicative, exceptive, exclusive, and other such propositions, and receive a detailed analysis at Ockham's hands.

Further divisions of the categorical proposition are (1) into affirmative and negative; (2) into singular, indefinite, particular, and universal; (3) into propositions of past, present, or future time; and (4) into propositions of direct form or of oblique form—a distinction conceded by Ockham to be more

---

[1] S. tot. log., II, I, 3or: "Propositio cathegorica est illa quae habet subiectum et predicatum et copulam et non includit plures tales propositiones. . . . Propositio hypothetica est quae ex pluribus cathegoricis est composita. Et illa dividitur in quinque species secundum communem opinionem, scil. in copulativam, disiunctivam, conditionalem, causalem, et temporalem." The *Consequentiae*, which will be discussed in Chapter VII, exhibits the topical syllogism, the enthymeme, and all non-demonstrative reasoning, in terms of the conditional or implicative form of the hypothetical proposition.

[2] S. tot. log., II, 1, 3or: "est sciendum quod propositio dicitur modalis propter modum additum in propositione, sed non quicunque modus facit sive sufficit ad faciendum propositionem modalem, sed oportet quod sit modus predicabilis de tota propositione."

grammatical than logical, and which, along with other possible distinctions of similar type, he is willing to leave to the "studious" for investigation.[1]

Having completed this enumeration, Ockham turns to the analysis of the principal types of proposition that can be generated from these distinctions. He first takes up categorical propositions of present time—singular, particular and indefinite, and universal; then those of past and future time; then modal propositions; and finally the *exponibilia*.

Singular categorical propositions of present time, such as are not equivalent to a hypothetical proposition, require for their truth only this—that the subject term and the predicate term stand, or (if it is a negation) do not stand, for the same individual thing, at the time of predication. If it be objected, says Ockham, that when subject and predicate stand for precisely the same individual thing, then the same thing is predicated of itself, producing a tautology, the answer is: *non sequitur*. Because one term is a sign of something of which another term is a sign, it does not follow that they are the same term, or that they have the same meaning. In the proposition "Socrates is white," something that is a concrete qualitative term is predicated of something that is a proper name, and hence subject and predicate are entirely distinct and different from each other. If the proposition is true, the two terms stand for one thing, but each term has meaning independently of the other, and hence the proposition does not verify itself, nor is it a tautology.[2]

For a particular or indefinite proposition to be true, it is sufficient that the subject and predicate stand for some one individual, and that the predicate be not distributed. Hence

---

[1] S. tot. log., II, 1, 30r–30v.
[2] S. tot. log., II, 2, 31r: "ad veritatem propositionis singularis quae non equivalet multis propositionibus . . . sufficit et requiritur quod subiectum et predicatum supponant pro eodem." Ibid., 3, 32r: "Et si dicatur quod in tali propositione subiectum et predicatum supponunt pro eodem, ergo predicatur idem de seipso, dicendum est quod non sequitur, quia quamvis sit idem pro quo supponit subiectum et predicatum, tamen illud quod supponit non est idem."

the truth of a particular or of an indefinite proposition can be established by a singular proposition, while its falsity can only be established by a universal proposition. Where the terms are taken significatively, an indefinite proposition is convertible with the particular proposition composed of the same terms; but if the subject of the indefinite proposition is taken non-significatively, as in "man is a species," it is not convertible with the corresponding particular proposition "some man is a species" for the indefinite is true and the particular false. [1]

Universal propositions are differentiated according to the different "signs of universality" placed before the subject term, such as "all, every, any, each, none, any such, whichever-you-please, both, and neither." The discernment of differences in the manner in which a term is distributed by these various signs, and the attribution to terms, as properties, of the capacity to be distributed in these different ways, constituted the subject matter of the investigation of *distributio*, in such writers as Petrus Hispanus. Ockham lists these ways of distinguishing universal signs, pointing out such variations in conditions of verification as are involved in their differences in form, but he leaves the detailed examination of the grammatical distinctions among such terms to the "studious." [2]

The condition for the truth of a universal affirmative proposition of present time, is that the predicate stands for each individual for which the subject term stands. Where the universal proposition is of present time, it is not the case that the subject term stands for every individual for which it *can* stand—i.e., its actual or indicated supposition does not coincide with its potential supposition, which is determined by its meaning in abstraction from *any* determinate time reference. It is for this reason that Ockham, in various places throughout his logical works, denies that propositions such as "Every man is an animal" are necessary propositions, unless it is understood that the copula "is" refers not merely to present time, but to

[1] S. tot. log., II, 3, 31v.
[2] S. tot. log. II, 4–6, 32r–33r.

every time. Since, however, every time includes the future, and the future exists only potentially, the terms of necessary universal propositions must be understood to stand for what is *or* for what can be.[1]

The chief difference in the formal conditions of truth, for propositions of past or future time, as compared with propositions of present time, is that in propositions of present time the predicate stands for that for which the subject term stands, with respect to the same time of its existence. But in the case of propositions of past or future time, the two terms may not be verifiable of their *supposita* simultaneously at all, either in the past, present, or future—as in the proposition "This white thing will be black." For such propositions to be true, it is required that the subject stand, at the time of predication, for things for which the predicate could have stood (if the proposition is of past time) at the time indicated by the form of assertion, or for which the predicate will be able to stand (if the proposition is of future time) at whatever future time the verb or copula consignifies. Thus, for "this white thing will be black" to be true, the subject term must now denote something of which, at some future time, the term "black" can be a sign. By the above rule we can see why the statement *creans semper fuit Deus* is true, although the statement *creans est Deus* may not always have been true—i.e., before the creation it would have been false.[2]

---

[1] S. tot. log., II, 4, 32r: "ad veritatem talis universalis (*scil.* an affirmative categorical universal proposition) non requiritur quod subiectum et predicatum sint idem realiter, sed requiritur quod predicatum supponat pro omnibus illir pro quibus supponit subiectum, ita quod de illis verificatur; et si ita sit, universalis est vera nisi aliqua causa specialis impediat, et hoc est quod communiter dicitur quod ad veritatem universalis sufficit quod quaelibet singularis sit vera." Ockham rejects, as did most of his contemporaries, the older notion, found for example in William Shyrsewood, that a universal proposition is false unless at least three individuals exist for which its terms stand. Cf. Prantl, p. 19, Anm. 64. Concerning the supposition of terms *pro eo quod potest esse*, in necessary categorical propositions, see S. tot. log., III, II, 5, fol. 64v, and the discussion of this question in Chapter VI, *post.*, pp. 228–34.

[2] S. tot. log., II, 7, 33v: "Unde illa est differentia inter propositiones de praesenti et propositiones de praeterito et de futuro, quod predicatum in propositione de praesenti stat eodem modo quo stat subiectum . . . sed in propositione de praeterito et futuro est variatio, quia predicatum non tantum supponit pro illo . . . pro quo . . . verificatur in propositionibus de

The problem of whether future contingent propositions are determinately true or false in advance of the occurrence of the fact asserted or denied by them, was a subject to which many mediæval writers devoted long discussions, in which the attempt was often made to explain how such propositions could on the part of God be known from all eternity to be true or to be false, without thereby ceasing to be contingent. Ockham, in his commentary on the *De interpretatione*, gives a faithful statement of Aristotle's reasoning, and of his conclusion that future singular propositions are not determinately true or false at the time of predication. He makes no attempt to adjust this conclusion to the theological truth that God has determinate foreknowledge of all future events, nor does he even attempt to suggest by analogy, as St. Thomas does, the mode of God's foreknowledge. Logic, for Ockham, is concerned with the forms of discursive thought, whereby what exists or what can exist apart from, and independently of, our thinking processes, can be understood to be as it is or as it can be, by propositions which are true. But since propositions, for human minds, are precisely those signs which have a reference to time, it is not within the province of the logician or of the discursive scientist to explain how an intellect that transcends all temporality can know a contingent proposition, such as is formed by the human mind with a future time reference, to be determinately true or false. This question Ockham leaves to the theologians. In two *Quaestiones de futuris contingentibus*, printed in the 1496 edition of Ockham's *Golden Exposition*, he examines the problem of divine foreknowledge of the free acts of the human will, and concludes that it is

---

praeterito vel futuro, quia ad hoc quod talis propositio sit vera non sufficit quod illud de quo predicatum verificatur sive per verbum de praesenti sive per verbum de futuro sit illud pro quo subiectum supponit, sed requiritur quod ipsum predicatum verificetur de illo pro quo subiectum supponit secundum quod denotatur per illam propositionem; sicut supposito quod Sortes sit modo albus, vel fuerit per totum diem hodiernum albus, et non ante; tunc haec est falsa 'Sortes fuit heri albus,' et tamen *album* vere predicatur de Sorte et tamen *heri* non predicabatur de Sorte; ideo haec est modo falsa de praeterito 'Sortes fuit heri albus.' Similiter si Sortes nunc primo sit albus, haec est falsa 'Sortes fuit albus' et tamen Sortes fuit illud de quo modo 'album' predicatur."

impossible to express the mode in which God knows future contingents.[1]

While Ockham points out the possibility of distinguishing many kinds of modal propositions besides the four discussed by Aristotle, he does not discuss the meanings of modal terms at all, in his treatise on the proposition, except insofar as such meanings are involved in illustrations of the rules of analysis of such propositions. It is sufficient, for purposes of exhibiting the formal conditions of the truth of modal propositions, to distinguish between the two ways in which modal terms enter into such propositions. Either the modal term functions as predicate, as in the statement "That every man is an animal is necessary," or it functions as an adverb modifying the copula, as in the statement "Every man is necessarily an animal." The first form is said to be *cum dicto*, and the second *sine dicto*. Any modal proposition understood as if it were stated *cum dicto*, whether actually so stated or not, is said to be taken *in sensu composito;* otherwise *in sensu diviso.*

[1] Exp. aur., 108r: "Ad evidentiam istius capituli est primo sciendum quod intentio philosophi est dicere quod in talibus futuris contingentibus neutra pars contradictionis est vera vel falsa determinate, sicut res non determinatur magis ad fore quam ad non fore; et ideo diceret quod Deus non plus scit unam partem contradictionis esse veram vel falsam quam aliam; imo neutra scitur a deo quia ex quo neutra pars est vera sicut determinat hic philosophus, et secundum eum primo Posteriorum, nihil scitur nisi verum, sequitur quod neutra pars est scita. Tamen secundum veritatem et theologos aliter est dicendum quod Deus determinate scit alteram. Quare autem hoc sit in theologia habet declarari." Ibid., 110v: "impossibile est exprimere modum quo Deus scit futura contingentia." Cf. Aquinas, *in Peri Hermenias*, I, IX, Lect. XIV (Leonine ed., pp. 69–70), who gives an analogical explanation, or suggestion, as to how God's mode of fore-knowledge is to be pictured by the human mind.

Ockham's unwillingness to justify, philosophically, the truth of theology which here appears to contradict the philosophical analysis of future contingents, is not a case of the so-called averroist theory of double truth—at least not in its bad sense (indeed, it becomes probable, as averroist writings are more carefully examined, that the averroists themselves were not such hypocrites as some have pictured them). Cf. Doncoeur, "Le Nominalisme de G. Occam" (*Revue Neo-scolastique*, 1921, pp. 20–5), who makes the same point. The justification of such a separation of theology and philosophy can be found in the writings of St. Thomas himself; for, according to Thomas, the truth of human discourse is measured by created things, while things are measured by the intellect of the Creator. Ockham's refusal to synthesize the principles of human knowledge with the principles of the divine creative understanding, is a refusal to synthesize created things with God—a praiseworthy invincibility against the lures of "pantheism" and, theologically speaking, of Pelagianism.

For a modal proposition *cum dicto* (or *in sensu composito*) to be true, it is sufficient that the modal term be truly predicable of the proposition into which the modal term has been introduced or of which it has been affirmed. But for a modal proposition *sine dicto*, or *in sensu diviso*, to be true, it is required that the predicate be verifiable in the same modality of demonstrative pronouns which stand for each of the individual things for which the subject term of the modal proposition stands. Thus the statement "Every man is necessarily an animal," taken *in sensu diviso*, is true only if we can state, with respect to each of the individuals for which the term "Every man" stands, that it is "necessarily an animal." In most cases a singular modal proposition *in sensu diviso* is equivalent to a singular proposition *in sensu composito*; thus "This man is necessarily an animal" would be true under the same conditions as "That this man is an animal is necessary," would be true. But in the case of universal propositions the two senses must always be distinguished, and even in the case of singular propositions, the senses must be distinguished wherever the terms are such that they cannot be verified simultaneously of a demonstrative pronoun indicating what they stand for. Thus, "It is possible that the white is black," is false *in sensu composito* (for "possible" cannot be verified of "The white is black" as a proposition of present time); but "The white is possibly (or can be) black," may be true.[1]

Aristotle, in the eleventh chapter of the *De interpretatione*, discusses the question of when a categorical proposition is equivalent to more than one affirmation, in such manner that

[1] S. tot. log., II, 9–10, 34r: "Est sciendum quod ad veritatem talium propositionum (i.e., *in sensu diviso*) requiritur quod predicatum sub propria forma competat illi pro quo subiectum supponit, vel pronomine demonstranti illud pro quo subiectum supponit, ita scil. quod modus expressus in tali propositione vere predicatur de tali propositione de inesse in qua ipsummet predicatum predicatur de pronomine demonstrante illud pro quo subiectum supponit. . . . Secundo notandum quod tales propositiones de modo consimiliter se habent ad suas singulares sicut propositiones de inesse, et ideo impossibile est quod talis universalis sit vera vel falsa vel contingens vel necessaria nisi quaelibet singularis sit necessaria vel contingens." This of course does not apply to modal propositions *in sensu composito*.

its subject or predicate is not a significative unity. Thus he says that "if a man is a shoemaker and also good, we cannot construct a composite proposition and say that he is a good shoemaker." On the other hand, if a man is an animal and also a biped, we can infer that he is a two-footed animal. Ockham, in his *Golden Exposition*, points out that Aristotle is here concerned not so much with the question of whether a proposition with a composite subject or predicate involves, as a condition of its truth, the truth of more than one proposition; but that he is concerned chiefly with the question of the conditions under which the truth of two propositions, taken separately, allows us to infer the truth of a single proposition in which the two subjects or predicates are combined as a single composite expression.[1]

We may, however, ask the other question—i.e., if the subject term of a categorical proposition signifies what it stands for not *per se*, but through connoting or implying the existence of something for which it does not stand, is not such a proposition equivalent to two distinct propositions, since it cannot be true unless two distinct propositions are true? For example, the statement "Every white man is an animal" will be true only if some men are white; the composite subject "white man" signifies men by connoting the actual existence in them of whiteness, and thus implies, as a condition for its standing for individuals signified by "man" or by "animal," that the following contingent proposition be true: "some men are white." Ockham holds that all such propositions, though categorical in form, are equivalent to hypothetical propositions, and require exposition—i.e., their truth depends on the truth of two distinct propositions, or, in any case, on the co-existence ("con-tingency") of two distinct kinds of things—substance and quality.

[1] Arist., De int. 11, 20b 35. Exp. aur. III, 118r: "Hic determinat philosophus de enunciationibus habentibus aliquod extremum compositum ex pluribus terminis, et dividitur in duas partes, quia primo ostendit qualis est talis propositio. Secundo quomodo ad divisim a coniunctis si est bona consequentia et quomodo non." Ibid., 119r: "Notandum est hic quod philosophus non loquitur praecise de propositione quae est plures, sed etiam indifferenter de propositione quae est plures et de aliqua quando non semper valet consequentia a divisis ad coniuncta."

The principal varieties of *exponibilia*, or of categorical propositions equivalent to hypothetical ones, are: (1) Those in which privative, fictitious, or infinite terms (e.g., "not-man") appear; (2) Those in which a relative pronoun, such as "who," appears; (3) Reduplicative, exceptive, and exclusive propositions; (4) Propositions which state that something "begins to be" or "is ceasing to be"; and (5) Propositions in which are included connotative and relative terms that determinately imply that actual existence of something other than the things for which the terms of the proposition stand.[1]

Propositions with privative, fictitious, and infinite terms generally require two exponents. An example of the privative type is: "He is blind," which is equivalent to "He has not sight, and is naturally capable of having sight." An example of the infinite type is: "An ass is a not-man," which is equivament to "an ass is something, and is not a man." Fictitious terms are those which cannot stand for anything for which the term "being" or "something" can stand, unless the fictitious term is taken non-significatively, or with simple or material supposition. An example of a proposition with a fictitious term, is "A vacuum is an absence of body," and for such a statement to be true the following hypothetical proposition would have to be true: "The absence of body is something, and it is a vacuum." Since "something" cannot be verified of "absence of body" taken significatively and *divisim*, the proposition is false. If, however, we say "The word *vacuum* means whatever the phrase *absence of body* means," our statement may be true, for we are then making a statement about a word, affirming that another expression can be substituted for it without altering the truth or falsity of any proposition in which it enters; this statement, however,

---

[1] S. tot. log., II, 11, 34v: "Dicto de propositionibus cathegoricis quasi simplicibus, dicendum est de propositionibus equivalentibus propositionibus hypotheticis. Et est sciendum quod quaelibet cathegorica ex qua sequuntur plures propositiones cathegoricas tanquam exponentes eam, hoc est, exprimentes quid illa propositio de sua forma importat, potest dici propositio equivalens propositioni hypotheticae. Huiusmodi sunt . . . propositiones exclusivae, exceptivae, et reduplicativae, et huiusmodi sunt etiam omnes propositiones in quibus ponuntur termini connotativi et relativi . . . etc."

can be true regardless of whether or not "vacuum," or "absence of body," can enter into any true proposition significatively.[1]

Propositions in which a relative pronoun appears, such as "A man who is white, is running," require exposition, as follows: "A man is white and he is running." If such a proposition is universal in form, it may have one of two senses. Thus "Every man who is white is running," may be equivalent to "Every man is white, and *every* man is running," or it may be equivalent to "Every man is white, and every *such* man is running." These senses should be distinguished, for avoidance of the fallacy of amphibology, as may be done by the use of commas; e.g., "Every man who is white, runs," or "Every man, who is white, runs."[2]

Reduplicative propositions receive a thorough analysis at Ockham's hands, which is of interest with reference to his argument concerning the difference between the concrete and abstract forms of genera and species of substance. As we observed in connection with this question, Ockham held that the abstract forms signify nothing *in re* other than what is signified by their concrete counterparts, so that the abstract form, as far as its signification is concerned, is synonymous with the concrete form. The difference between "man" and "humanity," according to Ockham, is not a difference in things signified, but a difference in usage. "Humanity," being used as equivalent to the reduplicative expression "Man *qua* man," cannot be used wherever the word "man" is used, even though it signifies nothing distinct from the individual things signified by "man." The reason for this is made evident by the analysis of reduplicative propositions, which require four, or in some cases five, exponents.[3]

Affirmative propositions with a reduplicative subject, such as "Socrates *qua* man is coloured," are either implicative of a condition, or of a cause. In the first case, they have four exponents, as follows: (1) "Socrates is coloured"; (2) "Socrates

[1] S. tot. log., II, 12–4, 35r–35v.   [2] S. tot. log., II, 15, 35v.
[3] Cf. *Ante*, ch. ii, pp. 57–63.

is a man"; (3) "Every man is coloured"; and (4) "If a man is, he is coloured." In the second case, where the reduplicative expression is intended to indicate not merely a condition, but a cause, an additional exponent is required. Thus the statement "Fire insofar as it is hot is calefactive," is true only if the following propositions are true: (1) "Fire is calefactive"; (2) "Fire is hot"; (3) "Every hot thing is calefactive"; (4) "If anything is hot, it is calefactive"; and (5) "That which is hot is the cause of calefaction."[1]

Further distinctions and rules, with respect to negative reduplicatives, and with respect to reduplicatives which include a negation in the subject term, are given in detail, but need not concern us here. What is significant is the fact that Ockham distinguishes "Socrates inquantum homo," from "Socrates," by logical and not by metaphysical means. Because the reduplicative proposition introduces by its form the condition that a universal proposition must be true for the reduplicative proposition to be true, the failure to analyse it into its exponents makes it *appear* to be a statement about "humanity" as exemplified in Socrates. What Ockham insists on, is that in such propositions we are not making a statement about an abstract form that is distinct from individuals, or, in the instance adduced, from the man called Socrates; all we are doing, says Ockham, is to affirm that something is true of Socrates which is also true of every man that exists, or of any man that existed in the past or that might exist in the future, with the further indication that Socrates is a man.

When we speak of "man as such," we are not referring to anything that is not an individual man, but rather we are making a single reference to all individual men that have been,

[1] S. tot. log., II, 16, 36r: "Ex praedictis colligi potest regula talis: quod a propositione reduplicativa ad suam praeiacentem est semper consequentia formalis, quia semper sua praeiacens est una exponens reduplicativae, et ideo sequitur formaliter 'homo inquantum animal est sensibilis, ergo homo est sensibilis.' . . . Ex istis sequitur quod multae propositiones quae a multis conceduntur tam in philosophia quam in theologia, sunt simpliciter falsae de virtute sermonis, cuiusmodi sunt tales: 'creatura inquantum est in deo, est realiter divina essentia' . . . 'homo inquantum creatura est non ens,' . . . etc."

are, or can be. The unity of the things signified, is a function of our mode of signification, and not of a *per se* unity of individual men as "parts" of some one thing called "humanity." Properly speaking, therefore, it is false to say that "Socrates *has* humanity," just as it is false to say that "Socrates is humanity"—not because "humanity" stands for anything that is not an individual man, but because it can only stand for all men taken together. And in the same way, when "humanity" is the subject of a proposition, since it stands conjunctively for all individual men, only a predicate that signifies all individual men at all times, can be truly predicated of it. In mathematics, similarly, where we talk about "quantity" as if it were something distinct from things divisible or things numerable, we have the same situation. The abstract term is equivalent to the reduplicative expression "quantum insofar as it is a quantum," and hence, without signifying any metaphysically distinct entity called "quantity," the abstract term "quantity," and the abstract terms included in the category of quantity, can receive as true predicates only those terms that could be predicated in *universal* propositions of their concrete counterparts.[1]

Exclusive and exceptive propositions also require exposition. An exclusive proposition, such as "Only man is an animal," requires for its truth the truth of two propositions: "Man is an animal," and "Nothing other than man is an animal." An exceptive proposition, such as "Every man except Socrates, is running," is exponible by "Socrates is not running, and every man other than Socrates is running." There are numerous varieties of exclusive and exceptive propositions, but their analysis is along the same lines, and can be passed over.[2]

Propositions in which something is said to "begin to be" or to "cease to be" something, are analysed into two exponents. Thus, "Socrates begins to be white" is equivalent to "Socrates is white and just now was not white." Likewise, "Socrates

[1] Cf. *ante*, ch. iv, pp. 145–151, for Ockham's criticism of the notion of quantity as something distinct from quanta.
[2] S. tot. log., II, 17–8, 37r–38v.

ceases to be white" is equivalent to "Socrates is white and a moment hence will not be white."[1]

Apart from these propositions which require exposition on account of syncategorematic words present in them, or on account of negative connotation in their terms (as in the case of privatives like "blind"), Ockham states that all categorical propositions with connotative or relative terms, are equivalent to hypothetical propositions. This does not mean, however, that a proposition such as "Every man is risible," or "Every body is calefactible," is exponible, unless taken as of present time only; for in these cases the connotative term does not indicate that something distinct from the things for which it can stand exists *in* or *with* the things for which it can stand— i.e., the being together ("con-tingency") of distinct causes is not implied.

The kind of proposition that is exponible on account of containing a relative or connotative term, is the kind which contains a term that connotes the existence, *together with* the things for which it stands, of something for which it does not stand but which it consignifies. Thus "white," standing for a surface, does so by indicating the existence in it of the quality "whiteness," unless the proposition is in the mode of possibility —in which case the contingent fact is not implied as a condition of the truth of the proposition, at least if the proposition is universal. But in a proposition such as "Socrates is white," or "Every man is white," contingent fact is implied. Similarly, "father" can stand for any individual who has a son, only by indicating the existence of a substance (i.e., the son or daughter) distinct from what it stands for—unless, again, the proposition is universal and *de possibili*.[2]

---

[1] S. tot. log., II, 19–20, 38v–39r.

[2] S. tot. log., II, 11, 34v: "sciendum est quod quaelibet propositio quae habet talem terminum est habens exponentes quid importatur per talem propositionem, sed diversae propositiones habent diversas exponentes propter diversos terminos connotativos vel relativos, ideo sufficit dicere de aliquibus ut per illas sciri posset proportionabiliter de aliis quomodo exponuntur. Unde sciendum est quod quandocunque ponitur in propositione concretum cui correspondet abstractum importans rem informantem aliam rem, semper ad veritatem talis propositionis requiritur duae propositiones quae possunt vocari exponentes eius, et una debet esse in recto et alia in obliquo, sicut ad veritatem istius 'Sortes

Ockham states that although Aristotle refers to propositions such as "This man is a man" as instances of essential and *per se* predication, he is, in such cases, using the expression "predication *in quid*" or "*per se*" in a loose sense. Essential predicates attach necessarily to their subjects; but the term "man" does not stand necessarily for something for which the term "this man" stands. The reason is, that the term "this man" has personal supposition only if the person using it can, at the time of predication, point to an individual man—i.e., the term "this man" presupposes the existence of something (*scil.* an act of pointing, or a person who can point) for which it does not stand. Hence, while it is necessarily true that every man is a man, when he exists, and while it is necessarily true that every man is an individual man, it is not necessarily true that an individual indicated by the pronoun "this," is a man, or that an individual man should be so placed that he could be denoted by the word "this."[1]

The most interesting and significant part of this analysis is found in its application to universal propositions. Those which have, as subject or predicate, a term that connotes something for which it does not stand, as existing *in* or *together with* the things for which it does stand, are in every case exponible, and such propositions are always contingent and never necessary or *per se* true. Thus the statement "Every man is white," is exponible, because it indicates the existence *in* the individuals for which its terms stand (*scil.* individual men) of the quality "whiteness" which is really distinct from them.

If now we apply Ockham's principle to the analysis of the

---

est albus' requiritur quod haec sit vera 'Sortes est,' et quod haec sit vera 'Sorti inest albedo'; similiter ad veritatem istius 'album currit,' requiruntur illae duae 'aliquid currit' et 'illud habet albedinem,' et ita est de aliis."

[1] S. tot. log., II, 11, 35r: "intelligendum est quod proprie et stricte accipiendo 'predicari per se et in quid,' quod scilicet est necessario predicabile, sic nulla talis species 'homo,' 'asinus,' 'numerus' et huiusmodi predicatur in quid et dicitur per se de aliquo, maxime in propositione de inesse et de praesenti, et hoc quia nulla talis est necessaria, 'Sortes est homo,' 'asinus est asinus,' 'iste numerus est numerus,' 'iste motus est motus,' et huiusmodi." Here Ockham indicates, against Porphyry, that the *infima species* is not a predicable in direct predication —i.e., science is not of the particular.

universal propositions of demonstrative science, such as are said to be necessary and *per se* true, we find that the possibility of such propositions being necessary, *per se*, and non-exponible, depends entirely on the question of whether or not Ockham's "nominalistic" solution of the problem of universals is correct. For example, the proposition "Every man is an animal," which is said to be necessary and to be *per se primo modo*, is actually so only on condition that neither term indicates the existence, *in* or *with* the things for which it stands, of anything distinct from them. And since, according to Ockham, genera and species of substance signify nothing distinct from the individuals for which they can stand, the necessity of such propositions is preserved. But if we insist, with the mediæval "logical realists," that genera and species of substance signify, or consignify, really distinct "parts" *in* the individuals denoted by them, or if we hold that "humanity" and "animality" signify things *in re* distinct from the individuals signified by "man" and by "animal," then such propositions as "Every man is an animal" would be exponible and contingent.

Or let us take the proposition "Every man is rational." Here the predicate is connotative, and indicates the intellective soul. According to Ockham, the essential differentia stands for the individuals for which its subject stands, not by connoting the existence *in* individual men of a substantial form really distinct from their individual nature, but by signifying a "part" of their actually undivided nature—i.e., signifying this nature *partly*. If, however, we take the view that there is a real distinction between substantial form and prime matter, and consider that the essential differentia indicates the existence *in* matter of a substantial form distinct from it, then the essential differentia cannot be regarded as necessarily predicable of the specific term of whose definition it is a part, and all such propositions as "Every man is rational" will be exponible and contingent.

Finally, we may apply Ockham's principle of analysis to the proposition "Every man is risible," which is said to be necessary and *per se secundo modo*, because the term "man" is

included in the determinate nominal definition of "risible."
Now according to Ockham, "risible" is predicated necessarily
of "man" because there is no distinction *in re* between a substance and its potentialities of change—i.e., "risible" stands
for individual men by indicating the power of laughter, which
according to Ockham, is not anything distinct from the
individual substances which are said (improperly) to "have"
the power of laughing. According to Ockham, individual
men do not *have* the power of laughing, as they have heat in
them or whiteness—they *are* the power of laughter. But if,
with most of Ockham's mediæval contemporaries, we hold that
there is a real or metaphysical distinction between a substance
and its potentialities, propositions which are called *per se
secundo modo* will not be true *per se*, or necessary, but will be
exponible and contingent, because their truth will be a function
of the togetherness in existence of entities which, being distinct
in being, might be and yet not "be together." Thus the thomists, by insisting on a "real" distinction between the soul and
its faculties or powers, unconsciously destroy the necessity of
such propositions as "Every man is capable of knowing," and
thereby destroy the necessity of the principle by which St.
Thomas argued against the averroist doctrine of the separated
active intellect![1]

One further condition on which the necessity of scientific
propositions depends, and which will be taken up later in
more detail, is this—no proposition is necessarily true or true
per se, whose terms are taken as standing for the things they
can stand for, merely in present time. All such propositions
are exponible and contingent, because determinate temporal
connotation implies the co-existence or contingency of substance and quality in the act of change (time being the measure
of motion or change), whereas propositions that indicate the
co-existence of distinct things are never necessary but are

---

[1] Cf. *ante*, ch. iv, p. 142, Note 2. Also Exp. aur., I, 27v: "Ex isto sequitur
quod risibilitas non est alia res formaliter ab homine sibi inhaerens sicut nec
calefactivitas est aliqua alia res formaliter inhaerens calori. Sed sicut 'calefactivitas' non importat nisi principium calefactivum a quo potest esse calor, ita
'risibilitas' non importat nisi hominem qui potest habere actum ridendi."

always exponible and contingent. Hence Ockham states that the propositions of demonstrative science must be understood not as statements about the existence of things in time, but as statements about things which *can* exist in time. Science, in other words, is not about changes (events), but about principles or potentialities of change (causes).[1]

From this analysis of exponible propositions it can be seen how Ockham's treatment of the problem of universals and of individuation, and his analysis of the categories, forms the foundation for the all important aristotelian distinction between demonstrative science and dialectical generalization or hypothesis. If all general propositions were exponible, and hence contingent, the aristotelian conception of science as demonstrative knowledge of necessary universal truths, would be pure illusion. But, as Ockham seeks to show, those who refer the distinctions between genera, species, differentiæ, and properties, to really distinct things co-existing *in* the individuals denoted by them, automatically destroy the distinction between essential and accidental predication, and between necessary and contingent propositions. As has been stated before, Ockham's logical nominalism is the *sine qua non* of his metaphysical realism.[2]

---

[1] Ockham, at this point, merely touches briefly on the question of whether all universal propositions are exponible, and dismisses the question as follows, S. tot. log., III, II, 11, 34v: "Sed dubitari potest an quaelibet propositio universalis habeat tales exponentes; videtur quod sic, quia quaelibet talis habet plures singulares. Dicendum est quod propositio universalis in qua ponitur hoc signum 'uterque' vel 'neuter' de virtute sermonis equivalet propositioni hypotheticae, sed illa in qua ponitur 'omne' vel 'nullus,' vel 'quilibet' non sic, quia quamvis habeat multas singulares tamen hoc non est necessarium, quia sicut demonstratus est prius haec est vera 'omnis fenix est' quamvis non sit insi una fenix." For his full discussion of the character of scientific propositions, see the next chapter, on Demonstration.

[2] The concluding portion of Part II of the *Sum of All Logic*, dealing with the conversion of propositions, is treated sufficiently, in its main features, by Prantl (pp. 392–6), to justify the omission of an exposition of it here. The treatment is not marked by any unorthodox features—the principal addition to Aristotle is found in the use of the distinction between *sensus divisus* and *sensus compositus* in stating the rules for the conversion of modals. Ockham also shows that the equivalences between convertible propositions (i.e. of formally convertible ones) is a function of the maintenance of the indicated supposition of the terms, so that conversion requires no "middle," and is immediate.

III

Ockham's analysis of the syllogism, contained in the first division of Part III of his *Sum of All Logic*, resembles his analysis of the categorical proposition to the extent that it is a differentiation of forms of discourse, through reference to different ways in which logically distinguished parts are put together to form a unity. While the divisions of Part III of the *Sum of All Logic* that are concerned with demonstration, topical reasoning, and fallacies, are also concerned with syllogism, they are not concerned with the syllogism as such, but rather with the manner in which knowledge, opinion, and error may be produced syllogistically through premises which are either evident, probable, or neither evident nor probable.

Aristotle's prefatory remarks concerning demonstrative, topical, and dialectical premises, in the first chapter of the *Prior Analytics*, indicate two things: (1) that the formal analysis of the syllogism is relevant to the fields of inquiry to which the later books of the *Organon* are devoted, and (2) that the distinctions between premises as demonstrative, topical, etc., are not to be taken into consideration in the *Prior Analytics*. In this treatise the premise is defined simply as "a sentence affirming or denying one thing of another," and it is differentiated as universal or particular, assertoric or modal, without reference to whether, in point of fact, it is true or false, known or believed.[1] Ockham's division of syllogisms on the basis of the epistemic character of their premises, is somewhat more systematically expressed than that of Aristotle, and is interesting enough to repeat *verbatim*.

---

[1] Cf. Arist., Anal. Priora I, 1, 24a 10–24b 16. Our justification for including the treatment of Ockham's analysis of the syllogism *in communi* in the same chapter with his analysis of the categorical proposition, may well be questioned, since Ockham does not group them together. This arrangement is dictated partly by reasons of convenience, and partly because Ockham's *method* of analysis is purely formal in both treatises—i.e., his analysis of syllogistic forms, as of propositional forms, is carried out without reference to the meanings of terms of first intention, or to determination of the truth or falsity of propositions formed from them.

Of syllogisms some are demonstrative, some topical, and some neither topical nor demonstrative. A demonstrative syllogism is one in which, from necessary propositions evidently known, first knowledge of a conclusion can be acquired. But a topical syllogism is from probable premises. And probable premises are those which appear (*scil.* to be true) to all or to the majority or to the wisest; and this description is to be understood thus, that probable premises are those which are true and necessary but not known *per se* and not syllogistically demonstrable from premises known *per se*, and which, further, are not evidently known through experience, nor demonstrable from such—but which, on account of their truth, appear to be true to all or to the majority or to the wisest. And, to be brief, let this be the description of probable premises: Probable premises are necessary truths, which are neither principles nor conclusions of demonstration, but which on account of their truth appear (to be true) to all or to the majority or to the wisest. By the first particular are excluded all contingent and all false propositions; by the second all principles and conclusions of demonstrations; and by the third are excluded certain necessary truths which however appear to be false to all or to the majority. And thus the articles of the Faith are not principles of demonstration nor conclusions, nor are they probable, for they appear false to all or to the majority or to the wisest—taking "wisest" here for the wise men of this world, and particularly for those using natural reason, because it is in this manner that the wise man is understood in the description of science or philosophy.

From these things it follows that the topical syllogism never errs either materially or formally, and it also follows that no one, in the natural course of things, can know evidently and demonstratively, with respect to any topical syllogism, that it is a topical syllogism, although he can have faith that it is one.

The syllogism which is neither demonstrative nor topical can be divided, because one kind is from improbable premises, and the other from premises that are not improbable; or, one kind errs in its matter, and the other kind does not err in its matter.[1]

The definition of the syllogism as such, which is applicable in common to demonstrative, topical, and all other kinds of syllogism, is given by Aristotle as follows: "A syllogism is discourse in which, certain things being stated, something other than what is stated follows of necessity from their being so." Whether the premises are true or false, known or believed, is

[1] S. tot. log., III, I, cap. 1, 44v.

irrelevant to the production of a syllogism; the most that can be said, with regard to the truth or falsity of the parts of a syllogism, is that the conclusion cannot be false if both premises are true, though the contrary may be the case.[1]

Before taking up the generation of the figures and modes of syllogisms, and distinguishing those whose premises are assertoric from those whose premises are modal, etc., Ockham states certain *preambula*, indicating that every syllogism is composed of two premises and a conclusion, and of three terms, called major, minor, and middle. He then distinguishes the three figures according to the position of the middle term in the two premises, stating that there is no fourth figure, since the difference in position of the middle term in the so-called fourth figure is merely due to the transposition of major and minor premises of the first figure. Consequently no other conclusions follow than those produced in the first figure.[2]

The generation of the modes of the first figure is exhibited through an enumeration of the sixteen possible combinations of universal affirmative, universal negative, particular affirma-

[1] Arist., An. Priora I, 1, 24b 18-9. Ockham, S. tot. log., III, I, 1, 44v: "Sillogismus est oratio in qua ex duabus praemissis dispositis in modo et figura de necessitate sequitur conclusio; et ad illam diffinitionem nihil refert an praemissae sint verae vel falsae; hoc tamen est generale, quod nunquam praemissae sunt verae et conclusio falsa, quamvis possit esse econverso."

[2] S. tot. log., III, I, 2, 44v: "Positis divisionibus et distinctionibus sillogismi, de quibusdam membris dividentibus in speciali est dicendum. Et primo de uniformi generatione sillogismorum de inesse, secundo de uniformi modalium, et tertio de mixtis. Circa primum est primo dicendum de sillogismis ex omnibus de inesse et de praesenti, secundo de aliis, sed antequam accedatur ad propositum videnda sunt quaedam preambula. Primum est quod tantum sunt duae praemissae et una conclusio in sillogismo et tantum tres termini, scil. major extremitas, minor extremitas, et medium. Est autem medium quod ponitur in utraque praemissarum, major extremitas quae cum medio termino ponitur in majori propositione. Minor extremitas est quae ponitur cum medio in minore propositione, hoc est, in secunda propositione. Secundum est quod tantum sunt tres figurae. Prima est in qua medius terminus subiicitur in prima propositione et predicatur in secunda. Secunda figura est in qua medius terminus predicatur in utraque. Tertia figura est in qua medius terminus subiicitur in utraque. Et non est apponenda quarta figura, quia si medius terminus predicatur in prima propositione et subiicitur in secunda non erit nisi transpositio propositionum positarum in prima figura et ideo non sequitur alia conclusio quam illa quae sequitur ex praemissis dispositis in prima figura. . . ."

tive, and particular negative propositions, and through the elimination of those modes which are invalid. Two ways of distinguishing the valid from the invalid modes are mentioned: (1) If we consider the syllogism as the exhibition of the connection of major and minor term, with respect to their indicated supposition, through the middle term, then every valid form of the syllogism can be recognized by the fact that it is regulated (immediately in the first figure and mediately in the others) by the *dictum de omni et de nullo ;* (2) If we consider the syllogism as a *consequentia,* or as equivalent to a hypothetical proposition with a conjunctive antecedent, its valid forms can be distinguished from the invalid forms inductively, since no instance of the valid forms can be found in which a false conclusion follows from true premises.

Ockham states that there is no *demonstration* of the validity of a valid mode in the first figure, but only the inductive or dialectical proof afforded by the second method mentioned above. That this second method is not strictly demonstrative is plain from the fact that it argues from the apparent truth of every conclusion produced through one of the valid modes from premises which are evident or apparently true to the validity of the mode by which such a conclusion is produced. This inductive procedure enables us to distinguish the valid modes from the invalid ones, and to state our distinctions in the form of rules governing the production of valid syllogisms. We can, furthermore, defend these rules dialectically, by challenging anyone to find a proposition generally held to be false (or held to be false by the majority or the wisest) which would follow through one of the valid modes, from premises conceded to be true by everybody, or by the majority, or by the wisest. But we cannot use these rules as principles for the demonstration of the validity of syllogisms formed according to them, because the validity of the rules is based on the validity of the instances of which the rules are generalizations; and the apparent validity of these instances is referred, in the inductive procedure, to judgments concerning the truth or falsity of actual propositions which, though generally conceded to be true, are not known in the strict and demonstrative sense.[1]

The other way in which a valid syllogism can be distinguished from one that is not formally valid, does not presuppose, as ground of induction, determinate knowledge or belief with respect to the truth or falsity of any propositions which can be conclusions of a demonstrative syllogism. Every syllogism regulated according to the *dictum de omni et de nullo*, either immediately (as in the first figure) or mediately (as in the other figures), is valid, and every syllogistic arrangement of terms and propositions not so regulated, is not valid, and is not a true syllogism. This also is not a demonstration, but rather a definition of what a syllogism is. As a definition, however, it has distinct advantages from the logical point of view; for it refers only to terms and to ways in which one term can be affirmed or denied of another, and does not presuppose determinate knowledge of the truth or falsity of demonstrable propositions, nor any postulates concerning the truth or falsity of such propositions. All that it presupposes is the existence of terms—i.e., that there are signs (mental, spoken, or written) such as can stand, in discourse, for things for which some, but not all, other terms can stand. From this definition of the term, Ockham's whole analysis of the categories and of the categorical proposition, can be derived; and in the same way, the *dictum de omni et de nullo*, as the principle by which a syllogism can be distinguished from an arrangement of terms

---

[1] S. tot. log., III, I, 3–4, 45r–45v: "Ista narrata (*scil.*, the manner in which the modes of the first figure are generated) non possunt probari nisi per modum quo probat Aristoteles, probando quod sunt quatuor modi utiles, per hoc quod non contingit inferre instantiam, unde servando talem modum arguendi ex duabus universalibus affirmativis, 'omnis homo est animal, omne risibile est homo, ergo omne risibile est animal,' impossibile est invenire instantiam ubi praemissae sunt verae et conclusio falsa. . . ." Ockham uses the word *probare*, and not *demonstrare*, because a dialectical proof is not a demonstration, but rather a "proving"—in the sense of "testing"—of a thesis. Ibid.: "Et est hic advertendum quod ad probandum combinationem inutilem vel modum inutilem non oportet invenire instantiam in terminis substantialibus sicut quidam errantes dicunt, sed sufficit invenire instantiam in quibuscumque terminis sive substantialibus sive accidentalibus sive quibuscumque." Cf. *ante*, ch. iv, pp. 129–130, on Boethius' restriction of the *dictum de omni* to predication *in quid*, and Ockham's criticism.

and propositions that is not a syllogism, presupposes nothing more than what is involved in Ockham's definition of a term.

Aristotle's statement of the *dictum de omni et de nullo*, in the *Prior Analytics*, is as follows: "Whenever three terms are so related to one another that the last is contained in the middle as in a whole, and the middle is either contained in, or excluded from, the first as in or from a whole, the extremes must be related by a perfect syllogism."[1] Previously Aristotle had said: "That one term should be included in another as in a whole is the same as for the other to be predicated of all of the first."[2] The mediæval statement of this rule was more brief: *nihil est sumere sub subiecto quin de eodem dicatur predicatum*. As Ockham points out, this definition of the perfect syllogism is not to be understood as if it were required that the major term should be *truly* predicable of everything of which the middle term is predicated—for if that were the case, syllogisms could be formed only from true propositions, and we would have to know whether the premises of a syllogism were true before we could determine whether or not it was a syllogism. It is sufficient, says Ockham, that the *form of affirmation*, by which the major term is predicated of the middle term, be such that the predicate is indicated to stand for everything for which the subject can stand, and that the form of the minor premise be affirmative, for a syllogism to result.

Aristotle, in stating his rule by reference to the relation between three terms, is to be taken literally—he is talking about terms, related through forms of affirmation or denial, and not about "real" relations between things signified by the terms. Syllogisms, as such, are arrangements of terms as parts of affirmations and denials; to produce a valid syllogism regulated by the *dictum de omni et de nullo*, we do not have to consider the meanings of terms, or the truth or falsity of propositions, but we do have to know how to *state* the major premise

[1] Arist., An. Priora I, 4, 25b 32–5.
[2] Arist., An. Priora I, 1, 24b 26–30.

as a universal affirmation or denial, and the minor premise as a universal or particular affirmation.[1]

The question of whether the syllogism is to be considered primarily as an ordering of terms in intension or primarily as an ordering of terms in extension, has no place in Ockham's discussion. The existence of the syllogism presupposes the existence of terms, and terms have intentional character precisely insofar as they have determinate capacity to stand for individual things for which some, but not all, other terms can stand. The analysis of the syllogism as such, requires the distinction between affirmative and negative propositions which are either universal or particular; and these distinctions in turn rest on the general recognition of what is involved in the definition of the *term*, as such—namely, its determinate capacity to stand for things when combined through predication with other terms. But although the existence of the syllogism presupposes the existence of terms whose nature is their determinate capacity to stand for many individuals, and thus presupposes both that terms are of determinate character (i.e., have "intension"), and that they can stand for things (or have "extension"), the analysis of the syllogism as such does not involve any reference *either* to the meanings or definitions of terms, *or* to knowledge of their *true predicative relations* to each other—*scil.*, as genus, differentia, property, or accident. The arrangement of three terms in three propositions, according to the specifications expressed in the *dictum de omni et de nullo*, constitutes a syllogism in the first figure, whether it is

[1] S. tot. log., III, I, 2, 45r: "Est autem dici de omni quando nihil est sumere sub subiecto quin de eodem dicatur predicatum. Quod est sic intelligendum: non quod predicatum vere conveniat cuilibet de quo dicitur subiectum, quia tunc non esset dici de omni nisi in propositionibus veris; sed sufficit quod per talem propositionem denotatur quod nihil sit sumere sub subiecto quin de eodem dicatur predicatum, et hoc denotatur per omnem propositionem universalem affirmativam." Ibid. 4, 46r: Here Ockham states that propositions of theology, dealing with the Trinity or with the dual nature of Christ, are not regulated by the *dici de omni*, because in these cases, a single thing is several really distinct things, which is not the case in natural things such as can be objects of finite understanding. It is interesting to observe that the principles and methods upheld by *multi moderni* or *multi errantes* in logic, and certain distinctions such as the scotist *distinctio formalis a parte rei*, which Ockham criticizes constantly insofar as they are introduced into logic or philosophy, apply very aptly to the statement of theological dogma, as indeed Ockham recognizes.

a demonstrative syllogism, a topical syllogism, or a syllogism composed of false statements or of improbable statements or of articles of faith.

The same principles of analysis are applied by Ockham to the modes of the second and third figures, these being regulated only mediately by the *dictum de omni et de nullo*. The methods of reduction (i.e., by conversion or *per impossibile*) of the modes of the second and third figures to the first, and the "weakened conclusions" that can be drawn through the first and second figures, are given in the traditional manner. Ockham includes the so-called "expository syllogism" under the third figure, laying down the following restrictions: (1) the middle term, which is subject in both premises, must be singular in the sense that it can stand only for one thing which is not many—a restriction which excludes not only terms having *suppositio communis* but also certain theological terms (such as the names of the Persons of the Trinity); and (2) the minor premise must be affirmative. Such a syllogism may be composed entirely of singular terms, and it is called expository because it is a method of exhibiting two terms as two ways of signifying or denoting some one thing. Possibly Ockham would have given as an example of such a syllogism, had he lived in recent years, the following: "Scott was the author of *Waverley*; Scott was the author of *Marmion*; therefore the author of *Waverley* was the author of *Marmion*."[1]

A number of rules are given for syllogisms in which one premise is of present time and the other premise of past time. Thus, in the first figure, if the middle term stands in the major premise for things which exist now, the minor premise must be of present time and not of past time. Or if the subject of

---

[1] S. tot. log., III, I, 16, 50r: "sciendum est quod sillogismus expositorius est qui est ex duabus praemissis singularibus dispositis in tertia figura quae tamen possunt inferre conclusionem tam particularem quam singularem sive indefinitam, sed non universalem. . . . requiritur quod subiectum supponit pro aliquo quod non est plures res quaecunque, nec est idem realiter cum aliquo quocunque quod est plures res sive respective sive absolute. . . ." Ibid., 50v: "et quia in creaturis nulla una res numero est plures res realiter quaecunque, ideo generaliter quando arguitur ex propositionibus singularibus praedicto modo sit sillogismus expositorius; hoc addito quod minor sit affirmativa."

the major stands for things which have existed (e.g., "Every thing that was alive two hundred years ago is dead"), then the minor premise must not be taken in present time.[1]

The rest of Ockham's analysis of the syllogism is taken up with a detailed and exhaustive statement of the rules for constructing uniform and mixed syllogisms from modal propositions, in the three figures. The distinction between the two senses of modal propositions (*sensus divisus* and *sensus compositus*), adds enormously to the complexity of this analysis, but brings to light many cases where syllogisms taken in one of these senses are valid, while if taken in the other sense they are invalid. The careful application of this distinction to modal syllogisms, as well as a more exhaustive examination of possible combinations of modes, and a more systematic statement of rules, is all that Ockham's analysis adds to the work of Aristotle on this subject. In addition, Ockham investigates, in a more cursory manner, the validity of syllogisms composed partly or wholly of exponible propositions, such as exceptives and reduplicatives, but finds relatively few valid varieties of such syllogisms. Finally, a brief paragraph on the hypothetical syllogism appears in which only the *modus ponendo ponens* is treated; that this final chapter is by Ockham seems questionable, since the previous chapter ends with the words: "Et ista de sillogismis ad praesens sufficiant."[2]

Prantl, seemingly appalled by the intricacy of Ockham's analysis of modal syllogisms, characterizes this part of the *Sum of All Logic* as sterile, and as one more instance of the bad effect on mediæval logicians of the "byzantinische Formalismus." Yet if one is patient and in not too much of a hurry, the careful reading of this part of Ockham's work is not without interest, for it has the rather good feature of exhibiting, in application to the most complex and subtly varied forms of

---

[1] S. tot. log., III, I, 17, 50v.

[2] This statement comes at the end of cap. 67, fol. 63v. Prantl, pp. 399-409, includes in his foot-notes a fairly adequate selection of citations from Ockham's treatment of the forms of syllogism, which is sufficient to indicate the manner in which he applies the principles and technique of analysis developed in the previous parts of his logical *Summa*, to the syllogism in its many forms.

discursive statement, principles of analysis which are intrin-
sically simple and intelligible, and which nevertheless are fully
adequate for making evident the form and construction of
the most complex syllogistic "fabrications." If the size of
the harvest is any indication of the fertility of the seed, we
should, on contemplating Ockham's thickly planted crop of
syllogistic forms, attribute sterility not to him nor to his principles, but rather to the modern temperament which is appalled
(and even the indefatigable Prantl wavers here) at the thought
of having to reap so great a harvest.[1]

With this brief indication of Ockham's treatment of the
syllogism as a form of complex signification, we reach the end
of that part of Ockham's logic which deals with terms and
with modes of combining terms into propositions and syllogisms. The analysis so far has been, in a strict sense, concerned
with *forms of discourse*, and not with the existence or non-
existence of things signified, or with the truth or falsity of
statements about such things. Where metaphysics has been
brought in, as with the "problem of universals," it has been
only in order to show how to keep from mixing metaphysics
with logic and with discursive science; what many of Ockham's contemporaries looked upon as metaphysical "problems," Ockham regarded as instances of equivocation with
respect to the supposition of terms. Such metaphysics as
is involved in Ockham's analysis, is involved in the existence
of terms—i.e., of acts of understanding which signify *things* and
which are capable of standing for them in propositions. *Ens,
unum, aliquid*, or the other transcendental terms, are inescap-
able except by complete silence—and although a metaphysics
which consists only of six convertible terms of absolute universality, may seem like a small thing, it cannot be shaken off, and
it need not be added to.

[1] Cf. Prantl, p. 401: "Wenn wir . . . bei Occam den hingebenden Fleiss
und die Verschwendung eines einseitigen Scharfsinnes anerkennen müssen, so
hat derselbe dennoch gerade durch jenen byzantinischen Formalismus das
Ganze derartig ertödtet, dass für eine besonnene Wissenschaftslehre oder Logik
hieraus keinerlei Frucht erwachsen kann . . ." etc. etc.

CHAPTER SIX

DEMONSTRATION AND DEFINITION

I

THE analysis of the term, of the proposition, and of the syllogism as such, which in Aristotle's *Organon* carries us to the end of the *Prior Analytics*, is a dissection of component parts or factors distinguishable in any kind of reasoned discourse, whether demonstrative or topical. Ockham, in the second division of Part III of his *Sum of All Logic*, undertakes to make use of this previous analysis in the statement of the characteristics and conditions proper to the kind of discourse that yields demonstrative knowledge and that exhibits indemonstrable principles.

Ockham's treatise on demonstration covers most of the material contained in the *Posterior Analytics*, but in somewhat different order, and with his characteristic language and methods of statement everywhere evident. Aristotle, being an urbane resident of Athens, makes his doctrine evident through inviting us to investigate and discuss problems and difficulties; Ockham, in mediæval fashion, seeks to follow the order in which that which is prior in the absolute sense comes first, and hence he defines his terms and sets forth his principles, leaving it to the pupil or reader to apply them in the solution of problems.

The general order of Ockham's discussion is as follows: (1) He states what a demonstrative syllogism is, enumerates the parts (terms and propositions) required in demonstrations, and indicates the respects in which they differ from terms and propositions which do not enter into demonstrative syllogisms. (2) He indicates how universal truths, both demonstrable and indemonstrable, may come to be known by experience without demonstration, and discusses the relation between knowledge of the fact and knowledge of the reasoned fact. (3) He discusses *a priori* demonstration, and the relation between demonstration and definition, in connection with the four questions enumerated by Aristotle in Book II of the *Posterior Analytics*.

In order to ascertain the conditions proper to demonstrative science, it is necessary to state the meaning of the word "demonstration." According to Aristotle, a demonstration is a "syllogism productive of knowledge." What a syllogism is, has already been indicated; but the word "knowledge," connoted by the term "demonstration," can be taken in more than one sense. Insofar as it is used strictly, as distinct from faith or opinion, Ockham discriminates three senses. (1) *To know* may mean evident grasp of a truth; and in this sense not only necessary propositions are said to be known, but also contingent ones evident in the act of perception. (2) *To know* may mean the evident grasp of a truth which cannot be false, and in this sense only necessary propositions are said to be known. (3) *To know* may mean the grasp of one necessary truth through the evident understanding of two necessary truths forming the premises of a syllogism, such that the conclusion is of itself capable of being doubted, but can be evidently known through the premises. And it is in this last sense that "knowledge" is connoted by the term "demonstration."[1]

[1] S. tot. log., III, II, 1, 63v: "Oportet autem primo scire quod secundum doctrinam Aristotelis demonstratio est sillogismus faciens scire; ista enim diffinitio, *scil.* 'faciens scire,' est diffinitio exprimens quid nominis illius termini 'demonstratio.' . . . Dico ergo quod omnes de demonstratione loquentes per hunc terminum 'demonstratio' non intelligunt nisi sillogismum facientem scire; sed quia 'scire' in diversis locis accipitur equivoce, videndum est quomodo 'scire' in hac diffinitione accipitur. Unde sciendum est quod quamvis 'scire' diversis modis accipi possit, tamen sufficit ad praesens dicere quod tribus modis dicitur. Uno modo 'scire' dicitur evidens comprehensio veritatis, et sic dicuntur sciri non tantum necessaria sed etiam contingentia, sicut scio te sedere et me vivere. Secundo modo dicitur 'scire' evidens comprehensio veritatis quae non potest esse falsa, et sic dicuntur sciri tantum necessaria et non contingentia. Tertio modo dicitur 'scire' comprehensio unius veritatis necessariae, per evidentem comprehensionem duarum veritatum necessarium, puta duarum praemissarum in modo et figura dispositarum; et illae duae veritates faciunt tertiam veritatem evidenter sciri quae aliter esset ignota, et sic accipitur 'scire' in praedicta diffinitione." Cf. Arist., An. Post. I, 2, 71b 18–24.
Aristotle uses the expression "scientific knowledge" (ἐπιστήμη or scientia) in this strict sense, in most of the Posterior Analytics (e.g., 100b 10–2, where

Since a demonstration is a syllogism, it must have three terms. But not all kinds of terms can enter into every kind of demonstration. Terms which imply the existence, *in* or *with* the things for which they stand, of things really distinct from them, cannot enter into affirmative assertoric premises; for propositions in which such terms appear, if affirmative and assertoric, are exponible and contingent. Such terms may, however, be parts of negative and modal premises. Thus, while the statement "Every body is hot" is contingent, the modal proposition "Every body can be hot," and the negative proposition "No colour is hot," are necessary. In the same way, terms whose nominal definitions include a contradiction, so that "being" is not predicable of them significatively in a proposition of possibility, cannot enter into affirmative categorical premises, though they may be predicates in negative premises.[1]

The terms which can be parts of *demonstratio potissima*, according to Ockham, are those signified by the following terms of

it is contrasted with νοῦς, by which indemonstrable principles are grasped); but sometimes he uses it in the broader sense as in Ockham's second definition. Ockham as a rule uses *scientia* for ἐπιστήμη, and *cognitio*, or *evidens cognitio*, as a more general term equivalent to "scire" in sense 2; he also uses *notitia intuitiva* to express νοῦς, whereby we recognize the being of what is signified by the essential definition.

In any case, "demonstration" must connote knowledge only in sense 3, of the three senses enumerated by Ockham; for if in sense 2, then scientific knowledge would involve infinite regress among necessary truths; and if in sense 1, sense perception would be a demonstrative syllogism, for a demonstration could then be defined as a "syllogism producing sense perception." While this is not as absurd as it sounds (certainly not to a pragmatist), it obviously is not what Aristotle means by "demonstration."

[1] S. tot. log., III, II, 1, 63v: "Omnis autem demonstratio componitur ex propositionibus et propositiones ex terminis. Unde quia terminorum et propositionum ex quibus constat demonstratio sunt quaedam conditiones propriae non omnibus terminis competentis, ideo primo dicendum est de conditionibus eorum; secundo de propositionibus requisitis ad demonstrationem; tertio de demonstratione." Ibid., 2, 63v: "Non omnes autem termini possunt ingredi demonstrationem affirmativam ex propositionibus mere de inesse et de praesenti, illi enim termini qui de nullo possunt predicari nisi contingenter vel falsis, ipsis sumptis significative, nunquam possunt esse partes demonstrationis talis. . . . quamvis in demonstratione negativa possunt esse, quia in negativa possunt de aliis necessario predicari. Similiter quamvis tales termini 'album,' 'nigrum,' 'calidum' et huiusmodi non possunt esse partes propositionum necessarium mere de inesse et de praesenti affirmativarum, tamen possunt esse partes propositionum de possibili necessarium, ideo talem demonstrationem ingredi possunt."

second intention: "subject," "definition," "attribute." In the strict sense in which these terms are here used, only absolute terms in the category of substance are "subjects," and only those terms which can stand for individuals signified by genera and species of substance, are "attributes." In a broader sense, mathematical demonstrations can be called *demonstrationes potissimae*, even though they do not fulfill these conditions. It is to be observed that affirmative assertoric premises in which attributes are predicated of their proximate subjects, are equivalent to propositions *de possibili* in which connotative terms indicating the actual contingent unity of distinct elements are predicated of the same subjects. Thus "Every body is calefactible," which is assertoric and necessary, is equivalent to "Every body can be hot," which is a necessary proposition *de possibili*.[1]

Since a proposition cannot be known to be true if the meanings of its terms are not unequivocally understood, Ockham states that *quid est* must be understood of every term that enters

[1] S. tot. log., III, II, 2, 64r: "Unde breviter secundum veritatem, demonstrationum de qua dicitur inferius omnes termini aliquam demonstrationem ingredi possunt, sed non omnes ingredi possunt demonstrationem potissimam de qua dicitur inferius. Termini autem qui demonstrationem potissimam ingredi possunt sunt praecise: passio, subiectum, et diffinitio . . . sciendum est quod passio . . . est quoddam predicabile distinctum a subiecto realiter importans illud idem quod importat subiectum, et aliquid plus vel saltem illud idem alio modo. Et eodem modo est de diffinitione. . . ." For the strict meanings of *passio, subiectum,* and *diffinitio,* cf. *ante,* ch. iii, pp. 106–11, 112 and 116. Concerning the demonstration of attributes of mathematical subjects, cf. S. tot. log., III, II, 40, 73v: "Verumtamen sciendum quod talis diffinitio subiecti non semper est propriissima diffinitio talis qualis est praecise substantiarum, sed frequenter diffinitio indicans partes integrales rei quales sunt diffinitiones mathematicorum, et de tali demonstratione potissima per quam demonstratur passio sive diffinitio exprimens quid nominis passionis de suo subiecto primo per diffinitionem subiecti tanquam per medium intelliguntur multae auctoritates in libro posteriorum. . . . quamvis omnis sillogismus ex necessariis et indemonstrabilibus faciens scire conclusionem prius ignotam sit demonstratio magis large sumendo demonstrationem, tali etiam demonstratione non potest una conclusio nisi unica demonstratione demonstrari quamvis aliis demonstrationibus possit unica conclusio multis demonstrationibus demonstrari . . . et per illas distinctiones et consimiles possunt solvi multa quae praedictis et etiam dictis Aristotelis in diversis locis repugnare videntur." Since mathematical attributes can usually be demonstrated in more than one way of their subjects, mathematical demonstration is *demonstratio potissima* only in a broader sense than is the case with physical demonstrations. Concerning the equivalence of "Every man possibly laughs" to "Every man is risible," cf. ch. iii, p. 104–5, on the word "property."

into a demonstration. That is to say, the meaning of the word must be grasped unambiguously, by a real definition or a nominal definition. Furthermore, since a proposition is true or false of what is signified by its subject term, and since there can be no evident knowledge of what is not true of anything at all, the existence of something signified by the subject term, as defined, must be understood.

With respect to the attribute, it is not always necessary to understand that it stands for something that can exist; if the major premise is negative, or equivalent to a conditional proposition, all that is required is that the meaning of the word be grasped unequivocally through a nominal definition. If, however, the major premise is affirmative and assertoric in form, then it is necessary to understand that the attribute is a sign of something whose existence can be apprehended by it, and for the same reason as in the case of the subject—namely, because the premises of a demonstration must be known evidently, and we cannot know an affirmative assertoric proposition to be true without understanding that something *per se* one is signified by both of its terms. According to Ockham, Aristotle's statement that sometimes the existence of what is signified by an attribute is presupposed, and sometimes not, is to be understood in this way.[1]

[1] S. tot. log., III, II, 3, 64r: "Non solum autem oportet istos terminos ad demonstrationem concurrere sed etiam quandoqunque demonstrationem ingrediuntur, antequam conclusio concludatur, oportet eos praecognoscere; non tamen semper oportet omnes aequaliter praecognoscere. De subiecto enim oportet praecognoscere quid est et quia est. Oportet enim praecognoscere de subiecto, cum sit terminus, quid significat; et haec praecognitio communis est omni termino cuiuscumque syllogismi vel argumentationis. Si autem sit demonstratio affirmativa et cathegorica, non oportet tantum de subiecto praecognoscere quid significat sed oportet praecognoscere quia est; hoc est, oportet praecognoscere quod esse non impossibiliter predicatur de subiecto significative sumpto. Et ratio est, quia ad hoc quod habeatur demonstratio oportet praemissas cognoscere, ergo oportet quod illa praemissa in qua predicatur aliquid de subiecto significative sumpto, vel econtra, sit cognita, et per consequens (quod) est vera; et si sit vera et scita esse vera, oportet quod sibi non competat impossibiliter esse, ex quo propositio est affirmativa. De passione autem, quamvis ingrediatur demonstrationem affirmativam, non oportet praecognoscere nisi tantum quid importatur per nomen, sed non oportet quod praecognoscatur quod sibi non repugnat esse, et hoc quidem verum est si major illius demonstrationis sit conditionalis vel equivalens tali; tunc enim non oportet, quantumcumque cognoscatur illa praemissa in qua ponitur passio, quod cognoscatur *esse* posse convenire passioni. Quando autem major est affirmativa non equivalens

Of the propositions required for demonstrations, some can be premises or conclusions of demonstrations, while others, though presupposed by demonstrations, are extrinsic to them and cannot be premises. Of these extrinsic principles, Ockham distinguishes two kinds, as follows:

(1) Some principles are presupposed, implicitly or explicitly, by all discursive thought and by all argument, and are such that their truth is recognized precisely insofar as any proposition is understood to be true or false. Such are the "laws of thought," and the metaphysical propositions composed of the convertible transcendental terms.

(2) Some principles are presupposed, not by all demonstrations, but only by those to which they apply. Thus every demonstration presupposes, implicitly or otherwise, the truth of a proposition in which "being" is predicated in the mode of possibility, of the subject of demonstration taken significatively. Only in cases where the demonstrator enters into argument with a person who questions the existence of the subject matter of the demonstration, are such propositions explicitly assumed—and, as Aristotle says, it is unprofitable for the demonstrator to argue with such people, since they literally do not know what they are talking *about*. More frequently such assumptions are expressly made in mathematics, as when we expressly assume that a figure of such or such a kind can be constructed or that its definition is not impossible; the reason for this is that the subjects of mathematical demonstrations have, strictly speaking, only nominal

---

conditionali, ita bene oportet praecognoscere de passione quia est, sicut de subiecto; nec hoc negat Aristoteles, sed vult quod quandoque oportet praecognoscer quia est de subiecto quamvis non oportet praecognoscere quia est de passione.

"Breviter ergo dicendum et quod secundum principia Aristotelis, de subiecto in demonstratione tam cathegorica quam hypothetica, et tam in composita ex una hypothetica conditionali et alia cathegorica, oportet praecognoscere de subiecto quid significat et quia est; et hoc est quod sibi non repugnat esse ita quod propositio predicans esse de illo non includat contradictionem. De passione autem, in demonstratione simpliciter cathegorica et affirmativa, oportet praecognoscere tam quia est quam quid est, propter eadem rationem propter quam oportet de subiecto praecognoscere quia est; sed in aliqua demonstratione non oportet de passione praecognoscere quia est, de eius autem diffinitione oportet praecognoscere quia est." Cf. Arist., An. Post. I, 1, 71a 11–71b 8; and I, 10, 76a 31–6.

definitions, so that the meaning of the word can be apprehended without experience of the existence of things for which it can stand, and hence the pupil can, in such cases, know what he is talking about, without being sure of its possible existence.

Other extrinsic principles of this second type are: (a) the axioms common to arithmetic and geometry, which cannot in their generalized form be premises of demonstration in either science, but must be "appropriated" to their subject genera; and (b) propositions which have for their subjects absolute qualitative terms. Thus "All heat is calefactive," which can only be known by contingent experience, cannot without equivocation be used as a premise for demonstrating "calefactive" of "the hot" or of "fire." Yet the proof that all fire is heat-giving, from the major premise "Whatever is hot is heat-giving," presupposes the other proposition as a prior, but extrinsic, truth.[1]

Another distinction among propositions required for demonstrations is that some are demonstrable and some are indemonstrable. The latter kind are called principles (whether extrinsic or intrinsic), and are subdivided as follows: (1) Some are knowable evidently by experience of contingent fact, without

---

[1] Arist., An. Post. I, 7, 75a 37–75b 19; I, 10–1, 76a 31–77a 35; and I, 32, 88a 18–88b 29. Ockham, S. tot. log., III, II, 4, 64r: "Est autem sciendum quod propositionum requisitarum ad demonstrationem quaedam sunt partes demonstrationis sicut praemissae et conclusio, et quaedam non sunt partes demonstrationis et vocantur dignitates et maximae, vel suppositiones quae sub propria forma non ingrediuntur demonstrationem, virtute tamen illarum propositionum aliquo modo sciuntur praemissae demonstrationis. V.g., ista est una propositio prima praecise nota per experientiam, 'omnis calor est calefactivus,' quae non potest esse pars demonstrationis saltem potissimae et universalis, virtute tamen istius tenent tales demonstrationes: 'omne calidum est calefactivum; omnis aer est calidus; ergo omnis aer est calefactivus.' Istae sunt distinctae propositiones, 'omnis calor est calefactivus,' 'omne calidum est calefactivum,' et prima est prior et secunda posterior, et tamen secunda non potest proprie demonstrari per primam, et secunda ingreditur demonstrationem et non prima, et tamen virtute primae tenent multae demonstrationes quas non potest ingredi . . . Propositio autem requisita ad demonstrationem non tanquam pars subdividitur quia quaedam est talis quod necesse est quemlibet docendum eam habere; cuiusmodi sunt tales, 'quodlibet est vel non est,' 'quodlibet est affirmatio vel negatio,' et huiusmodi. Quaedam sunt tales quas non est necesse quemlibet docendum eam habere, sed necesse est aliquos arguentes eas habere, sicut est de istis: 'aliquid est mobile' . . ."; here Ockham adds, as instances, such mathematical communia as "If equals are taken from equals, equals remain," etc.

demonstration—and such are the extrinsic principles enumerated above. (2) Others are said to be known *per se*, by the fact that the meanings of their terms cannot be grasped without the necessary truth of the proposition being immediately known—at least if the mind judges of it at all. Such propositions are those whose terms are understood through determinate definitions, and not merely through nominal descriptions. How terms come to be grasped through definitions, and consequently how such propositions come to be known *per se*, is the question that occupies Aristotle in Book II of the *Posterior Analytics*. It will be dealt with when we come to that part of Ockham's treatise which is concerned with the question *quid est* and with the relation of definition to *a priori* demonstration.[1]

Ockham next takes up the properties of the different kinds of propositions required for demonstration, first dealing with those which are common to all principles and conclusions, and afterwards taking up those which apply only to conclusions or only to premises. Of the common properties, the first and most obvious is that of *necessity*. From the definition of what a demonstration is, it is evident that both the conclusion and the premises must be necessarily true; and since the extrinsic principles required by demonstrations are required precisely because they are prior and better known than the premises, they also must be necessarily true.[2]

[1] S. tot. log., III, II, 4, 64r: "Propositio autem quae est pars demonstrationis subdividitur, quia quaedam est praemissa tantum, quae scilicet est indemonstrabilis; quaedam est conclusio tantum, quae scilicet potest demonstrari sed non potest esse principium demonstrationis . . . quaedam est praemissa et conclusio, quae potest demonstrari per alias praemissas et potest esse principium demonstrandi aliam conclusionem. Alia divisio potest esse quia propositionum requisitarum ad demonstrationem quaedam sunt principia, quaedam sunt conclusiones. Principia dicuntur illae propositiones quae non sunt conclusiones et tamen requiruntur ad demonstrationem sive sint partes demonstrationis sive non sunt partes eius. Et vocantur principia prima, quae subdividi possunt, quia quaedam principia prima per se sunt nota, quibus scilicet intellectus statim assentit ipsius terminis apprehensis, ita quod si sciatur quid significant termini statim sciuntur. Quaedam autem principia prima non sunt per se nota sed tantum per experientiam sunt nota, sicut est de ista propositione, 'omnis calor est calefactivus,' et de multis aliis quae non possunt fieri notae nisi per experientiam, de quibus specialiter loquitur Aristotles in primo Metaphysicae et in secundo Posteriorum in fine."

[2] S. tot. log., III, II, 5, 64v: "Istis praemissis videndum est de proprietatibus propositionum ad demonstrationem requisitarum. Illarum autem proprietatum

Necessary propositions are, according to Aristotle, eternal and imperishable. "Therefore," he says, "no attribute can be demonstrated nor known by strictly scientific knowledge to inhere in perishable things."[1] Does this mean that the subject term of a demonstrative proposition can only signify something eternal and imperishable? If this were so, then only God could be that of which a scientific proposition is true; for a term like "material substance," which means precisely those things which are changeable and corruptible, obviously does not signify what is eternal and imperishable. Or is it to be understood that the propositions themselves are eternal and imperishable entities of some sort, or that the concepts or "ideas" of which they are composed are themselves eternal? If that were the case, then scientific knowledge would be possible only to an eternal intelligence, since obviously no human soul that has begun to be and that exists in time, can of itself be that in which propositions or concepts have *eternal being*.

Averroes, choosing this second alternative, followed it to its logical conclusion by denying that individual human souls have any natural power of knowledge beyond sense perception of particulars; hence he identified both the "active" and "possible" intellects mentioned in the *De anima* with an eternal separated intelligence. The augustinians tended to choose the first alternative, conceiving human science of created things to be true science, or wisdom, only insofar as created things were referred, like symbols, to eternal exemplars

---

quaedam sunt communes omnibus propositionibus requisitis ad demonstrationem, quaedam sunt propriae praemissis, quaedam sunt propriae conclusionibus; quaedam sunt propriae principiis non ingredientibus demonstrationem.

"Una enim proprietas communis omni propositioni requisitae ad demonstrationem est necessitas; nulla enim propositio requisita ad demonstrationem est contingens vel impossibilis sed quaelibet est necessaria. Quod enim conclusio est necessaria patet ex diffinitione demonstrationis, quia demonstratio est sillogismus faciens scire propositionem necessariam; ergo conclusio erit necessaria; sed necessarium quamvis posset inferri ex contingentibus vel impossibilibus non tamen potest sciri per impossibilia vel contingentia, ergo necessario praemissae propter quas scitur conclusio sunt necessaria; sed propositiones rectificantes demonstrationem sunt priores et notiores praemissis; ergo illae sunt necessariae." Cf. Arist., An. Post. I, 6, 74b 5–75a 37.

[1] Arist., An. Post. I, 8, 75b 23–4.

contained in the divine Wisdom, or understood as symbolic of the mystery of the Trinity. Both of these alternatives can be understood as developments of the metaphysical point of view implicit in Porphyry's treatment of the predicables.[1]

According to Ockham, it is unnecessary to choose either of the above alternatives, which assume that it is *things* or *concepts* that are necessary, or imperishable, or incorruptible, in their being. In this sense, however, only God can be called necessary, eternal, and incorruptible. But according to Aristotle, science is of necessary *truths*, and only propositions can be called true or false—and they are true not by reason of their existence in a mind, but by reason of the existence of something signified by their terms. Hence it is in this same sense that they are to be called necessarily, or eternally, true.[2]

---

[1] Cf. *ante*, ch. iii, pp. 82–94. For the arab doctrine of the separated Intelligence, and the illumination theory of science built around it, see Aquinas, Contra Gentiles, II, c. 73–8; cf. especially c. 74, where Aquinas identifies this theory with platonism: "Sed si diligenter consideretur, haec positio, quantum ad originem, parum aut nihil differt a positione Platonis. Posuit enim Plato formas intelligibiles esse quasdam substantias separatas, a quibus scientia fluebat in animas nostras; hic autem ponit (*scil.* Avicenna) ab una substantia separata, quae est intellectus agens secundum ipsum, scientiam in animas nostras fluere. Non autem differt . . . utrum ab una vel pluribus substantiis separatis nostra causetur scientia; utrobique enim sequetur quod scientia nostra non causetur a sensibilibus; cuius contrarium apparet per hoc quod qui caret aliquo sensu caret scientia sensibilium quae cognoscuntur per sensum illum." Cf. also Aquinas, In Post. An. I, Lect. XVI, where the eternity of the object of science is interpreted as the invariability of the relation between cause and event, when, as, and if the event occurs or the cause exists, etc. For the augustinian view, and the doctrine of analogy, cf. Gilson, *La philosophie de S. Bonaventure* (Paris 1929), esp. ch. ii, iv, and vii.

[2] S. tot. log., III, II, 5, 64v: "Et ita patet quod omnes propositiones requisitae ad demonstrationem sunt necessariae, et sicut sunt necessariae ita sunt perpetuae et incorruptibiles; quod non est sic intelligendum quod illae propositiones sunt quaedam entia necessaria et perpetua, hoc enim falsum est; solum enim Deus est perpetuus et incorruptibilis, nec aliquod aliud a Deo potest esse perpetuum simpliciter et incorruptibile quin per aliquam potentiam possit fieri non ens. Propter quod sciendum est quod 'perpetuum,' 'necessarium,' 'incorruptibile' capiuntur dupliciter. Uno modo dicitur aliquid necessarium, perpetuum, et incorruptibile quia per nullam potentiam potest incipere vel desinere esse, et sic Deus est perpetuus, necessarius, et immortalis. Aliquando dicitur necessarium, perpetuum, et incorruptibile, propositio quae, si formetur, non potest esse falsa sed vera tantum; et illo modo demonstratio est necessariorum, perpetuorum, et incorruptibiliorum; hoc est, ex propositionibus quae non possunt esse falsae sed verae tantum." Cf. Arist., An. Post. I, 11, 77a 5–9: "So demonstration does not necessarily imply the being of Forms nor a One beside a Many, but it does necessarily imply the possibility of truly predicating one of many," etc.

Under what conditions, then, can a proposition be true in such manner that it is incapable of being false? The truth of an affirmative proposition is a function of the existence of that which is signified by its terms, according to the indicated form of supposition exhibited in the form of affirmation. As we have already noted, exponible propositions, such as imply the actual contingent unity of distinct things, are contingent, and can become false by motion *ex parte rei*. It has also been stated that propositions of merely present time, are exponible and contingent—for they imply not only that the predicate stands for things signified by the subject, but that such things exist *now*, or co-exist with the speaker who affirms the proposition. Hence Ockham states that affirmative assertoric propositions of merely present time (*mere de praesenti*), whose terms signify corruptible things, are not necessary.

Aristotle, according to Ockham, sometimes speaks as if such propositions could be necessary. This may be explained by the fact that, according to the Stagyrite, the world is eternal, the spheres incorruptible, and mundane things perpetual in kind even though corruptible in their instances. Under such circumstances, we could be sure that if we had come to possess a concept of essential nature through experience of some instance in the past, some instance of what the concept signified would be actually existent now and at any future time in which we might use the concept as subject of a proposition of merely present time. For Aristotle, knowledge that a thing is capable of existing *per se*, which we possess if we have actual experience of such a thing in any instance, gives warrant for stating that some instance of *such* a thing actually exists at any given time.[1]

---

[1] S. tot. log., III, II, 5, 64v: "Ex quo patet quod quamvis repugnat dictis Aristotelis, tamen secundum rei veritatem nulla propositio quae importat res corruptibiles mere affirmativa, mere cathegorica, et mere de praesenti, potest esse principium demonstrationis vel conclusio, quia quaelibet talis est contingens." Cf. ibid., 7, 65r: "quamvis secundum opinionem Aristotelis, qui ponit quod in perpetuum fuit et erit generatio, multae propositiones cathegoricae de praesenti et de inesse sunt per se, tamen secundum veritatem tales de terminis importantibus praecise res corruptibiles sive creatas non sunt per se, quia non sunt necessariae sicut dictum est." Elsewhere Ockham makes the same statement, but adds that Aristotle would agree to his qualification. Thus, S. tot. log., I, 26, 11r: "Est

But in Ockham's opinion it is unnecessary to limit Aristotle's intentions, with respect to necessary propositions, in this manner. Aristotle's discussion of the sense in which a scientific proposition must be necessary, envisages two conditions: (1) We cannot understand what a thing essentially is, without understanding that it is something; and hence he says that if a proposition is necessarily, eternally, and essentially true of something, something *must* exist of which it is true, and of which the subject term is a sign. (2) Scientific knowledge, as distinct from sense perception or from the intuition of *present* occurrences, is of universal character; i.e., a scientific proposition is true of every instance, at every time, and not of this or that instance, or of the instances existing at this or that time. Now it is not necessary to take this as meaning that a scientific proposition is true of instances which exist at the time the proposition is stated, unless such instances do happen to exist at that time. Nor is the proposition, properly understood, false if no instances exist at the time of predication—for if this were so, then a scientific proposition, however true it might be of instances existing at the time it was stated, would not be true of the instances existing at other times. But Aristotle states that a scientific proposition is true of every instance, and at every time.[1]

The intention of Aristotle is clear enough. But the formal character of necessary propositions requires, in Ockham's view, a more accurate description. A strictly necessary proposition, according to Ockham, is, if assertoric and affirmative

---

autem sciendum quod quamvis de quocunque, significative sumpto, predicatur diffinitio, et diffinitum predicatur significative sumptum et econverso, et quamvis propositiones cathegoricae de possibilibus equivalentes tali et similiter conditionalis, ex diffinitione et diffinito composita, sint necessariae . . . tamen nulla propositio talis affirmativa de inesse et mere de praesenti est necessaria. Unde illa est simpliciter contingens, 'homo est animal rationale' . . . et hoc quia si nullus homo esset, quaelibet talis esset falsa. . . . Verumtamen Aristoteles qui ponit quod tales sunt necessariae, 'homo est animal,' 'asinus est animal,' poneret quod tales sunt necessariae secundum sensum iam dictum."

[1] Cf. Arist., An. Post. II, 2, 90a 35–9; and II, 7, 92b 17–8; where he insists that the existence of knowledge presupposes the existence of something known. Cf. also ibid., I, 4, 73a 27–33, and I, 31, 87b 27–88a 17, where he insists that science is not of the "this," except accidentally and in the sense that perception is a *sine qua non* of our coming to have universal knowledge of perceptible things.

in form, to be understood as equivalent either to a necessary proposition *de possibili* (in the sense that its terms stand for what can be), or to a hypothetical proposition. This does not mean that scientific propositions are equivalent to hypothetical propositions in the sense that they are exponible. For they do not, like exponible propositions, imply the contingent unity of distinct things. The existence of an individual thing is not something distinct from its nature, contingently combined with it; rather it is because they are not distinct, that the grasp of the essential nature, involved in understanding the terms of a necessary proposition, presupposes, as a necessary antecedent, awareness of the *existence* of such essential nature in some instance.   In the same way, if we take a scientific proposition as equivalent to a proposition *de possibili*, so that it is presupposed that individual things *can* exist such as are signified by the terms, the same condition is brought out— for we cannot recognize or conceive what *can* exist *per se*, unless we have apprehended some actual instance of it.[1]

Propositions whose terms stand for corruptible things, are true only of the kind of things that exist in time; hence they

---

[1] S. tot. log., III, II, 5, 64v: "Et ideo dico quod nulla talis potest esse principium vel conclusio demonstrationis (i.e., no proposition that is affirmative, categorical, and mere de praesenti); hoc tamen non obstante dicendum est quod multae propositiones compositae ex talibus terminis possunt esse principia vel conclusiones demonstrationis quia propositiones conditionales vel equivalentes eis possunt esse necessariae. Haec enim est necessaria simpliciter, 'si homo est, animal est,' et ista 'si homo ridet, animal ridet,' et ista 'omnis homo potest ridere,' sumpto subiecto pro his quae possunt esse; et propositiones eodem modo eis equivalentes sunt necessariae. Et ex isto patet quod non obstante quod genera et species et quaecunque alia universalia distincta a cognitione Dei sint simpliciter corruptibilia sic quod possunt esse nihil; tamen de eis possunt fieri demonstrationes et scientiae, propter hoc quod non obstante quod possunt simpliciter destrui, tamen de eis possunt formari propositiones necessariae quae possunt sciri scientia proprie dicta. Ex isto etiam patet quomodo de contingentibus potest esse scientia quia secundum quod veniunt in demonstrationem sunt necessariae; hoc est, quod propositiones formatae ex terminis importantibus talia contingentia, quae veniunt in demonstrationem, sunt necessariae, quae non sunt mere de praesenti et de inesse cathegoricae et affirmativae; sed vel sunt negativae vel hypotheticae vel de possibili vel aliquo modo eis equivalentes." Ockham's discussion is undoubtedly thoroughly aristotelian in its fundamental point of view; but he attempts, to a degree Aristotle did not, to state the character and conditions of necessary knowledge of contingent things, in precise logical terms. It is at one and the same time an explicit recognition of the relativity of knowledge to existence, and an explicit exclusion of particular existence as that which is known.

are true of things which exist in *some* "present time." But time is not an absolute entity, according to Ockham, but a mode of signifying something that is in motion or at rest, through reference to limits or divisions of change by which its motion or rest can be measured. Now an exponible proposition, or a proposition of merely present time, signifies what moves or is at rest, by consignifying something distinct from it as simultaneous with it—i.e., by indicating its time as measured by another. But a scientific proposition is understood as true of the things for which its terms stand, in their own time, and not by consignifying the time of some other motion or rest distinct from them. Thus the time in which things signified by the subject of a necessary proposition, exist, is referred to *their* existence, and not to the existence of the proposition in the mind of the demonstrator—and consequently not to the time of the existence of the proposition.

In this way Ockham makes evident the two conditions of necessity envisaged by Aristotle—(*a*) that scientific knowledge is of propositions whose terms are, precisely insofar as their meaning is grasped, understood by the existence of something which they mean; and (*b*) that scientific knowledge is universal in character and consequently distinct from the immediate perception of *present* existence.

That the above interpretation accords with Aristotle's intentions, is indicated fairly clearly in his *dici de omni*, as stated in the *Posterior Analytics :* "I call 'true in every instance' what is truly predicable of all instances—not of one to the exclusion of others—and at all times, not at this or that time only; e.g., if animal is truly predicable of every instance of man, then if it be true to say 'this is a man,' 'this is an animal' is also true, and if the one be true now the other is true now." Which is in itself an indication of Ockham's statement that necessary propositions are equivalent to hypothetical propositions—equivalent, that is, in the sense that they are true of each thing signifiable by the subject term, in the time of its own existence, so that their truth is not a function of the co-existence or contingent unity of distinct things. Ockham points out that the *dici de omni* of the *Posterior Analytics* differs from that of the *Prior Analytics* in that it is here required that the universal proposition be true, whereas in the *Prior Analytics* it was required only that the major premise be universal in form, so that the predicate is *indicated* to stand for every thing signified by the subject.[1]

Not only must every principle or conclusion of demonstration be a necessary truth, but it must be true *per se*—i.e., by the essential nature of that for which its terms stand. This condition, of being true "essentially and as such," is stated by Aristotle as an inseparable companion property to the requirement that scientific propositions be true *de omni*, or in every instance and at every time.[2] Since the essential nature of that which is signified by a term is exhibited by the real definition of the term, it is by the immediate or mediate connection of the terms through essential definitions, that a proposition can be recognized as true *per se*. Following Aristotle's *Posterior Analytics* and Robert Grosseteste's commentary on it, Ockham gives the following statement of the property of being essentially true, and of the two modes of essential predication:

Briefly, therefore, it is the intention of Grosseteste (*Lincolniensis*) and of Aristotle, that when the predicate defines the subject

---

[1] Arist., An. Post., I, 4, 73a 27–33. Ockham, S. tot. log., III, II, 6, 64v: "Alia conditio tam praemissarum quam conclusionis demonstrationis est quod tam praemissa quam conclusio potest esse de omni." The use of the verb "potest esse" here is probably due to the fact that it is not necessary that there be many instances of what is signified by the subject; the brevity of Ockham's treatment of *de omni*, in the sense of "true of all," suggests that he preferred to express this requirement as a corollary of "necessary," leaving the expression *de omni* as properly expressive of *indicated* universality, whether true or not, as in the *Prior Analytics*. This might also account for his mild way of stating the requirement, and the use of the verb "potest esse" instead of "debet esse" or "oportet esse." Ibid.: "Est autem de omni non quando praedicatum convenit alicui contento sub subiecto et alicui non, nec quando uno tempore competit et alio tempore non competit sibi. Sed quando praedicatum competit omni contento sub subiecto et omni tempore. Unde differentia est inter dici de omni de quo loquitur Aristoteles in primo Priorum, et inter dici de omni de quo loquitur in primo Posteriorum; nam ad hoc quod aliquid dicatur de omni in Prioribus non requiritur nisi quod per talem propositionem denotatur praedicatum praedicari de tali subiecto universaliter, sive vere praedicatur de eo sive non. . . . Ad dici de omni de quo loquitur Aristoteles in primo Posteriorum requiritur quod praedicatum vere competit subiecto universaliter sumpto et pro omni tempore."

[2] Arist., An. Post. I, 4, 73a 33–73b 26.

essentially, or defines a term *per se* superior to the subject (i.e., predicable of the subject *in quid*), either as its definition or as part of its definition, or conversely, then it is a *per se* proposition. And the first mode is when the predicate defines the subject or defines a term essentially superior to the subject; whence, if such propositions (as the following) were necessary, they would be essentially true: "Every man is a rational animal," "Every man is an animal," "Every man is rational," "Every man is composed of a body and a soul"—for in all these the predicate defines the subject. Likewise the following would be essentially true if they were necessary: "Every man is a body," "Every man is a substance," "Every man is composed of matter and form," "Every man has matter"; because although these predicates do not define the subject, nevertheless they are predicated essentially of terms *per se* superior to the subject, and hence they would be essentially true.

The second mode, however, is when the subject or a term essentially superior to the subject, defines the predicate or defines a term essentially inferior to the predicate; whence this proposition, if it is necessary, is essentially true: "Every man is risible," because in the definition expressing what the word "risible" means, the term "man" is placed. Likewise this is essentially true if it is necessary: "Every man is susceptible of contrary determinations," because in the definition of the predicate is placed "substance" or "body", which is essentially superior to the subject, the subject being "man." For "man" defines this predicate "being susceptible of *such* contraries," pointing to some (contrary determinations) which can only be found in a man; and this predicate (*scil.* "being susceptible of *such* contraries") is essentially inferior to the general term "susceptible of contraries." And thus this proposition is essentially true, "Every man is susceptible of contraries."

From the above it is plain that all such propositions are *per se*: "Every man can become white," "Every matter can receive a form," "Every creature can be created by God," "God is creative," "Heat is calefactive," and so with others of this kind. It must be added that what has been said is to be understood of affirmative propositions.[1]

Not only may affirmative propositions be essentially true in the above two ways, but negative propositions which are composed of absolute terms, may be *per se* true if neither term is an element in the definition of the other. This is the case of "atomic disconnection," as in the proposition

[1] S. tot. log., III, II, 8, 65v.

"No man is an ass." We can also form a *per se* negative proposition from an affirmative one that is essentially true, if its terms are convertible, by denying the predicate of any or all subjects other than the subject of the affirmative. For example, if "Every man is risible" is *per se secundo modo* and of convertible terms, then "Everything other than a man is not risible," is also true *per se*.[1]

The inseparability of the property of being "essentially true," and that of being "true in every instance," is indicated by Ockham in his insistence that no proposition is true *per se* unless it is necessary. Hence, since singular propositions about corruptible things, and propositions of merely present time, are not necessary but contingent, it is not in the strict sense correct to say that a proposition such as "This man is a man," or "Every man now living is an animal," are *per se* true. And the reason for this is that such propositions, being capable of becoming false through destruction of the particular instances for which, to the exclusion of other instances, their terms stand, are contingent and not necessary.[2]

It remains to define the meaning of "universal," and of the expression "primary subject." According to Aristotle, the universal is that which is *de omni* and *per se*, and immediate,

---

[1] Arist., An. Post. I, 15, 79a 33–79b 23. Ockham, S. tot. log., III, II, 7, 65r: "Est autem sciendum quod omnis negativa necessaria, in qua terminus subiectus et predicatus sunt mere absoluti et non relativi nec connotativi, est per se; unde haec est per se, 'omnis homo non est asinus.'" Absolute terms which define each other were excluded in these words: "Nam aliquae negativae sunt per se, in quibus tamen predicatum non diffinit subiectum nec econverso."

[2] S. tot. log., III, II, 7, 65r: "Large dicitur propositio per se quando subiectum cadit in diffinitione predicati vel econverso, vel per se superius ad unum diffinit reliquum vel diffinitur per reliquum; et illo modo haec est per se: 'omnis homo est animal,' et ista 'omnis homo est rationalis,' et ista, 'omnis homo est risibilis'" etc. . . . "Aliter accipitur 'per se' stricte, et sic cum prioribus conditionibus ad hoc quod propositio sit per se requiritur quod ipsa sit simpliciter necessaria, ita quod nec potuit nec potest esse falsa. . . . Unde sic accepto 'per se' haec non est per se: 'homo est animal,' quia potest esse falsa, puta posito quod nullus homo sit. Verumtamen propositiones de possibili et eis equivalentes compositae ex talibus terminis sunt per se; unde ista est per se: 'omnis homo potest esse animal,' sumpto subiecto pro eo quod potest esse. . . . requiritur quod sit predicatio propria et directa per quod excluduntur propositiones ubi inferiora predicantur de suis superioribus particulariter sumptis, et subiecta de suis passionibus, et una passio de alia passione; propter hoc quod tales propositiones, quamvis sint necessariae, non tamen sunt per se strictissime accipiendo 'per se' . . . ."

in the sense that the attribute is convertible with the subject.[1] Such a proposition is, in Ockham's terminology, *primo vera*, and is described as follows: "A proposition is immediately true (*primo vera*) when the predicate does not belong more immediately, than to its subject, to any subject more general than its subject, nor to any subject not predicable of its subject. And such a predicate, with respect to such a subject, is called 'universal,' and that subject is called the 'first subject' of that predicate, at least if it is predicable in the second mode of essential predication."[2]

The first requirement indicated in Ockham's description —that the attribute be not more immediately predicable of a term more general than its subject—excludes the three ways mentioned by Aristotle in which we may fall into error in assigning universality to a proposition. The first case is when we attribute the predicate to some single instance, because of the fact that it happens to be unique; thus we might ascribe a property of the sun to "this sun," instead of to "any sun," because we only know of one instance of a sun (i.e., of a star with satellites). Secondly, the predicate may be attributed to several species instead of to a common genus convertible with these species taken together, because

---

[1] It is difficult to find English equivalents for the Greek in which Aristotle states the meaning of "universal." The mediæval Latin reproduces the Greek very closely, but almost any English version, to be intelligible, has to be expanded by the introduction of words which tend to distort or "colour" the meaning. I give below the Greek from An. Post., I, 4, 73b 26–7 and 32–3; then a mediæval Latin version (the one given in the Leonine edition of Aquinas' commentary); and finally, the lengthy version of the Oxford edition of Aristotle in English.

Greek: καθόλου δὲ λέγω ὃ ἂν κατὰ παντός τε ὑπάρχῃ καὶ καθ' αὐτὸ καὶ ᾗ αὐτό . . . . τὸ καθόλου δὲ ὑπάρχει τότε, ὅταν ἐπὶ τοῦ τυχόντος καὶ πρώτου δεικνύηται.

Latin: Universale autem dico quod, cum de omni sit, et per se, et secundum quod ipsum est. . . . Universale autem est tunc cum in quolibet et primo demonstratur.

English: "I term 'commensurately universal' an attribute which belongs to every instance of its subject, and to every instance essentially and as such. . . . An attribute belongs commensurately and universally to a subject when it can be shown to belong to any random instance of that subject and when the subject is the first thing to which it can be shown to belong."

[2] S. tot. log., III, II, 8, 65v: "Est autem propositio primo vera quando predicatum nulli subiecto cómmuniori illo subiecto, nec alicui subiecto non predicabili de illo subiecto, prius competit quam illi subiecto. Et tale predicatum respectu talis subiecti vocatur universale, et illud subiectum vocatur primum subiectum illius predicati, saltem si sit predicabile secundo modo dicendi per se."

of the absence of a name for their common genus. Thirdly, we may not recognize the difference between a species and its proximate genus, and thus attribute the universal to the species when its true first subject is wider than this species. The requirement that universal propositions be *per se* and necessary, excludes the case where attributes of some common subject are predicated directly of each other.

The second requirement indicated in Ockham's description —that the attribute be not more immediately predicable of a term that is *not* predicable of its subject, excludes the case where an attribute like "calefactive" is predicated of "the hot." For since it is because heat is present in a thing that it is called hot, the property of being "calefactive" is more immediately predicable of "heat" than of "the hot" —but "heat" is not predicable at all (unless equivocally) of "the hot." Consequently the proposition "Every hot thing is calefactive," though indemonstrable, is not *primo vera*, but presupposes as a prior and extrinsic principle the universal proposition "All heat is calefactive."[1]

[1] S. tot. log., III, II, 8, 65v: After stating the three ways in which we are likely to err through attributing a predicate as universal to a term actually inferior to its first subject (stated by Arist., An. Post. I, 5, 74a 4–74b 4), Ockham says: "Istis modis primo peccatur attribuendo universale alicuius communioris minus communi; per secundam particulam excluditur concretum alicuius abstracti cui primo competit. Unde si nihil esset calefactivus nisi calor, tunc hoc predicatum 'calefactivum' non competeret primo 'calido,' quia haec non esset primo vera 'omne calidum est calefactivum,' sed haec est primo vera 'omnis calor est calefactivus,' quia haec non potest esse vera 'omne calidum est calefactivum' nisi haec esset vera 'omnis calor est calefactivus,' sed econtrario bene potest; et ita est prior et per consequens 'calefactivum' predicetur primo de 'calore.' Et si dicatur quod quando predicatur primo aliquid de aliquo, de nullo predicatur nisi de quo predicatur suum proprium subiectum, sicut de nullo predicatur 'esse risibile' nisi de quo predicatur 'homo,' sed 'esse calefactivum' predicatur de 'calido' de quo tamen non predicatur 'calor,' ergo 'calor' non est primum subiectum 'calefactivi'; dicendum est quod universale nunquam predicatur de aliquo nisi de quo predicatur suum primum subiectum vel contentum sui primi subiecti, unde de quocunque predicatur 'calefactivum,' de eodem predicatur 'calor' vel 'calidum,' si 'calefactivum' sit universale primo competens 'calori.' . . . " The priority of 'calor' over 'calidum' is due to its being more abstract—not by predication, but by analogy or generalization. A parallel instance is the priority of "quantity" over "number" and "magnitude," of which terms "quantity" is predicated equivocally or analogically. Cf. Arist., An. Post. I, 6, 75a 28–75b 20; and II, 17, 99a 4–16.

II

Having stated the properties common both to principles and conclusions of demonstration, Ockham next states that every conclusion of demonstration is a dubitable proposition, such that it is not known *per se* without demonstration, by the mere grasp of the terms through definitions of essential nature. That the conclusion of demonstration must, of itself, be capable of being doubted, is evident from the fact that a demonstration is a syllogism producing knowledge; for that which is immediately known *without* demonstration cannot be made known, at least in the same sense of "knowledge," *by* demonstration. On the other hand, we may come to know a demonstrable proposition without demonstration, by experience—but the kind of knowledge thus obtained is not of the same character as knowledge by demonstration. If we gain knowledge of a demonstrable proposition by experience, without demonstration, we know the fact but not the reasoned fact, and though we may not question the truth of the proposition, we can still ask why it should be so.[1]

[1] S. tot. log., III, II, 9, 65v: "omnis conclusio demonstrationis est dubitabilis ita quod non est per se nota. Cum enim demonstratio est sillogismus faciens scire, et nihil facit scire aliquod praescitum, necesse est si apprehendatur conclusio sine praemissis quod illa conclusio potest ignorari . . . quamvis autem omnis conclusio demonstrationis sit dubitabilis propositio, non tamen oportet quod semper dubitetur quousque per demonstrationem certificetur, quia conclusio demonstrationis duabus viis cognosci potest. Aliqua enim cognosci potest per demonstrationem quando ex notitia praemissarum devenitur in notitiam conclusionis. Alia autem non solum sic cognosci potest sed cognosci potest per experientiam illo modo quo Aristoteles docet primo Metaphysicae et secundo Posteriorum principia cognosci per experientiam. Sicut enim aliquis potest per experientiam cognoscere quod omnis talis herba sanat, ita potest per experientiam cognoscere quod luna sit eclipsabilis." (66r): "Oportet etiam scire quod non solum omnis conclusio potest dubitari sed etiam aliqua principia demonstrationis sunt dubitabilia quamvis non omnia, unde omnia principia quae non nisi per experientiam cognosci possunt dubitabilia sunt quantumcumque sunt prima ita quod ex aliis demonstrari non possunt."
Cf. Quodl. V, Qu. 2 (McKeon's *Selections*, vol. II, pp. 375–80): and also S. tot. log., III, II, cap. 11, 66r: "Verumtamen aliquando praescitur conclusio sine ipsas praemissas, quod dupliciter potest contingere, unomodo quia quandoque est praecognita per experientiam, et quandoque per alias praemissas. Non enim est inconveniens quod eadem conclusio per diversa principia

240   WILLIAM OF OCKHAM

Not only can we acquire evident knowledge of the truth of demonstrable propositions by experience, and without demonstration, but there are many indemonstrable propositions which can only become known through experience. Such, for example, are the extrinsic principles presupposed by demonstrations, which, though they are necessary truths, cannot become evidently known except through experience of contingent fact. If we have not perceived something actually moving, we cannot know that "Something is movable"; but if we do know what it is to be "moveable," we *must* have learned this by experience of actual motion, and hence the principle "Something is moveable" is necessarily true.

After stating that indemonstrable principles, as well as many demonstrable conclusions, can become known through experience and without demonstration, Ockham gives a brief account of the manner in which universal propositions come to be known through experience of particular contingent fact. His exposition is based on the last part of Book II of the *Posterior Analytics*, and on Book I of the *Metaphysics*, where the process of coming to grasp universal principles in experience of contingent fact, is described genetically.

Since it has been said that some principles and some conclusions can be known through experience, how principles or conclusions come to be known in this way should be briefly indicated. Wherefore it must be known that the imagination, when some sensible thing has been apprehended by the senses, can imagine the same thing, and not only the imagination but also the intellect can apprehend it. And when thus apprehended, the intellect can know evidently other contingent conclusions; for example, if heat is felt by the senses, the intellect can apprehend this same heat, and can know that this thing is hot and that when it is approximated to another thing it makes the other hot, and that this other would not be hot unless this hot thing had previously been approximated to it; and in this way the intellect knows evidently this proposition "this hot thing makes something hot." This proposition being

demonstretur." This is especially true in mathematics, where various demonstrations are often equally productive of knowledge; in physics, the same conclusion may become evident in the act of perception (e.g., that the moon can be eclipsed), or by *a posteriori* reasoning, or by *a priori* demonstration.

known, and it being known that when something is present in one individual it can be present in others, then the intellect grasps this universal proposition: "every heat is heat-giving," for there is no reason why one instance of heat should be more heat-giving than another. This proposition being thus known by experience, a universal proposition is known; and it is the universal proposition which, if it cannot be known otherwise than in this way through sense perception, is a principle of art and of science. If however it can be known in this way, and besides this can be known without sense perception through propositions that are known, stated as syllogistic premises, then it is a conclusion of science and demonstration.

It is however to be noted that sometimes such a proposition has as subject term a *species specialissima*, and sometimes it has as subject a term more general than it. That which has for its subject a *species specialissima* can be evidently known through the grasp of one singular proposition; thus, it being evidently known that this heat *makes* something hot, it can be evidently known that every instance of heat *can make* something hot. Whence the evident knowledge of one such singular contingent proposition, such as "this heat makes something hot," suffices without other singular propositions for the acquisition of evident knowledge of the universal.

If however the universal should have for its subject term something more general than a *species specialissima*, then, as a rule or always, it is required that some singular should be known of each of the species contained under it; and thus for knowing such a proposition several singulars are required. It ought also to be noted that frequently, in order to acquire knowledge of the universal proposition, many singulars are required even though the subject of the universal is a *species specialissima*; for in most cases a singular contingent proposition cannot be evidently known without many apprehensions of single instances, whence it is not easy to know that this herb cured a certain invalid and that it was not this doctor who cured him. And so with many other cases, for it is not easy to grasp that which is experienced, because the same effect in species can exist through many causes specifically different.[1]

[1] S. tot. log., III, II, 10, 66r: Cf. Arist., An. Post. II, 17, 99b 3–5: "We conclude, then, that the same effect may have more than one cause, but not in subjects specifically identical." Cf. also Exp. aur. I, 16v: "omnis disciplina incipit ab individuis, unde philosophus secundo Posteriorum et primo Metaphysicae vult quod ex sensu quod non est nisi singularium fit memoria, ex memoria experimentum, et per experimentum accipitur universale quod est principium artis et scientiae, et ita sicut omnis cognitio nostra ortum habet a sensu, ita omnis disciplina ortum habet ab individuis, licet nulla doctrina tractare debeat de singularibus signanter, seu nulla scientia proprie dicta est de individuis sed de universalibus pro individuis."

Ockham's conviction that we have intellectual grasp of singulars, rests on the fact that sense perception (as distinguished from sensation or from mere change or movement of the sense organs) involves *recognition*, while recognition involves the grasp of something in abstraction from the immediate occasion which is the *present* contingent fact. I cannot perceive that something is hot unless I distinguish two factors whose conjunction constitutes the contingent fact—namely, heat, and that in which heat is present. If this discrimination were not involved, there would be no perception of a *fact*, for our apprehension of something as a fact is precisely our recognition of the "being conditioned" indicated by the word contingent. To discriminate distinct factors whose conjunction constitutes a contingent fact, is, however, to grasp these factors as distinct from each other, and hence as indivisible or individual, in themselves. We may apprehend heat by getting a hand burned on a stove, but as soon as we form the evident singular proposition "this is hot," an act of discrimination, and of abstraction from *mere* immediacy, is involved. The affirmation of the singular proposition, which is an act of synthesis of two modes of signifying an existent thing, is at the same time an analysis of the concrete connotative predicate into absolute terms.[1]

As Aristotle indicates, even in the act of perception the rudimentary universal is present—the concept "individual

[1] In the selections from Ockham's *Quodlibeta* translated by R. McKeon (*Selections from Mediæval Philosophers*, vol. II, pp. 360–80), the character of evident contingent knowledge is brought out; neither sense nor intellect, alone, suffice for evident knowledge of sensible particulars, but both sense and intellect are involved in the intuition of singulars, from which abstractive or universal knowledge arises. The following sentences from these *Quodlibeta* indicate this point: (p. 366): "I say that our understanding does know sensible things intuitively, because our understanding knows evidently the first contingent proposition concerning sensibles: therefore it has an incomplex conception sufficient to cause this complex conception evidently; but abstractive knowledge of sensibles does not suffice; therefore, etc." (p. 367): "I say that the sensitive seeing does not suffice to cause assent to a contingent proposition however much it may suffice to cause an act in the sensitive appetite . . ." (p. 368): "sensitive sight is the partial cause of intellectual sight, but it is not the partial cause of the act of assenting without the intellectual seeing, for complex knowledge presupposes incomplex knowledge in the same subject; just as the will cannot proceed to action, unless knowledge precedes in the understanding, howeversomuch intuitive knowledge there be in sense."

man" is presupposed by the expression "this man" as well as by the expression "every man."[1] Fact is the occasion of our grasp of meaning; but apprehension of something *as being a fact*, is impossible except insofar as we have grasped meaning in abstraction from the particular occasion. Hence, as Ockham indicates, we may have evident knowledge of a universal truth, *if* our grasp of the constituents of a contingent fact is determinate and unambiguous. Thus the two ways in which we gain evident knowledge of fact from contingent experience, give rise to two distinct types of "extrinsic principles." Where our experience is of the presence of a perceptible quality in something distinct from it, we acquire evident knowledge of it as the principle by which one substance contingently affects another, and thus know that heat, for example, is the proximate principle of calefaction. But from the same experience we acquire evident knowledge not only of the nature of heat, but of the existence of something calefactible—or, stated more generally, of changeable substance. And in this way, through experience of contingent fact, we discriminate that which is absolute in our ways of coming to know (*scil.*, the qualities by which we perceive in the first instance) from that which is absolute in the order of being—*scil.*, substance. And thus we acquire from sense experience a starting point for inquiry, experiment, and the dialectical processes which elicit (though they do not produce) the intellectual intuition of determinate essential nature, by which the true middle term is recognized in demonstration. The discussion of the grasp of essential nature, and its relation to demonstration and definition, is not relevant at this point,

---

[1] Arist., An. Post., 100a 17–100b 1: "though the act of perception is of the particular, its content is universal—is man, for example, not the man Callias." The distinction between "particular" and "individual," though not used explicitly either by Ockham or Aristotle, is useful in exhibiting the meaning of a statement like the above. We perceive the "particular" in the sense that what we perceive is contingently involved in a particular fact or event; yet to perceive something as a factor or cause of an event, is possible only insofar as we conceive this "something" as *per se* distinct from that with which it is conjoined in the fact—and this is to conceive the individual (undivided) nature as cause, and as independent of the particular effect or event through which it came to be apprehended.

but belongs to the investigation of *a priori* demonstration and of its intrinsic principles. Knowledge by experience, as described here by Ockham, yields evident knowledge of extrinsic principles, and also knowledge of demonstrable facts—though where we come to know the demonstrable without demonstration, our knowledge is inferior, for we do not know the reason of the fact, nor do we really have determinate knowledge of what the fact is, or of precisely *what* has occurred, until we learn the reason through demonstration.[1]

From the foregoing it is obvious that not every universal proposition, in which an attribute is predicated of its first subject, is demonstrable; for it is not only definitions that are indemonstrable, and propositions composed of absolute terms, but also many universal propositions *per se secundo modo* are indemonstrable, and knowable only by experience of contingent fact, or else through intuitive grasp of essential nature, in demonstration, such as presupposes experience of instances

[1] Cf. Quodl. V, Qu. 2 (McKeon's *Selections*, vol. II, pp. 375–80) on the difference in our manner of knowing a demonstrable proposition by experience alone, and by demonstration. Since the necessity of a demonstrable proposition cannot be known without demonstration, mere experiential knowledge of it causes us to recognize its truth, but not that by which it must necessarily be true; hence we cannot, by induction or *a posteriori* reasoning, acquire knowledge of a demonstrable proposition as necessary, without an additional intuitive act, on the part of the intellect, by which the principle of the *a priori* demonstration is recognized as the reason of the fact. This is indicated on p. 380, as follows: "the necessary is not known through the contingent syllogistically as through premises, but evident contingent knowledge can be the efficient cause partial to causing evident knowledge in respect of the necessary."

Cf. Sent. Prolog., Qu. 1, z (cited by Abbagnano, p. 58, Note 1): "Notitia intuitiva rei est talis notitia virtute cuius potest sciri utrum res sit vel non. . . . Similiter notitia intuitiva est talis quod, quando aliqua cognoscuntur quorum unum inhaeret alteri, vel unum distat ab altero loco, vel alio modo se habet ad alterum, statim virtute illius notitiae incomplexae illarum rerum, sciret si res inhaereret vel non inhaereret, si distet vel non distet, et sic de aliis veritatibus contingentibus. . . ." The second kind of *notitia intuitiva* is always involved in evident contingent knowledge, but it presupposes the first kind, at least to the degree that we apprehend the *genus generalissimum* of substance, as something *per se* one and distinct from quality. More determinate grasp of the being of substances is had intuitively in the determinate grasp of essential nature (e.g., "animal," "man"); but this more determinate grasp cannot be had by sense experience alone, nor by the intellectual intuition of any one singular instance, but only when we pass beyond mere interest in fact, and seek the cause or the reason of facts already known in the other (non-demonstrative) way.

in specifically different subjects. Thus the proposition "All heat is heat-giving" can in no way be demonstrated—for if we attempted to demonstrate it with the nominal definition of "heat-giving" (i.e., "productive of heat" or something similar) as middle term, we would merely beg the question. This is evident, because the nominal definition of the attribute must be understood prior to the demonstration—for otherwise we could not know the major premise.[1]

Ockham distinguishes four kinds of commensurately universal propositions with connotative attributes, two of which are indemonstrable *a priori*, and two of which are demonstrable. The indemonstrable types are as follows: (1) The attribute may stand for the things signified by the subject, by connoting a quality or pair of qualitative contraries as potentially existent in the things for which it stands; such attributes may be said to signify their *supposita* as passive potentialities (material causes) of the qualitative change connoted by them; (2) The attribute may stand for its *supposita* by connoting something distinct from them that is not potentially existent *in* them, but which nevertheless can be a sign of their existence; such attributes may be said to signify their *supposita* as active principles (efficient or final causes) of change.

An example of the first type is where a term like "calefactible" is predicated of "body" as its first subject; an example of the second type is where a term like "calefactive" is predicated of "heat," or "creative" of "God." Propositions of these two kinds, which indicate their *supposita* as potential factors in contingent events such as involve other factors

---

[1] S. tot. log., III, II, 12, 66r: "Ex praedictis patere potest quod non quaelibet propositio in qua predicatur passio de suo subiecto, potest esse conclusio demonstrationis; haec enim est talis: 'omnis calor est calefactivus,' si nihil sit calefactivus nisi calor; et tamen ex quo non potest evidenter cognosci nisi per experientiam, manifestum est quod demonstrari non potest. Et si dicatur quod illa potest sic demonstrari: 'omne productivum caloris est calefactivum; omnis calor est productivus caloris; ergo calor est calefactivus,' ubi per diffinitionem passionis concludatur passio de subiecto—Dicendum est quod haec non est demonstratio sed petitio principii, unde universaliter quando pro medio accipitur diffinitio quid nominis, in tali illatione est petitio principii. Cuius ratio est, quia ante omnem demonstrationem et ante omnem conclusionem debet praecognosci quid nominis tam subiecti quam passionis."

distinct from them, are never demonstrable, and can be known only by experience.[1]

The other two types of universal propositions, which are demonstrable and in which *quia est* need not be known of the attribute, are as follows: (*a*) The attribute may stand for its *supposita* through connoting a synthesis of integral parts, *and* something distinct from them which does not exist in them; e.g., "having internal angles equal to two right angles," which is a universal attribute of "triangle," connotes the equivalence of the synthesis of parts which defines "triangle" to the synthesis of the same elements ("unit" and "magnitude") which defines "two right angles." (*b*) The attribute may stand for its *supposita* through connoting their parts negatively, as if they were not *per se* one; thus "corruptible," whose first subject is "material substance," indicates the possibility of substances ceasing to be individual ("undivided"), which is the same as indicating that they can cease to be. Thus the middle term, by which such an attribute is demonstrable of its first subject, is the essential definition of the subject; and the attribute is demonstrable through this essential definition only because its nominal definition indicates nothing extrinsic to the things for which it stands. Such attributes are, however, rare; and hence the demonstration of an attribute of its first subject, *a priori* or by the definition of the subject, is scarcely ever possible in the science of nature.[2]

---

[1] S. tot. log., III, II, 12, 66r–66v: "Est ergo sciendum quod aliqua propositio in qua predicatur passio de suo subiecto primo est demonstrabilis et aliqua non . . . aliqua passio praecise importat in recto idem quod subiectum et in obliquo aliquam formam realiter sic inhaerentem . . . ut 'calefactibile' respectu sui subiecti primi . . . alia passio praecise importat in recto illud idem quod importatur per subiectum, et in obliquo importat aliquam rem non sibi inhaerentem nec essentialem nec accidentalem . . . ut 'creativum.' Nam 'creativum' nihil importat nisi deum in recto, et creaturam in obliquo, sicut patet ex diffinitione exprimente quid nominis quae est 'aliquid potens creare aliquid'."

[2] S. tot. log., III, II, 12, 66v: "Alia autem passio importat idem in recto quod importat subiectum, et in obliquo importat partes illius, et etiam rem non sibi inhaerentem . . . exemplum tertii, 'habens tres angulos aequales duobus rectis'; nam ista passio in recto significat triangulam et in obliquo partes eius, et etiam alios angulos qui non sunt partes eius. . . . Alia autem passio importat idem in recto quod importat subiectum et negative in obliquo importat partes subiecti . . . ut 'corruptibile' respectu 'substantiae'; nam 'corruptibile' in recto et affirmative significat substantiam illam quae est corruptibilis; negative

Of propositions in which attributes are demonstrable of their first subjects nearly all are to be found in mathematics; and these are demonstrated through the nominal definitions of their subjects, for in the strict sense mathematical terms have only nominal definitions. Mathematical attributes do not indicate potentialities *in re*, in the contingent order, but they are intelligible as syntheses of the elements of quantitative definitions, in abstraction from change and from any except the "intelligible matter" involved in the notion of the potentially, but not actually, differentiated continuum. Thus the indefinable concepts, and the extrinsic principles or axioms, are sufficient for the definition and demonstration of all mathematical terms and propositions; and these indefinable concepts (e.g., "unit" and "magnitude"), and the common axioms, can become known through any experience of contingent fact, through reflection on the formal character of the proposition by which contingent fact is expressed.[1]

Ockham takes pains to point out that when Aristotle talks about the *a priori* demonstration of attributes, through definitions, of their *first* or immediate subjects, he is to be understood as referring principally to mathematical demonstration—an interpretation that is quite consistently supported by the illustrations offered by Aristotle, which in such cases are usually drawn from mathematics. The same holds good of those places

---

autem vel in obliquo significat partes eius quod patet ex diffinitione exprimente quid nominis quae est 'aliquid cuius partes possunt non esse vel cuius una pars potest ab alia separari'."

[1] S. tot. log., III, II, 12, 66v: In speaking of all four types of proposition, in which an attribute is predicated of its first subject, Ockham sums up as follows: "De prima passione universaliter dico quod nulla talis potest demonstrari de suo subiecto primo, quia si talis passio ignoretur de suo subiecto primo, non potest sciri de eo nisi per experientiam tantum; patet inductive, et eodem modo dicendum est de passione secunda. Sed passio tertio modo dicta et quarto potest demonstrari de suo subiecto, quia potest ignorari de suo subiecto primo quamvis sciatur quid significatur per subiectum et quid etiam significatur per passionem. Postea autem cognito cuius et quales sunt suae partes, sine ulteriori experientia de passione, potest eadem passio sciri de subiecto, et hoc per diffinitionem exprimentem illas partes quae in obliquo vel negative importantur per passionem. Et tales demonstrationes sunt mathematicae propter quod in eis parva vel nulla requiritur experientia, et demonstrantur de eis semper vel frequenter per diffinitionem subiecti tanquam per medium."

where Aristotle states that we do not need to know the existence of that for which the *attribute* can stand, though we must
know that the *subject* exists; it is only in mathematics, where
we can demonstrate the attribute of its first subject through
the nominal definition, that we do not require experiential
knowledge of the existence of something for which the attribute
can stand. In such cases, however, our grasp of the primary
elements of the definition must have arisen through experience.
As Aristotle states, all knowledge acquired by demonstration
and argument proceeds from pre-existent knowledge—hence
the starting point must always be intuition of *being*.¹

It remains to determine the meaning of the words "principle," and "prior," and to discuss the distinction between
knowledge of the fact and knowledge of the reasoned fact. A
proposition is called a first principle, according to Ockham,
not because there is no other proposition prior to it in any sense,
but because it is indemonstrable, and has no proposition prior
to it in the demonstrative order. Thus the laws of thought
and the metaphysical principles are prior to any premise of
demonstration, because presupposed by any premise of demonstration; but no premise is demonstrable from them. Similarly, a proposition like "All heat is calefactive" is prior to
"Whatever is hot is calefactive," though the latter cannot be
demonstrated from the former.²

¹ S. tot. log., III, II, 12, 66v: "Et quia in paucis scientiis proprie habemus
diffinitiones a priori nisi in mathematicis, in quibus communiter passio demonstratur de suo subiecto proprio per diffinitionem subiecti tanquam per medium, ideo
frequenter dicit Aristoteles quod passio est demonstrabilis de suo subiecto et quod
diffinitio est medium; non quod omnis passio est demonstrabilis de suo subiecto
subiecto proprio, sed quod omnis passio est demonstrabilis de aliquo subiecto,
et in mathematicis ut semper vel frequenter passio est demonstrabilis de suo
subiecto primo. Nec intendit Aristoteles quod in omni demonstratione medium
sit diffinitio, sed intendit quod in omni demonstratione in qua demonstratur
passio de suo subiecto primo medium est diffinitio; in aliis non oportet." Cf.
Arist., An. Post. I, 12, 78a 10–2. Also cf. *ante*, pp. 223, 224, text and notes.

² S. tot. log., III, II, 13, 66v: "Post praedicta videndum de proprietatibus
principiorum demonstrationem ingredientium quae non possunt esse conclusiones.
. . . Unde non ideo dicuntur principia esse prima quia nulla sit propositio
quocunque modo prior eis: hoc enim non est verum, nam secundum opinionem
Aristotelis aliqua est propositio necessaria negativa prima, et tamen omni negativa
est aliqua affirmativa prior, per quam tamen affirmativam demonstrari non
potest, cum non sit processus in infinitum in demonstrationibus." Cf. Arist.,
An. Post. I, 25, 86b 30–8.

It may be said, furthermore, that to every premise of demonstration some truth, which is not prior to it in the demonstrative order, is nevertheless prior to it in the contingent order, in the sense that it is presupposed by the premise, or in the sense that the premise could not have become known if this other truth had not become known. Thus the proposition in which "being" is predicated, in the mode of possibility, of a subject term of demonstration taken significatively, is presupposed by knowledge of the truth of the premise in which that term appears. For we cannot know that the premise is true of something for which its terms stand, without knowing that something can exist for which the terms *can* stand. Hence an affirmative premise, assertoric in form, presupposes as extrinsic principle a proposition predicating "being," in the mode of possibility, of the subject term; or else such a premise must be taken as equivalent to a proposition *de possibili* or to a conditional proposition, in which case the form of statement of the premise itself indicates the antecedent condition without which it cannot be known to be true. The point, of course, is the thoroughly Aristotelian one that we cannot know the truth of a principle except insofar as we grasp the essential nature of that which is signified by its terms; but, as Aristotle insists, we cannot know *what* a thing is, or its essential nature, without knowing to exactly the same degree *that* it is.[1]

We have, therefore, a double order of priority in knowledge —the condition of our actually knowing the truth of indemonstrable premises, is our antecedent grasp of the being of that which

[1] Cf. Arist., An. Post. I, 2, 71b 32-3: The premises must be "antecedently known, this antecedent knowledge being not our mere understanding of the meaning, but knowledge of the fact as well." Ibid., II, 7, 92b 5: "He who knows what human—or any other—nature is, must know also that man exists; for no one knows the nature of what does not exist—one can know the meaning of the phrase or name 'goat-stag,' but not what the essential nature of a goat-stag is." Ockham, S. tot. log., III, II, 14, 67r, referring to propositions which predicate merely nominal definitions of terms conventionally defined by them, says: "Ista autem prioritas non habet locum in illis propositionibus quarum una accipit diffinitum et alia diffinitionem exprimentem quid nominis tantum, et hoc quia significatum vocabuli non potest sciri sine diffinitione exprimente quid nominis si habet quid nominis. Potest autem significatum vocabuli haberi sine diffinitione exprimente quid rei, quamvis habeat diffinitionem exprimentem quid rei. . . . Arguendo a diffinitione exprimente quid nominis ad diffinitum est petitio principii, non autem a diffinitione exprimente quid rei ad diffinitum."

is signified by the terms, a grasp which cannot be acquired except through experience of existing instances. Thus in the order of *coming to know* principles of demonstrative science, evident contingent propositions are prior, because presupposed. The discrimination of the elements of the contingent fact, which are signified disjunctively by the terms of the contingent proposition, immediately yields the extrinsic principle of a demonstration concerning the subject—*scil.*, the extrinsic principle in which "being" is predicated in the mode of possibility of the subject term. For example, if we have evident knowledge of the demonstrative premise "Every body can be hot," we *must* have known an evident contingent proposition, "This body is hot," and hence we knew that "being" is predicable *de possibili* of "body" and of "hot," taken significatively. But this is precisely the antecedent condition of our knowledge of the demonstrative premise; and if we do not assume it as an extrinsic principle of our demonstration, we must indicate it in the demonstration itself by taking the premises as equivalent either to conditional propositions or to propositions whose terms stand for *things that can exist.*[1]

On the other hand, demonstrative science is of propositions which state not *that* something is, in the unqualified sense, but which state *what* such things can be, in the qualified sense. That is, we demonstrate attributes of a subject, and not that the subject exists.[2] Hence in the demonstrative order one

---

[1] S. tot. log., III, II, 13, 66v: "Oportet autem scire quod quamvis principia demonstrationis sint prima sic quod non sunt demonstrabilia, tamen aliqua propositio non necessaria quae non est principium demonstrationis potest esse prima. Unde sicut est ordo inter propositiones necessarias quod aliqua est prima vel prior et alia posterior, ita est ordo inter propositiones contingentes quod aliqua est prior vel prima et alia posterior, sicut ista 'Sortes est' est prior ista 'Sortes est homo,' quia sequitur tanquam a priori, 'Sortes est et Sortes non est non homo, ergo Sortes est homo,' et ita de aliis."

[2] Arist., An. Post., I, 10, 76a 31–5. The translation, in the Oxford edition, of ἀρχή ("principle") by "basic premise", and also of λαμβάνειν (in Latin "accipi") by "be assumed," is rather misleading. It is not the existence of a premise that is presupposed by knowledge of the premise, but the existence of the *thing* signified by the subject *term*. Aristotle is not contrasting "premise" with attribute—but subject with attribute. And λαμβάνειν does not mean what we mean in English by "assume"—i.e., "suppose" or "take for granted"—but it means here that the existence of what is signified by the subject of demonstration *must* have come to be known, or must have been *received*, antecedently or in some other way than by argument or instruction.

DEMONSTRATION AND DEFINITION 259

The problems which arise in connection with the middle
by which analytic knowledge of fact is had, are principally
found in connection with the questions *si est* and *quid est,* and

---

nem 'quia' fiat quaestio, sed magis est nota terminandi et respondendi; scito
autem quod haec propositio est vera, sicut scito quod luna eclipsatur, et scito
quod est aliquod medium per quod certificari potest quod luna eclipsatur, et
scito quid est illud medium utpote scito quod est aliquis effectus vel aliquid
aliud per quod certificari potest quod luna eclipsatur, contingit ulterius quaerere
quare et propter quid luna eclipsatur. Unde potest aliquis scire evidenter quod
luna eclipsatur et per consequens habet aliquod medium per quod scitur quod
luna eclipsatur; tamen potest ignorare causa quare luna eclipsatur, et ita potest
quaerere propter quid luna eclipsatur et tunc est alia quaestio, *scil.* propter
quid, et tunc quaeritur propriissimum medium per quod potest sciri quod luna
eclipsatur. . .

"Aliter potest demonstrator dubitare de aliquo an sit, utpote dubitat an deus
sit vel esse possit, et tunc quaerit an sit medium deveniendi in notitiam huius.
Hoc autem scito, quaerit ulterius quid est, sicut scito quod deus est, quaerit
ulterius quid est deus, et tunc quaeritur medium propriissimum per quod sciri
potest quod res est. Et istae duae quaestiones non ponuntur in numerum, quia
subiectum et predicatum non significant res distinctas distinctis modis. Ex
praedictis patet quod omnis quaestio vel quaerit si est medium deveniendi in
notitiam prius quaesiti, sicut quaestio quia et quaestio si est, vel quaerit quid
est illud medium, sicut quaestio quid est et quaestio propter quid est.

"Ex quo patet quod omnis quaestio est quodammodo quaestio medii. Sed
sciendum est quod medium non accipitur hic pro medio syllogistico sicut dicit
Lincolniensis, sed vocatur hic medium omne illud per quod decurrit ratio in
notitiam prius ignoti, et ita experientia potest hic vocari medium. . . . Oportet
etiam scire quod quandoque omnes istae quatuor quaestiones exiguntur ad
aliquam conclusionem vel terminos illius conclusionis demonstrabilis, de quibus
non est necessaria praecognoscere quia est; et in illo casu verum est quod dicit
Lincolniensis, *scil.* quod quaerentes duo, *scil.* si est et quia est, non quaerimus
aliud quam illud per quod fit discursus inferentia, *scil.* medium syllogisticum
ordinatum inesse debito ad extrema.

"Patet . . . quod diffinitio exprimens quid nominis passionis praesupponitur
omni quaestioni, et quod prima quaestio est quaestio si est de passione, quae
quaerit medium vel viam deveniendi in notitiam passionis quod est possibilis;
hoc est, quod 'esse' de ea possibiliter predicatur. Secunda autem quaestio est
quaestio quid est de passione, quia sicut illud quod sua diffinitio exprimens
quid nominis explicat in generali, ita quaestio quaerit in speciali, quod quidem
quaesitum est generale ad illud propter quod luna eclipsatur, quia corpus opacum
est commune ad terram. Scito autem si est et quid est de passione, quaeritur
ulterius an passio sit predicabilis de illo subiecto et quod est medium deveniendi
in notitiam illius, quo scito quaeritur in speciali causa propter quam passio
competit isti subiecto; et ita quid et propter quid quaerunt idem, sed quaestio
quid est de passione quaerit magis in generali, et quaestio propter quid magis
in speciali, et propter ista vult philosophus quod in tali processu quaestio quid
est et propter quid quasi idem sunt, et quod medium et causa idem sunt, quia
medium syllogisticum explicat causam frequenter in tali processu, propter quam
ita est a parte rei sicut denotatur esse per conclusionem demonstrationis. In
multis autem casibus non sunt ista vera nec multa alia quae dicit Aristoteles
circa istam materiam, nec in aliis vult ea intelligi generaliter."

Cf. Arist., An. Post., II, 1–2, 89b 21–90a 34. On "necessary truth" cf. *ante,*
pp. 227–33; on exponible propositions, cf. ch. v, pp. 205–209.

the way in which their answers can become evidently known. For in affirmative demonstration the middle term is a genus of the subject term, and is itself the first subject of the attribute; but to know that the terms are thus related, is to know what the definitions of subject and attribute are—i.e., to understand them through definitions of essential nature, and not merely through nominal definitions.

Now we cannot, Porphyry to the contrary notwithstanding, use rules of definition or the method of division, to prove that one term is related to another as genus to species, or to prove that a defining formula is a real definition predicable convertibly and significatively of its *definiendum*. As Aristotle says, never yet by defining anything did we get knowledge of it; but in connection with *demonstratio propter quid*, we face the paradox that knowledge of the reasoned fact is impossible without essential definition, while on the other hand essential nature, or real definitions, are not demonstrable.[1]

Ockham does not, like Aristotle, state the question of definition and its relation to demonstration as a problem, but gives the aristotelian solution by following a different method. After stating the four questions mentioned by Aristotle at the beginning of Book II of the *Posterior Analytics*, and indicating the sense in which each of them is concerned with the existence or nature of a "middle," Ockham sets out to investigate the way in which the answers to these questions, as applied to the different kinds of terms and propositions entering into demonstration, can become known. Obviously the main part of his discussion is taken up with the problem of essential definition —the answer to the question *quid est*. For once we understand how the definition of terms, through the essential nature of the individual existences for which they stand, is possible, our knowledge of the premises, and hence of the conclusion, of a syllogism of the reasoned fact, is readily explained.

The first question dealt with is that which asks if a thing can exist. This question (*si est*) is, for Ockham, equivalent to asking if a term signifies an essential nature—for what is *a* thing,

---

[1] Arist., An. Post. II, 3, 90b 14–6.

capable of existing *per se* outside the mind, is precisely an essential or individual nature. Now to ask the question *si est* of a term, we must have some definite concept, or complex of concepts, in mind, by which the *word* is, for us, distinguished in meaning from other words. If the word is an absolute term, we cannot possess the concept corresponding to it and yet be ignorant of the existence of individual things or natures signified by it—for an absolute term (or absolute concept) is an act of understanding that which is *per se* one and individual in nature, without connotation or implication of any fact or circumstance or particular time. If a man possesses the concept "body," or "whiteness," he is aware of the possible existence of that which is a body and of that which is capable of having whiteness present in it. And if he does not possess these concepts, he cannot ask whether things signified by them can exist, though he may ask this question of the *words*—but in that case he understands the words through nominal definitions or complex descriptions.[1]

[1] S. tot. log., III, II, 25, 69v: "Et est primo sciendum quod quaestio si est terminatur per hoc quod evidenter cognoscitur si res est, quod fit si sciatur propositio in qua esse existentiae per propositionem de inesse vel de possibili predicatur de subiecto; ideo videndum est quomodo talis propositio evidenter cognosci potest. Et oportet scire quod talis propositio dubitabilis vel habet pro subiecto nomen mere absolutum affirmativum, vel aliquod aliud nomen pro subiecto, puta nomen negativum vel connotativum vel respectivum; et propositio mentalis vel vocalis tali mentali correspondens in qua subiicitur nomen absolutum mere affirmativum nullomodo cognosci potest evidenter nisi res importata per subiectum intuitive et in se cognoscitur—puta nisi aliquo sensu particulari sentiatur, vel nisi sit intelligibile non sensibile et ab intellectu videatur illomodo proportionabiliter quo potentia visiva exterior videt visibile.

"Unde non potest quis evidenter cognoscere quod albedo est vel esse potest nisi viderit aliquam albedinem, et propter hoc quamvis credere possit narrantibus quod leo est et quod pardus est, et sic de aliis, tamen talia evidenter non cognoscit. Verumtamen ad sciendum evidenter tales propositiones non oportet sic apprehendere omnia significata per subiectum sed quandoque sufficit unum solum apprehendere, et quandoque plura; et ita talis quaestio si est non poterit terminari nisi per experientiam, hoc est, per notitiam sensitivam quae est principium experientiae, et de tali loquitur philosophus cum dicit, 'Qui ignorat quid est nescit si est; quemadmodum habemus quia est, sic habemus quid est,' unde quantum aliquis scit de aliquo tali quid est, tantum scit si est et econverso.

"Et si dicatur de deo scimus quod est et tamen nescimus quid est, dicendum est quod nullam propositionem mentalem in qua subiicitur terminus omnino simplex et mere absolutus conveniens deo vel supponens pro deo possumus pro statu isto habere; possemus enim scire de eo quid est, si sciremus si est. Possumus tamen habere propositionem mentalem in qua subiicitur terminus communis deo et aliis, et ideo de aliquo contento possumus scire quid est et si est, et quantum

To ask *si est* of a connotative term, is to ask whether it has a first subject—i.e., whether it is predicable as property of some absolute term. The answer to this question is demonstrable only in those cases in which an attribute is demonstrable of its first subject through a nominal definition—and this, as we have seen, is rarely possible except in mathematics, where both subject and attribute are defined synthetically, the elements of definition and also the rules of synthesis or axioms being common to both terms. In other cases, as where the attribute stands for its *supposita* by connoting something really distinct from them potentially existent in or with them, *si est* cannot be demonstrated, but can become known only through experience of existing things. Thus to answer *si est* with respect to the term "calefactible," is to know if anything can be hot—in this case the question is answered at the same time that the existence of *heat* is apprehended by us, for to apprehend heat is to apprehend the hot, and to apprehend the hot is to apprehend what can be hot—i.e., the calefactible.[1]

---

scimus si est, tantum scimus quid est et econverso. Ex quibus patet quod talis propositio nullo modo potest demonstrari nec a posteriori nec a priori, nisi forte dicatur quod propositio particularis large sumendo demonstrationem dicatur posse demonstrari; sicut si haec sit nota praedicto modo, 'omnis albedo est vel potest esse,' et arguatur sic: 'omnis albedo est vel potest esse; aliquis color est albedo; ergo aliquis color est vel potest esse.'" Cf. Arist., An. Post. II, 8, 93a 18–20, and 27–8.

[1] S. tot. log., III, II, 26, 69v: "Si autem propositio dubitabilis in qua predicatur esse existentiae per propositionem de inesse et de possibili habeat pro subiecto nomen connotativum vel respectivum vel negativum vel unum compositum ex multis nominibus talibus, quandoque potest demonstrari et quandoque non; talis enim propositio semper equivalet uni propositioni in qua predicatur passio de suo subiecto saltem large sumendo passionem—sicut ista propositio 'eclipsis est' equivalet isti 'aliquid eclipsatur,' et ista 'calefactivum est' equivalet isti 'aliquid est calefactivum,' etc., . . . et ideo sicut dictum est de propositionibus quibus equivalent quod sunt demonstrabiles vel non, ita dicendum est de istis. Si tamen dicitur quod nulla est demonstratio nisi quando major potest esse prius tempore cognosci quam conclusio ita quod major potest esse nota et conclusio potest ignorari et tamen apprehendi, potest dici quod aliquae tales propositiones sunt demonstrabiles et aliquae non, puta quando passiones sunt demonstrabiles de suis propriis subiectis, sunt tales propositiones demonstrabiles; quando autem passiones non sunt demonstrabiles de suis subiectis primis, tunc non sunt demonstrabiles—ut ista 'calefactivum est vel potest esse' demonstrari non potest sed tantum scitur per experientiam sine sillogismo in quo major potest esse nota et conclusio apprehendi et ignorari." Cf. *ante*, pp. 245–7, with reference to which attributes are demonstrable of their first subjects, and what types are not.

The question *si est* can only be answered with respect to a term, to the extent to which something that is *per se* one— i.e., essentially a *thing*—is signifiable by it. If we leave out of consideration the *word* of which the question *si est* is asked, paying attention to the concept by which the word is understood, the question *si est* is always equivalent to the question *quia est* asked of a proposition in which a connotative term is predicated of an absolute term or of the word "something" taking the place of an absolute term. Consequently, we must consider whether it is possible to know that an attribute signifies existence, without the apprehension of some determinate kind of essential nature, whose existence is implied by the attribute's capacity to stand for "something," being presupposed.

According to Aristotle, it is impossible to know that something exists, without being aware of definable form—i.e., without grasping, to precisely the degree in which existence is known, *what* exists. Similarly, it is impossible to know what something essentially is, without being aware of its existence.[1] In view of this parallelism between our awareness of existence and our awareness of essential nature, it might seem that the words "essence" and "existence," for Aristotle, are two ways of signifying what is one and the same thing. And this is exactly the interpretation which Ockham adopts, though perhaps the majority of the scholastic interpreters of Aristotle were of the opposite opinion. As is usual in such cases, however, the opposition is not clean cut, for the scholastics who insisted on a real distinction between essence and existence, usually understood by "existence" the "being conditioned" which by Ockham is understood as *co-existence* or contingency. In this sense, therefore, the distinction between essence and existence is equivalent to the distinction between a thing considered *divisim*, without determinate reference to anything else, and the same thing considered together with something else, as "part" of a contingent event or relation.

[1] Arist., An. Post. II, 8, 93a 18–20: "we cannot apprehend a thing's definable form without apprehending that it exists. . . ." (27–8) "the degree of our knowledge of a thing's essential nature is determined by the sense in which we are aware that it exists."

Now the point of view which is revealed in Ockham's whole analysis of terms and of propositions, is that "togetherness" is not a metaphysical thing or principle, but that a term which signifies two distinct things as "parts" of a factual whole, signifies nothing other than the two distinct things, their "togetherness" being not a third metaphysical element, but rather a function of a human mode of signification. For Ockham, there is no cause of motion extrinsic to the thing which is moved, and the thing which moves it: but mover and moved are of themselves the sole causes of the fact that motion occurs. In saying that they are the sole causes of the event, it does not follow that they are themselves uncaused causes—though this inference was usually made by those who objected to the identification of essence and existence, on the ground that it placed created things on a par with the First Cause. On the contrary, it is because the existence or essential nature of finite things is to act and to be acted upon, that such things *are* the immediate and adequate principles or causes of the events in which they are involved. And for precisely this reason, it is only the existence and essence of the individual things for which the terms of a proposition stand, if the proposition is not of present time only, that make the proposition true. If the proposition is of present time only, or if it is singular or particular in form, its truth depends also on the existence of the mind apprehending something as "now" or as a "this." But with universal and necessary propositions, such as are conclusions of demonstration, the sole reason of truth is the existences for which the terms stand—and since we cannot apprehend and conceive what is not a *thing* and a *what*, the possibility of knowing a necessary truth by its reason or cause depends on whether or not our apprehension of essential nature is also an apprehension of individual existence.

If, as Ockham maintains, the essential nature of an individual thing is not other than its existence, then if we can have determinate concepts of essential nature we can know facts by their actual causes—the "is" which connects the terms of a necessary proposition, will be certified by the *ens* which is determinately grasped when the middle term of the demonstration is understood. But if the existence of a man is other than his essential nature, at the same time being the cause of the truth of the proposition "Every man is risible," then the grasp of the essential nature of "man," through the real definition, would be possible even if no man ever existed, and consequently it would be possible without any propositions concerning individual men being true. But if this were the case, the possession of a demonstration of a scientific proposition would not be knowledge of a necessary truth; and the connection of the extreme terms with the middle would be mediated by "existence" as a further, but indeterminate or infinite, middle.

Ockham's treatment of the question of essence and existence, therefore, is exactly parallel, in principle and end, with his treatment of the question of whether genera and species of substance are connotative terms signifying "universal things" inhering in individuating matter. If existence is something distinct from what exists, so that essences exist by reason of something that is not essentially anything, then the only reason of existence is mere existence—not any *kind* of existence (for that would be essence), but indeterminate, undifferentiated, and unintelligible "thisness." Ockham's position, here as elsewhere, is directed to the clarification and simplification of the relation of science to metaphysics. If all finite concepts, substantial as well as accidental, are attributes *predicable* of existence as such, so that the primary subject of every term is other than the determinate form signified by the term, science becomes identical with logic and metaphysics, and metaphysics becomes a discursive *process* or *end*less dialectic. Such is the philosophy of internal relations implicit in Porphyry's treatise on the predicables, and in the so-called "realist" theories of the universal, when these theories involve a metaphysical distinction between essential nature and a principle of individuation, between form and formless matter, or between essence and existence *in* existing things. To Ockham, such a position is the destruction of science and of the whole aristotelian philosophy, because it makes motion prior to the mover and moved, predication prior to signification, and the cause of truth or fact (*scil.* being) indeterminate and unintelligible.

It is to be considered in what way existence is related to a thing, and whether the being and the existence of a thing are two things distinct from each other outside the soul. It seems to me that they are not two such things, and that existence does not signify anything distinct from things. For if it did, then it would be either a substance or an accident; not an accident because then the existence of a man would be a quantity or quality, etc., which is obviously false as appears by induction. Not can it be said that it is a substance, because every substance is matter or form or the composite, or an immaterial substance. But it is apparent that none of these can be said to be existence, if existence is something other than the essence of a thing. Further, if they were two things, either they would form an essential unity or they would not. If so, then one would have to be act and the other potentiality, and consequently one would be matter and the other form, which is absurd. If, however, they did not form an essential unity, then they would make up a mere aggregation. . . . Further, if they were two things it would not involve contradiction for God to conserve an essence in the world without its existence, or conversely to conserve its existence without it, each of which is impossible.

Therefore it is to be said that essence and existence are not two things, but that these two words "thing" and "to be" signify one and the same, but one does so as a noun, and the other as a verb; and for this reason one cannot conveniently be used in place of the other, since they do not have the same function. Whence "to be" can be placed between two terms, as in saying that a man *is* an animal (*hominem esse animal*), and it is not thus with the word "thing" or "essence."

Hence "to be" signifies the thing itself. But "being" (*entitas*) signifies the first simple cause when it is said of it in signifying it as not dependent on another. When, however, it is predicated of others it signifies those very things that are dependent and ordered to the first cause, and this is the case because those things are not things unless they are thus dependent and ordered to the first cause; just as, at some times, they do not exist. Whence, at a time when a man is not dependent, and thus does not exist, so at that time he is not a man; and therefore it is no more to be imagined that the essence is indifferent to existence and non-existence, than that it is indifferent to being an essence or not an essence . . . ; hence such arguments as these, "an essence can

exist and not exist, therefore existence is distinct from essence,"
and "an essence can be under opposites, therefore essence is
distinct from existence," do not hold, any more than does the
following: "an essence can *not be* an essence, and it can be an
essence, therefore essence is distinct from essence."

Existence and essence are no more two things than essence and
essence, and this is the opinion of Grosseteste when he says, in his
commentary on Book II of the *Posterior Analytics*, that "everything
said of the first cause proves only that the essence itself of the first
cause is entirely simple, but what is said of other things proves
only their order and dependence on the first essence which exists
per se, and this ordering or dependence does not multiply anything
in the essence which depends on the first Being, whether it is
inquired concerning the first Being or concerning a thing dependent
on the first Being, if it exists. . . ."

The reason, however, why the saints and others say that God is
his own existence and that this is not the case with creatures, is
because God exists in such manner that he cannot not exist, but
rather he necessarily exists and does not exist by reason of anything
else. A creature, however, exists in such manner that it is not
necessary that he exist, just as it is not necessary that he be a thing,
for he is a thing by the agency of another. And thus in God there
is nothing other than God by which God exists; but in the creature
these differ, because that which is the creature, and that by which
he exists, are distinct *simpliciter* just as God and creatures are
distinct.[1]

Having thus indicated that things are not related to themselves, nor to other things, by a third principle called "existence," Ockham takes up the question of how we come to
know the answer to the question *quid est*, and to possess the
concepts of individual existence or nature that are involved
as "middles" in demonstration of the reasoned fact. As
Aristotle states, the nature of the thing and the reason of the
fact are identical; hence if we can determine how we come to
recognize essential nature, we will thereby determine how
demonstrative science is acquired.[2]

Essential definitions are of two kinds: the most proper kind
(*diffinitio quid rei proprie dicta*), which may be called "intrinsic
essential definitions," are distinguished from definitions *per*

[1] S. tot. log., III, II, 27, 70r.   [2] Arist., An. Post., II, 2, 90a 14.

additamentum, which may be called "extrinsic essential defini-tions." An example of the first kind is "rational animal," as definition of "man"; an example of the second kind is "act of an organic natural body," as definition of "soul." The first kind of definition is proper to material substances, for only things signifiable by parts forming a *per se* unity, are definable in this way. *Extrinsic* real definitions can be had of absolute qualitative terms, as when we define "whiteness" (*albedo*) as "the colour most dazzling to sight." [1]

Intrinsic essential definitions are composed of genus and differentia, the genus being an absolute concept indicating precisely the undivided being of the things signified by it, and the differentia being a connotative term which stands for such individuals by indicating a determinate or abstracted part of their individual nature. It is to be considered how the parts of an essential definition are known to be predicable *per se primo modo* of the specific term whose definition they constitute. [2]

[1] S. tot. log., III, II, 28, 70r: "videndum est quomodo terminatur quaestio quid est; hoc est, quomodo potest evidenter cognosci propositio in qua predicatur diffinitio de diffinito. . . . Diffinitio exprimens quid rei est illa quae non est necessaria disputanti scienti significatum vocabuli; sicut ad hoc quod aliquis sciat quid significat hoc nomen 'homo' non est necessarium scire quod homo componitur ex tot partibus vel ex talibus partibus. Unde quilibet potest disputare cum alio quamvis ignoret diffinitionem exprimentem quid rei; sed ignorata diffinitione quid nominis exprimente, non potest quis cum alio disputare . . . non est igitur diffinitio exprimens quid rei necessaria disputanti, quia talis diffinitio non tantum exprimit quid nomen significat sed exprimit etiam quid res est.

"Talis autem diffinitio duplex est, quaedam enim diffinitio talis est quae nihil importat extrinsecum rei, alio modo quam importat rem vel partem rei, et talis diffinitio vocatur diffinitio propriissime dicta, quae non potest esse nisi substanti-arum vel nominum substantiarum, quia talis diffinitio non potest esse nisi com-positorum tanquam illorum quorum essentia exprimitur per orationem, cuiusmodi composita per se una non sunt nisi substantiae. Talis est diffinitio 'animal ration-ale,' cum sit 'animal' genus et 'rationale' differentia, quia 'animal' importat totum hominem et 'rationale' importat partem hominis sicut suum abstractum. Alia est diffinitio importans quid rei, quae simul cum hoc quod importat rem importat vel exprimit aliquid aliud quod non est de essentia rei, sicut est diffinitio *animae* quae est ista: 'anima est actus corporis physici organici, etc.,' ut habetur in 2. De anima, quae importat animam et corpus quod non est pars animae nec anima, et ista vocatur diffinitio per additamentum, et tales diffinitiones importantes quid rei convertuntur cum nominibus mere absolutis affirmativis."

[2] S. tot. log., III, II, 29, 70r: "Diffinitio exprimens quid rei non data per additamentum semper continet pro prima parte aliquod genus diffiniti, et pro alia parte vel aliis partibus continet differentiam vel differentias essentiales vel aliquos obliquos significantes per se et primo partes rei; et istae partes (scil. genus et differentiae) sunt diversae. Nam genus importat totum, aliae partes significant seu important partes determinatas rei sive partes distinctas. Prima

Since there is no "middle" between a thing and its essential nature, and since both genus and differentia signify nothing other than the essential nature of a thing, it is obvious that *a priori* demonstration of such a definition is impossible. In the case of the genus, according to Ockham, *a posteriori* proof is likewise impossible; for if a property commensurate with the genus were used as middle term of an *a posteriori* syllogism, *si est* would have to be known of it prior to the inference, (for properties of substances are not demonstrable of their first subjects)—but to know *si est* of the property is to possess a concept of individual nature convertible with the property, and this is to conceive the genus. Hence a proposition such as "Man is an animal" can in no way be known through demonstration, since both terms are absolute, and incapable of being understood significatively except through experience of the existence of individuals signified by them. Ockham describes the process as follows:

This is the process; that first a man is apprehended through some particular sense, and then the same man is apprehended by the intellect, this apprehension giving rise to a general notion common to all men; and this notion is called a concept, intention, or passion, this concept being common to each man. Once it exists in the intellect, the intellect immediately knows that a man is something, without argument; subsequently, some animal other than a man, or some other animals, being apprehended, an idea (*notitia*) common to every animal is elicited (*elicitur*); and this general notion is common to every animal, and is called a passion or intention of the soul, or a concept common to all animals. When this exists in the soul, the intellect can combine this concept with the previous concept, and when they are compounded by way of the verb "is," the intellect immediately assents to that proposition without any reasoning. And thus any such proposition in which a genus is predicated of a term which it properly defines, is had without syllogism; and this is universally true of every genus with respect to the species which is of absolute character, because such a proposition is immediately known if the terms are clearly apprehended.[1]

pars diffinitionis, puta genus, nec a priori nec a posteriori potest demonstrari de diffinito, sicut quod homo sit animal demonstrari non potest, sed propositio talis sine sillogismo acquiritur mediante notitia intuitiva."
[1] S. tot. log., III, II, 29, 70r.

Against the objection that propositions in which a genus is
predicated of its species, are not as a matter of fact immediately
evident to everybody, Ockham replies that if anyone possesses
simple and proper concepts of existence corresponding to
the words of such a proposition, then it cannot be doubted
but must be immediately evident. But where a person understands such terms only through descriptions, or by complexes of
accidental notions none of which is proper to the thing
though the whole complex is convertible with the specific
term, it is possible to doubt such a proposition—and the reason
for this is that such a person does not actually know that such
a thing can exist, though he may have faith that it does,
on account of his belief in what others have told him. But
if such a person, after using a specific term like "lion" without
having any single concept proper to it, but only a descriptive
concept or complex of accidental concepts of what the word
means, later comes to experience the existence of individual
lions, he will then know that a lion is essentially an animal
—assuming that he has a proper concept of animal, acquired
from experience of other animals. Thus his newly acquired
proper concept of "lion" would, in a sense, be a middle by
which "animal" would be known to have belonged to his
previous "descriptive notion" of what the word "lion"
meant. This, however, would be only a verbal demonstration,
though according to Ockham Aristotle sometimes speaks of
demonstration as proving the genus to belong *per se primo
modo* to the species. Where he does speak in this manner, however, it is such cases as the above that he has in mind—for our
grasp of the existence of things signified by an absolute term,
in abstraction from contingent fact or circumstance, cannot
precede our intuitive apprehension of what such terms mean.[1]

A proposition in which an essential differentia is predicated

[1] S. tot. log., III, II, 29, 70r: "Ad secundum dicendum est quod quaelibet
talis propositio mentalis in qua subiiciuntur et predicantur tales conceptus mere
absoluti, est per se nota, quia statim sciuntur cognitis terminis; tamen non quaelibet propositio vocalis est per se nota, nam ex quo voces significant ad placitum,
voces mere absolutae possunt imponi eodem de quibus habemus *vel* alii habent
tales conceptus, et tunc aliquis qui tales conceptus non habet potest scire significata
vocabulorum et simul cum hoc potest nescire eam, eo quod alios conceptus mentales non habet, sed habet conceptus mentales plures quorum aliqui si componan-

of its species can, in some cases at least, be demonstrated *a posteriori*, though never *a priori*. Thus a man, being himself a sensitive being, could have a concept of "sensitive soul," and might also be aware of certain effects or actions whose occurrence would presuppose the capacity of sense perception in anything performing such operations. Then, seeing some living bodies (such as those sea creatures which are near the border line between plant and animal), and wondering whether they are sensitive or not, he might prove that all such living bodies as these are sensitive, by some observed behaviour or reaction such as presupposed the capacity to feel. It is by such *a posteriori* reasoning, according to Ockham, that Aristotle made evident the fact that all perceptible substances have materiality as an essential principle or part of their undivided being—their capacity to change and to be generated and destroyed, being the middle terms of the induction.[1]

tur ad invicem, totum resultans ex eis erit convertibile cum illa voce, et ita talis propositio vocalis non erit per se nota, quia non quaelibet notitia qua scitur quid termini significant sufficit ad sciendum talem propositionem; et sicut illa propositio vocalis non est per se nota, ita illa mentalis quae componitur ex conceptibus compositis non est per se nota, quia potest haberi quamvis nesciatur. Unde ego modo de facto scio quid significat hoc nomen 'leo,' et scio quid significat hoc nomen 'animal,' et tamen ignoro istam propositionem 'leo est animal' quamvis credam eam esse veram; et habeo propositionem mentalem cuius subiectum est unum compositum ex multis notitiis incomplexis quarum nulla est simplex et propria leoni, sed propositionem mentalem cuius subiectum est simplex et mere absolutum proprium leonibus non habeo, quia si talem propositionem mentalem haberem statim sine sillogismo scirem eam. Sed nunquid propositio mentalis in qua subiicitur tale compositum, et etiam propositio vocalis, sunt demonstrabiles ex quo sunt dubitabiles? Potest dici quod large accipiendo demonstrationem tales sunt demonstrabiles, et hoc quia conclusio potest esse ignota et dubia, et postea, scita propositione majore in qua predicatur idem predicatum de conceptu mentali acquisito per notitiam intuitivam rei, et scita minore in qua predicatur idem conceptus de subiecto conclusionis, potest conclusio fieri nota; et ita talis propositio large accipiendo demonstrationem potest fieri nota per demonstrationem ex quo potest concludi sillogismo faciente illam conclusionem esse evidenter notam quae prius erat dubia vel apparuit esse falsa." Cf. ibid., c. 31, 71r: "Verumtamen de subiecto quale nos habemus de facto non est forte inconveniens diffinitionem posse demonstrari saltem large capiendo demonstrationem. Et per istum varium modum probandi possunt exponi multae auctoritates Aristotelis, quae videntur tam inter se quam praedictis repugnare; quandoque enim loquitur de uno modo demonstrandi et quandoque de alio, et quandoque loquitur de predicatione diffinitionis de diffinito simplici et proprio, quandoque loquitur de predicatione diffinitionis de diffinito composito et proprio tantum."

[1] S. tot. log., III, II, 30, 71r: "Quamvis propositio in qua predicatur genus absolutum de specie mere absoluta, composita ex conceptibus simplicibus, demonstrari non possit nec a priori nec a posteriori, tamen propositio in qua

From the foregoing it is apparent that no 'definition of a species or genus can be *proved* to be its essential definition; for although *a posteriori* proof of the differentia is in some cases possible, the genus can only be known by experience and intuitive abstraction. The order in which we may come to acquire the concepts from which an essential definition is formed, may be two-fold: for we may come to have an intuitive conception of some of the essential parts, without being aware of the undivided nature of the whole, and in such a case we do not grasp the essential nature of the thing, nor possess a real definition, until we have abstracted the generic concept through experience of existing instances of individuals signified by the term which is defined. Or we may first recognise the generic character, later coming to differentiate the essential principles or parts by which the species is distinguished from other species ordered under the same genus; and in this process of building up the definition, *a posteriori* inference may be involved in our recognition of the differentiæ.[1]

---

predicatur differentia de specie tali a posteriori demonstrari potest. Nam differentia, sicut dictum est prius, importat unam partem in obliquo, cum igitur per effectus demonstrari potest talem rem habere talem partem, ideo per effectum demonstrari potest differentia talis de specie tali. Verbi gratia, si aliquis habet notitiam propriam animae sensitivae, et per consequens sciat quid significat hoc vocabulum 'sensitivum,' et videat aliquod corpus cuius habeat notitiam simplicem et propriam talibus corporibus, et tamen ignorat an habeat animam sensitivam— iste, per aliquos effectus cuilibet tali corpori competentes, potest demonstrative probare quod omne tale corpus habet animam sensitivam, et per consequens quod est sensitivum; et per talem modum probavit Aristoteles per transmutationem et motum quod in istis generalibilibus et corruptibilibus est materia distincta a forma, et per consequens quod sunt materialia, cum tamen *materiale* est differentia essentialis eorum."

[1] S. tot. log., III, II, 31, 71r: "Est ergo duplex modus deveniendi in talem diffinitionem. Unus est per notitiam intuitivam partium illius rei. Qui enim intuitive cognosceret partes rei statim posset formare conceptus demonstrabiles importantes illas partes in obliquo et importantes totum in recto. Sed adhuc non est necesse quod habeat diffinitionem, quia defficeret sibi genus quod non potest haberi nisi per notitiam intuitivam alicuius singularis, aut eius speciei vel aliquorum singularium diversarum specierum; quo habito potest intellectus illum conceptum praeponere aliis conceptibus demonstrabilibus et sic habetur diffinitio, quod si predicatur de diffinito erit illa propositio evidens sine omni sillogismo et ita indemonstrabilis erit.

"Si autem partes non omnes rei intuitive videantur sed totum videatur intuitive, non tamen videns possit discernere inter omnes partes totus; si tamen hoc sit possibile tunc illa pars quae est genus accipitur per notitiam illam et per notitiam alteri vel aliorum singularium. Alii autem conceptus demonstrabiles a

While there is no way in which essential definitions can be demonstrated to be essential definitions, since the undivided nature by which the defining formula has significative unity can only be apprehended intuitively in experience of existing instances, Ockham points out that the rules given in the *Topics* can be of much assistance in organizing the materials presupposed by the abstractive or intuitive act which is the grasp of essential nature or of the explanatory "middle." Dialectical criticism and synthesis are also useful in eliminating irrelevant lines of inquiry, whereby we can distinguish the accidental from the peculiar predicates, detect ambiguities, and make distinctions. Our grasp of essential nature, and of the reasoned fact, is not an inference nor a process, but an act of intelligence; on the other hand, the materials must be provided, and hence controlled experience and systematic methods of inquiry, such as are developed in the *Topics*, aid us in making an unambiguous statement of each separate problem, and thereby tend to elicit the intuitive act by which the explanatory and essential principle is "seen."[1]

The art of definition (*ars definiendi*) is the method of division, whereby the parts of an essential definition are checked and properly ordered. Ockham states the two methods of division indicated by Aristotle, and shows how they presuppose, and in no sense demonstrate, the knowledge that such or such terms signify the essential nature of the things defined. All that the method of division proves, even in a broad sense of the word "prove," is that a certain group of words stated

posteriori concluduntur a diffinito et ita accipitur diffinitio sic quod una pars per notitiam intuitivam et aliae per effectus, et tunc istis habitis est talis propositio nota in qua predicatur diffinitio de diffinito; nec hoc negat Aristoteles, sed intendit Aristoteles principaliter hoc probare quod per nullum sillogismum a priori potest fieri evidenter notum quod talis diffinitio predicatur de diffinito, et quod sufficienter exprimit essentiam diffiniti."

[1] S. tot. log., III, II, 31, 71r: "Sic ergo apparet per quem modum pars diffinitionis scitur de diffinito et per quem modum diffinitio scitur de diffinito. Et ad istum processum multum faciunt regulae datae in VII Topicorum; per istud tamen non habetur ars diffiniendi, sed ars diffiniendi accipitur per divisionem. Unde quamvis aliquis sciat evidenter omnes propositiones in quibus predicantur partes diffinitionis de diffinito, si tamen nesciat illas partes in una oratione recto ordine ordinare, nescit diffinire nec habebit diffinitionem. Unde qui sic ordinaret partes diffinitionis hominis 'rationale animal mortale,' non haberet diffinitionem." Cf. Arist., Topica, VII, 3, 153a 6–154a 12.

in a certain order has the logical character of an essential definition; hence the definition itself is taken non-significatively in the procedure of division, so that what we prove by it is a proposition like this: "The expression *rational animal* is a definition." But we cannot prove, by division or by the definition of what a definition is, that "Man *is* a rational animal," the terms being taken significatively or with personal supposition.[1]

Extrinsic essential definitions (*diffinitiones per additamentum*) are formed from an absolute term which signifies the essential character of a thing, plus one or more terms predicable

[1] S. tot. log., III, II, 31, 71r: "Est ergo ars diffiniendi per quam partes diffinitionis debite ordinantur et hoc est per divisionem, ut prius ponatur genus, deinde dividatur genus et accipitur illa differentia quae scitur competere diffinitio quamvis hoc nesciatur per divisionem sed aliquo modo praedictorum modorum; deinde adhuc subdividatur et sic procedendo et addendo quousque perveniatur ad orationem convertibilem. Duobus autem modis contingit sic divisive procedere: Unomodo ut primo dividatur genus, secundo accepta differentia quae competit diffinito, dividatur illa differentia vel genus convertibile cum illa differentia," etc. . . . "Aliter contingit per divisionem procedere ut semper idem dividatur et non diversa, sicut si debeat diffiniri ternarius, et accipitur primo genus ternarii, puta numerus, et dividitur numerus prius sic 'et numerorum alius par alius impar,' et addatur ista differentia 'impar' isti generi 'numerus,' sic: 'numerus impar.' Deinde dividatur idem genus, scil. 'numerus,' et non hoc totum 'numerus impar,' nec aliud convertibile; sic 'numerus alius utrobique primus, alius non utrobique primus,' etc., et addatur ista differentia 'utrobique primus' isti toti 'numerus impar,' etc." Ibid., 71v: "In primo processu non solum oratio tota est convertibilis cum diffinito, sed etiam una differentia est convertibilis cum diffinito, et de tali modo accipiendi diffinitionem loquitur Aristoteles VII Metaph.; in secundo processu nulla pars diffinitionis est convertibilis cum diffinito sed quaelibet erit in plus, et tota oratio erit convertibilis. Sed hoc generale est quod nihil scitur de diffinito per divisionem nisi dicas quod tota oratio nunc scitur per divisionem propter hoc quod intellectus primus non componit talem propositionem; sed quicquid scitur de diffinito scitur per aliam viam. Hoc tamen haberetur in fine quod scitur quod haec oratio est diffinitio talis diffiniti; non tamen per hoc scitur quod haec diffinitio significative sumpta predicatur de diffinito significative sumpto; et hoc vult Aristoteles quando probat per divisionem non sillogizatur nec demonstratur diffinitio de diffinito significative sumpto, inquantum scilicet explicat quid est res, sed hoc potest praecedere artem diffiniendi. Sed per artem diffiniendi partes diffinitionis debite ordinantur et per hoc scitur quod talis oratio est diffinitio talis diffiniti; et hoc intendit Lincolniensis quando dicit methodus diffinitiva concludit orationes tales, 'animal rationale mortale est diffinitio hominis,' et haec est oratio composita ex secundis intentionibus et non est haec oratio oratio diffinitiva solum explicans quid est homo, sed haec est oratio predicativa huius secundae intentionis 'diffinitio' de hac diffinitione 'animal rationale mortale'; propter quod Aristoteles et Lincolniensis volunt quod nunquam diffinitio potest demonstrari de diffinito per diffinitionem diffinitionis, quia per tale medium non potest demonstrari diffinitio significative sumpta sed semper praecise de propria diffinitione supponente pro se et non pro suo significato."

per se secundo modo of the term defined. While these differentiating properties may in some cases be demonstrable of the term defined, the genus is not, and hence definitions of this kind cannot be demonstrated of the *definiendum*, since the grasp of the genus is always presupposed and is had only through intuitive apprehension of existing instances. Thus, if whiteness were defined as "the colour most dazzling to sight," the genus could in no way be demonstrated and could only be known by the intuitive grasp of the common character of the different colours; nor could the extrinsic differentia placed in this definition become known without experience of whiteness having this effect. Hence no kind of essential definition, by which an absolute term is defined *per se*, can be known by demonstration to be the definition of that which it defines, because the genus is never demonstrable of its species, but is formed in the mind through intuitive apprehension of the undivided existence of the things signified by it. Consequently essential definitions—i.e., definitions of things which, in Aristotle's words, have no "cause of their substantial being other than that being itself," are indemonstrable statements of essential nature.[1]

[1] S. tot. log., III, II, 32, 71v: "Diffinitio data per additamentum non solum explicat essentiam rei sed etiam simul cum hoc explicat aliquid aliud a re et hoc vel negative vel affirmative, et ideo talis diffinitio non solum componitur ex aliquo predicabili per se primo modo sed etiam componitur ex aliquibus predicabilibus secundo modo, quae sunt passiones diffiniti; et ideo ad sciendum quomodo diffinitio talis scitur de diffinito videndum est quomodo diversae partes diversimode sciuntur de eodem; unde illa pars quae explicat essentiam rei, quae est genus, non potest sciri de diffinito per syllogismum sed per notitiam intuitivam alicuius rei tantum, sicut dictum est prius. Aliae autem partes diffinitionis diversimode sciuntur de diversis diffinitionibus secundum quod diversae passiones diversimode sciuntur de diversis subiectis. Sicut quaedam passiones demonstrantur de subiectis suis primis, et quaedam non possunt demonstrari de subiectis suis primis sed tantum possunt per experientiam sciri de subiectis; ita partes tales diffinitionis possunt demonstrari vel demonstrative probari de diffinitis, et quaedam non possunt demonstrari de eis; et sicut quaedam passiones possunt demonstrari a priori de subiectis et quaedam a posteriori, ita quaedam partes talis diffinitionis possunt probari de diffinitis a priori, et quaedam a posteriori. Verbi gratia, si haec sit diffinitio 'albedinis', *color disgregativus visus*, prima particula quae est genus albedinis nullomodo potest demonstrari de albedine sed tantum potest fieri evidenter nota per notitiam intuitivam et non per syllogismum, et secunda autem particula potest fieri nota per experientiam. Si enim nullus experiatur albedinem disgregare visum nullus sciret an albedo esset disgregativa visus. . . . Constat itaque ex praedictis nulla diffinitio alicuius mere absoluti affirmativi et simplicis potest de diffinito demonstrari quia semper una pars est indemonstrabilis de tali diffinito."
Cf. Arist., An. Post. II, 9, 93b 21–8.

Connotative terms, such as may be attributes in demonstrative syllogisms, are described by Aristotle as "things which have a cause distinct from themselves," or which have a "middle." All such terms have, in Ockham's terminology, nominal definitions; besides this, some of them have, in a sense, real definitions. The first distinction between connotative terms is between those of which "being" is predicable in the mode of possibility, the term being taken as having personal supposition, and those of which being cannot possibly be verified. This latter type includes such words as "goat-stag," "vacuum," "infinite body," and in general, words whose nominal definitions include a contradiction or an absolute negation. Such terms have nominal definitions predicable of them only if they are taken non-significatively; e.g., the word "vacuum" is defined properly as "a word equivalent to the expression *absence of body*."[1]

Other connotative terms are such that they, and their nominal definitions, can stand significatively for individual existing things. Such terms may be said to have two sorts of definition—(*a*) merely nominal (*quid nominis tantum*), as when we define "white" as "that in which whiteness is present"; and (*b*) what is called a "material definition," as when we define "calefactive" as "a *body* receptive of heat," placing its first subject in the definition as material part. It is a definition of this kind which is, in certain cases, demonstrable *a priori*—namely, in those cases where the attribute defined is demonstrable *a priori* of its first subject. The reason is that these *determinate* nominal definitions, which include the first subject as material part, differ only in form from propositions *per se secundo modo*, and hence if the corresponding proposition is immediate and indemonstrable, so is the material definition of the attribute.[2]

[1] S. tot. log., III, II, 33, 71v: "Non solum autem diffinita absoluta diffiniuntur, sed etiam diffinita connotativa, et illa sunt in duplici differentia. Quaedam enim sunt talia de quibus significative sumptis impossibiliter predicatur 'esse,' cuiusmodi sunt: 'chymaera, hircocervus, vacuum, corpus infinitum,' et huiusmodi. Alia sunt de quibus non impossibiliter predicatur 'esse,' sicut 'album, nigrum, risibile, calefactivum, creativum,' et huiusmodi. Prima habet praecise diffinitiones exprimentes quid nominis, sicut 'chymaera' habet diffinitionem exprimentem quid hoc nomen 'chymaera' significat, sed non habet diffinitionem experimentem quid est illa res quam 'chymaera' significat, quia nulla talis res est, nec esse potest."

[2] S. tot. log., III, II, 33, 71v–72r: "Alia autem connotativa, hoc est illa quae

The distinction was generally made by Ockham's contemporaries between the "formal definition" of a connotative term, and its "material definition." The former is one which stands for the things signified by its definendum through indicating a qualitative form, or a final cause, extrinsic to the essential nature of the things for which it stands. Such would be the definition of "calefactive" as "something receptive of heat," in which the essential nature of that which *is* receptive of heat is not determinately indicated. Similarly, an extrinsic final cause may be indicated, as when we define a "saw" as "that by which we can cut wood," it being immaterial to the meaning of the word, whether the saw is made of metal or of anything else, so long as it fulfills its purpose. But in some cases we can prove that some determinate kind of material is a *sine qua non*, or material cause, of the existence of that which is formally indicated in the nominal definition. If, for instance, nothing that was not metallic could cut wood, we could prove from the formal definition of a saw that every saw is a metallic substance; and thus we would have a *quasi*-demonstration of a material definition of "saw." The syllogism would be as follows: "Everything by which wood can be cut is metallic, sharp, and of such or such shape, etc.; every saw is something by which wood can be cut; therefore every saw is metallic, sharp, and

significant diversa vel idem diversimode, hoc est affirmative vel negative, in recto vel in obliquo, vel aliquibus talibus diversis modis, possunt habere duplicem diffinitionem; unam quae exprimit quid nominis tantum, et aliam diffinitionem quae exprimit quid rei. Illa autem quae exprimit quid nominis tantum est propriissima diffinitio talis diffiniti, propter quod vocatur a non nullis diffinitio formalis et diffinitio secundum speciem. Alia exprimens quid rei, quae non est propriissima diffinitio talis diffiniti; propter quod frequenter dixi quod tale connotativum non habet diffinitionem nisi exprimentem quid nominis tantum et non diffinitionem exprimentem quid rei, quia talis oratio non est propriissima diffinitio talis diffiniti, imo forte non est diffinitio sua; et propter hoc talis diffinitio vocatur diffinitio materialis ab aliquibus. Verbi gratia, hoc nomen 'ferra' potest dupliciter diffiniri; uno modo sic, 'ferra est aliquid quo possumus dividere lignum,' ita quod haec sit sua diffinitio quid nominis exprimens quid debemus intelligere per hoc nomen 'ferra'; ita quod si sit aliquid cui non convenit haec oratio, eo ipso non significatur per hoc nomen, saltem in recto. . . ." The other definition would be "Ferra est aliquid ferrea et acuta, quo possumus dividere lignum"; but this would not be the proximate definition, because it is immaterial to the meaning of "ferra" whether it be made of iron or of something else— e.g., ice.

of such or such shape, etc." The conclusion of this syllogism
yields one definition of "saw," and the syllogism as a whole is
equivalent to a complete definition expressing both material
and final causes, differing from the demonstration only in
form—*scil.*, a saw is "a sharp metallic substance, of such or
such shape, etc., by which wood can be cut." Such *quasi*-
demonstrations of definable form are confined to connotative
terms whose formal definitions can be understood without the
material part being apprehended, as is the case with all names
of artificial things. But the definitions of absolute terms, or
of the concepts corresponding to them, are indemonstrable
statements of essential nature, and cannot be demonstrated
but come to be grasped only through the intuitive apprehension of individual (i.e., undivided) nature actually existent.[1]

The balance of Ockham's treatise consists in a brief indication of the ways in which the questions *quia est* and *propter*

[1] S. tot. log., III, II, 34, 72r: "videndum est quomodo istae diffinitiones possunt
cognosci de diffinitis, et est sciendum quod generaliter diffinitio exprimens quid
nominis non potest demonstrari de diffinito, sed illa praesupponitur omni demon-
strationi vel omni sillogismo. Si talis diffinitio sit vocalis vel signum ad placitum
institutum tantum scitur per doctrinam in addiscendo ab aliis loquentibus
significata vocabulorum vel instituentibus talia signa ad significandum; et ideo
de tali diffinitione non est magna difficultas, quamvis propter ignorantiam talium
diffinitionum multae difficultates et infinitae opiniones et multae opinionum
varietates tam in philosophia quam in theologia consurgant; sed de alia diffinitione est major difficultas.

"Et est sciendum quod tales diffinitiones possunt esse diversae; quandoque
enim praeter diffinitionem exprimentem quid nominis potest a qualibet causa
sumi diffinitio; si ibi sint quatuor causae et si ibi tantum sit causa finalis et
efficiens, potest ab utraque illarum sumi diffinitio; et illae diffinitiones quae
sumuntur a causa formali et finali vocantur diffinitiones formales; illae autem
quae sumuntur a causa materiali et efficiente vocantur diffinitiones materiales.
Et illae diffinitiones sic se habent quod diffinitio materialis potest demonstrari
per diffinitionem formalem; v.g., supposito significato vocabuli huius termini
'domus,' et praesupponatur diffinitio exprimens quid nominis, qua nota, acquiritur
sine demonstratione diffinitio sumpta a causa finali 'domus,' ut sciatur quod
demus est cooperimentum prohibens nos a frigore, ventis, et pluvia et caumatibus
et huiusmodi; quo facto potest demonstrari quod domus componitur ex lignis,
lapidibus, et sic de aliis huiusmodi, per tale argumentum: 'omne prohibens nos
a frigore, pluvia, etc., componitur ex lignis, lapidibus, etc. (ex quo scitur quod
talia possunt resistere frigori et pluviae etc.); sed domus est cooperimentum
prohibens nos a frigore, etc.; ergo domus componitur ex talibus.' . . . Ista ergo
conclusio ignota fit nota non per experientiam sed per propositiones notas dis-
positas in modo et figura, et ita una diffinitio demonstratur per aliam de diffinito;
sed hoc nunquam verum est nisi quando diffinitum est connotativum, sicut sunt
omnia nomina artificialia." Cf. Arist., An. Post., II, 10, 93b 28–94a 13. Cf.
also Aquinas, In Post. An., I, Lect. XVI, and II, Lect. VIII.

quid est are answered—i.e., of the types of *a priori* demonstration of the reasoned fact, according to the different ways in which definable form is revealed in the premises. Not only can we demonstrate conclusions through syllogisms whose middle terms are absolute, but the middle may indicate an extrinsic cause or condition, the premises being grasped as necessary and *per se* through definitions indicating efficient or final causes. Such types of demonstration are discussed by Aristotle in the eleventh and twelfth chapters of Book II of the *Posterior Analytics*. After enumerating these types of demonstrative "middles," Ockham again indicates the contrast between physical and mathematical demonstrations, pointing out that the latter involve attributes of which *si est* need not be known, since proof is through nominal definitions regulated only by the common axioms and consisting of syntheses of common defining elements, such as "unit," "magnitude," "part," and "whole." While the answer to the question *quia est*, asked of a proposition whose terms are not immediately connected, may be had by demonstration, Ockham indicates the equivalence of the question *propter quid est* to the question *quid est* in the following respect: its answer can never be had by *a priori* demonstration, but only through experience, intuition, and by *a posteriori* demonstration in those cases where the convertibility of middle and major has been established from other principles than the one which appears in the conclusion of the *a posteriori* argument. Thus all demonstrative knowledge reduces to indemonstrable principles and definitions grasped intuitively through experience of the actual; and infinite regress in *a priori* demonstration, as well as circularity in arguments through reciprocally related premises and conclusions, are excluded.[1]

[1] S. tot. log., III, II, 35-41, 72v-74r. On the difference between physical and mathematical demonstrations and attributes, cf. *ante* p. 223, Note 1; pp. 246-8; pp. 255-6 (on physics as subalternate to mathematics). S. tot. log., III, II, 41, 74r: "Quaedam enim principia nec a priori nec a posteriori demonstrari possunt . . . et quaedam sunt alia principia prima quae non nisi per experientiam et nullo modo per effectus evidenter sciri possunt. Quaedam autem principia, licet a posteriori possunt demonstrari, tamen talis demonstrans per illud principium nisi aliunde acquirat notitiam eiusdem non demonstrabit conclusionem . . . et ista de demonstratione sufficiant."

The foregoing discussion of the questions *si est* and *quid est* indicates the manner in which definable nature is presupposed by all inquiry, and the sense in which it is the *means* or "middle" of all knowledge of the reasoned fact. We cannot question nature or existence, but our questions and our doubts are inevitably concerned with things of our own doing—with syntheses, or "fabrications" which, in the case of discursive thought and signification, are composed of terms or concepts. Existence is not a problem of human thought, but it can, and does, terminate problems and doubts which arise concerning our syntheses of signs; for no argument is as convincing as the actuality of the thing.

The things which we can be said to know, in the strict sense of this word, are the things which can be questioned; and since the being and nature of an existing thing needs no witness of itself to make it what it actually is, our uncertainties, and consequently our proofs, are concerned not with the things that exist by nature, but with our ways of signifying them. In short, knowledge is of the true—of propositions—and it is distinct, as regards its object, from that act of *recognition of being*, which is *intelligentia* (νοῦς) or intuitive apprehension, by which we grasp the object of definition.

Ockham's analysis of terms, propositions, and arguments, like that of Aristotle, exhibits science as a human activity which, though requiring motion and material change as antecedent condition, is constituted as *knowledge*, by the act of intelligence or of recognition of that which is intelligible and actual. It is because the actual is only recognized and, as it were, received or comprehended by us, to the extent that we seek to signify it and communicate it, that speculative science must involve the "fabrication" of propositions and syllogisms. We must prepare the cradle for the baby to be born. But we are not certain about the cradle's adequacy until the baby is in it. It is much the same with knowledge of the fact alone, and knowledge of the reasoned fact—the former expects, or presupposes, what the latter reveals.

CHAPTER SEVEN

THE *CONSEQUENTIAE*—CONCLUSION

I

THE demonstrative syllogism, considered not as an inferential process but as the act of knowing a necessary truth through recognition of the individual nature of the things for which its terms stand, is the form and expression of scientific knowledge. In such a syllogism, a truth concerning individual existents that are principles of change, is known in such manner that no contingent circumstance or extrinsic time reference, and no factor attributable to the personal history of the man who knows the truth, is involved as a part of what is known. Such contingent conditions are of course presupposed by the contingent fact that this particular man did acquire this knowledge; but his way of coming to know a truth, and his act of judgment by which the proposition is formed in his mind, are not the things that he knows in knowing such a proposition to be true.

Science, for Ockham, is neither a history of events nor a biography of the soul, but rather it is the grasp of a synthesis of significant terms as an adequate sign of individual things *qua* principles of change or of their own becoming. It is knowledge of the reasoned fact, of the truth of a proposition by the nature of the things of which it is true; for according to Aristotle, the reason of the fact is identical with the nature of the thing. This conviction of Ockham's, that the reason of fact is individual nature, and that knowledge of truth is the recognition of a complex of terms as an adequate sign of what is individual in nature, is fundamental to his entire exposition of the logic of terms. It underlies his treatment of the problem of universals, of the *Categories*, of the necessary proposition, and of demonstrative principles.

Perceptual judgments yield evident knowledge of contingent fact, the cause of assent being the intuitive apprehension of distinct things existing together. In evident knowledge of truths which are necessary, on the other hand, the cause of our assent is not things of distinct nature apprehended together, but individual things grasped by their own nature in abstraction from particular environment or conjunction with other things. When we have evident knowledge of a necessary truth, it is the truth of a proposition that is known, and not the individual things *of* which the proposition is true; what we judge to be true is not the existence by which our judgment is true, but a proposition formed in our mind as a sign of that existence. The object of *knowledge* is always a proposition, but though our assent is to the proposition, the reason of our assent, and of the truth of the proposition, is not the synthesis of terms that is the object of knowledge, but the being of the things signified by the terms so compounded.

The difference between knowledge and opinion is not a function of different kinds of propositions, but of different causes of assent. In knowledge, our conviction that a proposition is true, rests on nothing other than our recognition of the being of what its terms stand for, without implication of anything other than the essential nature of just such things. But when we do not have knowledge, but only opinion, our conviction rests not on an intuitive recognition of *what it is to be* an individual such as is signified by the subject term, but on our belief that other true propositions imply the truth of this one.[1]

It is possible, therefore, for a man to apprehend a demonstrative syllogism, with proper concepts corresponding to its

[1] Arist., An. Post. I, 33, 88b 30–89b 9. Aristotle classes as objects of opinion those propositions assented to as true, but not as incapable of being other than they are. Evident contingent knowledge would, by this criterion, be knowledge rather than opinion, insofar as the connection was recognized as true only for the immediate present time. But for scientific purposes, such immediate contingent judgments are pre-logical, the real difference being between evident knowledge of universal propositions, and opinion concerning propositions of the same form.

terms, without thereby having demonstrative knowledge of the conclusion. For he may assent to the conclusion in the manner in which we assent to propositions through opinion or belief, by referring the truth of the conclusion to the truth of the premises, by way of the implicative relation expressed in the rule of syllogistic construction. In such a case the conclusion is not known to be true *per se* by the being of the individual things for which its terms stand, but assent is given to it by reason of a consequential relation of logical character of which this particular arrangement of terms and propositions is an instance. A consequential relation between propositions or terms, however, is not attributable to things *in re*, but only to human ways of synthesizing or "fabricating" complex signs from incomplex signs. Hence, if real science is distinct from logic, and a true proposition something more than an instance of human synthetic activity exemplifying a rule of discursive construction, it is evident that a syllogism taken merely as an inference is not a demonstration, and is not productive of knowledge but only of opinion.[1]

Ockham's treatise on the conditional proposition (the *Consequentiae*) is concerned with precisely this way of assenting to propositions, involving reference to other propositions and to an implicative connection attributed to them because of the logical properties of the terms or of the form of statement. The conditional proposition is, in Ockham's view, the appropriate form of non-demonstrative argument, because the "middle," which is the reason of assent to the connection

---

[1] Arist., An. Post. I, 33, 89a 16–24: "The truth perhaps is that if a man grasp truths that cannot be other than they are, in the way in which he grasps the definitions through which demonstrations take place, he will have not opinion but knowledge; if on the other hand he apprehends these attributes as inhering in their subjects, but not in virtue of the subjects' substance and essential nature, he possesses opinion and not genuine knowledge; and his opinion, if obtained through immediate premises, will be both of the fact and of the reasoned fact; if not so obtained, of the fact alone. The object of opinion and knowledge is not quite identical; it is only in a sense identical, just as the object of true and false opinion is in a sense identical." Ibid., 89a 35: "the apprehension that animal is an element in the essential nature of man is knowledge; the apprehension of animal as predicable of man but not as an element in man's essential nature is opinion: man is the subject in both judgments, but the mode of inherence differs."

asserted, is not a term of first intention taken significatively, but a term or proposition taken non-significatively as an exemplification of some kind of logical form. If, for example, a demonstrative syllogism is taken merely as an inference, and not as a significative unity, it is properly speaking a conditional proposition, the two premises forming a conjunctive antecedent, the conclusion a consequent, and the "middle" which is the reason of assent to the conclusion, being the *dictum de omni* or rule of syllogistic form.[1]

Ockham makes an exhaustive classification of the kinds of consequential relations that can be generalized from the examination of the logical properties of the terms and propositions used in the demonstrative sciences. His treatise is almost entirely concerned with formal implication—that is, rules developed on the basis of the previous analysis of the logical characteristics of statements of demonstrative principles and conclusions; and hence it may be said that Ockham's treatment of implication and inference presupposes throughout, as the foundation for its rules, the logic of terms and of the analysis of meaning, exhibited in Aristotle's *Posterior Analytics* and in the preceding books of the *Organon*. While Ockham seems to be aware of the possibilities of constructing a logic of material implication, such as is found nowadays in the symbolic systems, such a logic does not appear to interest him very much, since it is of little or no practical use as an instrument of scientific investigation or of *significant* argument and discussion.

The most important of the many distinctions among consequential relations enumerated by Ockham at the beginning

---

[1] Ockham, S. tot. log., III, III, 1, 74r: "Habito de sillogismo in communi et de sillogismo demonstrativo agendum est nunc de argumentis et consequentiis quae non habent formam sillogisticam, cuiusmodi sunt Enthimemata. Et primo praemittendae sunt quaedam distinctiones de consequentiis ex quibus omnibus faciliter patere poterit studioso quid de omnibus sillogismis non demonstrativis est intelligendum." Cf. ibid., 37, 92r: "Sciendum est quod totum quod praecedit consequens vel conclusionem dicitur antecedens. Et ideo antecedens aliquando est una propositio cathegorica et aliquando continet plures, ut patet in sillogismo; et tunc quamvis una illarum propositionum sit vera conclusio poterit esse falsa, sed si quaelibet illarum sit vera, conclusio non poterit esse falsa si sequatur ex eis."

of his treatise, are the following: (1) Some consequences
hold only *ut nunc*, or for a particular time, while others are
simplex, such that the antecedent could at no time be true
and the consequent false; (2) Some hold by an intrinsic middle,
and others by an extrinsic middle; (3) Some consequences
are formal, and others material; (4) Some consequences
are composed of terms having simple or material supposition,
and others of terms having personal supposition. The distinction between intrinsic and extrinsic middles, by which
antecedent and consequent are connected, is given by Ockham
in the following words:

That consequence holds by an intrinsic middle when it holds
because of some proposition formed from the same terms, such as
this consequence, "Socrates is not running, therefore a man is not
running," which holds by reason of this middle, namely "Socrates
is a man." . . . But a consequence holds by an extrinsic middle
when it holds through some general rule which does not refer to
these terms rather than others, such as this consequence, "Only
a man is an ass, therefore every ass is a man," which holds through
the general rule "an exclusive affirmative and a universal affirmative, with terms transposed, are convertible" . . . and through
such an extrinsic middle every syllogism holds. And if it is said
against this distinction that this consequence "Socrates is not
running, therefore a man is not running," holds through the
extrinsic middle "from singular to indefinite and from inferior to
superior, a negative being placed after the copula, is a valid
consequence," and that therefore it does not hold by an intrinsic
middle, it is to be said that it holds through the extrinsic middle
mediately and as if remotely or insufficiently; because by that
general rule something additional is required, namely that Socrates
is a man, and hence it holds more immediately and sufficiently
through the middle," Socrates is a man," which is an intrinsic
middle.[1]

---

[1] S. tot. log., III, III, 1, 74r: "Prima distinctio est ista quod consequentiarum
quaedam est ut nunc, et quaedam est simplex; consequentia ut nunc est quando
antecedens pro aliquo tempore potest esse verum sine consequente, sed non pro
isto tempore; sicut ista consequentia est bona ut nunc, 'omne animal currit ergo
Sortes currit,' quia pro illo tempore pro quo Sortes est animal non potest antecedens esse verum sine consequente et tamen pro aliquo tempore potest antecedens
esse verum sine consequente. Consequentia simplex est quando pro nullo tempore
poterit antecedens esse verum sine consequente sicut ista consequentia est simplex:
'nullum animal currit ergo nullus homo currit,' quia nunquam poterit antecedens

Formal consequences are those which hold by an intrinsic middle immediately and an extrinsic middle mediately, or which hold by an extrinsic middle only. Material consequences are those which do not hold in either of these ways, but merely because of what the terms stand for. Material implication is illustrated by the consequence, "A man runs, therefore God is," the principle being the following: a necessary proposition is implied by any proposition, since in such a consequence the consequent cannot be false (being necessary) when the antecedent is true.

Ockham first states a number of rules for consequences which hold by an intrinsic middle exemplifying a predicative relation between the terms that appear in antecedent and consequent. Thus, from the truth of a proposition with subject distributed, we can infer the truth of a proposition whose subject is inferior to the other by predication, and also distributed; e.g., "Every animal is mortal" implies "Every

---

esse verum sine consequente . . . alia distinctio consequentiae est talis quia aliquando consequentia tenet per medium intrinsecum, aliquando per medium extrinsecum. Illa consequentia tenet per medium intrinsecum quando tenet virtute alicuius propositionis formatae ex eisdem terminis sicut ista consequentia: 'Sortes non currit, ergo homo non currit,' tenet virtute istius medii, *scil.* 'Sortes est homo.' . . . Sed tunc consequentia tenet per medium extrinsecum quando tenet per aliquam regulam generalem quae non plus respicit illos terminos quam alias, sicut ista consequentia: 'Tantum homo est asinus ergo omnis asinus est homo,' tenet per illam regulam generalem 'exclusiva affirmativa et universalis affirmativa de terminis transpositis convertuntur.' . . . et per talia media extrinseca tenent omnes sillogismi; et si dicatur contra istam distinctionem quod ista consequentia 'Sortes non currit ergo homo non currit,' tenet per illud medium extrinsecum 'a singulari ad indiffinitam et ab inferiori ad superius posposita negatione est bona consequentia,' et per consequens non per medium intrinsecum —dicendum quod tenet per illud medium extrinsecum mediate et quasi remote et insufficienter, quia per illam regulam generalem requiritur plus, *scil.* quod Sortes sit homo et ideo magis immediate et sufficiens tenet per illud medium 'Sortes est homo' quod est medium intrinsecum." A *consequentia materialis* is "quando tenet praecise ratione terminorum et non ratione alicuius medii extrinseci respicientis praecise generales conditiones propositionum"—e.g., "homo currit ergo deus est. . . ." A *consequentia formalis* is (a) when it holds solely by an extrinsic logical rule, and (b) when it holds "per medium intrinsecum immediate et mediate per medium extrinsecum"; e.g., "Sortes non currit, ergo homo non currit."

On material consequences, cf. ibid., 37, 92r: "necessarium sequitur ad quodlibet, et ideo sequitur 'tu es asinus ergo tu es deus,' et sequitur 'tu es asinus ergo deus est trinus et unus,' sed tales consequentiae non sunt formales, ideo illae regulae non sunt multum usitatae."

man is mortal," the intrinsic middle being the proposition "Every man is an animal." Such a consequence is an enthymematic equivalent of a syllogism. Other rules of the same sort indicate that definitions, descriptions, and synonyms can be substituted for the equivalent terms defined, described, or related as synonyms, without altering the truth value of the proposition. Similarly, if one term is predicable convertibly of another, as property or differentia, we may infer the proposition whose subject is thus convertible with the subject of the other.[1]

Similar rules, equally obvious for the most part, are stated for other affirmative consequences, and for negative ones. Some of the illustrations given for these consequences are of interest. For example, in illustrating the rule that the consequence from inferior to superior, without distribution and in affirmative propositions, is valid, Ockham points out that the application of this rule shows many generally accepted propositions to be false, since they imply false consequents. Thus the statement, "A white man is an accidental aggregation," is false since it implies the obviously false proposition. that

[1] S. tot. log., III, III, 2, 74v–75r: "a superiori distributo ad inferius distributum est bona consequentia . . . quando enim predicatio superioris de inferiori est necessaria, tunc est consequentia simplex." Since every consequence *ut nunc* holds only by reason of a present occasion of synthetic judgment, Ockham states that of consequences *ut nunc* one does not differ formally from another, though one may be equivalent to more true singular propositions than another. This is precisely the situation in contemporary systems of material implication— Ockham's discussion of *consequentiae* exhibits a perfectly conscious grasp of the possibilities of developing a system of material implication, but since he is primarily interested in logic as an instrument of science and for the determination of truth and falsity, the possibilities of divorcing it from this use and of developing a self-sufficient mathematical calculus of equivalences, without reference to determinate signification, did not appeal to him.

The numerous rules regulating various kinds of *consequentiae*, being for the most part of technical interest only, will not be cited in these notes, since a sufficient sampling of them, in condensed form, has been offered by Prantl, pp. 411–9, Anm. 1016–42. A detailed study of Ockham's *Consequentiae*, concerned with its character as a well-integrated dialectical system exhibiting the application of generalizations regarding forms of synthesis of terms, to problems involving the recognition of differences in forms of signification as well as in forms of attribution or synthesis, should be both interesting and profitable to those who conceive logic as a calculus. Such an investigation is, however, beyond the scope of the present study; hence it seems hardly worth while to do again what Prantl has already done—i.e., give a bare, and condensed, citation of the rules of consequentiae without discussion of their import as parts of the system.

"A man is an accidental aggregation"; or the statement that "Prime matter is without form," is false since it implies the obviously false proposition, "Matter is without form."[1]

Another rule of similar character states that from a proposition whose subject is modified by an adverb or by a word preceded by a preposition, we may infer a proposition without this modification of the subject. Though this rule is qualified in its application, it exhibits the falsity of a number of propositions upheld by the *moderni*, and especially by the scotists. Thus it was often said that "Every created thing is *of itself* nothing," which, by Ockham's rule, implies the following manifestly false proposition, "Every created thing is nothing." Similarly, "All matter *of itself* is without form" cannot be true if the following proposition, implied by it, is false: "All matter is without form." This rule has special application to propositions with reduplicative subjects, such propositions always implying similar ones without the reduplicative expression. If it were true, as some *moderni* of scotist and neo-thomist tendencies maintained, that "Socrates *qua* man is not distinct from Plato," it would follow that "Socrates is not distinct from Plato." Or if the scotists—who held that the specific nature is not really distinct from the individual nature but distinct *in* the thing by a "formal distinction"—state that "The specific nature is *really* the individual differentia," they must concede the consequent that "The specific nature *is* the individual differentia."[2]

Consequences holding by extrinsic middles, are regulated by what may be called "analogies of proportion." Thus where

[1] S. tot. log., III, III, 3–6, 75r–75v. The examples referred to are from cap. 6 (75v): "ab inferiori ad superius est bona consequentia sine distributione et affirmativa, et talis est simplex. . . . Ex isto patet quod omnes tales sunt falsae, 'homo albus est aggregatum per accidens,' 'asinus intellectus est ens diminutum,' 'materia prima caret forma,' 'homo albus differt ab homine' . . . quia illae inferunt istas propositiones falsas: 'homo est aggregatum per accidens,' 'asinus est ens diminutum,' 'materia caret forma,' 'homo differt ab homine,' . . . per istam regulam quae nunquam deficit: ab inferiori ad superius sine distributione est bona consequentia si termini supponant personaliter et significative."

[2] S. tot. log., III, III, 6, 76r: "a prepositione sumpta cum suo casuali vel a terminatione equivalenti adverbio vel prepositioni et suo casuali, ad illam sine tali addito, est bona consequentia; sicut sequitur, 'homo necessario est animal, ergo homo est animal,' 'homo dat denarium cum tristitia, ergo homo dat

two abstract terms bear the same logical relation to their concrete counterparts, then if one of the abstract terms is predicable of the other, its concrete counterpart will be predicable of the concrete form of the other. For example, "If justice is a virtue, then the just are virtuous." Another rule is equivalent to the mathematical principle that if equals are added to equals the results are equal; e.g., if it is valid to infer "A man runs, therefore an animal runs," then it is valid to infer "A white man runs, therefore a white animal runs." This rule is applicable only when the added term is fully categorematic, either adjectival or substantival, and not equivalent to a syncategorematic term or expression.[1]

Other consequences that hold by extrinsic middles, are those based on relations of opposition between terms or between propositions. Thus the negation of one predicate may be inferred from the affirmation of its contrary with respect to the same subject. Or from the affirmation of a positive follows the negation of the privative, and vice versa. As an illustration of this rule Ockham uses one of his favourite examples: "Matter is not deprived (*privata*), therefore matter is informed by a form."[2]

---

denarium.' . . . Ex isto patet quod omnes tales propositiones de virtute sermonis sunt falsae: 'quaelibet creatura de se est non ens,' 'quaelibet materia de se caret forma,' 'idem sub una ratione est prius et sub alia ratione est posterius,' etc."— for all these imply propositions of the same terms without the adverbial modification, such as are manifestly false and impossible. Ibid.: "Quicquid etiam predicatur de aliquo cum dictione reduplicativa absolute sine tali dictione vel aliquo equivalenti predicatur de eodem. Ex quo patet quod omnes tales consequentiae sunt bonae: 'natura specifica est realiter differentia individualis, ergo natura specifica est differentia individualis' . . . et sic de multis aliis quae tamen consequentiae negantur a modernis."

[1] S. tot. log., III, III, 7, 77r: "dicendum est nunc de regulis inferentibus affirmativam ex affirmativa per medium extrinsecum . . . si principale de principali, et coniugatum de coniugato, et casus de casu, et econverso; et vocatur coniugatum concretum et principale abstractum, et casus adverbium sequens; unde sequitur, 'iustitia est virtus, ergo iustus est virtuosus,' et 'qui iuste aliquid facit, aliquid virtuose facit.' . . . si aliqua consequentia sit bona eodem addito utrobique, adhuc erit consequentia bona; sicut si ista est consequentia bona, 'homo currit ergo animal currit,' ista consequentia est bona, 'homo albus currit ergo animal album currit'." *A fortiori* arguments rest on the same rule; but Ockham brings in many qualifications, since in such arguments there is always danger of the fallacy of figure of speech.

[2] S. tot. log., III, III, 9, 78v: "ex affirmatione contrarii sequitur negatio alterius contrarii, sicut sequitur 'Sortes est albus, ergo Sortes non est niger.'

From the relations of opposition between propositions rules are formulated for other consequences, the discussion of equipollences, repugnances, and impertinences being enriched, in Ockham's customary fashion, with the distinctions between the two senses (*divisus* and *compositus*) in which modals may be taken. Most of this material is derived from Aristotle's treatment of the same subject in the *De interpretatione*, Ockham's restatement being more detailed, systematic, and academic.[1]

The major portion of the *Consequentiae* is devoted to an exhaustive statement of the four modes of predication which, according to the *Topics* of Aristotle, are exhibited in every problem or proposition that is a subject of argument. Recognition of these modes of predication is presupposed in the application of the rules for all those consequences that hold by intrinsic middles—for in such cases the intrinsic middle indicates that one term is either inferior, superior, or convertible, by universal predication, to another term. In establishing such a relation between terms, we are not talking about things signified by terms of first intention, but about such terms themselves, as elements of propositions believed or conceded to be true. Hence the rules governing the identification of genus, differentia, property, and accident, indicate consequences whose terms have simple or material supposition; for the consequential relations are between terms, and not between things that exist by nature apart from human discursive operations.

The section of Ockham's treatise which deals with the predicables is extremely detailed. The treatment is positive in character, and not merely concerned, as in Ockham's exposition of Porphyry, to remove the metaphysical implications of the porphyrian introduction to the *Categories*.

. . . Et ex isto patet quod in motu idem subiectum primum non est simul sub contrariis. . . . A negatione contrarii ad positionem alterius est bona consequentia"—this rule is qualified as holding only when there is no intermediate, and it is also stated that such consequences are *ut nunc* only, unless "being" is predicable necessarily of the subject. Ibid.: "A positione habitus sequitur negatio privationis et econverso . . ."; e.g., "'Sortes est videns ergo Sortes non est caecus,' 'materia non est privata ergo materia est informata forma'."

[1] S. tot. log., III, III, 10–6, 79v–82r.

Following the *Topics* with a microscopic eye, and with in-exhaustible patience, Ockham states sixty-nine rules for identifying a term as a genus with respect to a subject. He then differentiates between the broad and strict usages of the term "property," and gives many rules for identifying this mode of predication. The whole problem of definition is again discussed, this time from the dialectical point of view; i.e., in order to indicate how, from the way in which a term is predicated of different subjects in propositions whose truth is conceded, it may be shown to be, or not to be, part of the essential definition of some subject term. The predicable "accident" receives very cursory treatment, indicating that Ockham, like Aristotle, conceived the subjects of dialectical or topical inquiry to be universal propositions and not contingent truths.[1]

On the question of the different senses of "same" and "diverse," Ockham notes Aristotle's distinction between numerical, specific, and generic identity, but takes exception to the scotist notion that things numerically diverse are specifically identical except through signification. For if we say that Socrates and Plato are identical in species, we mean that a numerically identical specific term or concept is predicable of the numerically diverse proper names "Socrates" and "Plato," taken significatively. Or if we say that in the contingent proposition "The white thing is heavy," the terms are numerically identical, all we mean is that they stand for a numerically identical thing, though they, and their definitions, are numerically diverse. Nothing, in short, is one without being numerically one; if we say that what is numerically diverse can be specifically one, we only mean that a single specific term signifies more than one single thing, and not that a single thing is itself not a single thing.[2]

The discussion of induction, or of inferences establishing a universal proposition by the truth of singular propositions, is

---

[1] S. tot. log., III, III, 17–28, 82r–87v.
[2] Cf. Arist., Topica I, 7–8, 103a 6–103b 19; and VII, 1–2, 151b 27–153a 5. Ockham, S. tot. log., III, III, 29, 87v–88r.

brief, and would scarcely be encouraging to those who hoped to find in Ockham an anticipation of Sir Francis Bacon or of J. S. Mill, with respect to inductive method. As was indicated in the examination of Ockham's theory of demonstration, and of the way in which indemonstrable universal truths come to be known by experience, the universal proposition is not derived by way of inference from a synthesis of singular propositions. Rather it is by conceiving the constituents of a contingent *fact* in abstraction from each other, that we grasp the individual nature of a *thing* through a universal concept. Universal propositions are functions of univocal terms or concepts, and not of a process of adding singular contingent propositions together by a synthetic operation assumed to be prolonged indefinitely.[1] The only form of inductive consequence from singular affirmatives to a universal affirmative, is that of "perfect induction" in those cases where the universal subject is restricted to a limited number of things signified. If, for example, we wished to establish by argument from singular propositions, the universal proposition "Every person in this room is wearing glasses," it could be done in this way. But such a method is of small use for establishing scientific truths, and most of Ockham's discussion is concerned with the ways in which universal statements can be overthrown by singular propositions which contradict them.[2]

---

[1] Cf. *ante*, ch. vi, pp. 242–4; also ch. v, pp. 189–92.

[2] S. tot. log., III, III, 31–5, 89r–91r. For assertoric propositions of present or past time, the following rule is given: "Quaelibet universalis affirmativa vera de praesenti non equivalens propositioni de futuro, et de inesse, habet aliquam singularem veram; si autem sit falsa non oportet quod habeat aliquam singularem falsam sed sufficit quod nulla singularem habeat . . . si omnes singulares alicuius propositionis sint verae, universalis est vera . . . si universalis affirmativa sit falsa oportet quod aliqua singularis sit falsa . . . ad hoc quod aliqua singularis sit alicuius universalis requiritur quod subiectum universalis predicatur de subiecto singularis." On propositions of future time Ockham notes that according to Aristotle no future contingents or singulars can be determinately foreknown, and hence there can be no induction of future universals from future singulars. The induction of modal universals from modal singulars is regulated by rules similar to those for assertoric propositions, except for the distinctions founded on the *sensus divisus* and *sensus compositus*. Modal universals of possibility are not capable of being inferred from singular propositions of possibility, even if taken in any finite number of instances; the reason is that not everything

After giving a number of rules, drawn from the *Topics*, by which equivocation can be detected, Ockham concludes his discussion of implication with the statement of the most general rules for consequences. These are the rules which abstract from all formal conditions applicable to terms, and consider nothing beyond the "truth-value" relations between any two propositions. The rules are as follows: (*a*) a true proposition never implies a false one; (*b*) a false proposition may imply a true one; (*c*) if one proposition implies another, the contradictory of the consequent implies the contradictory of the antecedent; (*d*) whatever is implied by the consequent is implied by the antecedent; (*e*) whatever implies the antecedent implies the consequent; (*f*) a proposition in the mode of possibility does not imply a proposition in the mode of impossibility; (*g*) the impossible implies any proposition; and (*h*) the necessary is implied by any proposition. These generalizations have a familiar modern sound, as if from Cambridge; but after stating them Ockham says: "such consequences are not formal, hence these rules are not much used."[1]

---

that is possible when considered by itself, is compossible with other possibilities. Thus we can say "This future contingent is possible," successively with respect to all future contingents, and yet we cannot infer that "All future contingents are possible," because taken together they are not a single possibility, but some may render the others impossible. In the same way, singular contingents do not imply a universal contingent proposition *in sensu composito*, nor vice versa.

The significant and quite aristotelian point of Ockham's discussion of induction is that it can take place only insofar as the subject of the universal is known to be a univocal sign of the things for which the subjects of the singular propositions stand. Hence, if the universal proposition is of scientific character (*de omni, per se,* and necessary) its subject will be an absolute term, and the identification of singular subjects as signs of the things for which the universal term can stand, will presuppose recognition of the universal term as a more immediate subject of the attribute than the singular. Thus definition and abstract signification is presupposed by induction, and the collection of particular facts is an aid primarily to the act of abstraction or analysis by which the constituents of the particular fact are distinguished; we could not infer that all animals are mortal from the observation of the death of millions of dogs, horses, etc., unless in each instance we recognized the singular subject as something essentially signified by "animal" —but if we grasped this, we would already have recognized that the universal term "animal" was a more immediate subject of the attribute "mortal" than the term "dog" or than the term "this horse," etc. The grasp of the universal, through experience, is not a function of synthesis, except accidentally, but of analysis of the contingent fact by recognition of the essential character of its constituents, a recognition which is of itself the grasp of a universal reason.

[1] S. tot. log., III, III, 36–7, 91r–92r.

A short discussion of *obligationes* and *insolubilia*, in the accustomed manner of fourteenth century logicians, appears at the end of Ockham's treatise on *Consequentiae*. As Prantl points out, this has all the earmarks of an interpolation, appearing in the text rather abruptly as if added to the end of Ockham's treatise, and ending with an incomplete discussion of paralogisms and ways of dealing with them. The *obligationes* are forms of agreement concerning things to be assumed for purposes of argument, and the exposition indicates how to state such agreements without leaving loop-holes which would afford one's adversary the chance of gaining an advantage in the argument. This topic is not very relevant to logic, and since the treatment of it is probably not from Ockham's pen, it can conveniently be passed over.[1]

The *Sum of All Logic* ends with a fairly brief treatise on fallacies, which follows Aristotle's *De sophisticis elenchis* in the traditional order and manner. Ockham contests the statement made by some of his contemporaries, that fallacies *in dictione* are distinguished from fallacies *extra dictionem* by the fact that the former are fallacies of thought or speech, and the latter fallacies *a parte rei*. Rather the first kind are those which would not occur except for the fact that our thoughts are expressed by written or spoken signs, while the second kind of fallacy applies not only to our modes of synthesis of words, but of concepts as well.[2] It is worthy of note that the one form of fallacy to which Ockham devotes many pages of detailed discussion is that of "figure of speech." This is perhaps the most frequent source of error in philosophy, for it is involved in the attribution of characteristics and distinctions that belong to signs, to the things of which they are signs. This habit, which in the long run reduces to the equivocal use of

---

[1] S. tot. log., III, III, 38–43, 92r–93v. Cf. Prantl, p. 419.
[2] S. tot. log., III, IV, 1, 94r: "Et ideo falsum est quod dicunt aliqui quod fallaciae in dictione sunt a parte vocis, et fallaciae extra dictionem a parte rei, quia non plus sunt istae ex natura rei quam illae. Sed debet dici quod fallaciae in dictione sunt illae penes quas secundum omnes modos peccant sophistica argumenta composita ex signis voluntariae instituti. Fallaciae extra dictionem sunt illae penes quas peccant argumenta tam composita ex signis voluntarie institutis quam composita ex signis naturaliter significantibus."

terms with respect to their significative and non-significative forms of supposition, results in the confusion of logic, natural science, and metaphysics, and gives rise to what may be called indifferently a "logical realism" or a "metaphysical nominalism." Whatever name may be given to it, it is what Ockham opposes as the worst error in philosophy, destructive of all truth, reason, science, and of the whole philosophy of Aristotle.[1]

The foregoing sketch of Ockham's treatment of hypothetical inference will perhaps be sufficient to indicate his thoroughly non-metaphysical conception of dialectic and of the materials (relations between signs) with which it is concerned. The treatise on *Consequentiae* is a long one, and was perhaps influential, among Ockham's nominalistic followers of the fourteenth and fifteenth centuries, to a degree disproportionate to its importance in Ockham's logic as a whole. Nominalism, in the sense in which this term is generally used with reference to late mediæval philosophy, might in fact be described as the kind of philosophical attitude which results from too great an interest in the subject matter of Aristotle's *Topics*, combined with a tendency to forget that the *Topics* is preceded, in aristotelian logic, by an analytic treatment of incomplex forms of signification, and of the demonstrative syllogism.

Fundamentally Ockham's treatment of the dialectical method is that of Aristotle, for it presupposes, as the *raison d'être* of formal relations of implication between propositions, the demonstrative order and definable form. There would be little justification for the distinctions between genus,

---

[1] S. tot. log., III, IV, 10, 99v–103r, is devoted to the fallacy of figure of speech. Cf. Ockham's remarks concerning those who attribute the properties of terms, as predicables or as parts of propositions, to things signified by them, ch. ii, p. 47, Note 1.

The *Summa totius logicae* ends, in the 1508 edition (106v), with the following "explicit"— slightly laudatory by mediæval standards, though perhaps not by the standards of the 16th century:

Explicit magna constructio logicae fratris Guielmi Occham Anglici sacrarum litterarum Magistri ac omnium logicorum acutissimi, Inviolatae scholae invictissimorum nominalium inceptoris ex professione fratrum Minorum, in omnium disciplinarum genere doctoris plusquam subtilis, quam noviter correxit Marcus Beneventanus Monachus Celestinorum Beati Benedicti, Sacrarum litterarum professor, ac Rerum Mathematicarum Amator.

definition, property, and accident, if there were no such thing as a demonstrative syllogism, or if predicative relations between terms did not rest ultimately on the nature of things signified by them, rather than on the mere capacity of the human mind to combine them into propositions.

The rules of formal implication rest, for the most part, on the assumption that the things signified by a single subject term are signifiable in certain definite ways by other terms, analogous to the ways in which the terms involved in demonstrative syllogisms signify the things of which the demonstration is true. In demonstrative knowledge, our grasp of what the terms signify enables us to state necessary propositions composed of such terms, such propositions being either immediate and indemonstrable, as in the case of principles or premises, or else demonstrable through such immediate truths. Once in possession of such a nexus of necessary propositions concerned with a single subject of demonstration, we may reflect on the logical relations exhibited in the syllogism between its parts, and formulate rules by which such logical relations may be discerned in other statements which are believed to be necessarily true but which are not known demonstratively or through recognition of essential nature.

In this way Aristotle's division of propositions or problems into those which indicate a genus, definition, property, or accident, is exhibited by Ockham as dependent on his previous analysis of signification and demonstration. It provides a systematic method of inquiry and criticism through which, from knowledge of fact alone, we may come to grasp the principles by which those facts can be explained and known demonstratively. Dialectic is not, however, a method by which first principles can be demonstrated or constructed according to rules of definition; rather it is a method by which problems can be distinguished and stated unequivocally, relevant facts gathered and organized, and the requisite materials provided for an act of intuitive recognition of essential character and individual nature to take place—if we have "quick wit."

II

The character of a philosophy is not adequately revealed by a summary statement of its most general concepts, nor by indicating its resemblances and differences with respect to other philosophies, but rather by following it step by step in its detailed statement, measuring it by the adequacy of its own principles and methods to the analysis of each problem. The unity and force of Ockham's exposition of logic, and the philosophical implications of what is called his nominalism, become evident only in the detailed examination of his discussion of terms, signification, forms of statement, and demonstration. It is by such a method that we have sought to exhibit the philosophical character of Ockham's logical nominalism, and the realistic and non-discursive metaphysics underlying it. In summing up, we may draw a few conclusions, of general character, concerning the import of Ockham's philosophical discussions as they might be viewed historically, against the background of the mediæval tradition in which they arose.

For better or for worse, Ockham made a profound mark on the thought of the later middle ages, precipitating a conflict of philosophies which in the eyes of many historians was the death struggle of the scholastic tradition. That Ockham's teachings in logic and physics had considerable influence in encouraging scientific investigations along new lines, destined to lead to the interests and methods of inquiry that have predominated in the modern period, can scarcely be doubted. But to what degree Ockham's own conception of the principles and methods of natural philosophy, was perpetuated or developed by the later nominalists, and to what extent Ockham can be considered a "forerunner" of the modern scientific spirit, is a problem that cannot be settled even with a remote degree of historical accuracy, until the available but largely unexamined sources of the late period of scholasticism receive adequate and accurate study.

298 WILLIAM OF OCKHAM

To appreciate the powerful effect of Ockham's logical teaching on the fourteenth century, we must try to determine in what basic respects his conception of science and of scientific principles, differs from the point of view which predominated in practically the whole mediæval period. What single problem, we might ask, was omnipresent in the twelfth and thirteenth century scholastic discussions, and in the pagan and christian philosophers and commentators that inspired these discussions?

In St. Augustine one question is always present—that of the mode of dependence of the temporal on the eternal, of changeable things on the unchangeable, and of the soul on its creator.[1] While the influence of christian revelation on the speculations of the scholastics is not to be overlooked, these speculations were nevertheless philosophical constructions, paralleled outside of the christian realm, among arabs, jews, and greeks. Socrates' precept, *nosce te ipsum*, has been taken as a point of departure for speculative thinking in every age of philosophy; and the augustinian quest for the actuality and unity which can measure the potentially infinite range of human understanding and of human thirst for the good, gives rise in the christian tradition to epistemologies and cosmologies of a philosophical content and method, whose equivalents are found in classical, infidel, and modern secular philosophies as well.

That augustinism, from a philosophical point of view, was not alone in its interest in the soul's relation to God, or in its conviction that the exploration of this implicit relationship is the method of discovering the foundation of all scientific certitude, is not hard to show. Even before St. Augustine was born, the fifth chapter of the third book of Aristotle's *De anima* began to be expanded, by commentary or paraphrase and by new analogies and distinctions, into a metaphysical cosmology. It is in this chapter that Aristotle touches on the act of intelligence, or νοῦς; and in spite of the fact that it is

[1] Cf. Gilson, *Introduction à l'étude de S. Augustin* (Paris, 1931), ch. i and ii, for an excellent exposition of this central theme of St. Augustine's thought.

to this immediate or intuitive unity of the soul with the substance of things apprehended by sense, that all scientific knowledge is referred at the end of the *Posterior Analytics*, Aristotle can find scarcely anything to say about it. It would be naïve to consider this comparative silence an accident; and it would seem risky, from the viewpoint of accurate interpretation, to make Aristotle's cautious suggestion of a possibly analogy, with respect to the distinction of potentiality and act, between intellect and sense perception, the basis of a literal cosmological system. Yet this is what was done by the neo-platonists, by the whole line of arab and jewish philosophers, and by those of the scholastics who sought to accommodate an averroist or avicennist interpretation of Aristotle to the augustinian tradition.

Aristotle seems fully to have appreciated the futility of trying to go behind that which is presupposed by all discursive thought—the act of apprehending determinate being. Hence he does little more than indicate that the act of understanding something that is undivided or indivisible in nature, is immediate, as though the soul actually intelligent were *identical* with the nature actually understood. But we have only to turn to Alexander of Aphrodisias and Themistius, to see the beginnings of a long series of attempts to make intelligence *continuous* with the intelligible, through inter-mediaries. Alexander distinguishes material intellect, possible intellect, active intellect, and "adept intellect"; the neo-platonists expanded these degrees of continuity and difference, within νοῦς, into a whole hierarchical order of emanations and illuminations linking the human soul with a primordial Absolute; an Absolute which is indeterminate and infinite, hence suitable as a principle of continuity between the soul and all finite objects of its understanding. The pseudo-Dionysius, with his celestial hierarchy and ascending stages of illumination, christianized the neo-platonist realm of intelli-gences. And among the arabs, like Al-farabi, Avicenna, Averroes, or the jew Avencebrol, as well as among those scholastics who borrowed their aristotelianism from these sources, the same preoccupation is found; all were concerned with the dialectical regress from the soul as it is *de facto*, to the source of its intellectual light, and to the warrant, in eternity, for its knowledge of reasoned fact concerning inferior or sensible things.[1]

That man should be able to know true universal propositions, or to desire a good transcending any and every finite thing, was what aroused the wonder and interest of the mediæval thinkers who had inherited greek philosophy and the hebrew and christian theological traditions. Their interest in natural philosophy was metaphysical—to explain some kind of change by reference to finite causes of motion, was not a satisfactory explanation for them. They wished to comprehend the reason of fact *as such*, referring all instances of true knowledge to a First Truth prior to these instances and prior likewise to the determinate things signified by the terms of such propositions. Such a first truth could be found nowhere in the realm of perishable and finite things, but was to be sought through reflection on the soul's acts of knowledge and of assent to truth, in abstraction from any *determinate* objects of understanding or of assent. Psychology and logic were thus made instruments, and in a sense media of expression, of a metaphysics which sought to reveal continuity between the human soul and an actually infinite intelligence. Physics, likewise, was not merely a science of things chargeable, in which kinds of motion were explained by the existence and nature of kinds of moveable things. Rather it became a cosmology and metaphysics as well, the existence of finite causes being referred to an absolute source of finite existence, and the explanation of change being linked up with the story of creation *ex nihilo*.

In the thirteenth century this problem, of the relation of the finite to the infinite, and of substances to a single and infinite Substance on which they are dependent, was central

[1] The latin version of Alexander of Aphrodisias' treatise Περὶ Νοῦ, together with an interesting discussion of its influence on Al-kindi, Al-farabi, and Averroes, is published in "Alexandre d'Aphrodise," by G. Thery, O.P. (*Bibliothèque Thomiste*, VII, Kain, 1926).

to all discussions. Due to the influx of the aristotelian writings, the field of debate was greatly widened, and the older solutions underwent considerable modification. Thus St. Thomas, criticizing the arabs for robbing finite substances of their proper causal being, and criticizing them also for denying to the human soul any essential power of understanding, opened up a naturalistic approach to physics and logic that had been lost for the most part during the previous thousand years. Yet the context of St. Thomas' discussion was the traditional one. Although he argued against the notion that human science involves an illumination or regress to an intelligible realm above the soul, he tempered his arguments with a parallel exposition, in analogical terms, of the augustinian point of view, adjusted to the literal treatment derived from Aristotle.

In Duns Scotus we find a synthesis, under the ægis of the older tradition, of the elements which Aquinas had so carefully distinguished. For all his intricacy and subtlety, Duns Scotus presents a symmetrical and fully conscious treatment of the whole range of philosophical subjects, cemented together by the concept of infinity—a concept literally applicable to God, and involved analogically in the existence and understanding of all finite things. Every finite thing is exhibited as a unity of metaphysical "parts" which are neither identical nor really distinct, their mode of existence being a reflection of the Actual Infinite which sustains them in existence and in their changes. "Being" is predicable, for Duns Scotus, not only analogically but also univocally, of all things; hence to refer a truth to the being of a finite nature involves reference also to the Being which is infinite. Similarly, for Duns Scotus, every finite concept must be resolved to a concept of infinite potentiality and a concept of completely abstract and impotent form—as if reflecting, in each act of human understanding, the synthesis of creative power and unrealized form, involved in creation *ex nihilo, as represented in discursive thought.*[1]

[1] Cf. F.-X. Maquart, "Faut-il reviser les jugements des thomistes concernant la doctrine de Scot?" in *Revue de Philosophie*, N. S. IV, Nos. 5–6, Sept.–Dec. 1934, pp. 400–35. Also the discussion in Gilson, "Avicenne et le point de depart de

The contrast between the attitude, interests, and methods revealed in Ockham's discussions of science and its principles, to those of his mediæval predecessors, is marked. He not only restores to determinate concepts of essential nature their absolute primacy as principles of science, but he definitely repudiates the whole idea of trying to account for the being of such natures, by absolute principles distinct from them or prior to them. The whole programme of seeking for some single supreme ground of certainty, some first truth present to the soul or capable of being discovered through reflection on *forms of thinking as such*, is cast aside; and science is exhibited as a purely analytic grasp of determinate fact by determinate principles of explanation.

Ockham's basis of criticism of the augustinian programme might be expressed in its most general form as follows:

(1) We cannot explain the existence of finite substances as such, by trying to conceive what they would be if they were non-existent, and then adding to the result the notion of existence as such—for out of the indeterminate, added to the non-existent, we can derive nothing.

(2) We cannot explain the existence of determinate concepts or acts of understanding, in human mind, by first assuming

---

Duns Scot" (*Archives d'histoire doctrinale et litteraire du moyen âge*, II, 1927, pp. 89–150). Duns' notion of the concept *ens* as a univocal sign of pure potentiality, metaphysically distinct from every form, and also his method of indicating parallel "real-formal" distinctions corresponding to logical distinctions among concepts, are indicated in the following passage from Opus Oxon. I, Dist. III, Qu. 3, art. 2, 1: "Sicut ens compositum in re componitur ex actu et potentia in re, ita conceptus compositus per se unus componitur ex conceptu potentiali et actuali, sive ex conceptu determinabili et determinante. Sicut igitur resolutio entium compositorum stat ultimo ad simpliciter simplicia, scilicet ad actum ultimum et potentiam ultimam, quae sunt primo diversa, ita quod nihil unius includit aliquid alterius . . . ita oportet in conceptibus omnem conceptum non simpliciter simplicem, et tamen per se unum, resolvi in conceptum determinabilem et determinantem, ita quod ista resolutio stet ad conceptus simpliciter simplices, scilicet ad conceptum determinabilem tantum, ita quod nihil determinans includat, et ad conceptum determinantem tantum, qui scilicet non includit aliquem conceptum determinabilem. Ille conceptus tantum determinabilis est conceptus *entis*, et determinans tantum est conceptus ultimae differentiae; ergo isti erunt primo diversi, ita quod unum nihil includit alterius."

individual things to be *per se* unintelligible, and individual human beings to be *per se* unintelligent, and then adding a light from Infinity to these incapacities. If the human mind is not of itself able to apprehend the nature of existent things, insofar as such things are experienced through the senses, then no extrinsic illumination, and no synthetic procedure of compounding phantasms or brain-images, will make the human mind intelligent, or make individual things intelligible to a man.

(3) The essence of God, "creativity," and the absolutely unconditioned or infinite, are not principles of *human* knowledge; the principles of our knowledge, which Aristotle says are indemonstrable and must be "received" prior to demonstration, are the concepts of essential or individual nature by which we grasp the objects of definition. These are the first principles, and metaphysics is the science of first principles not in the sense that its terms signify principles prior to these, but in the sense that its terms signify these principles *qua* first, analogously.

If we consider the different questions, raised in various parts of Ockham's logical works, on which Ockham differs radically from the scotists, the contrast between his conception of science, and that of the earlier mediæval writers, is brought out forcefully. Logic is, for Ockham, an art and not a speculative science; for Duns Scotus it is speculative, and deals with a conceptual order that parallels a synthetic structure internal to things. But according to Ockham, the logician is interested in the discursive operations of the mind, not because they reveal a common structure internal to things *qua* adequated to mind, but because *an accurate grasp of what is constant in human modes of apprehension and of complex signification, makes possible an accurate differentiation between things apprehended or signified.*

If we can know the order in which the coloured glasses are held up to our eyes, we can determine whether the landscape itself has changed colour or not. Similarly, if we catalogue all our ways of apprehending and signifying things, we can distinguish differences due to the nature of different things signified, from differences due to variations in our mode of signification. In short, Ockham does not conceive logic as an instrument of metaphysics, or as a science of the soul which exhibits the order of partial exemplifications of truth to a Truth by which all things are true; but he conceives it as an analysis of the forms of signification and statement used in the sciences of nature, useful because it enables us to distinguish the characteristics of discourse attributable to our ways of signifying things, from the elements whose character is a function of the essential nature of the things signified.[1]

Ockham's discussion of the various theories of what the concept or intention is, illustrates the same basic attitude. The act of understanding (νοῦς) is presupposed by any explanation of the act of understanding that we may try to give; hence we might as well define the concept as *the mind recognizing something*, and dispense with the useless (and, if taken literally, dangerous) paraphernalia of active intellect, intellectual "light," and intelligible form, as intermediates between the man actually intelligent and the thing actually understood. Ockham's distinction between natural and conventional signs, and his view of the concept as a natural sign of the individual existences for which it can stand, is pertinent to his criticism of those who would make human intelligence dependent on a third and extrinsic element apart from the individual things signified.[2]

Again, in discussing the categories of quantity and relation, Ockham's principle is similar. One thing is not related to another thing by a third thing called a relation, nor is one thing equal to another by a third thing called equality— once this step is taken, it has to be repeated indefinitely, and then every event and every co-existence becomes unintelligible except to a mind capable of comprehending an actual infinite. The same applies to terms which signify one thing as potentially

[1] Cf. *ante*, ch. ii, pp. 31–38.
[2] Cf. *ante*, ch. ii, pp. 47–52; and ch. iii, pp. 82–89.

determined or conditioned by another; the potentiality of laughter, for example, is not anything distinct from the man who is said improperly to have this potentiality—he does not have it, but he is it. Science, for Ockham, is not of the contingent, not of the "togetherness" of distinct things—nor, for that matter, of indistinct things. Rather it is of propositions whose terms signify what is *per se* one and individual in nature, without determinate implication of the co-existence of any other things; what seems to carry the most weight with Ockham, in his reading of Aristotle, is the statement in the *Posterior Analytics* that the reason of the fact is *identical* with the nature of the thing.

Is Ockham's point of view anti-metaphysical? To those who conceive metaphysics as a discursive science, and as a cosmological system explaining the existence of the world of finite things by exhibiting it as a construction or concretion of formless potentiality and impotent "eternal objects," Ockham's criticisms of his contemporaries are criticisms of metaphysics. On the other hand, metaphysics may be conceived as a non-discursive science, whose principles are not contraries or factors in synthesis, but rather concepts which signify every determinate actuality as analogous, *qua* actual, to every other actual thing. If metaphysics is conceived in this way, then Ockham's criticisms of his contemporaries constitute a defence of pure metaphysics against a dialectic which confuses forms of discursive thought with the things discourse is about, and which exhibits judgment (or synthesis of distinct elements) as prior in the absolute sense to *the recognition of actual being*.

If there is no other object of thought, or reason of truth, than the structure of discourse itself, reflected back to the thinking mind by an undifferentiated "receptacle" or substratum of existence, then Ockham's distinctions between signs and things signified, or between truths and the individual natures of which they are true, are specious distinctions. If, furthermore, the principles of metaphysics are identical, or parallel, with the principles of logic or of discursive thinking, as they appear in the scotist statements attacked by Ockham, the word "nominalism" loses its philosophical significance, since in this context the predicative relations between concepts are formally indistinguishable from the "factual relations" which are taken as constitutive of what we call "real things."

Against the background of Ockham's non-discursive metaphysics, however, the word "nominalism" is significant. Ockham takes logic as a statement of the ways in which human beings fabricate complex signs, and true propositions, from incomplex concepts significant of individual finite natures. He is a nominalist in logic precisely because he recognizes as first principles of knowledge things which are prior to, and distinct from, the *forms of synthetic construction* with which logic deals. As we have indicated before, Ockham is a nominalist in logic because he is a realist in metaphysics and in his conception of the sciences of nature—the *forms* of discursive signification are to be attributed to the nature of the human soul, as its characteristic mode of activity *qua* intelligent; but the *truth* of discourse is exhibited as a function of the nature and being of things distinct from it, signified by the concepts of which discourse is composed. In this way Ockham refers knowledge to determinate and finite causes; to individual things intelligible to individual men, and to individual men capable of signifying such things and of stating true or false propositions about them.

In one sense Ockham's naturalistic conception of science was not an innovation in the scholastic world. Much of the work of St. Thomas was designed to show how science of nature, composed of literal universal propositions, was possible without positing any intermediate factor between the individual human being—with his sensory equipment and the intellectual capacity of grasping essential nature in abstraction from particular contingent occasions—and the individual perceptible things of which human sciences are true. But the interest of Aquinas was in adjusting this view of science to the augustinian tradition, and in stating the relationship between what we know by experience and reason, and what we know by faith and revelation. St. Thomas was a theologian primarily, and a man of science only secondarily; as indicated in his discussions of the averroist theory of knowledge, it was largely because the illumination theory of science endangered vital christian dogmas, that he attacked it.[1]

The novelty of Ockham's position was its full separation of the sphere of natural knowledge from that of faith, and from the metaphysics that took God as its starting point and the relation of the finite to the infinite as its problem. Ockham was a man of science, whose theology was neither incompatible with his philosophy and metaphysics, nor confused with it. His method was analytic, and his principles those yielded by analysis of determinate subjects of investigation—each problem being distinguished and stated through reference to the *kinds of things* involved in that single problem, and its solution sought in its own terms, or by its "proximate middle." Ockham was an empiricist, but not of the seventeenth century type; he referred knowledge to experience, but not to experience of the unintelligible by man deprived of his intelligence. He was a secular philosopher, at least in comparison with his scholastic predecessors; not in the sense of those later secular philosophers who dealt with problems of theology without revelation, but in the sense that problems of theology and of the primordial genesis or absolute cause of all things, were not in his estimation scientific or philosophical problems.

Ockham's influence on the interests, methods, and attitudes of fourteenth and fifteenth century investigators of nature, was undoubtedly important. The whole tendency of his discussions, in logic and physics, was against the notion that to have any specific certitude we have to have certitude of

---

[1] Gilson, *The Philosophy of St. Thomas* (transl. by Bullough, Herder, St. Louis, 2nd ed. 1929), ch. ii, brings out very clearly the notion that St. Thomas' chief preoccupation was in defining and harmonizing the autonomous realms of faith and reason. It could be said, indeed, that Aquinas' defence of the autonomy of reason, and of man's natural power to know, against the averroist denial of the possibility of man knowing necessary truths without illumination from above, was prompted just as much by the fact that the christian scheme of things demands it, as by an interest in science of nature for its own sake.

existence in general or of some absolute and supreme truth which guarantees, once and for all, judgments that we may make about finite things. Thus he gave confidence to those who wanted to take up specific problems, one at a time, and solve them in their own terms. Ockham's logic was a warrant for the constancy of human forms of signification, sufficient as an instrument of analysis in scientific inquiry; but it neither assumed, nor required, any metaphysical guarantee extrinsic to the proper principles of the real sciences—i.e., extrinsic to the natures of whatever things those sciences were concerned with. Logic, for Ockham, was not a set of scientific principles, but an art concerned with the ways in which the concepts proper to any natural science can be distinguished, and exhibited as principles, with respect to the propositions or truths that are the conclusions of that science.

It is not hard to see, therefore, how Ockham's followers, taking this attitude and adopting this method, went in for physical investigations of an empirical character, looking for principles only in relation to specific problems suggested by experience of definite types of natural occurrences. A rather striking instance is found in Nicolas of Orêsme, an immediate follower of Ockham, who set out to investigate the planetary motions of the solar system. After stating both the geocentric and heliocentric solutions of the problems, he indicated that in relation to the observed facts making up the conclusions of the demonstration, either hypothesis was explanatory of the problem; being stated as a mathematical problem, it called for a mathematical solution, and two different solutions were equally possible, at least until further observation should yield facts that might alter the statement of the problem.[1]

The development of mathematical physics, starting in the fourteenth century and continued until our own times, took a direction that had been opposed by Ockham on the same

[1] Cf. Duhem: "Un précurseur français de Copernic: Nicole Oresme (1377)", in *Revue générale des sciences pures et appliquées*, 15 Nov. 1909; also "François de Meyronnes et la question de la rotation de la terre," in *Arch. Franc. Hist.*, 1913, 23.

grounds that he had opposed the confusion of logic and physics. His whole discussion of the category of quantity, and his constant contrast of physical demonstrations with mathematical demonstrations, aimed to show that quantitative terms, and their definitions, do not signify primary causes, but are ways of signifying substances or qualities *coniunctim*, as elements of *analogous* contingent facts. To give a metaphysical import to the rules of synthesis regulating mathematical construction is, from Ockham's point of view, as destructive of the science of nature as was the scotist conception of logic as a speculative science of metaphysical import. The object of Ockham's criticism was the augustinian notion of the created world as nothing but a system of partial, and hierarchically ordered, exemplifications of a First Truth by which all truths are true; equally opposed to Ockham's position is the modern conception of the universe as nothing but a system of relations exemplifying principles of mathematical synthesis as such. What is nowadays called "nominalism" is far closer to the logical realism and discursive metaphysics upheld by the scotists and criticized by Ockham, than to the philosophical position which earned for Ockham the title of nominalist.[1]

Since Ockham's professed aim, in his logical works, was to give an accurate interpretation of Aristotle, and a statement of logic purified of metaphysical implications alien to the philosophy of Aristotle, we may consider the question of how good an interpretation of the Stagyrite his exposition of logic was. Obviously only Aristotle himself is qualified to say who is to be called an authentic aristotelian, and he is beyond the reach of our appeals. On the other hand, we may state the problem in another way, and ask if Ockham's conception of the principles and methods of science is not closer to that

---

[1] At what point, in late mediæval or early modern times, the successors of Ockham abandoned his qualitative conception of change for a quantitative theory, is a problem of considerable historical interest. The cartesian dichotomy of being into *res cogitans* and *res extensa* is, obviously, far removed from Ockham's point of view, though it revives, in a new form, most of the metaphysical "problems" of the older augustinian tradition, which Ockham regarded as purely dialectical problems irrelevant to science.

of Aristotle than the point of view which had predominated
in earlier mediæval statements and which in Ockham's time
was upheld by the scotists. The answer to this question also
involves the assumption of an interpretation of Aristotle, as
the measure of later statements; but without presuming to
be in possession of any special revelation as to the intentions
of the founder of the peripatetics, we may at least point to a
few factors relevant to the question.

That Aristotle conceived logic as an analysis of *forms of
discourse*, seems to follow from the language he uses in each of
the treatises composing the *Organon*. The *Categories* is concerned with "forms of speech that are in no way composite,"
the *De interpretatione* with distinctions between *noun* and *verb*,
affirmation and *denial*, *sentence* and *proposition*. The *Analytics*
deal with *syllogisms*, or "reasonings" and with ways in which
the predicative connection between two terms can be exhibited
as a function of a "middle." Ockham's thesis, that the
categories are not classifications of things which exist by
nature, or of "parts" of them, and that predicative relations
between terms are not to be referred to similar "real" relations
distinct from the things related, is at least a thoroughly
defensible position in the interpretation of the *Organon*. While
Aristotle never seems to mention what kind of a science or
art logic is, this very fact gives more support to Ockham's
conception of it as an analysis of forms of discourse, than to
the scotist conception of logic as a speculative science. Further,
if Ockham's interpretation is the more accurate, Aristotle's
apparent lack of concern with the "problem of universals"
in the *Categories* or *Analytics* is explained quite easily; only one
who is a nominalist in logic can be excused from dealing with
the problems of logical realism, or from leaving metaphysics
out of logic.

Another interesting point is the fact that Ockham, in
discussing what a "natural sign" is, or what the act of understanding is *as such*, is just as laconic as Aristotle is in the *De
anima*, or at the end of the *Posterior Analytics*—where he
(Aristotle) indicates the primacy, with respect to discursive

science or knowledge of demonstrative premises, of intelligence (νοῦς). Since there is no prior "middle" connecting the understanding of determinate being with the determinate being that is understood, a cosmological explanation of human intelligence *as such* is neither given nor required; in this Ockham seems to return to the attitude of Aristotle, and to depart from the attitude which had predominated throughout the mediæval period.

Most of all, Ockham's aristotelianism is indicated by his complete adoption of the thesis that the reason of the fact is the being of the things of which the fact is true. It is in defence of this principle that Ockham opposes the traditional "real distinction" between essence and existence within finite things, and the scotist "formal distinction" that is more than a logical distinction. The augustinian conception of knowledge, in all of its many statements, involves reference of determinate truth and of finite existence to an infinite and superior reason of all truth and of all existence, and as a consequence involves, as condition of literal demonstration, infinite regress. Aristotle's *Posterior Analytics*, on the other hand, is very largely concerned to show that science and demonstration do not involve infinite regress or circularity. Here again Ockham seems closer to Aristotle than the *moderni* whose logical realism he opposes.

The principles of each science, for Ockham as for Aristotle, are proper to that science, indemonstrable, and grasped only through intuitive recognition of determinate nature. The originative source of knowledge and of abstract concepts is exhibited as sense experience of existing things. Yet science is not identified with sense perception, nor with the intuitive recognition of being; it presupposes these, but is itself an act of assent to the truth of a proposition, *by* recognition of the being of things signified or "meant" by its terms.

Such is the "nominalism" of William of Ockham. For Ockham there was no problem of knowledge *überhaupt*, as there had been for his predecessors, and as there was to be for his seventeenth century successors; nor was there any problem of existence *as such*, as there had been before him and as there was to be for the seventeenth century. Problems, as Aristotle indicates in the *Topics*, are propositions; hence existence, and our awareness of what exists, are not problems to be solved, but means of solving our problems.

BIBLIOGRAPHY

A

EDITIONS OF OCKHAM'S WRITINGS

Guilhelmi de Ockham anglici super quatuor libros sententiarum subtilissimae quaestiones earumdemque decisiones. Lugduni, 1495. This edition includes as a supplement Ockham's *Centiloquium theologicum.* The commentary on the first book of the Sentences was also published separately at Strasbourg in 1483.

Quodlibeta septem. Parisiis, 1487. Another edition, Argentinae, 1491; also includes the *De sacramento altaris.*

De sacramento altaris et de corpore Christi. Parisiis, 1490; Venetiis, 1516. This text, with translation into English, is published in *The De Sacramento Altaris of William of Ockham,* by T. B. Birch (Lutheran Literary Board, Burlington, Iowa, 1930).

Expositio aurea et admodum utilis super artem veterem edita . . . cum quaestionibus Alberti parvi de Saxonia. Bononiae, 1496.

Summa totius logicae. Parisiis, 1488; Bononiae, 1498; Venetiis, 1508, 1522, 1591; Oxoniae, 1675. In some editions this is entitled, "Tractatus logicae . . . divisus in tres partes."

Summulae in libros physicorum. Bononiae, 1494; Venetiis, 1506; Romae, 1637. Also called "Philosophia naturalis."

Quaestiones in octos libros physicorum. Argentori, 1491, 1506; Venetiis, 1506; Romae, 1637.

Dialogus inter magistrum et discipulum. Lugduni, 1495.

Defensorium contra Joannem XXII. Venetiis, 1513.

Gulielmi de Ockham Epistola ad Fratres Minores. Ed. by C. K. Brampton, Oxford, 1929.

The De Imperatorum et Pontificum Potestate of William of Ockham. Ed. by C. K. Brampton, Oxford, 1927.

Unbekannte kirchenpolitische Streitschriften aus der Zeit Ludwig des Bayern, II Teil, Rom, 1914; by R. Scholz; pp. 392–480.

Monarchia II, Frankfort, 1614, ed. by M. Goldast, contains most of the polemical and political writings.

B

SECONDARY SOURCES ON OCKHAM

ABBAGNANO, N.: *Guglielmo di Ockham* (Lanciano, 1931), 392 pp.

BAEUMKER, C.: "Die christliche Philosophie des Mittelalters," in *Die Kultur des Gegenwart* (Berlin-Leipzig, 2nd. ed. 1922), pp. 418–23.

BAUDRY, L.: "Fragments inconnus de Guillaume d' Occam: Le Tractatus de principiis theologiae," in *Journal des Savants*, Janv.–Mars, 1927, pp. 46–55.
"Les rapports de Guillaume d'Occam et de Walter Burleigh," in *Archives d'histoire doctrinale et litteraire du moyen-âge*, IX (1934).
"À propos de la théorie occamiste de la relation," in *Archives d'histoire doctrinale et litteraire du moyen-âge*, IX (1934).

BECKER, H.: "Gottesbegriff und Gottesbeweis bei Wilhelm von Ockham," in *Scholastik* 3 (1928), pp. 369–93.

BUHLE, J. G.: "Lehrbuch der Geschichte der Philosophie," *B. V*, pp. 635–69 (Göttingen, 1800).

BURNS, C. D.: "William of Ockham on Continuity," in *Mind*, Oct., 1916, pp. 506–12.
"Ockham's Razor," in *Mind*, Oct., 1915, p. 592.
"William of Occam on Universals," in *Proc. of the Arist. Soc.*, N. S., vol. XIV (1914), pp. 76–99.

BRUCKMÜLLER, Fr.: *Die Gotteslehre Wilhelms von Ockham* (Munich, 1911).

CANELLA, G.: *Il Nominalismo e Guglielmo d'Occam, studio critico di storia della filosofia medievale* (Firenze, 1907).

DE WULF, M.: *History of Mediaeval Philosophy* (Messenger's transl., Longmans, London, 1926), vol. II, pp. 176–86 on Ockham.

DONCOEUR, P.: "La theorie de la matière et de la forme chez Guillaume Occam," in *Revue des sciences philosophiques et théologiques*, Paris, 1921, pp. 21–52.
"Le mouvement, temps, et lieu d'apres Occam," in *Revue de philosophie*, Mai, 1921.
"La relation chez Occam," in *Revue Neoscolastique*, 1921, p. 5 ff.

DUHEM, P.: *Études sur Leonard de Vinci*, II, pp. 189–94; III, pp. vi–ix.
"Le temps et le mouvement selon les scolastiques," in *Revue de philosophie* 14 (1914).
"Un précurseur français de Copernic: Nicole Oresme (1377)," in *Revue générale des sciences pures et appliquées* 15 (Nov., 1909).
"François de Meyronnes et la question de la rotation de la terre," in *Arch. Franc. Hist.*, 1913, 23.

EICHBERG, W.: "*Untersuchungen über die Beziehungen der Erkenntnislehre Spinozas zur Scholastik mit besonderer Berücksichtigung der Schule Ockhams*," (Borna–Leipzig, 1910, (Diss.)

EHRLE, F., Card.: "Die Sentenzenkommentar Peters von Candia," in *Franziskanische Studien, Beiheft* 9 (Munster, 1925); pp. 78–95 on Ockham.

ERDMANN, J. E.: *Grundriss der Geschichte der Philosophie*, I, pp. 462-73 (Berlin, 1896).

FEDERHOFER, F.: "Die Psychologie und die psychologischen Grundlagen der Erkenntnislehre des Wilhelms von Ockham," in *Philosophisches Jahrbuch* 39 (1926).
Die Erkenntnislehre des Wilhelm von Ockham (Diss., Munich, 1924).
"Die Philosophie des W. von Ockham im Rahmen seiner Zeit," in *Franziskanische Studien* 12 (1925), pp. 273–96.
"Ein Beitrag zur Bibliographie u. Biographie des W. von Ockham," in *Philosophisches Jahrbuch* 38 (1925), pp. 26–48.

FERET, P.: *La faculté de théologie de Paris et ses Docteurs les plus celèbres*: *Moyen Age*, vol. III, pp. 339–350 (Paris, 1894–1897).

FRANCK, A.: "Guillaume Occam et les franciscains du XIVe siècle," in *Reformateurs et publicistes de l'Europe* (Paris 1864), pp. 153–200.

GILSON: *La philosophie au Moyen Age* (Payot, Paris, 1930); pp. 249–66.

HEIM, K.: *Das Gewissheitsproblem in der systematischer Theologie bis zu Schleiermacher* (1911), pp. 206–19.

HARRIS, C. R. S.: *Duns Scotus* (Oxford, 1927), vol. I, pp. 272–300.

HAURÉAU, B.: *Histoire de la philosophie scolastique*, II, 2, pp. 356–430 (Paris, 1872).

HERMELINCK, H.: *Die theologische Fakultät im Tübingen vor der Reformation*, 1906. On Ockham's relation to Gabriel Biel.

HOCHSTETTER, E.: *Studien zur Metaphysik und Erkenntnislehre Wilhelms von Ockham* (Diss., Berlin, 1927).

HOFER, J.: "Biographische Studien über Wilhelm von Ockham," in *Archivum Franciscanum Historicum* 6 (1913), vol. II, pp. 211–233; vol. III, pp. 439–65; and vol. IV, pp. 654–69.

KUGLER, L.: *Der Begriff der Erkenntnis bei Wilhelm von Ockham* (Diss., Breslau, 1913).

KÜHTMANN, A.; *Zur Geschichte des Terminismus* (Leipzig, 1911).

KROPATSCHECK, Fr.: "Ockham und Luther," in *Beitrage zur Förderung christlicher Theologie IV* (1900), pp. 51–74.

LITTLE, A. G.: *The Grey Friars in Oxford* (London 1892), pp. 224–234.

LINDSAY, J.: "The Logic and Metaphysics of Occam," in *The Monist*, vol. XXX, No. 4, pp. 521–47 (Oct., 1920).

LÖWE, J. H.: *Der Kampf zwischen Realismus und Nominalismus im Mittelalter* (Prague, 1876).

MANSER, G. M.: "Drei Zweifler am Kausalprinzip im XIVten Jahrhundert," in *Jahrbuch für Philosophie u. Spekulative Theologie*, 27 (1912), pp. 405–37.

McKEON, R.: *Selections from Mediaeval Philosophers*, vol. II (Scribners, 1930), pp. 351–59, and pp. 360–421 (transl. of parts of *Quodlibeta*).

MICHALSKI, K.: "Les courants philosophiques à Oxford et à Paris pendant le XIVe siècle," *Bulletin international de l'Académie Polonaise des sciences et des lettres*, (Cracovie, 1922), pp. 63–8.
"Le criticisme et le scepticisme dans la philosophie du XIVe siècle," *Bulletin international de l'Académie Polonaise des sciences et des lettres, Classe d'Histoire et de Phil.* (Annee, 1925; Cracovie, 1926), pp. 41–122.
Les sources du criticisme et du scepticisme dans la philosophie du XIVe siècle (Cracovie, 1924).

MUSCHIETTI, C.: *Breve Saggio sulla filosofia di Guglielmo d'Ockham* (Bellinzona, 1908).

POOLE, R. L.: *Illustrations of the History of Mediaeval Thought* (London, 1920). *Dictionary of National Biography*, XIV, pp. 802–7.

PELZER, A.: "Les 51 articles de Guillaume Occam censurés en Avignon en 1326," in *Revue d'histoire ecclésiastique*, 1922, t. XVIII, pp. 240–70.

PRANTL: "*Geschichte der Logik im Abendlande*," vol. III.

RITTER, H.: *Geschichte der christlichen Philosophie* (Hamburg, 1845), vol. VIII, pp. 574–604.

ROUSSELOT: *Etudes sur la philosophie médiévale* (Paris, 1842), pp. 200–91.

SEEBERG: *Lehrbuch der Dogmengeschichte*, III, 2, pp. 520–28, 602–21, and 643–48 (3rd ed., Leipzig, 1913).

SIEBECK, H.: "Ockhams Erkenntnislehre in ihrer historischer Stellung," in *Archiv für Geschichte der Philosophie* X, 3 (Berlin, 1897), pp. 317–39.

STÖCKL: *Geschichte der Philosophie des Mittelalters*, vol. II.

TENNEMANN: *Geschichte der Philosophie*, vol. VIII, i, pp. 840–903 (Leipzig, 1810).

THORBURN, W. M.: "Occam's Razor," in *Mind* (Apr., 1915), pp. 287–88. "The Myth of Occam's Razor," in *Mind* (July, 1918), pp. 345–53.

VERWEYEN, J.: *Das Problem der Willensfreiheit in der Scholastik* (1909), pp. 238–42.

UEBERWEG-GEYER: *Geschichte der Philosophie: II, Die Patristische und Scholastische Zeit* (11th ed., Berlin, 1928), pp. 571–83 on Ockham.

WERNER, K.: "Die nominalisierende Psychologie des späteren Mittelalters," in *Sitzungsbericht der Wiener Akademie*, vol. XCIX (1882), pp. 254–302. *Die Scholastik des späteren Mittelalters II*, 1883. *Der hl. Thomas von Aquino*, vol. III (1889), pp. 114–21.

WILLMANN, O.: *Geschichte des Idealismus*, vol. II.

C

OTHER REFERENCES

ARISTOTLE: references are to the Oxford English Translation, edited by W. D. Ross; Oxford, 1928, etc.

AQUINAS: Comm. in *Periherm*, and in *Post. An.* (Leonine edition, Opera omnia, vol. I, Rome, 1882).
Contra Gentiles (Lethielleux ed., Paris, 1925).
Qu. Disp. De Veritate (Lethielleux ed., Paris, 1925).
Summa theologica, I (Lethielleux ed., Paris, 1927).

BOETHIUS: Logical works in Migne *Patrologia Latina*, vol. LXIV.

DUNS SCOTUS: *Opera omnia* (Waddings edition, 1639).
Op. oxon., Bks. I and II (Quaracchi, 1912).

GILSON, E.: "Pourquoi S. Thomas a critiqué S. Augustin," in *Archives d'histoire doctrinale et litteraire du moyen âge*, I, 1926, pp. 5–128.
"Avicenne et le point de depart de Duns Scot," ibid., II, 1927, pp. 89–150.
Introduction à l'étude de S. Augustin (Vrin, Paris, 1931).
La philosophie de S. Bonaventure (Vrin, Paris, 1929).
The Philosophy of St. Thomas Aquinas (transl. by E. Bullough); 2nd ed., Herder, St. Louis, 1929.

GROTE, G.: *Aristotle*, vol. I (London, 1872).

JOYCE, G. H.: *Principles of Logic* (3rd ed., Longmans, 1929).

MAQUART, F. X.: "Faut-il réviser les jugements des thomistes concernant la doctrine de Scot?" in *Revue de Philosophie*, N. S. IV, No. 5–6, Sept.–Dec., 1934; pp. 400–35.

McKEON, R.: "De anima; Psychology and Science," in *Journal of Philosophy*, vol. XXVII, No. 25, Dec. 4, 1930.

MILL, J. S.: *System of Logic* (London, 1892).

PAETOW: *The Arts Course at Mediaeval Universities with Special Reference to Grammar and Rhetoric*" (Ill. Un. Press).

SIMONIN, H. D.: "Les Summulae Logicales de Petrus Hispanus," in *Archives d'histoire doctrinale et litteraire du moyen âge*, V, 1930, pp. 267–78.

THÉRY, G.: *Alexandre d'Aphrodise* (Bibl. thomiste VII, Kain, 1926).

WALLERAND, G.: "Les Oeuvres de Siger de Courtrai," *Les Philosophes Belges*, vol. VIII (Louvain, 1913).

WEBER, A.: *History of Philosophy* (transl. by Thilly, N. Y. 1925, revised ed.).

WINDELBAND, W.: *History of Ancient Philosophy* (Cushman's transl., 3rd ed., N. Y., 1899).

INDEX OF PROPER NAMES

317

SUBJECT INDEX

A

a posteriori syllogism, 252–5;—demonstration of essential differentiae, 271–2
a priori demonstration, 252–3, 257–80
absolute terms, 54–7
absolute nature, or *natura indeterminata*, in scotist epistemology, 89–90; Ockham's criticism of it, 61–3, 91–2
abstract terms, 57–65
accident, 105–6
act of understanding, 49–50
antiqui, Ockham's defence of them, 7, 61
apprehension vs. *judgment*, 177–80
Aristotle's four questions, 258–60; *si est*, 260–3; *quid est*, 267–78; *quia est* and *propter quid est*, 278–9
ars definiendi, 273–4
attribute, 116
augustinism, 10, 298, 300

C

categories, Ockham's analysis of them, 118–75; basis of his analysis, 135–6, 172–5
concept (see *intention*); the concept according to Averroes, 85
concrete vs. *abstract* terms, 57–65
coniunctim, 121
conjunctive signification, 21
connotative terms, 55–7; their definitions, 276–8
consequentiae, Ockham's treatise on them, 283–94
contraries, logical, 141, 154–5, 159, 168–9; physical, 168–9
conversion, of propositions, 209, Note 2

D

de omni (see *dictum de omni*)
definition, kinds of, 106–11; its relation to demonstration, 259–80
demonstratio potissima, 222–3

demonstration. Ockham's treatment of it, 220–80; meaning of the term *demonstration* defined, 221; are definitions demonstrable? 259–80
denominative terms, 126
descriptions, 111
dialectical method, treated by Ockham in manner of Aristotle, 295–6
dialectical reasoning exhibited by Ockham under the form of the hypothetical proposition, 283–4
dictum de omni of the Categories, 129–30; of the Prior Analytics, 213–15; of the Posterior Analytics, 233–4
differentia, 102–4
diffinitio per additamentum, 267–8, 274–5
diffinitio quid nominis, 110
diffinitio quid rei, 106–10; " natural " vs. " metaphysical " form, 106–9
disjunctive signification, 121
disposition, as quality of the first species, 162
divisim, 121
division, method of, 273–4
dubitable proposition, 239

E

equivocal signification, 125
ens in potentia and *ens in actu*, 122–3
ens per se and *ens per aliud*, 122
esse obiectivum, 49
essence and *existence*, problem of, 263–7
essential definitions, 267–75
eternal—in what sense applicable to necessary truths, 228–30
evident propositions, 177–8
exceptive propositions, 204
exclusive propositions, 204
experience, as source of evident knowledge of indemonstrable propositions, 240–4
expository syllogisms, 217
extension vs. *intension*, 216
extrinsic principles of demonstration, 225–6

319